Pamphlets of Protest

Pamphlets of *Protest*

AN ANTHOLOGY OF EARLY AFRICAN-AMERICAN
PROTEST LITERATURE, 1790–1860

EDITED BY

RICHARD NEWMAN   PATRICK RAEL   PHILIP LAPSANSKY

ROUTLEDGE
NEW YORK AND LONDON

Published in 2001 by
Routledge
29 West 35th Street
New York, NY 10001

Published in Great Britain in 2001 by
Routledge
11 New Fetter Lane
London EC4P 4EE

Library of Congress Cataloging-in-Publication Data

Pamphlets of protest : an anthology of early African-American protest literature, 1790–1860 / [compiled by] Richard Newman, Patrick Rael, and Philip Lapsansky.
    p.   cm.
Includes bibliographical references and index.
    ISBN 0-415-92443-X   —   ISBN 0-415-92444-8 (pbk.)
    1. Afro-Americans—Civil rights—History—18th century—Sources. 2. Afro-Americans—Civil rights—History— 19th century—Sources. 3. Afro-Americans—Politics and government—18th century—Sources. 4. Afro-Americans—Politics and government—19th century—Sources. 5. Anti-slavery movements—United States—History—19th century—Sources. 6. Protest literature, American. I. Newman, Richard. II. Rael, Patrick. III. Lapsansky, Philip.

E184.6 .P36 2000
323.1'196073—dc21   00–038254

Contents

Acknowledgments

This project has been a collaborative endeavor from its inception. The book began as a series of conversations among the editors about black pamphleteering. It then evolved with the help of numerous scholars, students, and many others. It is a pleasure to thank them now in print: at Routledge, Derek Krissoff encouraged the editors at the earliest possible stage and remained a constant source of encouragement and insight. Deirdre Mullane helped broaden the project, making it a much larger and more important piece of scholarship. She not only encouraged our effort but generously offered her commentary on the introduction and made substantive comments on every one of the pamphlets. The editors also wish to thank the New York State African-American Research Council (particularly Anne Pope), whose early financial assistance allowed the project to move forward in an expeditious manner. Finally, the staff at the Library Company of Philadelphia provided invaluable aid in researching the pamphlets themselves. The Library Company remains a treasure of early African-American history and literature.

Rich Newman would like to thank the following people at the Rochester Institute of Technology for their support and assistance. The Faculty Research Council provided two grants which facilitated data entry and research. Glenn Kist, Paul Ferber, Andrea Walter, Ken Nelson, Rebecca Edwards, and Frank Annunziata deserve special mention for their encouragement and aid. Other individuals rendered critical assistance in the form of editing and inputting pamphlets. Thank you also to Donald Yacavone, Nicole Peradotto, Ann McDonald, Ginnie Capozzi, Annette Fazio, Ruth Newman, and Robert Newman. Finally, RIT students who took a course entitled "Black Protest Before the Civil War" offered invaluable comments and suggestions which have helped make *Pamphlets of Protest* a better book.

Patrick Rael would like to thank Bowdoin College for financial assistance from its Faculty Research Fund, and acknowledge the research assistance of Eric Henry, Courtney Mongell, and Tina Nadeau. He is grateful for the loving support of Nicola Denzey.

The editors would be remiss if they did not thank the many scholars who blazed a trail in African-American history and literature—from Benjamin Quarles and Herbert Aptheker to Charles Davis, John Blassingame, Henry Louis Gates, Francis Foster Smith, Wilson Moses, Sterling Stuckey, Leon Litwack, Gary Nash, C. Peter Ripley, Ira Berlin, James and Lois Horton, Jean Yellin, and James Stewart, among dozens of others too numerous to mention.

We wish to dedicate this book to future students of African-American history and literature, and to Dorothy Porter, who remains a teacher to us all.

*   *   *

One final note on the choice of pamphlets appearing in this volume: The editors faced the dilemma confronting most compilers—too much fascinating material to publish at once. Our list is not exhaustive. We hope that interested students and scholars will study the pamphleteering tradition in future works on black protest.

Introduction:

The Theme of Our Contemplation

Writin' is Fightin'.
—Ishmael Reed

For too long others have spoken for us.
—*Freedom's Journal*, 1827

Between the 1790s and 1860s, African-American writing became a prominent part of both black protest culture and American public life. Although denied a political voice in national affairs (as well as in most state governments), black authors produced a wide range of literature to project their views into the public sphere. Autobiographies and personal narratives told of slavery's horrors; newspaper essays railed against racism in its various forms; and poetry, novellas, reprinted sermons, and speeches preached an ethos of racial uplift and national redemption. Pamphleteering became one of the most important parts of this tradition. Yet while scholarship on African-American writing and culture has proliferated to an unprecedented degree in the past two decades, few works have focused solely on the pamphleteering genre. To take one important example, the monumental *Norton Anthology of African-American Literature*—an invaluable teaching resource and the most comprehensive collection of black writings designed for scholarly and classroom use—skims over pamphlet literature, particularly in the period before 1830. Its survey of "Black Writing in the Age of Slavery" moves briskly from Phyllis Wheatley's poems of the 1770s to David Walker's "Appeal" in the 1830s without mentioning the names of prominent black pamphleteers such as Richard Allen, William Hamilton, James Forten, and Daniel Coker. *The Norton Anthology* then moves into the slave narrative genre to pick up the story of black writing.[1]

Pamphlets of Protest focuses exclusively on black pamphleteering between the American Revolution and the Civil War: its formation as a distinct genre, its characteristics and evolution, and its meaning in both American and African-American culture. Pamphlets played a consistently important role in black intellectual life and protest. Black pamphleteers read one another, cited one another, learned from one another. Henry Highland Garnet offered perhaps the most illuminating example of such collaborative effort in his 1848 edition of Walker's "Appeal," which he published alongside his own famous "Address to the Slaves of United States." Garnet never met Walker—never heard his voice—except in the pages of the man's pamphlet. Although the "Appeal" had gone out of print after Walker's untimely death in 1830, old editions circulated in black communities. Garnet found the words fresh and revolutionary; he vowed to reprint the pamphlet—to further preserve Walker's legacy. Similar references to pamphlets appear often in the black activist tradition. The first black newspaper, *Freedom's Journal* (founded in 1827), republished James Forten's 1813 pamphlet protesting racist laws in Pennsylvania so that the "younger generation" might learn the trade of written protest. William C. Nell's *Colored Patriots of the Revolution*, a black history text written in the 1850s, spoke glowingly of an early pamphlet produced by Richard Allen and Absalom Jones. And Martin Delany's 1852 book *The Condition, Elevation and Destiny of the Colored People of the United States, Politically Considered* cited Nell's pamphlet version of *Colored Patriots*. In the same year, both Delany and Henry Bibb urged readers to consult a new pamphlet on black emigration by female activist Mary Ann Shadd.[2] The list goes on.

Frederick Douglass famously said, "Power concedes nothing without demand. It never did and it never will."[3] Black activists fought for racial justice from the beginning of the American republic until the country's near demise during the Civil War and through the twentieth century. Black pamphleteers were a consistent part of this struggle. Their writings presented a diversity of black protest thought that demanded change and in no small way helped to achieve it.

Read by Thousands: Pamphleteering and the Creation of Black Printed Protest

When African Americans began issuing pamphlets during the 1790s, pamphleteering already enjoyed a long and varied history in Western culture. During the 1600s the English Civil War prompted a pamphleteering battle between the revolutionary Diggers and their monarchist foes. The pamphlet also became one of the main protest vehicles of American Revolutionaries over a century later, introducing colonial and British audiences to the likes of Thomas Jefferson, James Otis, Thomas Paine, and countless other writers. Similarly, the French revolutionaries of 1789 waged a public war against the ancien régime through a mountain of pamphlets.[4]*

To these protesters separated by time and topic, pamphlets offered versatility. One might define the pamphlet as something between a broadside and a book. Adaptable as an argumentative essay, a short narrative of events, or a bare-bones sketch of an organization's proceedings, the pamphlet could be used by all manner of activists. At the same time the pamphlet offered a media form that promised to preserve words and deeds in a discrete, individual, and long-lived object. As Bernard Bailyn writes in his definitive study of American Revolutionary-era pamphleteers, the pamphlet was both a medium of the moment—allowing protestors to publish quickly their views—and a substantial document that could stand the test of time. Neither books (which until the 1830s and a revolution in binding techniques remained expensive) nor broadsides (one-page posters that did not treat matters in any extended way) provided this ideal combination.[5]

African-American pamphleteers recognized the utility of the form and appropriated it after the American Revolution to battle racial subjection. Between the 1790s and 1860s, black writers produced hundreds of pamphlets. These documents captured a range of debate and testified to the remarkable diversity of black literary culture and thought. Just as Richard Allen and Absalom Jones could use the pamphlet to correct racial stereotypes in the 1790s, so too could David Walker use the genre to mobilize the black masses in the 1820s. Female writers such as Maria W. Stewart wrote pamphlets explicating women's role as racial reformers, black emigrationist Martin Delany's pamphlets encouraged his brethren to leave America altogether, and black nationalists from Henry Highland Garnet to T. Morris Chester issued pamphlets celebrating racial pride. Black conventions from the 1830s to 1860s certainly recognized the significance of pamphleteering. Indeed, one of the first things most conventioneers did was appoint a publishing committee, whose members ensured that the convention's proceedings would be presented "in pamphlet form," as a Pennsylvania meeting put it 1848. Particularly in the early national era, when no national black newspaper existed, and even later on, when black newspapers operated on a tenuous basis, the pamphlet provided an important and consistent literary outlet for black activism.[6]

In this vein, the pamphlet must also be understood as a part of a broader struggle by black Americans to assert themselves in the public sphere. Often denied the right to vote (and therefore to participate in formal politics), African Americans viewed public protest as the central means of waging a liberation struggle. Public protest took many forms, from petitioning governments to organizing parades to giving speeches. Writing became one of the most important of these protest tools.

How did writing assume such importance within black public protest? And just where did pamphleteering fit? Answers begin with orality, for many written documents began as spoken words. Slave narrators like Sojourner Truth often dictated their life story to a white amanuensis. Black orators often polished their sermons or speeches, turning them into pamphlets. Published proceedings captured in written form the often vociferous debates which erupted on the convention floor. The rise of print culture, then, did little to displace the use of the spoken word. Orality remained a vibrant part of black protest throughout the nineteenth century, in the North as well as the South.

Nonetheless, print assumed disproportionate importance in black protest circles by the early 1800s. The rise of print culture among blacks occurred in a society with a rapidly expanding culture of letters. African Americans utilized the explosion of inexpensive printed matter permitted by the new technologies of a burgeoning industrial economy. By 1850, nearly four times as many daily newspapers circulated throughout the country as there had been two decades earlier, and the costs of production had plummeted by 600 percent.[7] The significance of these changes on American culture can hardly be overestimated. As Benedict Anderson has suggested, print culture in general permitted the consolidation of national identity; Americans could "come to visualize in a general way the existence of thousands and thousands like themselves through print-language."[8]

While of course sectional rivalries undermined the larger project of national unification, no such barrier hampered the forging of a unified black identity through the promotion of literacy. As Henry Louis Gates, Jr., explained in his seminal work, *The Signifying Monkey*, "the production of literature was taken to be the central arena in which persons of African descent could . . . establish and redefine their status within the human community." By creating a literary identity and tradition, black authors would transcend white stereotypes. Print also allowed blacks to "talk" to one another and white society in new ways. Throughout the North (and in parts of the South) following the Revolution, free and recently liberated blacks established an increasing number of educational institutions and reform groups that emphasized the significance of print in the black freedom struggle. In Philadelphia alone between the 1780s and the late 1820s, African Americans formed over forty such groups to promote moral uplift, economic achievement, religious instruction, and literacy. "Perhaps there never was a period," Prince Saunders proclaimed to the Pennsylvania Augustine Society in 1818, "when the attention of so many men was so vigorously awakened to a sense of the importance of the universal dissemination of . . . instruction." Happily, Saunders continued, the Augustine Society focused on the "intellectual, social, moral and political improvements of the rising generation of the people of our complexion." In Newport, Rhode Island, free blacks created the African Benevolent Society and the African Union Society following the Revolution to promote education and group uplift. Both New York's and Boston's black communities operated several debating societies and educational institutions, underwriting speakers and pamphlets on a variety of issues relating to racial reform. In most black communities, by the first decade of the nineteenth century, increasing numbers of pamphlets were "published by the order of the society" or "published at the request of the author."[9]

In this manner, print carried black voices through space and time: space, so that a broader national community of black leaders and white citizens could see African-American arguments; and time, so that subsequent generations of black as well as white readers could refer back to African-American documents. Early pamphlets did more than retain the memory of black activists, they provided templates for those who followed. In 1792, Prince Hall issued his famous "Charge" to Boston's black community, urging his brethren to join benevolent societies, gain literacy, and remain pious, respectable citizens. A pamphlet edition of the "Charge" made its way to other cities, particularly Philadelphia. It remained a model for future black reformers. Print also allowed black writers to enter into the most restricted spaces of slavery. Crates of Walker's "Appeal" circulated in Virginia, Georgia, and South Carolina in the early 1830s, alarming both Northern and Southern politicians. Similarly, slave narratives could be found in parts of the slave South, particularly cities with larger concentrations of free blacks.[10]

Blacks' efforts to cultivate a public literary identity transformed African-American protest. As both literary scholars and social historians have shown over the past several decades, enslaved African Americans created a rich culture whose content they shielded from masters' eyes. What slaves did or thought was often unknown. Frederick Douglass commented that one was either "within the circle" of the enslaved's world or oblivious to its complex meanings.[11] Written protest, on the other hand, sought to let as many people as possible see what black activists thought. In short, print made black protest an explicit and undeniable part of American culture. Richard Allen and Absalom Jones highlighted the meaning of black written protest in their struggle to correct white printer Matthew Carey's slanders against Philadelphia's black community during the Yellow Fever epidemic of 1793. "Mr Carey's first second and third editions are gone forth to the world, they noted, "and, in all probability, will be read by thousands."[12] Who would rebut Carey's claim that many blacks had ransacked white houses and exploited white sickness for monetary gain? Black writers like Allen and Jones understood the need to fill this void. From the 1790s onward, black activists self-consciously dedicated themselves to creating a literary voice which could reach beyond any local African-American community and confront white citizens on a much broader basis. They sought to counter what they termed the "public mind"—an expanding world of public ideas which, by fostering racial prejudice, lay at the roots of their plight.

To the post-Revolutionary generation of Americans, the idea that black writers would engage people outside of their own community—the public—was one of two things: inconceivable or dangerous. Many whites just did not think that blacks, let alone slaves, ought to be part of any dialogue over slavery, abolition, or racial justice. Even white abolitionists found the black view hard to take seriously in the early fight against slavery. In 1800, the American Convention of Abolition Societies looked to "engage some suitable literary character" to produce a "history" and "analysis" of slavery in the United States, for such a writer would best be able to capture the essence of slavery's horror and thus captivate people's minds. Black authors were not contacted or even considered.[13]

A more interesting example of whites' efforts to deny the legitimacy of black public speech comes from a 1790 newspaper debate in New York City in which a writer going by the name of "Rusticus" sought to prove that black inferiority went hand in hand with slavery. For this reason, "Rusticus" observed, abolition was mere folly. "Before we can form a clear idea upon [emancipation]," he wrote in his first article, "we must first acquaint ourselves with the name, nature and circumstances of the thing"—of African Americans. "Thus I was compelled to travel over large philosophical and historical grounds, to find the place of the wool hairy negro in the order of nature." And Rusticus's eventual conclusion about "the thing"? The African was somewhere between apes and men in nature's order, making slavery a thoroughly warranted institution.[14]

Imagine, then, Rusticus's surprise upon encountering this reply from a writer named "Africanus": "I am a SHEEP HAIRY negro, the son of an African man and woman, who by a train of fortunate events ... was let free when very young ... received a common English school education, and have been instructed in the Christian religion. [I am] a master of a trade ... and am encouraged by several spirited, noble, and generous Americans who are pleased to praise me for employing my time so much more rationally (as they say) than most white men in the same station of life. And please don't consider me as the link in the creation by which the monkey hangs to the gentleman." His purpose, Africanus noted quite bluntly, was simple: "I hope the penning of my thoughts shall appear worthy of a place in your paper ... as an opponent to the Philosophic Rusticus." And so Africanus continued, in his own set of essays, to refute Rusticus's claims that Africans were unworthy, un-Christian, and uncivilized creatures whose only purpose was to occupy the lower rungs of backbreaking service to white society. "I will conclude by answering the last question of Rusticus," Africanus summed up. "The American and the African are one species—the law of nature declares it. And I, a sheep hairy African negro, being free and in some degree enlightened, feel myself equal to the duties of [any] spirited, noble, and generous American freeman."[15]

"Africanus," like later slave narrators and generations of black pamphleteers, made his mark. Other white writers were astonished—both that a black man could write such a letter, and that an editor might publish it. The mere presence of African Americans in print constituted an affront to white supremacy, and a powerful argument for equality. When blacks' arguments proved profound enough to require rebuttal—as in the case above, or with Jones and Allen's reply to Matthew Carey—white critics virtually conceded blacks' right to participate in the public life of the nation. Black writers had to be reckoned with. A well-known Patriot in America and England, Matthew Carey worried that his reputation would be tarnished if he did not reply to the "abuse liberally bestowed" upon him by Allen and Jones. To "justify his [own] character" before the public, Carey reprinted Allen and Jones's charges and then explained his initial comments about blacks' conduct. Carey had vowed to let the "two free Africans'" pamphlet pass "without notice." He quickly changed his mind, however, thinking "it might be advisable" to reply in print.[16]

While Northern critics occasionally fell for the bait, Southern slaveholders often knew better. They understood that print offered blacks the ears of a broader public, one that might include sympathetic whites. An unknowing South Carolina editor discovered this in 1790, when he printed the appeal of a slave named "Yambo." Writing in the *Columbia Herald* to convince slaveholders that harsh treatment of slaves worked against masters' economic interests, "Yambo, An African, in South Carolina" pleaded for an end to routine whippings and beatings. In the weeks after "Yambo" appeared, the editor was flooded with a host of "unpleasant replies" from slaveholders decrying "the insertion of the piece." He issued an unprecedented quasi-apology to his readership, explaining that people should know his warm feelings toward protecting slavery.[17]

For first-generation pamphleteers in particular, then, the stakes of literacy were high. The written word was a validation of thought and learning. William Hamilton, a leading member of New York City's black community during the early republic, commented in an 1809 speech to the African Society for Mutual Relief that their expressions of thanks "do much pleasure to my feelings," though "your request for the publication of my address is a higher compliment." This, Hamilton continued, would give him a further opportunity to confront the opinions "advanced by men who claim a pre-eminence in the learned world, that Africans are inferior to white men in the structure of both body and mind." Early white abolitionists had been urging African Americans to concentrate not simply on virtuous habits and industry (advice they gave to blacks repeatedly) but on writing as well. But abolitionists were sure that *they* would have to teach blacks about the connection between writing and literacy, on the one hand, and citizenship on the other. "A careful attention to the moral and literary improvement of the rising generation is justly considered by all as essential to the civil and religious welfare of society," the American Convention of Abolition Societies reported in its annual address of 1805.[18]

Throughout the 1790s and early 1800s, black writers illustrated that they did not need such lectures. To the contrary, members of a rising generation of free black community figures sought to usurp white abolitionists' mission of policing the morals of the black rank and file, arguing that they could just as easily serve as purveyors of moral advice and admonition. The overall number of black writers was small, a mere fraction of the free black population, and authors often emerged from a black elite, defined by education, occupation, and social contacts with prominent whites. Through their capacity to safely supervise the suspect morals of nonelite blacks and carefully manage the race's increasingly important public image, these literary elites asserted their authority as leaders. Yet while they demonstrated to a white public their capacity to police their own as a play to consolidate their own authority as leaders, mere self-interest does not adequately describe their motives or roles. African-American protestors of all classes and stations believed in the broad importance of literacy to the freedom struggle. As James Forten wrote to one Massachusetts congressman who supported black petition rights in 1800 when eighty-four other statesmen would not, "700,000 of the human race are concerned in our" memorial. Forten, like other leaders in Northern black communities, realized that those whose voices could be heard had a duty to speak and publish for the race—not simply their local lodge or organization or community, but *the* African-American community. Such efforts challenged white "friends" to relinquish their moral guardianship of blacks. The very capacity of black spokespersons to patronize nonelite blacks constituted a powerful argument for the removal of barriers to blacks' "elevation," such as the denial of the elective franchise. Many early black leaders argued that, now under the guidance of a "respectable" leadership, blacks could be left to work out their own destiny, unencumbered by the legal and extra-legal constraints which hampered their freedom.[19]

All this could be accomplished in print, black writers hoped. The increasing emphasis upon written forms of protest following the Revolution prompted a rather remarkable cultural transformation among African Americans: from a predominantly oral tradition to one which recognized the importance—the necessity—of employing print culture for racial redemption. "The enterprise in which we are engaged is of so novel a nature," Samuel Cornish and John Russworm wrote to white abolitionists in 1827 about starting *Freedom's Journal*, "that it will require some time to elapse, before our people can set a value upon [it]. . . . In the meanwhile, we must look to our friends in different parts of the Globe to stay our feeble hand." Despite the novelty of a black paper, by the time of *Freedom's Journal*'s inauguration, black writers had long since established a viable literary identity. [20]

As the black literary tradition gained force, slave narratives and pamphlets became well-established genres. Although they both contributed mightily to black printed protest, critical differences marked the two forms. The slave narrative genre preceded black pamphleteering, dating to the 1760 publication of former slave John Marrant's autobiography. While former slaves produced a few narratives in the 1790s and early 1800s, these tales did not become characteristic of African-American protest until much later. Indeed, only seventy full-length narratives were produced between the Revolutionary era and the Civil War—on average, about ten per decade. Slave narrators were crafty and even subversive writers, as scholars from Jean Yellin to William Andrews have shown. And many did not utilize white editors. But narrators did not enjoy the same editorial freedom as pamphleteers. For example, most slave narratives featured an introduction written by a notable white abolitionist. One thinks immediately of William Lloyd Garrison and Wendell Phillips prefacing Douglass's work, or Lydia M. Child fronting Harriet Jacob's work. For white audiences, these interlocutors vouched for a narrator's authenticity. Then, too, the demands of a white, Northern, middle-class audience—hungry for stories of heroic individual struggle and black suffering—lent later slave narratives a somewhat formulaic quality. Genre convention suggested a consistent plotline: the author is either born in or winds up in slavery, relates graphic tales of labor and violence under the lash, escapes bondage through hard work and ingenuity, and eventually is befriended by abolitionists, whereupon he or she claims his or her independent identity in a printed autobiography. As William Andrews has shown, black autobiographies were sometimes shaped by white editors and copyists, who might, for example, overemphasize religiosity as a means of black redemption or the kindness of white abolitionists. Slave narrator Henry Bibb's editors excised many angry references to whites and highlighted the aid of white reformers on the Underground Railroad. Bibb's second edition, published by himself, told a somewhat different story, with Bibb emphasizing his own agency in fleeing slavery and a none-too-subtle anger at apathetic whites.[21]

Pamphlet literature proved much less predictable, owing to the breadth of genres appearing under the form. This breadth, combined with greater control over the production process, considerably enhanced black authors' editorial autonomy. The gentle and moderate William Whipper could use the pamphlet to make logical and learned arguments for black moral reform, and do it in a highly prosodic manner. Yet so too the explosive Henry Highland Garnet could use pamphlets to call for slave rebellion and the more intellectually inclined Martin Delany could use them to articulate arguments for black emigration. Control over production and content freed black authors from the narrow constraints of a single genre, permitting black expression to blossom. Pamphleteers could roam a wide field of rhetorical possibilities unavailable to the slave narrator. They could aim their words directly at whites, as did Robert Purvis in his "Appeal of Forty Thousand," or intend them only for blacks, as was the case with T. Morris Chester's "Negro Self-Respect and Pride of Race." It is sometimes difficult to generalize about the content of the pamphlets, especially as the tradition grew, and this is precisely the point: the value of the pamphlet lay in the very possibility inherent in it, the luxury to experiment it permitted, and the access it promised to a variety of audiences. These were no trivial matters. They embodied the autonomy which defined an ideologically diverse movement. The documents contained in *Pamphlets of Protest* may reveal no consensus on strategy or tactics. Some scholars have pointed to these differences as hindering the pre–Civil War freedom struggle, yet the mere capacity to entertain such a wide range of emancipatory options constituted a tangible, valuable expression of liberty. "He who would be free must himself strike the first blow," black leaders were fond of quoting. When African Americans put pen to paper, they did just that.[22]

Justice for All: African-American Pamphleteers in the Early National Period

Emerging during a period of rapid change in the new American nation—a nation black colonists helped create but were not fully a part of—the first generation of black pamphlet writers claimed a space in the Republic by fighting for their rights in print. If writing protest literature was a means to an end, that end was destroying slavery and achieving racial equality. The cohort of pamphleteers working between the 1790s and the 1820s established a foundation for future black antislavery struggles by focusing squarely on these broad concerns. Indeed, subsequent generations of writers continually returned to the dominant themes of first-generation pamphlet writers: abolition and black political equality. As Frederick Douglass commented in 1848, James Forten remained one of the most influential figures in his protest thought; Douglass's heart would "swell with pride" at every mention of the name. Why? Forten had been one of the first activists to write extensively about blacks' claims to freedom and justice for all.[23]

America's struggle for independence, and more precisely American Revolutionary ideology, decisively shaped the worldview of early pamphleteers. To begin with, the Revolution put slavery on the defensive, as American philosophers and statesmen of the 1770s pictured bondage as anathema to their national struggle for liberty. Black colonists furthered their own cause by adopting Revolutionary ideology as their own. In 1773, for example, a group of Massachusetts slaves petitioned the colonial legislature for their freedom, stating that they too were entitled to be "free born individuals." From the Revolution proper in 1776 through the 1790s, antislavery sentiment became abolitionist policy in various ways: Northern states such as Pennsylvania, Connecticut, Massachusetts, and Rhode Island abolished slavery by legislation or judicial decree; Southern states eased restrictions on private emancipation, which allowed many guilty masters (temporarily committed to Revolutionary principles) in Maryland and Virginia to free bondspeople; and statesmen promised to end the overseas slave trade in the near future. "It seems like a time not too distant will witness the end of slavery," Rhode Island abolitionists gloated to a European reformer in 1790.[24]

Yet slavery remained a dominant part of the American landscape. The nation's new constitution guaranteed that masters would have a right to retrieve fugitive slaves throughout the Union, the overseas slave trade functioned legally until 1808 (South Carolina imported forty thousand African slaves between 1800 and 1807), new slave states such as Tennessee, Kentucky, Alabama, and later Missouri entered the Union, and the domestic slave trade grew, as many Northern masters sold their property south to avert gradual abolition laws.

Black pamphleteers tried to sustain antislavery momentum. This was particularly important by the early 1800s, when a series of slave revolts shook the Americas. Indeed, Gabriel's rebellion (a plot by Virginia slaves to take Richmond in 1800) and the Haitian revolution (the only successful slave revolt in the Western Hemisphere) scared even white reformers, and bolstered the arguments of antiabolitionists in places like South Carolina and Georgia, who asserted not only that black slavery was a necessary part of American national development but that black freedom would destroy the white republic. As one Southern politician shouted when blacks tried to petition Congress to stop the overseas slave trade in 1800, "We the People" did not include blacks.[25]

Not so, early black pamphleteers replied. Was not the War for Independence a battle against oppression? Were not black calls for freedom part of an American ideology which valorized the fight against tyranny? A collective "yes" poured forth from the black press. "Freedom is the theme of our contemplation," one black Bostonian wrote in an 1808 piece. "Did not Americans think freedom a privilege truly to be enjoyed when her mother nation [England] was about to invade her? Well, if so desirable to America as that, why then are Americans not willing to have it universal?" New York activist George Lawrence, in an 1813 address, asserted that, if Americans were "not ignorant of their own Declaration, they must enforce it" by removing slavery, for "this government is founded on principles of liberty and equality." Those "noble sentiments 'we hold these truths to be self-evident'," the Reverend Peter Williams of New York wrote in 1808, must also be applied to "the bleeding African," who still pleads to Americans, "am I not a man and a brother?"[26]

Within the broader effort to end slavery and racial injustice through appeals to Revolutionary ideology, early pamphleteers focused on a number of issues: ending the overseas slave trade, curbing the fugitive slave law, stopping the passage of oppressive measures in the North, and encouraging free blacks to embrace moral reform principles as a path to elevation. Beyond any particular issue, first-generation pamphleteers maintained their importance as spokespersons in national debates over slavery and race. While founding fathers such as Thomas Jefferson hoped the sensitive race issue might wither or just go away, black pamphleteers responded with a slew of documents, all underscoring a simple point: Slavery and racial injustice still existed in the land of the free. Black pamphleteers would not let white Americans forget such glaring contradictions.

Black writers emphasized certain rhetorical tactics in this endeavor. They focused intensively on urging white statesmen and politicians to craft abolition laws in states where slavery still existed and laws guaranteeing black equality in states where slavery already had been abolished. First-generation pamphleteers adamantly claimed the principles of the Revolution for black Americans, but they also framed their appeals in a careful manner. In 1827, Nathaniel Paul of Albany extolled the virtues of New York's final manumission decree (that all slaves born before 1800 would be unequivocally liberated) by listing the names of the bill's legislative supporters and by calling artfully on other statesmen throughout the land to fight against the institution of slavery. "Strange indeed is the idea that such a system fraught with wickedness," he observed, "should ever have found a place in this otherwise happiest of all countries—a country the very soil of which is said to be consecrated to liberty."[27]

Despite the strategic imperative of a deferential discourse, early pamphleteers could—and did—veer into more accusatory language. By the 1810s, as abolitionism stalled and the American Colonization Society entered the scene with a plan to rid America of free blacks, some pamphlet writers stripped away layers of surface geniality. New York City pamphleteer William Hamilton (one of the most important black leaders of the early republic) in an 1815 essay indirectly labeled white slave traders the personification of evil and Euro-American apologists for slavery as peculiarly cunning. Africans, on the other hand, were benevolent and wise. Russell Parrott of Philadelphia described the emotional scarring rendered by the slave trade, conjuring images of the way barbarous white traders ripped apart families, the shrieks of children sold away from parents, the collective loss endured by those who survived the Middle Passage.[28]

Because many of these documents originated as addresses to black churches or debating clubs, it is not surprising to find such vivid language. Nor is it surprising that a deferential tone assumed more prominence when such speeches became written appeals. Even in their most angry moments, Hamilton and Parrott refrained from haranguing their white reading public—their pamphlets seldom utilize direct pronouns, for example—although Hamilton refers to slaveholding nations as cursed and "bloated with pride."

Daniel Coker and James Forten perhaps best exhibited the early strategy and style of black pamphleteers. Both writers used the pamphlet to address white leaders and to fight racial injustice on broad grounds—Coker (who hailed from Maryland) to battle Southern bondage, Forten (from Philadelphia) to combat Northern racialist laws. Both exhibited a deferential yet adamant style characteristic of black (as well as white) essayists in the post-Revolutionary period. And both explicitly spoke to the importance of writing in the black struggle for justice. Coker's 1810 "Dialogue Between a Virginian and an African Minister" skillfully integrated African-American protest against slavery into a highly learned dissection of white racial stereotypes. Indeed, the power of his pamphlet is not simply its message that slavery is wrong but also that white society must take seriously black views—properly couched in respectful terms, of course. A classic example of both parody and morality play, the "Dialogue" re-creates a conversation between an African-American minister (Coker) and a slaveholding Virginian. Coker had to be careful not to portray his black preacher as a triumphant hero. Then too, he had to watch his tone—too pedantic and white readers might dismiss his sketch as an emotional outburst by blacks unworthy of their consideration. If the audience were white slaveholders, and the aim to support broad manumission plans, then Coker had to lead his hesitant audience without lecturing them. In the "Dialogue," the Virginian distances himself from abolitionism, stating that it is "strange" and "repugnant to reason" even to consider wide-scale emancipation. The terms of the debate are seemingly set: they revolve around white Biblical perspectives and resistance to black views.[29]

Although his "Dialogue" unfolds with all due deference on the part of the African minister, Coker turns the tables on the master all the same, refuting the Virginian's claims about black inferiority and biblical support of slavery. Examining his biblical arguments, for example, Coker's minister points the planter's attention to a fuller reading of God's word which would refute the dictum, "servants obey masters." He also makes clear that blacks have as much right to weigh in on formal and public debates over slavery as anyone in America. Coker's epigram is telling: "I said I will answer also my part; I also will show my opinion, for I am full of matter." When the planter says that slavery is legal, and emancipation would take away his property rights, Coker replies that "this is an important objection, and it calls for a serious answer." His detailed reply surveys the history of bondage but comes back to blacks' view of the issue: "You say emancipation would be unjust, because it would deprive men of their property; but is there no injustice on the others side?" Indeed, he argues, "Let us consider the injustice on both sides." On one side, in other words, was a right to property in men—admittedly illegitimate according to both Jefferson and the planter!—and on the other side, a right to human freedom, a more just claim. Coker sublimates his black perspective into a scales-of-justice argument. And on that high plane, human freedom must win.

Coker's "Dialogue" makes two points seminal to early pamphleteers: slavery cannot stand up to ideological scrutiny, and those with power (white masters and statesmen) must act benevolently on behalf of oppressed blacks. James Forten's 1813 pamphlet "Series of Letters by a Man of Colour" adopted these same techniques, even where he favored a polemical address to Coker's literary dialogue. Perhaps the most fully articulated attack on Northern racial prejudice in early national America, Forten's pamphlet had a dual aim: to remind Pennsylvanians that their own state history was a glorious story of freedom (from William Penn's goal of creating a utopian colony to the forming of Pennsylvania's race-neutral constitution in 1790), and that this state history was part of a broader national struggle of freedom. A new law that threatened out-of-state blacks who settled but did not register in the Quaker State (lest they be sold into slavery) violated these noble traditions.

Unlike Coker's critique (which addressed Southern masters and was published in Maryland), Forten's "Letters" accused Northern Americans of forgetting their Revolutionary struggle against tyranny. But like Coker, Forten pleaded for aid from benevolent politicians. As Forten even stated, "Blacks had no wish to legislate"; they would settle for righteous actions made on their behalf.

Whether or not Forten believed these words, his literary persona understood the sensitivities of his white readers. He had to mobilize them without challenging their republican sensibilities. Forten expertly did this by alluding to America's Revolutionary commitment to liberty and justice for all. The Declaration of Independence, the Constitution, the very notion that "all men are created equal"—surely, Forten observed in his "Letters," these were meant to be expansive rather than restrictive documents. They embraced "the Indian and the European, the savage and the saint, the Peruvian and the Laplander, the white man and the African, and whatever measures are adopted subversive to this inestimable privilege, are in direct violation of the letter and spirit of our Constitution, and become the subject of the animadversion of all." Now, Forten blasted, even states like Pennsylvania were restricting African Americans' movement and threatening to take away the liberties blacks thought they enjoyed. "This is the only state in the Union wherein the African race have justly boasted of rational liberty and shall it now be said that they will be deprived of protection by the laws?" "All men are born equally free," he continued, and "the motto of our state legislature ought to be: 'The law knows no distinction.'" But Pennsylvania legislators seemed to have "mistook this sentiment, and do not consider us men." Forten's exasperation was exceeded only by his faith in appealing to the governing public on these patriotic grounds.[30]

It is important to emphasize once again how significant early black pamphleteers were to the freedom struggle. Activists from Forten's and Coker's generation were the first blacks to speak consistently for the race in public. Their literary struggle appropriated the black public voice from white leaders, who traditionally spoke for blacks not just in political venues but in most corners of public life. In addition, first-generation black pamphleteers' style of appealing to the public eventually influenced Garrison's generation of white antislavery activists. The world's oldest antislavery group, the Pennsylvania Abolition Society, functioned from the 1770s through the 1830s, but it had a markedly different style from black activists. Early white reformers favored conservative, legalistic attacks on bondage, and they frowned upon emotional appeals to the public by blacks—such sentiment threatened the goodwill of tractable slaveholders, promising the continued possibility of their compliance. Garrisonians, on the other hand, embraced black public protest, publishing more material by African-American authors in the *Liberator*'s first few years than had decades of early white abolitionists. Garrison also credited blacks for influencing his anti-colonizationist views, particularly his meetings with writers such as James Forten and William Watkins.[31]

In a world defined by elite patronage in general, and in which blacks required white aid for racial redress in particular, early pamphleteers remained conscious of their strategy: compelling whites to use their power benevolently for black rights. For Hamilton and Parrott, Forten, Paul, and Coker, white society had an obligation to secure black freedom. These black pamphleteers saw themselves as intermediaries between their people and those most capable of freeing them.

Deference versus Demand: The Antebellum Generation of Black Activists

The antebellum period (1820s–1850s) saw hope and disillusionment mix in African-American protest circles. On the one hand, a more aggressive white abolitionist movement emerged after 1830, taking its cues from decades of black activism. For the first time in American reform institutions, black abolitionists and white worked together, vowing that their consciousness-raising efforts would bring slavery and racial injustice to an end. Reformers soon clashed when these ideals faded. More importantly, African Americans faced a worsening racial front in the United States: the enslaved population grew sizably (doubling between the 1830s and 1860s), Southern masters instituted even harsher control over bondsman in the wake of both Nat Turner's slave rebellion in Virginia in 1831 and the rise of immediate abolitionism, and Northern states stripped free blacks of various rights. Pennsylvania and New York disfranchised black voters. Ohio passed black codes which limited African Americans' rights to participate in local civic institutions such as school boards. And in Philadelphia, Boston, and New York, jobs, schools, and transportation remained segregated while white mobs often ran roughshod over both black and white reformers. National political developments multiplied the obstacles confronting black activists. In response to radical abolitionists' aggressive new tactics, pro-slavery apologists hardened their stances and mobilized their forces. Congress initiated a gag rule of abolitionist petitions between 1836 and 1844; the federal legislature also crafted a new fugitive slave law in 1850, making it easier for Southern masters to track down runaway fugitive slaves in the North; and the Supreme Court in the 1857 *Dred Scott* decision stated that black Americans had no rights that white Americans were bound to respect. Black reformers, in short, had no paucity of issues confronting them.[32]

African Americans expanded their protest efforts, too, and pamphleteers played a critical role in the evolving black reform movement. The pamphlet literature of this period is remarkable for its topical range. Black writers weighed in on timeless issues, such as ending Southern slavery and attaining full civil rights in the North; they also addressed a series of other concerns, including black women's rights, racial pride, and emigrationism. By 1860, it was virtually impossible to speak of a single black writing community, or a singular set of protest tactics.

In this manner, pamphlets serve as a critical means of examining an increasingly vocal debate among antebellum black reformers over the tactics required to achieve meaningful equality. For all generations of pre–Civil War activists, the struggle was to attain the natural rights promised by the Revolution. From the early national to the antebellum period, though, the pamphlet tradition changed as black activists expanded the range of tactics considered to attain that end. Whereas black activists in the first decades of the nineteenth century often followed the deferential tone suggested by the gradual emancipationists of a more genteel political climate, those of ensuing years increasingly embraced the radical temper of an expanded public sphere, its new era of mass politics, and its aggressive assertions of group interest.

Calls for moral uplift pervaded black protest literature from the first pamphlets of Jones and Allen's generation through antebellum-era writers such as Theodore Wright, William Whipper, and Frederick Douglass. According to many of its early adherents, the moral uplift of the race required blacks to master not just literacy but useful trades, upright behavior, and principles of religious piety. By embodying middle-class moral virtues blacks would gain respectability as well as eventual access to American civic institutions, such as the elective franchise. Faith in blacks' potential combined with an optimism in whites' ability to accept blacks as future equals fueled early adherents of moral uplift principles. William Whipper's 1828 address captured the highest aspirations of this philosophy. Speaking at an organizational meeting of a new literary society in Philadelphia, Whipper advocated mental improvement as a critical means of fighting oppression. Awakening the mind would lead to practical benefits as well as the cultivation of taste and higher sensibilities. It would also destroy racial prejudice, prepare blacks for citizenship, and confound slavery's advocates. What would proponents of slavery say if there were a black Jefferson? "It is the hope of benefiting our condition," Whipper wrote, "that has encouraged us to commence the present undertaking." In the face of black accomplishment, much of the (white) stigma attached to race would dissolve.[33]

Picking up on the moral suasion principles of first-generation activists, a sterling roster of writers also continued to press Americans to live up to the nation's highest ideals. The 1853 Colored National Convention's address, printed in Rochester, exemplified moral suasion strategies. Penned largely by Frederick Douglass, this "Declaration of Sentiments" pleaded with white citizens to demolish racial subjection. "Fellow-citizens!" he began. "We cannot announce the discovery of any new principle adapted to ameliorate the condition of mankind. The great truths of moral and political science, upon which we rely, and which we press upon your consideration, have been evolved and enunciated by you." Douglass then outlined the American creed as the continuing basis for African-American protest. "We point to your principles," the Rochester pamphlet stated, "your wisdom, and to your great example as the full justification" for black protests. Douglass's literary strategy mixed adamancy and deference in equal proportion. As he concluded, "We shall affect no especial timidity, nor can we pretend to any great boldness. We know our poverty and weakness, and your wealth and greatness. Yet we will not attempt to repress the spirit of liberty within us, or to conceal, in any wise, our sense of the justice and the dignity of our cause." Black Americans' patience might be sorely tested, but in Douglass's eyes they had no better foundation of protest than American ideals—and no better audience than white statesmen and citizens at large.[34]

Robert Purvis's "Appeal of Forty Thousand" similarly embodied this push for black rights in America. Published in 1837 to protest the new Pennsylvania constitution's disenfranchisement of black voters, the "Appeal" took aim at white statesmen who turned their backs on the Quaker State's liberal racial history. Like his father-in-law, James Forten, Purvis sought to cajole whites without repudiating American political values. Indeed, disenfranchisement violated America's republican faith and dishonored Pennsylvania's glorious past. The state had issued the world's inaugural gradual abolition law in 1780; it refused to put the word "white" in the 1790 constitution as a pretext for citizens' rights and liberties; and it often heeded the calls of earlier pamphleteers who chastised the government for even considering anti-black laws. And seemingly all for naught, Purvis exclaimed in the "Appeal." Like Douglass, Purvis chided Americans who talked proudly of liberty but then refused to grant it to African Americans. But like Douglass, too, Purvis appealed to whites for black redress, and he called on his black brethren to frame their appeals carefully.[35]

But the advance of white supremacy, North and South, challenged this strategy of moral reform, and the call for equality within American culture took on new dimensions in the post-1830s period. Increasingly, pamphleteers rejected efforts to appeal to whites' better natures. Instead, they sought a platform of power from which they might coerce rights from whites or even build their own nation where they might protect their own rights. David Walker marks the starting point of an expanding genre of black pamphleteering in antebellum America. To begin, he pioneered a new tactic of mass organizing—or building a black power base—as a way of securing rights. Walker's name has reverberated in African-American history since he first wrote his "Appeal" in 1829 and then mysteriously died a year later. Men and women who never knew Walker celebrated his words and deeds, from nineteenth-century pamphleteers such as Maria W. Stewart and Henry Highland Garnet to twentieth-century activists such as W. E. B. Dubois and Malcolm X. As Sterling Stuckey writes, "Walker's 'Appeal' is a cry of outrage for wrongs suffered by

[all] African Americans at the hands of whites." Walker's writing is sure, Stuckey contin- ues, and "his critique original in character."[36]

Walker's ideological importance has long been clear: he was one of the first black writ- ers to publicly urge African Americans of all classes and conditions to create a grassroots power base which compelled racial justice. But Walker's "Appeal" represented important developments *within* the black pamphleteering tradition, too. He expanded the vocabulary and uses of the pamphlet as a protest form. Stylistically, he incorporated the black vernac- ular (the rhythms of black speech, the cadences of African-American preaching) into a written analysis of white oppression. His vivid writing reflects a fiery oratorical tradition. According to Walker, the pamphlet could be used to illuminate emotions, not just exhibit high intellect. Walker urged activists to use his pamphlet as actors would use a play: they should perform it for those who could *not* read or write. The printed page thus becomes an expansive medium which connects reader and writer via words, emotions, and a common passion. In a certain sense, then, Walker's "Appeal" diverges strikingly from the dispas- sionate analyses favored by many first-generation pamphleteers such as Coker and Forten.[37]

Yet Walker did not fully repudiate learned analysis; in fact, Walker was the first black writer to speak fully to *both* black and white audiences. Walker's document interspersed analytical text with harangues and calls to militant black action. In one part of the "Appeal," he could offer a logical refutation of the racialist foundation of the American Colonization Society; in the next, he might declaim white hypocrisy and the debilitating effects of white oppression on all black Americans. Emotion and high intellect merge without apology. His language is strong, but it does not exclude: white as well as black can comprehend every word he uses. Even in the call-and-response sections, Walker mixes a black vernacular tradition with a clear outline of white horrors. "I have compiled a very imperfect list of cruelties," he writes at one point, so that the unprejudiced reader would see that black militancy was now justified. In doing this, he lives up to Jefferson's own standard of rebellion, illuminated for all the world to see in the Declaration of Indepen- dence: Oppressed people have a right to rebel if they construct a rational argument explaining the causes. Chief among black grievances, of course, for Walker as for Forten and Allen, was slavery in the land of freedom. "Must I read the Declaration to you?!!" Walker asks incredulously. Despite his edgy tone, however, Walker returns again and again to a model of logic which calls upon the writer to demonstrate the fallacy of another's position. By erecting an intellectual foundation out of myriad religious, political, and cultural strands, Walker asks all readers to take his militant stand seriously. In other words, Walker wanted a document that had literary substance, not just ferocious appeal. Indeed, white audiences immediately felt that Walker had issued an ultimatum to them. Walker could thus institute a new tactical approach to fighting subjection—by calling on blacks to organize en masse—while at the same time creating a documentary trail of white crimes for all the world to see. In this sense, Walker's "Appeal" melded with the early black pamphleteering tradition.[38]

After Walker's multifaceted literary act, the black pamphleteer had a much wider canvas with which to work. He (or she) could drop much of the subtle mode of expression previ- ously used out of fear of offending whites. He could directly address black readers (as well as white) in print. And he could use elements of the black vernacular without apology while still confronting a broader readership on the high plane of rationality. Perhaps most importantly, Walker illustrated that the pamphlet could contain a wider array of black reform thought. On the one hand, this energized new voices within the black pamphle- teering tradition, not simply well-established figures or elites; on the other hand, it prompted others to elaborate on Walker's black organizing tactics.

The work of Maria W. Stewart, a fellow Bostonian, nicely illuminates both of these trends. Stewart's "Productions," a collection of speeches published in Boston in 1835, focused on the ways blacks could create a power base in a world of utter racial discord. Inspired by Walker, Stewart called on her brethren and sisters to organize into a potent protest bloc and then demand an end to racial subjection. Quite striking is Stewart's early public recognition of Walker—this at a time when even white reformers such as William Lloyd Garrison distanced themselves somewhat from Walker's seemingly dangerous "Appeal." Not Stewart: for her, Walker was *the* energizing force in black life. "We have a great work to do," she exclaimed, echoing Walker. "Never, no, never will the chains of slavery and ignorance burst, till we become united as one."[39]

Stewart updated Walker's message by focusing on black women's organizing power. Like many female pamphleteers and speakers after her, Stewart realized that she faced a double dilemma. Men and women of both colors frowned on her call for women to break out of their domestic sphere. "What if I am a woman?" she asked. According to her biographer, Stewart was the first woman to address what was then known as a promiscuous audience of black and white, male and female spectators.[40]

Stewart called on black women to become an organizing vanguard within a national black community: "O, Ye daughters of Africa! Awake! Awake! Arise!" Like generations of black reformers, she advocated moral uplift; but like Walker, she believed that moral uplift would not prove black worth in the eyes of whites, it would unite blacks. She entreated mothers and daughters to join her crusade. "Oh Mothers, what responsibility rests on you! You have souls committed to your charge." At every level, from the family onward, black activists must create a black power base—a virtual nation within a nation. "I am of a strong opinion that the day . . . we unite, heart and soul, and turn our attention to knowledge and improvement, that the day of hissing and reproach among the nations of the earth against us shall cease." "Make a mighty effort," she calls out, "and ARISE."[41]

As Marilyn Richardson has observed, Stewart's bedrock faith was a liberation theology: faith led to emancipation. Interestingly, her pamphlet's use of religion marks yet another divergence from first-generation pamphleteers. Both Allen's "Address To Those Who hold Slaves" and Coker's 1810 "Dialogue" envisioned religion as a bridge of understanding between the races. Masters' emancipation would bring redemption to white society, for God would reward those who liberated blacks, and blacks would remain eternally grateful to their white liberators. Stewart, taking cues from Walker's liberation theology, condemns white masters and does not waste her time on those sinners who defy God. Rather, her theology is one of black redemption: God is on the side of the oppressed. Religion is not a balm, it is a guide to resistance. "Why sit ye here and die?" Stewart asked in an 1832 address at Boston's Franklin Hall. "If we say we will go to a foreign land . . . there we shall die. If we sit here we shall die." What should African Americans do in a land where slavery had grown demographically and geographically, and even free black rights had been further restricted in various states? The answer for Stewart, as for Walker before her and writers like Garnet and Delany after, was to mobilize black community resources and only then to challenge white society's oppressive principles. Stewart's biblical injunction comes from 2 Kings 7:1, a parable about famine in ancient Israel. After the Lord has helped drive out the oppressors, the oppressed discover that they have the community resources to survive. Act for self and community, the Good Book declares, and redemption will follow. For Stewart, the threat of death itself will not deter her. "Many will suffer for pleading the cause of oppressed Africa," she proclaims, "and I shall glory in being one of her martyrs."[42]

Both Walker and Stewart advocated new definitions of moral uplift in which blacks focused less and less on demonstrating their moral fitness for equality. Rather, they hoped that education and literacy would allow black Americans to rise as an all-powerful group which could not be denied rights and liberties. Even writers not strictly associated with these so-called "militant" pamphleteers reformulated their understanding of America's racial dynamics. In 1837, for example, Hosea Easton published "A Treatise on the Intellectual Character and Civil and Political Condition of the Colored People," which in no small way sought to recast the parameters of racial reform in terms David Walker would have understood. One of the earliest immediate abolitionists to travel the New England lecture circuit and to speak to integrated audiences in both small villages and cities, Easton came to question his early optimism in reform. According to Easton, so powerful were whites' prejudicial actions and beliefs that merely killing slavery would not end black oppression. Moreover, he indirectly critiqued moral uplift strategies, pessimistically noting that whites (in the context of the 1830s world) would simply never accept black equality. In short, racial power—not slavery—was the defining problem of American culture. Until Americans realized this, and until white citizens themselves relinquished their supremacist views, racial reform would only limp along.[43]

Where Easton fretted about white power, other pamphleteers sought to challenge oppression by emphasizing black power. It is no coincidence that as the racial context hardened during the 1830s, this period also witnessed the rise of a brasher black literary voice. David Ruggles's 1837 pamphlet outlining the work of the New York Vigilance Committee is a stunning example. Formed in 1835 to protect New York City's free black community from kidnapping threats, the Vigilance Committee also constituted a black countervailing force in a racially polarized society. Neither politics nor law offered blacks due process. It was up to African Americans themselves to form organizations committed to defending vigorously black rights and attacking racial oppression—even to the point of interfering with the return of fugitive slaves. Ruggles admitted that he previously shared an optimism in racial reform, thinking that slavery was doomed and only a segment of the American population shared the "base and unprincipled" opinions of slaveholders. Now he confronted a society pervaded by racist beliefs. "We find it difficult to name a class of the community, or a department of life," his pamphlet explained, "where the colored man is not exposed to oppression." In a civilized society, such evils "ought not to be tolerated." And now, the Committee proclaimed, they would not. Blacks would take on slave-catchers, racist judges, and anti-black citizens. Although the Underground Railroad had operated since the early 1800s, Ruggles's pamphlet marked another milestone in black protest by announcing explicitly that Northern blacks would help Southern slaves. According to one estimate, the Committee rendered aid to more than three hundred African Americans.[44]

In Ruggles's "Vigilance" pamphlet, as in Walker's "Appeal" and Henry Garnet's "Address to the Slaves" (published in 1848 but conceived in the early 1840s), power became a compelling organizing principle in and of itself. Entreating white leaders would get blacks nowhere, for white Americans did not deem blacks worthy of equal rights. In response, African-American leaders had to take matters into their own hands—by physical force if necessary. Garnet's "Address" was short on details, but big on this strategic point: Black slaves had not just a right but a duty to take their freedom by force. So convinced of this is Garnet that he lectures his enslaved brethren that they will not be guaranteed entry into heaven merely because they had been oppressed. Frederick Douglass feared that Garnet's essay contained "too much of the physical." But for Garnet, the physical merely emphasized the ideological: black Americans had to harness their own power to gain freedom, rights, and equality. They would never gain freedom by relying on white stewardship. Often criticized by other activists, such nationalist voices were muted in black conventions and in black newspapers. Garnet's "Address" was originally deleted from the minutes of the 1843 Buffalo Convention pamphlet. Doing what black pamphleteers had always done, Garnet exercised his own authorial control and self-published the address a few years later, together with Walker's "Appeal" (which had gone out of print since the early 1830s).[45]

By the 1850s, and continuing into the Civil War, a coterie of black nationalist pamphleteers expanded the tradition of Garnet and Walker. Demonstrating that nationalism was not a single movement but encompassed many strands of thought (from black pride within the American nation to forming a separate black nation outside of the United States), writers such as James Theodore Holly, Edgar Blyden, Mary Ann Shadd, T. Morris Chester, and Martin Delany emerged as a vanguard within a broader black reform movement.[46]

The emphasis on "black political autonomy and even independence" found its most cogent expression in Martin Delany's 1854 pamphlet, "The Political Destiny of the Colored Race." Written as the definitive statement of the black emigration convention then meeting in Cleveland, it was a fierce polemic on behalf of black nationalism. While Delany's 1852 volume *The Condition, Elevation, Emigration and Destiny of the Colored Race* treated this theme in a more in-depth manner, the pamphlet allowed him to distill his thoughts for a broader audience. It also captured an important moment in black protest. For the early 1850s saw competing national black conventions gather, one in Rochester in 1853 (led by Frederick Douglass and those black activists dedicated to reforming America from within), and Delany's convention in Cleveland the following year (which effectively repudiated America as a site for black redemption).[47]

Delany's pamphlet called on black Americans to form a separate national compact based on color and heritage as the only way to overcome American racial oppression. National self-determination was the principle that ruled the Western world, Delany believed. Like other oppressed groups (the Pilgrims, American colonists), African Americans must seek justice elsewhere. By accommodating American political culture in any way, he argued, African Americans fooled themselves into believing they would one day become equals with whites. But the white ruling class would never view blacks as equal. As Delany put it, white Americans would not "share power" with African Americans, whom they had always viewed as underlings. Realizing this, and their own power already as a "nation within a nation," blacks would have to form their own country.

The appeal of Delany's message was not necessarily its call for emigration. Although a number of emigrationist adherents could be found, most antebellum blacks did not embrace the scheme. Many were sympathetic, however, to Delany's prideful tone and emphasis on the need for blacks to operate from a position of power that whites would respect. Black Americans ought not request anything from whites, he asserted, and would actually work against their own interests should they try to do so. Rather, blacks possessed the historical background and cultural power necessary to equal America if they united. In short, Delany's pamphlet challenged black activists to rethink their tactics in a world polarized almost completely by race, in which raw force was proving itself the only effective principle of order.

By the mid-1850s, when Delany, James Theodore Holly, and other nationalist-emigrationists were in their heydays, the pamphlet tradition had witnessed a significant change in focus. The early pamphlets had been deferential, and many of the later ones were certainly less so. Yet care should be taken to not overstate the difference between early national and antebellum pamphlets. The former may appear to have solicited white favor, implicitly conceding that equality and civic participation depended upon garnering the approval of those with the power to bestow rights. The latter may appear to have ushered in a new era wherein blacks refused to curry favor, relying instead on a power-based politics which sought little from whites but separation. This was not necessarily the case. Black pamphleteers in the early national period had spoken to American elites not because they sought white approval first and foremost, but because they correctly intuited that freedom had brought them into a new place and time—an expanding and increasingly anonymous public sphere mediated by print. Their deference owed not to an unqualified desire for integration, but to the deferential style of politics that characterized their age and the Federalist-era patrons who had supported many early leaders.

Antebellum writers spoke to a broader American public through print. Two other things had changed by the late 1820s as well. First, African Americans themselves, free in ever-increasing numbers and increasingly literate, had become an important part of the public sphere to which black leaders spoke. Second, the tactic of deference had failed to yield the results expected by the inaugural generation of writers. Clearly, new strategies were called for, yet even they continued to address a public sphere composed primarily of white Americans. The absence of deference in the words of Walker, Garnet, and others did not render them separatists. It did not mean that their words were not intended for a broader public which included whites, and which still predicated itself on the possibility of altering the "public mind" on matters of race. In an age of mass politics, even those denied access to the formal institutions of politics might use the mechanisms through which resources were contested—the new and expanding media of print—to influence the process, whether they were self-annointed community leaders or not.

Hallmarks of the Genre: Tropes, Themes, and Styles

To persuade, cajole, enlighten, and energize, pamphleteers believed they had to master the written word. Authors displayed varying amounts of creativity within the genre, and the form came to contain distinctive modes of expression, some familiar within the history of rhetoric and others more familiar within the African-American protest tradition itself. Examining these tropes further underscores the depth of the pamphleteers' craft, for black writers wanted their work to have lasting weight and substance. They read as widely as possible, constantly meditated on appropriate literary strategies, and returned again and again to certain themes. Black pamphleteering was not just protest literature for a time— it exemplified African-American letters as a distinct and potent medium for all times.[48]

Henry Louis Gates's trope of the talking book is an obvious place to begin an examination of pamphleteering's literary characteristics. According to Gates, early African-American writers were concerned with inscribing themselves into the world of print culture. In this way, they might "talk" to their oppressors (who valued print) and claim a common humanity. The trope of the talking book went further, however, as Gates points out that generations of black writers spoke to one another by returning to certain central themes—some of which connected to African communicative traditions. "Signifying" became the most prominent of these patterns. From Olauodah Equiano to Toni Morrison, black authors signified on each other and thereby renewed the trope of the talking book.

African-American pamphleteers would have understood the concept of the talking book, for they used the pamphlet to talk to one another and meditate on the tradition they had created. Indeed, once black pamphleteering was established as a genre during the 1790s and early 1800s, black authors had an expansive literary universe in which to operate. They could "signify" on so-called American themes—and speak to white Americans—

by claiming their rights and liberty as outraged observers (a common trope of American Revolutionary essayists). They could "signify" on each other's work and ideas too. For example, in 1827, William Hamilton published a new pamphlet that celebrated slavery's end in New York. A reviewer in *Freedom's Journal* claimed that Hamilton's work laid bare "the inconsistency of men holding slaves" in America. Although the work "lacked a classical polish," the anonymous critic called it original, beautiful, and, in some places, "sublime." [49] The point here is that the work of black pamphleteers existed not simply in a world of particular topics. Through time and geographical space, black pamphlet writers forged, and then shared, a broad intellectual and rhetorical heritage. In short, black activists' words were shaped by more than their immediate context. Coherent structures of thought and expression undergirded the genre itself. One might say that the pamphleteering tradition was renewed with each new work, and that each new work borrowed from a canon of gestures, phrases, ideas, and shared meanings.

Black pamphleteers exhibited a self-consciousness about the written word. A mastery of language, writers from James Forten to David Walker to Martin Delany asserted, could mark black thought as timeless and significant. Marshaling words to fight racial injustice or outline the case for black nationalism could make a difference in a culture which so prized print. William Whipper called this literary strategizing the "pomp of words." Black activists could do no better, he claimed, than mastering the art of literary persuasion. Accordingly, the "pomp of words" required a familiarity with the rules of formal debate. "There is a right and wrong method of reasoning," William Whipper observed in a eulogy of British abolitionist William Wilberforce. "The former fires its premises on great fundamental truths, the latter is governed by our animal impulses." Whipper's literary persona displayed a quick wit and thoroughgoing understanding of history, logic, and rhetorical styles. His very self-consciousness of "enlightened" modes of debate was a claim to literacy and therefore intellectual achievement; moreover, his reasoned discourse placed him on an even plain with the Jeffersons of the world, while at the same time destroying the stereotype of incompetent blacks.[50]

As with slave narratives, a pamphleteer's demonstrated literary mastery could provoke anxiety in a white audience. For this reason, some black writers took the tack opposite Whipper's and feigned literary inadequacy to engage readers. Particularly for early black writers who desired a white audience, this ploy was critically important. Only after luring readers into their argument could black pamphleteers turn the tables and become authoritative lecturers on racial justice. In his 1834 pamphlet, "The Extinguisher Extinguished," David Ruggles apologized at the outset for any literary or rhetorical errors the audience might encounter. He hoped that readers would focus only on his broad critique of a white essayist's wrongheaded racial theories. "I have waited for abler pens to accomplish the work," Ruggles claimed. "But I am persuaded that abler pens will have nothing to do with it." Yet Ruggles delivered a wide-ranging and knowledgeable dismissal of "Dr. Reese's" case. In fact, by the end of the document, Ruggles is supremely confident that he has demolished the brief for black inferiority. He has mastered the art of persuasion. Even "gloss and sophistry," he announced, could not cover the rhetorical failings of the white essayist. Ruggles ends by pronouncing his foe's work "ridiculous nonsense."[51]

This style of seemingly shrinking before an audience only to provide an authoritative analysis was a time-tested rhetorical ploy.[52] By setting listeners or readers at ease through some self-deprecating comment, the speaker (or writer) prepares them for the ultimate message. Black pamphleteers gave this strategy a twist, emphasizing how far they had come in mastering rhetorical arts. Allen and Jones's 1794 pamphlet challenged white readers to understand the obstacles even free blacks faced in attaining education and literacy. White society tried "to prevent our rising from the state of barbarism," they argued, and then blamed blacks for not achieving more. "We can tell you from a degree of experience that a black man, although reduced to the most abject state of human nature . . . [can] think, reflect, and feel injuries." Indeed, they asserted, if whites were enslaved, they too would suffer intellectually as well as physically. On the other hand, if slavery and racism ceased to exist, blacks would "cultivate their minds with the same care" as whites and prove that blacks were not "inferior in mental endowments."[53] Ruggles echoed these sentiments in the 1830s: Not black nature but American racism suppressed black talent and subjugated African-descended peoples. "Now, make the case your own, reader. Suppose YOU were kidnapped in Africa," would you achieve so much? Ruggles asked.[54]

For African-American women, literary mastery presented even deeper problems and possibilities. Women of color faced quizzical responses from men and women of both colors. Maria W. Stewart's pamphlets famously addressed this issue, but so too did other writers.[55] The African Female Benevolent Society of Troy, New York, issued two pamphlets in the 1830s which wonderfully illuminated women's literary strategy. In one, Elizabeth Wicks expressed "unfeigned pleasure" in her task of eulogizing a deceased member but also apologized in advance, for "my abilities are small." Her sisters would therefore "make allowances for the feeble efforts I am about to make." However, Wicks's pamphlet transcended feigned inadequacies by providing a rousing exposition of the human will not just to survive in the face of obstacles, but to struggle, rise, and overcome. Her essay was a cogent expression of the Second Great Awakening, with an African-American edge: Humans can and must change their world to gain God's grace. Wicks highlighted black agency by putting a literary stamp on it. She asked her sisters in the North to remain concerned with "our brethren who are yet in bondage" in the South—and to take a particular interest in educating black youth in their own communities. By tending to these multiple community needs, black women would spread literacy and the Gospel far and wide and thus put racial subjection on the defensive. In the end, Wicks's authoritative call trumps her earlier claims of inadequacy. She commands: "I would say to you children, let not your days . . . be wasted away and utterly lost to every valuable and noble purpose."[56]

Tone became another defining characteristic of the pamphleteering genre. Like a dial that could be turned high or low, black pamphleteers modulated their tone to suit different audiences, emphasize different points, and accent certain views. David Walker's sharp tone is well known, but there were many gradations on the dial. Deference to authority marked one spot—a low tone, as in the early pamphlet of James Forten. A notch up, a sarcastic tone projected an impatience with white hypocrisy and apathy. Still another turn of the dial brought blasts of anger from Henry Highland Garnet or T. Morris Chester.

More than a literary trope, tone helps illuminate the problem of audience for black pamphleteers.[57] For early national writers such as Allen and Forten, a white audience translated into a potential power base. And that power base valued a polished discourse— one of apparent patience and deference to the nation's "betters." Returning to Daniel Coker's "Dialogue," for example, one notices how concerned he is with exhibiting a moderate tone to win over his intended audience. Indeed, the master sees the folly of his ways in defending slavery if only because of the subtle logic employed by Coker's black minister. At one point, the master even concedes, "I am convinced by your tone." While the black minister turns out to be the expert on slavery and racial justice, the Virginia slaveholder is allowed to retain feelings of superiority. Indeed, the black minister's humility highlights the triumph of a moderate tone: "I am glad to find you are not tainted with ingratitude," the Virginia master says as he departs, sure that blacks would not retaliate against their former masters in a world free of bondage.[58] In this manner, a deferential tone represented a calculated antislavery strategy to subvert the pro-slavery argument.

Subsequent generations of pamphleteers manipulated the tone dial to address new audiences and showcase new strategies.[59] For example, nationalists Martin Delany and T. Morris Chester used a sarcastic tone to target a black readership. Delany bristled at the thought that blacks believed themselves to be American citizens. Writing for the National Emigration Convention in 1854, Delany charged, "We have not addressed you as citizens, because you have never been." Delany's tone implicitly asked blacks to interrogate their own racial psychology. Although his explanation of white racial power bordered on the academic (as when he pointed out that black "degradation being once legally determined, color is sufficient to keep that distinction"), Delany's consistently direct and sharp tone underscored his call for an independent black nation. Liberation of the African race, he said, would come only outside of America, because then "the ruling elements and lawmakers would be [black]." Throughout his pamphlet, Delany refuses to call black Americans "freemen" or "citizens"; they are black "country men" who must form their own nation outside of the United States.[60]

The connections between speech (or the black vernacular) and tone are often quite striking. Chester's work on racial pride, in which he integrates speech and written argument to rousing effect, is one of the best examples from the pamphlet literature. Originally an address to the Colored Library Company of Philadelphia, Chester's pamphlet takes his audience through an alternate black history of America, which, he says, should be taught to black students. But the power of his text is its energizing tone—the words are designed literally to jump off the page and produce shouts of agreement. He transcribes audience responses to his oration in his written text: passages are marked with "Applause" and "Loud Applause"; and exclamation points indicate where his speech rises to new heights. "Tear down your portrait of Washington and raise Toussaint (loud applause!)" is one typical example. Chester was actually calling for more written accomplishment in black educational circles—textbooks, biographies, and histories. But his pamphlet did not ignore the importance of oral traditions in transmitting that message. As such, his essay works in both an oral and a written context, and, like the work of Walker, Stewart, Garnet, and many others, shows the close and continued connections between the two in black written protest.[61]

Convention pamphlets showed the strategic range of the tone dial. Combining transcriptions of debates as well as polished essays, these pamphlets were often infused with multiple—even contradictory—voices: from deferential to angry. The Buffalo Convention of 1843 achieved its fame for debates over whether or not to publish Henry Highland Garnet's "Address to the Slaves." Frederick Douglass opposed publication, as the convention minutes state, because Garnet's essay had "too much of the physical"—it condoned violent uprising by the enslaved. Buffalo delegates argued the matter for several days, eventually voting down the motion to publish the address as part of the official convention records. Thus, while Garnet's essay does not itself appear, his focus on direct confrontation between master and slave haunts the minutes in the form of vigorous debate among delegates.[62]

Pennsylvania's African-American leaders published a pamphlet from their 1848 state convention with a similarly wide range in tone. When addressing white citizens about blacks' lack of voting rights, the convention emphasized moderation, stating that "the successful prosecution of our cause depends much on the form and manner of our advocacy." The draft petition seeking re-enfranchisement also began in a deferential style: equal voting rights, black Pennsylvanians declared, "are deeply interesting to you and highly important to us," for anything which developed the "natural, intellectual, and physical resources of the state or nation enhances her strength." American nationalism would be bolstered by providing black equal rights. A few pages later, however, the Pennsylvania pamphleteers turned the volume up a bit by lecturing white citizens. Are blacks to be prevented from voting simply "because we're not white? Is this the light of the 19th-century! Gracious God!" Yet the address closed by ensuring that the citizens of the state understood the essentially moderate call for black voting rights: "The position [of disenfranchisement] we occupy is contrary to the spirit and genius of the people of this state."[63]

But a peek behind the scenes (in the convention's minutes, also published in pamphlet form) reveals the more consistently sharp and angered tone expressed by members of the convention. According to the minutes, "The people of Pennsylvania, by sanctioning the dis-enfranchisement of the colored citizens, have violated their republican faith, and brought dishonor and degradation" upon themselves. Similarly, "an appeal to the colored citizens" of the state maintained this attacking tone. Far from deferential petitioners, the appeal characterizes Pennsylvania blacks as proud freedom fighters demanding change. In fact, the state's refusal to grant the elective franchise "distributed a blow to our manhood"; black activism did not simply seek to correct a wrong in moderate terms, then, it hoped to retrieve an honor "worthy us."[64]

A third literary trope concerned autobiography. From the earliest pamphlets in the 1790s, black writers used autobiography as a critical frame of reference. Yet, while the first-person perspective pervaded the genre, autobiography served a somewhat different purpose in pamphlets than in the slave narrative genre. Autobiography required writers to alternate between personal memory and historical events—to make sense of a life by putting it in order and context. As V. P. Franklin observes, African Americans "used their personal experiences as a mirror" to reflect on a larger set of concerns.[65]

The pamphleteering genre did not recount personal experiences in this manner—it used the subjective to explain why positions were taken, how they were formed, who must understand them. For black pamphleteers, the first-person perspective was an important method of clarifying, critiquing, and illuminating the issues at hand: racist laws, white stereotypes, black nationhood. Autobiographical frames of reference broadened outward into a world of analysis, formal social debate, and intellectual activity. The trick was to go beyond the personal to the transcendent. It is no mistake that Allen and Jones helped inaugurate the pamphleteering tradition when they sought to respond to a public attack levied against Philadelphia's black community during the 1793 Yellow Fever epidemic. "We are solicited by a number of those who feel themselves injured," they commented, "to step forward and declare facts *as they really were*; feeling that from our situation, on account of the charge we took upon us, we had it more fully in our power to know and observe the conduct and behavior of those who were employed." Their "narrative" sought to set the record straight from an interior view of black testimony and experience. But Allen and Jones transcended this charge too by constructing a more general and thoughtful anti-slavery argument. In an early version of the nature-versus-nurture argument, they asserted that if slavery and racial oppression were eradicated, then black Americans would gain equal status with whites. Countering the words and common wisdom of Jefferson (who in *Notes on Virginia* argued that blacks were inherently unequal), Allen and Jones observed that slavery made conditions vastly unequal for black Americans. Once Americans demolished this social barrier, black Americans would prove themselves worthy members of free society. In the world of the 1790s, with only one-eighth of the black population free and only a few Northern states embracing gradual abolitionism, such words were strong intellectual refutations of white power. And they stemmed from the sting of Allen's and Jones's personal experience.[66]

"To speak or write on a subject relating to one's self is peculiarly embarrassing," Hosea Easton observed in 1837, "and especially so under a deep sense of injury."[67] Nonetheless, black writers had to meld their personal experiences—what an Easton pamphlet referred to as "the colored condition in America"—with a broader political and intellectual analysis of the nation's worsening racial dilemma. Easton did his part by examining the devastating impact of white racism on African Americans' collective psyche. From ancient African cultures of refinement and distinction to a present status as thoroughly subjugated people, Easton viewed black Americans' plight as desperate. As he put it, "a once noble people are now heathenish." Why? Easton identified slavery as Americans' original sin—one which had by the 1830s spread beyond Southern bondage itself and become entangled with all black people's existence. Like Allen, Coker, and even Walker, Easton highlighted African Americans' theoretical claim to rights (they gained them by "birth" in the country or by the "blood" they shed for the country). But only when whites truly recognized the validity of these claims—and the deep wound they inflicted upon black Americans—would black Americans be freed.[68]

Using personal perspectives to interrogate racial dilemmas, black pamphleteers challenged one of the rhetorical ideals of early national statesmanship: "disinterestedness."[69] Where white statesmen and philanthropists of the post-Revolutionary age professed a belief in separating their personal views and emotions from the Republic's well-being, black writers like Easton connected their personal and group experiences to what they believed was the nation's most pressing problem—that of race. James Forten's 1813 pamphlet critiquing a proposed Pennsylvania law restricting black movement made no pretense about his personal stake in the issue—indeed, the stake of all free black Americans, not to mention the integrity of American ideology itself. Forten's very title told readers of his racial position: "Series of Letters by a Man of Colour." He personalized his argument in other ways too. "Suppose I have a brother," he wrote, who seeks to visit from out of state. Will he be required to register? Would newborn babies be registered? From personal experience, though, Forten moved on to grander themes: the Declaration of Independence, Pennsylvania's constitution—documents which secured liberty without regard to racial classifications. Whites would not accept restrictions on their liberties; why should blacks' experience be any different in the so-called free North? Forten's experience, he makes clear, was merely a mechanism for understanding the fallacies which allowed whites to craft such discriminatory laws in the first place. Why should any person in America be enslaved on the basis of color?[70] William Watkins's 1855 pamphlet "Our Rights as Men" provided a cogent epigram to the trope of autobiography, distilling black collective experience into a broader claim for equal rights: "But sir," he asked readers, "if colored men helped achieve your liberty as well as mine, if your fathers and MY fathers found one common revolutionary grace, I ask you in the name of crushed and bleeding humanity, why should you . . . be elevated to heaven, and we be cast down to hell?"[71]

The autobiographical perspective played a somewhat different role for nationalists like Walker, Garnet, and Delany. Indeed, these writers confronted blacks with their own collective experience of oppression as well as their destiny as a people. For all three writers, in fact, it was critical that blacks used their experiential perspective to understand the lure of nationalism: African-descended people had experienced such miserable treatment in America that they could achieve racial justice *only* outside of the country in a separate black nation. Furthermore, these writers emphasized that African Americans could align themselves only with those who understood the psychology of collective oppression. Nationalists had one other goal in the use of ancestral memory in their appeals: the provision of hope and uplift. Garnet's "Address to the Slaves" directs his readers to think of their personal and collective situations together—the enslaved person on a Southern plantation, the plight of blacks everywhere. Then he reminds them that as a proud race they can combine forces to liberate African-descended peoples throughout America. "Let your motto be resistance," he famously proclaimed. "Remember, You are four millions." The intensity of feeling in Garnet's pamphlet is generated by the intensity of oppression felt by slaves. Garnet, like Walker and Delany, hopes to energize blacks by sublimating that intense feeling into a program for mass black action.[72]

A final and most fascinating trope of black pamphleteering was its focus on, and use of, history. Black writers in all genres—newspaper articles, poetry, and personal narratives—took up their pens to record a critical version of American history and society. David Walker firmly stated this concern when he announced that future writers, free from the racial bias of his white contemporaries, would "search the historical record" anew and discover his voice as a significant commentator on American culture. In short, pamphlets made the black view seem an inviolate part of the nation's past.

Convention pamphlets routinely utilized history as a trope validating black activism. For example, Ohio conventioneers John Mercer Langston and William Howard Day wrote essays that revisited their states' erratic racial record. In various addresses, they pointed lawmakers' and citizens' attention backward—to the ideals of the Revolution, early state constitutions which banned slavery in the Northwest, and the federal Constitution itself, which did not use the word slavery. Ohio's passage of black laws violated the overall meaning and words of the state's early constitutional history. In addition, recent "Caste legislation," an 1857 Ohio address argued, is "contrary to the drift and meaning of the United States Constitution." "We find no word 'white' in that instrument" to support Jim Crow laws. Furthermore, state discriminatory policies would be "contrary to the ancient and well-established policy of the fathers of the Republic." Reviewing this policy, via an Ohio judge's opinion, Mercer and Day claimed that "nearly all the states made colored persons electors." History is "on our side," they concluded. Only after the sojourn through history did Ohio blacks make their appeal: "Let us assure you, then," they said collectively to white citizens, "that no unjust and oppressive legislation shall ever drive us from this state. . . . Our position is as fixed and immovable as the pillars of this great state. Your history and your destiny shall be ours." For black citizens, then, the past remained a rousing call to action.[73]

Perhaps no single historical event outside the Revolution received greater attention from black pamphleteers than Andrew Jackson's proclamation of thanks to African-American soldiers during the war of 1812. In 1837, Robert Purvis cited Jackson's message in his missive against disfranchisement of black voters in Pennsylvania. The history of the Republic, Purvis charged, was intimately connected to black patriotism. Free blacks should not be denied the right to vote, in fact, because their fathers died on the battlefield of freedom too. "During the last war," Purvis remarked, "the free people of color were called to the defense of the country by General Jackson, and received [his] testimony to the value of their services." Purvis further pointed out that these black soldiers were "addressed as fellow citizens with whites." Their descendants deserved the benefits of this black service. As a pamphleteer, Purvis had a duty to bring this common history to the public's attention. Much later, in his work defending the formation of black militias, William Watkins referred to Jackson's message as evidence of whites' reliance on black military might in the nation's wars for freedom.[74]

Interestingly, pamphleteers highlighted black protest itself as a key feature of American history. David Walker's "Appeal" reprinted a newspaper essay by Richard Allen with a strong anti-colonization stand. According to Walker, Allen deserved a prominent place in the history of the debate over colonization every bit as much as "worthy" whites such as Henry Clay. Colonization, Walker stated, was merely "a plan to get the colored free people away from those of our brethren unjustly held in bondage." For proof, he cited Clay's address to a meeting of the American Colonization Society. A whitewashed history would end there, he maintains. Then Walker adds Allen to the mix, illustrating free blacks' opinion of the ACS. "Respecting colonization," Walker continues, "I shall give an extract from the letter of the truly Rev. Allen" from *Freedom's Journal*. Like Walker, Allen claimed that colonization sought only to exile free blacks and thereby secure Southern slavery by eliminating black protest. "Can we not discern the project of sending the free people of color away from their country?" Allen tersely stated. The plan intended to keep slaves away from "free men of color enjoying Liberty." For Allen, blacks had as much claim to American liberty as whites, for "the land which we have watered with our tears and our blood, is now our Mother country." For Walker, Allen's words were part of a corrected historical record: "I have given you, my brethren, an extract verbatim from the letter of that good man," Richard Allen. For those "thousands, perhaps millions of my brethren" who never heard of Allen, Walker announced they could now see his words in the "Appeal."[75]

Just as Walker referenced Allen as an icon of black history, so too did Maria W. Stewart's 1835 "Productions" claim Walker. The point was not merely to cite him as an inspiring figure but as an activist who had changed, she hoped, American history. Indeed, Stewart's work was one of the few black publications (excluding newspapers) that so explicitly paid homage to the man and his message. It is important to remember that Walker's "Appeal" went out of print for well over a decade after his death and that the context of the mid-1830s (with a newly aggressive and racially integrated abolition movement, urban rioting against racial reformers, and fallout from Nat Turner's slave rebellion of 1831) mitigated against Walker's message. Stewart's pamphlet skillfully recapitulated Walker's message without reprinting it.[76]

According to Stewart, the black community must "go forth and multiply" Walker's "fearless" example. Although steeped in a tradition of Afro-Christian belief, Stewart advocated a program of spiritual and educational uplift. Readers should not mistake her religiosity for pacifism, however. In fact, like Walker, she alludes to violence. Liberty and equality, she claims, are worth dying for. "Far be it from me to recommend to you, either to kill, burn, or destroy. But improve yourselves, express yourselves, rise!" To even mention such words in print during the 1830s was radical, but then, part of Stewart's purpose was to preserve and enlarge upon Walker's radical message. "Though Walker sleeps, Yet he lives and his name shall be had in ever-lasting remembrance." Her cause, she continues, is a war. "I have enlisted in the holy warfare," she noted, "and I mean to fight, until my voice expires in death." When she asks in another address to the African Masonic Hall, "Where are the names of our illustrious ones?" she has already provided part of the answer.[77]

Where Stewart meditated on a black individual's heroic example, Elizabeth Dungy, secretary of the African Female Benevolent Society of Troy, examined the inspiring work of African-American women. Ostensibly eulogizing a deceased benefactor of the Troy group, Dungy used the occasion to turn the spotlight on the members themselves. Formed in February 1833 with a handful of members dedicated to charity, education of youth, and spiritual uplift, the African Female Benevolent Society grew to over sixty members in just one year. After reading a yearly report, Dungy called members' attention to "Mrs. Jane

Lansing," a white reformer and one of the "brightest ornaments in the female hemisphere." In classic oratorical (and then written rhetorical) fashion, Dungy asked the audience if she could "intrude on your time a little longer." In that time, she skillfully returned to the society's founding goals—and members' importance in keeping the fight for justice and betterment alive. "What do I see," she asked, "when looking in to the crowd?" Three societies, three institutions "for the benefit of the people of color." Of course, this meant charity. But it also meant education of black youth. Indeed, Dungy spoke of the institution's investment in educating "the youthful mind," which had resulted in a rising literacy rate among the younger generation. "Cultivating the mind" was power, and the Society was doing it. "I congratulate you on your success," she stated, noting that both earthly and eternal reward would result from continued action.[78]

The 1860s and Beyond

The pamphleteering genre remained a critical part of African-American protest during and after the Civil War. Before Union armies recruited black soldiers, pamphlet writers debated African-American involvement in the war. Alfred Green's call for black men to make the war their own is perhaps the best-known example of a Civil War pamphlet. The tradition also traveled south with conquering Union armies and "black carpetbaggers," permitting the newly freed to express themselves to the public for the first time. When Norfolk, Virginia's black community, emerged from slavery in 1865, its members published a pamphlet asking Americans to grant them equal voting rights and educational opportunities.

In the North too, pamphlets provided a critical outlet for blacks challenging segregationist policies. Former Underground Railroad operative William Still published an important attack on Philadelphia's Jim Crow laws in 1867: "A Brief Narrative of the Struggle for the Rights of the Colored People . . . in Railway Cars." A range of other pamphlets in the North and the South were published during the 1860s and 1870s, meditating on black labor concerns, voting rights, the continuation of slavery outside of the United States, the development of segregationist policies in various parts of the country, and on and on.

Yet, paradoxically, slavery's destruction and the promise of political inclusion in these years may have also muted the autonomous voices of black leaders that had figured so prominently in the early national and antebellum eras. It might easily be imagined that the Civil War and Reconstruction—which liberated 3.5 million slaves and in which 180,000 fought—would have created an even greater outpouring of pamphlets, as blacks flexed their new political muscle. However, Reconstruction sacrificed the autonomy of black political expression on the altar of biracial democracy. For the first time, blacks could vote in large numbers. They did so under the banner of a Republican Party dominated by whites. This sacrifice paid only scanty dividends. For Reconstruction ended abruptly in 1877 and blacks were routed from positions of power. A century later, during a second Reconstruction, a modern civil rights movement would again wrestle with the problems of maintaining an autonomous black cultural voice while simultaneously accepting the aid of white allies.[79]

In the wake of Reconstruction, new generations of writers issued pamphlets to combat the restoration of white power. The demise of black political inclusion witnessed the reemergence of the pamphlet tradition and the institutional activities that had fed it. Indeed, while pamphleteers faced a world of rapidly worsening social and political relations between the end of Reconstruction and the turn of a new century (from disenfranchisement to a horrific rise in lynchings), the genre resurfaced as a mainstay of black protest, serving to publicize racial atrocities and calls for self-help, and to place demands before a national audience. Literary activists ranging from the unheralded John Palmer to Ida B. Wells emerged, as the lessons of the antebellum period—the futility of moral reform and the fickleness of a white public that too casually betrayed its founding precepts— were slowly learned again.[80] As a new century dawned, W. E. B. Dubois declared its central problem to be the one which had greeted the previous, and one which confronted the next generation: the problem of the color line. Just as modern civil rights reformers would utilize media to combat racial injustice, so did their pre–Civil War predecessors fight for freedom in print—not just in slave narratives or newspapers but in countless pamphlets of protest.

Notes

1. Henry Louis Gates, Jr., Nellie Y. McKay, et al., eds., *The Norton Anthology of African-American Literature* (New York: Norton, 1997). On black writing before the Civil War, see also C. Peter Ripley et al., eds., *The Black Abolitionist Papers* [BAPS], 9 vols. (Chapel Hill: University of North Carolina Press, 1985–1992); Eric Sundquist, *To Wake The Nations: Race in the Making of American Literature* (Cambridge: Cambridge University Press, 1993); William Andrews, *To Tell a Free Story: The First Century of Afro-American Autobiography, 1760–1865* (Urbana: University of Illinois Press, 1986); and Henry Louis Gates, Jr., ed., *The Schomburg Library of Nineteenth-Century Black Women Writers* (New York: Oxford University Press, 1986). A notable exception is Dorothy Porter, *Negro Protest Pamphlets* (New York: Arno Press, 1969).

2. Henry Highland Garnet, "Walker's Appeal, Together with [Garnet's] Address to the Slaves" (New York, 1848); *Freedom's Journal* serialized publication of James Forten's "Series of Letters by a Man of Colour" starting in January, 1827; William C. Nell, *Colored Patriots of the Revolution* (Boston, 1852); on Bibb and Delany's citation of Cary's works, see Jane Rhodes, *Mary Ann Shadd Cary: The Black Press and Protest in the Nineteenth Century* (Bloomington: Indiana University Press, 1998), 42–45, 49–50.

3. Frederick Douglass, quoted in Charles Davis and Henry Louis Gates, Jr,. *The Slave's Narratives* (New York: Oxford University Press, 1987), front page.

4. James Holstun, *Pamphlet Wars* (London: Frank Cass & Co., 1992). Pamphleteering did change as a polemical medium. In the early eighteenth century, pamphlets often were used to continue arguments beyond the capacity of colonial newspapers; by the Revolutionary era, pamphlets existed more as an autonomous piece of literature. I am indebted to James Green of the Library Company for providing this insight.

* There is debate over when the first black pamphlet was published. Phyllis Wheatley's poetry is one obvious place to start, in the 1770s. But if a pamphlet is defined as a piece of prose, the date must be pushed forward. Gary Nash cites a 1782 anonymous publication, "A Sermon on the Present Situation of Affairs between America and Great Britain Written by a Black." See Gary Nash and Jean Soderlund, *Freedom by Degrees* (New York, 1991), 97. Phil Lapsansky has not been able to verify the pamphlet's author as an African-American writer. Charles Evans, who compiled a massive list of American publications for the American Antiquarian Society (*The Evans Imprint Series*, Microcard Edition), gives primacy to Jupiter Hammon's pamphlets of the 1780s: "An Evening's Improvement. Showing the Necessity of Beholding the Lamb of God. To Which is Added A Dialogue. The Kind Master and Dutiful Servant" (Hartford, 1783), and "An Address To the Negroes in the State of New York" (New York, 1787). The latter work, a sermon to blacks that they must "get an honest living" and respect their masters while in bondage, approximates

somewhat a slave narrative, because it is introduced by two white printers. "As this Address is wrote in a better stile [sic] than could be expected from a slave," the Printers Carroll and Patterson state, "Some may be ready to doubt the genuineness of the production." It was from Hammon's own hand, they noted. Prince Hall's "A Charge" (Boston, 1792) also merits consideration. But Allen and Jones's "Narrative" was the first black pamphlet to bear a U.S. copyright: "Printed for the authors . . . 54th Pennsylvania District, copyright issued to Absalom Jones and Richard Allen as authors and propietors, 23 January, 1794." See Allen and Jones, "A Narrative of the Proceedings of the Black People . . . and a Refutation of Some of the Censures Thrown Upon Them in Some Late Publications" (Philadelphia, 1794).

5. Bernard Bailyn, *Ideological Origins of the American Revolution* (Boston: Belknap Press, 1967), Introduction.

6. See "Minutes of the State Convention of Coloured Citizens . . . at Harrisburg" (Philadelphia, 1849), 1–11.

7. Alexander Saxton, *The Rise and Fall of the White Republic* (London: Verso, 1990), 95–96.

8. Benedict Anderson, *Imagined Communities* (London: Verso, 1983), 74.

9. Henry Louis Gates, Jr., *Signifying Monkey* (New York: Oxford University Press, 1987); Prince Saunders, "An Address before the Pennsylvania Augustine Society" (Philadelphia, 1818). See also Elizabeth McHenry, "'Dreaded Eloquence': The Origins and Rise of African-American Literary Societies and Libraries," *Harvard Library Bulletin*, II, 2 (spring 1995), 32–56.

10. Prince Hall's "Charge" circulated among Philadelphia's black community. See Gary Nash, *Forging Freedom* (Cambridge: Harvard University Press, 1988), 218.

11. A *Narrative of the Life of Frederick Douglass Written By Himself*, in *The Classic Slave Narratives*, ed. Henry Louis Gates, Jr. (New York: Vintage, 1987), 263.

12. Richard Allen and Absalom Jones, "A Narrative of the Proceedings of the Black People During the Late Awful Calamity in Philadelphia" (Philadelphia, 1793).

13. Richard Newman, "The Transformation of American Abolition, 1780s–1830s" (Ph.D. diss., SUNY Buffalo, 1998), ch. 4–5.

14. Rusticus (New York, 1790). Rusticus and Africanus' letters appeared in the *United States Gazette* between March and April 1790.

15. Ibid.

16. See Matthew Carey, "Address to the Public" (Philadelphia, 1794), 1–8.

17. "Yambo, An African in South Carolina," in *Columbia Herald*, August 12, 14, 1790.

18. William Hamilton, "Address Before the African Society for Mutual Relief" (New York, 1809). See aslo Newman, "Transformation of American Abolition," ch. 4.

19. On black petitions and press, see Newman, "Transformation of American Abolition," ch. 4. The concept of a "black elite" comes from Julie Winch, *Philadelphia's Black Elite* (Philadelphia: Temple University Press, 1991).

20. Newman, "Transformation of American Abolition," ch. 4–5.

21. The defining characteristics of the slave narrative genre are explicated in a wide range of scholarship, including: Andrews, *To Tell A Free Story*; Gates, *The Signifying Monkey*; Robert Stepto, *From Behind The Veil*, 2nd. ed., (Urbana: University of Illinois Press, 1991); Jean Fagan Yellin, ed., *Incidents in the Life of a Slave Girl* (Cambridge: Cambridge University Press, 1987).

22. The original reads: "Hereditary bondsmen! know ye not, / Who would be free, them-

selves must strike the blow?" Lord Byron, *Childe Harold's Pilgrimage*, Canto ii, Stanza 76. William Pease and Ellen Pease, *They Who Would be Free* (Urbana: University of Illinois Press, 1993).

23. See Douglass's 1848 speech in Blassingame, ed., *The Papers of Frederick Douglass* (New Haven: Yale University Press, 1987).

24. The petition of Massachusetts' slaves appears in Herbert Aptheker, *A Documentary History of Negro Thought* (New York: The Citadel Press), I. 15.

25. See Newman, "Transformation of American Abolition," ch. 4.

26. "The Sons of Africa: An Essay on Freedom," written by a member of the African Society of Boston (Boston, 1808); George Lawrence, "An Oration on the Abolition of the Slave Trade, delivered . . . in the African Methodist Episcopal Church" (New York, 1813); Peter Williams, "An Oration on the Abolition of the Slave Trade, . . . delivered in the African Church" (New York, 1808).

27. Nathaniel Paul, "An Address Delivered on the Celebration of the Abolition of Slavery in New York" (Albany, 1827).

28. See Hamilton, "An Oration on the Abolition of the Slave Trade, Delivered in the Episcopal Ashbury African Church" (New York, 1815).

29. Coker, "A Dialogue Between a Virginian and an African Minister" (Baltimore, 1810).

30. Forten, "Series of Letters by a Man of 'Colour'" (Philadelphia, 1813).

31. Garrison, "Thoughts on African Colonization" (Boston, 1832), particularly section two, which features blacks' reprinted petitions and pamphlets opposing the American Colonization Society.

32. See Ripley et al., *BAPS*, vol. III, Introduction. See also Patrick Rael, *Colored Americans: Forging Black Protest in the Antebellum North* (Chapel Hill: University of North Carolina Press, 20001).

33. William Whipper, "An Address Delivered in Wesley Church" (Philadelphia, 1828).

34. "Proceedings of the National Convention . . . Held in Rochester" (Rochester, 1853).

35. Robert Purvis, "Appeal of Forty Thousand" (Philadelphia, 1838). See also Patrick Rael, *Colored Americans: Forging Black Protest in the Antebellum North* (Chapel Hill: University of North Carolina Press, 2001).

36. Sterling Stuckey, *Goin' Through the Storm* (New York: Oxford University Press, 1994), 88–91.

37. For a recent biography and appraisal of Walker's style, see Peter Hinks, *To Awake My Afflicted Brethren* (University Park: Penn State University Press, 1997).

38. David Walker, "Appeal to the Colored Citizens of the World" (Boston, 1829, 1830).

39. Maria W. Stewart, "Productions" (Boston, 1835).

40. Ibid.

41. Ibid.

42. Marilyn Richardson, *Maria W. Stewart: America's First Black Woman Political Writer* (Bloomington: Indiana University Press, 1987), Introduction.

43. For one of the most important analyses of racial reform, see James B. Stewart, "Racial Modernity," *Journal of the Early Republic* (winter 1998). On Easton, see Stewart and George Price, eds., *To Heal the Scourge of Prejudice* (Amherst: University of Massachusetts Press, 1999).

44. Ruggles, "New York Committee of Vigilence for the Year 1837" (New York, 1837).

45. See Garnet, "Address to the Slaves . . . with Walker's Appeal" (New York, 1848).

46. For an excellent analysis of issues relating to identity and emigration, see James Horten and Lois Horton, *In Hope of Liberty* (New York: Oxford University Press, 1998), ch. 7–8.

47. See Martin Delany, *The Condition, Elevation, Emigration and Destiny of the Colored People in the United States* (Originally published "By the Author" in Philadelphia, 1852); and Delany, "Political Destiny of the Colored Race on the American Continent" (Cleveland, 1854).

48. For the broader meaning of black letters, see Gates et al., eds., *The Norton Anthology of African-American Literature*, Introduction, as well as Gerald Early, ed., *Speech and Power: The African American Essay and Its Cultural Context from Polemics to Pulpit*, 2 vols. (Hopewell, N.J.: The Ecco Press, 1993).

49. See Hamilton, "An Oratory Delivered in the African Zion Church" (New York, 1827). And *Freedom's Journal*, July 13, 1827.

50. See William Whipper, "An Address Delivered in Wesley Church" (Philadelphia, 1828) and "Non-Resistance" (Philadelphia, 1837).

51. David Ruggles, "The Extinguisher Extinguished" (New York, 1834).

52. On the rhetorical traditions of African-American writers and lecturers, see especially Keith Miller, *Voice of Deliverance; The Language of Martin Luther King, Jr. and Its Sources* (New York: The Free Press, 1992); on American rhetorical styles in general, see Gary Wills, *Lincoln at Gettysburg* (New York: Oxford University Press, 1995). And Jay Fliegelman, *Declaring Independence: Jefferson, National Language and the Culture of Performance* (Stanford: Stanford University Press, 1993).

53. Allen and Jones, "A Narrative."

54. Ruggles, "The Extinguisher Extinguished."

55. On the dilemmas of female African-American writers and their responses, see Joanne M. Braxton, *Black Women Writing Autobiography: A Tradition Within a Tradition* (Philadelphia: Temple University Press, 1989); Francis Foster Smith, *Written By Herself: Literary Production by African American Women, 1746–1892* (Bloomington: Indiana University Press, 1993); and Jean Fagin Yellin's introduction to Harriet Jacobs's *Incidents in the Life of a Slave Girl*.

56. Elizabeth Wicks, "Address Delivered Before the African Female Benevolent Society of Troy" (Troy, 1834).

57. For an important analysis of audience/reader problems in black autobiography, see Robert Stepto, "Distrust of the Reader in Afro-American Narratives," in *Reconstructing American Literary History*, ed. Sacvan Berkovitch (Cambridge: Cambridge University Press, 1986); Francis Smith Foster, "Resisting Incidents," in *Harriet Jacobs and Incidents in the Life of a Slave Girl*, ed. Deborah M. Garfield and Rafia Zafar (Cambridge: Cambridge University Press, 1996).

58. Daniel Coker, "A Dialogue Between a Virginian and an African Minister" (Baltimore, 1810).

59. Stuckey illuminates the rise of a stronger, more self-consciously "black" literary tone in *Goin' Through the Storm*, ch. 5–7.

60. Martin Delany, "Political Destiny of the Colored Race on the American Continent" (Cleveland, 1854).

61. T. Morris Chester, "Negro Self-Respect and Pride of Race" (Philadelphia, 1863).

62. "Minutes of the National Convention . . . held at Buffalo" (New York, 1843).

63. "Appeal to the Voters of the Commonwealth of Pennsylvania" and "An Appeal to the Colored Citizens of Pennsylvania," both in "Minutes of the State Convention of the Colored Citizens of Pennsylvania . . . December 1848" (Philadelphia, 1849).

64. Ibid.
65. See V. P. Franklin, *Living Our Stories, Telling Our Truths: Autobiography and the Making of the African-American Intellectual Tradition* (New York: Scribner, 1995).
66. Allen and Jones, "A Narrative." Also, Jefferson, *Notes on the State of Virginia* (1786).
67. See Price and Stewart's excellent introduction to Hosea Easton, "A Treatise on the Intellectual Character . . . of the Colored People . . . and the Prejudice Exercised Toward Them" (Boston, 1837) in *To Heal the Scourge of Prejudice*.
68. Ibid.
69. See Gordon S. Wood, "Interest and Disinterestedness," in *Beyond Confederation*, ed. Stephen Botein, Richard Beeman and Edward Carter (Chapel Hill: University of North Carolina Press, 1987).
70. James Forten, "Series of Letters by a Man of Colour" (Philadelphia, 1813).
71. William Watkins, "Our Rights As Men" (Boston, 1853).
72. Garnet, "Address to the Slaves of the United States." On nationalist narratives, see Sterling Stuckey, *Slave Culture*; Wilson Jeremiah Moses, *Liberian Dreams: Back to Africa Narratives from the 1850s* (University Park, PA: Penn State University Press, 1998); and, on nationalism's gendered literary dimensions, Madhu Dubey, *Black Women Novelists and the Nationalist Aesthetic* (Bloomington: Indiana University Press, 1994).
73. "Address" of the Ohio Convention (1857). See Philip Foner and George Walker, *Proceedings of the Black State Conventions*, 2 vols. (Philadelphia, 1979), Vol. II, 318–330.
74. Robert Purvis, "Appeal of Forty Thousand Citizens, Threatened with Disenfranchisement, to the People of Pennsylvania" (Philadelphia, 1837); Watkins, "Our Rights As Men," 1853.
75. Walker, "Appeal."
76. Stewart, "Productions."
77. Ibid.
78. Elizabeth Dungy, "Address" (Troy, 1834).
79. Alfred M. Green, "Letters and Discussion on the Formation of Colored Regiments and the Duty of Colored People in Regard to the Great Slaveholders's Rebellion. . . ." (Philadelphia, 1862); "Equal Suffrage. Address From the Colored Citizens of Norfolk, Va., . . ." (New Bedford, Mass., 1865); William Still, "A Brief Narrative of the Struggle for the Rights of the Colored People . . . in Railway Cars" (Philadelphia, 1867).
80. See, for example, the following works from the period between 1880 and 1900: Ida B. Wells, "The Reason Why" (Chicago, 1893); "On Lynching: Southern Horrors" (New York, 1892, 1895, 1900); John Palmer, "Was Richard Allen Great?" The Daniel P. Murray Pamphlet Collection at the Library of Congress houses many of these works and is a wonderful source for scholars and students of black writing.

Absalom Jones and Richard Allen

The first patented pamphlet by African Americans was initially conceived to correct public misperceptions about black Philadelphians' conduct during the Yellow Fever epidemic of 1793. Matthew Carey, the celebrated printer, accused blacks of pilfering white homes as citizens fled the infected city. His pamphlet outraged the black community.

When no white authority stepped forward to condemn Carey, two black writers issued a written reply: "The Narrative." According to its authors, Richard Allen (1760–1831) and Absalom Jones (1746–1818), Carey's biased work would remain etched in the public mind unless blacks responded in print—the medium had a special power in American culture. Far from forming marauding bands, blacks helped whites in disproportionate numbers, even in the face of mounting black deaths. But the pamphlet transcended this theme by attacking the intellectual foundation of Carey's argument. Blacks were not the problem, as he claimed, slavery was; absent this institution, they could achieve all that whites had. It was one of the first fully articulated statements of nurture over nature: Remove the stigma of bondage and watch blacks become successful citizens.

Allen and Jones were both former slaves who had bought their own freedom and settled in post-Revolutionary Philadelphia. Over the next several decades, they helped establish the first independent black church in America, headed community organizations (such as the Free African Society), and shaped much of Afro-Philadelphians' protest strategies of moral uplift. Both believed in the importance of print as a vehicle for black protest. Jones published his own sermon on the ending of the slave trade as well as other treatises in 1808; Allen wrote a memoir at the end of his life and supported *Freedom's Journal* in the 1820s. Both were part of the first generation of free black protest leaders—"Giants," as they were later called. Their pamphlet heralds the emergence of a black literary voice, one firmly etched in print for all posterity to see.

"A Narrative of the Proceedings of the Black People During the Late Awful Calamity in Philadelphia"

(1794)

"... we are solicited, by a number of those who feel themselves injured thereby, and by the advice of several respectable citizens, to step forward and declare facts as they really were ..."

In consequence of a partial representation of the conduct of the people who were employed to nurse the sick, in the late calamitous state of the city of Philadelphia, we are solicited, by a number of those who feel themselves injured thereby, and by the advice of several respectable citizens, to step forward and declare facts as they really were; seeing that from our situation, on account of the charge we took upon us, we had it more fully and generally in our power, to know and observe the conduct and behavior of those that were so employed.

Early in September, a solicitation appeared in the public papers, to the people of colour to come forward and assist the distressed, perishing, and neglected sick; with a kind of assurance, that people of our colour were not liable to take the infection. Upon which we and a few others met and consulted how to act on so truly alarming and melancholy an occasion. After some conversation, we found a freedom to go forth, confiding in him who can preserve in the midst of a burning fiery furnace, sensible that it was our duty to do all the good we could to our suffering fellow mortals. We set out to see where we could be useful. The first we visited was a man in Emsley's alley, who was dying, and his wife lay dead at the time in the house, there were none to assist but two poor helpless children. We administered what relief we could, and applied to the overseers of the poor to have the woman buried. We visited upwards of twenty families that day -- they were scenes of woe indeed! The Lord was pleased to strengthen us, and remove all fear from us, and disposed our hearts to be as useful as possible.

In order the better to regulate our conduct, we called on the mayor next day, to consult with him how to proceed, so as to be most useful. The first object he recommended was a strict attention to the sick, and the procuring of nurses. This was attended to by Absalom Jones and William Gray; and, in order that the distressed might know where to apply, the mayor advertised the public that upon application to them they would be supplied. Soon after, the mortality increasing, the difficulty of getting a corpse taken away, was such, that few were willing to do it, when offered great rewards. The black people were looked to. We then offered our services in the public papers, by advertising that we would remove the dead and procure nurses. Our services were the production of real sensibility; -- we sought not fee nor reward, until the increase of the disorder rendered our labour so arduous that we were not adequate to the service we had assumed. The mortality increasing rapidly, obliged us to call in the assistance of five' hired men, in the awful discharge of interring the dead. They, with great reluctance, were prevailed upon to join us. It was very uncommon, at this time, to find any one that would go near, much more, handle, a sick or dead person.

Mr. Carey, in page 106 of his third edition, has observed, that, "for the honor of human nature, it ought to be recorded, that some of the convicts in the goal, a part of the term of whose confinement had been remitted as a reward for their peaceable, orderly behavior, voluntarily offered themselves as nurses to attend the sick at Bush-hill; and have, in that capacity, conducted themselves with great fidelity, &c." Here it ought to be remarked, (although Mr. Carey hath not done it) that two thirds of the persons, who rendered these essential services, were people of colour, who, on the application of the elders of the African church, (who met to consider what they could do for the help of the sick) were liberated, on condition of their doing the duty of nurses at the hospital at Bush-hill; which they as voluntarily accepted to do, as they did faithfully discharge, this severe and disagreeable duty. -- May the Lord reward them, both temporally and spiritually.

When the sickness became general, and several of the physicians died, and most of the survivors were exhausted by sickness or fatigue; that good man, Doctor Rush, called us more immediately to attend upon the sick, knowing we could both bleed; he told us we could increase our utility, by attending to his instructions, and accordingly directed us where to procure medicine duly prepared, with proper directions how to administer them, and at what stages of the disorder to bleed; and when we found ourselves incapable of judging what was proper to be done, to apply to him, and he would, if able, attend them himself, or send Edward Fisher, his pupil, which he often did; and Mr. Fisher manifested his humanity, by an affectionate attention for their relief.-This has been no small satisfaction to us; for, we think, that when a physician was not attainable, we have been the instruments in the hand of God, for saving the lives of some hundreds of our suffering fellow mortals.

We feel ourselves sensibly aggrieved by the censorious epithets of many, who did not render the least assistance in the time of necessity, yet are liberal of their censure of us, for the prices paid for our services, when no one knew how to make a proposal to any one they wanted to assist them. At first we made no charge, but left it to those we served in removing their dead, to give what they thought fit-we set no price, until the reward was fixed by those we had served. After paying the people we had to assist us, our compensation is much less than many will believe.

We do assure the public, that all the money we have received, for burying, and for coffins which we ourselves purchased and procured, has not defrayed the expence of wages which we had to pay to those whom we employed to assist us. The following statement is accurately made:

CASH RECEIVED

The whole amount of Cash we received for burying the dead, and for burying beds, is, £233 10 4

CASH PAID

or coffins, for which we have received nothing − − − − − − £33 0 0

For the hire of five men, 3 of them 70 days
each, and the other two, 63 days each,
at 22/6 per day – 378 0 0
– 411 0 0

Debts due us, for which we expect but little   – – – – – £110 0 0

From this statement, for the truth of which we solemnly vouch, it is evident, and we sensibly feel the operation of the fact, that we are out of pocket – – – – – £178 9 8

Besides the costs of hearses, the maintenance of our families for 70 days, (being the period of our labours) and the support of the five hired men, during the respective times of their being employed; which expences, together with sundry gifts we occasionally made to poor families, might reasonably and properly be introduced, to show our actual situation with regard to profit–but it is enough to exhibit to the public, from the above specified items, of Cash *paid and Cash received*, without taking into view the other expences, that, by the employment we were engaged in, we lost C 177 9 8. But, if the other expenses, which we have actually paid, are added to that sum, how much then may we not say we have suffered! We leave the public to judge.

It may possibly appear strange to some who know how constantly we were employed, that we should have received no more Cash than £ 2 3 3 10 4. But we repeat our assurance, that this is the fact, and we add another, which will serve the better to explain it: We have buried *several hundreds* of poor persons and strangers, for which service we have never received, nor never asked any compensation.

We feel ourselves hurt most by a partial, censorious paragraph, in Mr. Carey's second edition, of his account of the sickness, &c. in Philadelphia; pages 76 and 77, where he asperses the blacks alone, for having taken the advantage of the distressed situation of the people. That some extravagant prices were paid, we admit; but how came they to be demanded? the reason is plain. It was with difficulty persons could be had to supply the wants of the sick, as nurses;-applications became more and more numerous, the consequence was, when we procured them at six dollars per week, and called upon them to go where they were wanted, we found they were gone elsewhere; here was a disappointment; upon enquiring the cause, we found, they had been allured away by others who offered greater wages, until they got from two to four dollars per day. We had no restraint upon the people. It was natural for people in low circumstances to accept a voluntary, bounteous reward; especially under the loathsomeness of many of the sick, when nature shuddered at the thoughts of the infection, and the task assigned was aggravated by lunacy, and being left much alone with them. Had Mr. Carey been solicited to such an undertaking, for hire, *Query*, "what would *he* have demanded?" but Mr. Carey, although chosen a member of that band of worthies who have so eminently distinguished themselves by their labours, for the relief of the sick and helpless-yet, quickly after his election, left them to struggle with their arduous and hazardous task, by leaving the city. 'Tis true Mr. Carey was no hireling, and had a right to &, and upon his return, to plead the cause of those who fled-, yet, we think, he was wrong in giving so partial and injurious an account of the black nurses; if they have taken advantage of the public distress, is it any more than he hath done of its desire for information? We believe he has made more money by the sale of his "scraps" than a dozen of the greatest extortioners among & black nurses. The great prices paid did not escape the observation of that worthy and vigilant magistrate, Mathew Clarkson, mayor of the city, and president of the committee-he sent for us, and requested we would use our influence, to lessen the wages of the nurses, but on informing him the cause, i.e. that of the people overbidding one another, it was concluded unnecessary to attempt any thing on that head; therefore it was left to the people concerned. That there were some few black people guilty of plundering the distressed, we acknowledge; but in that they only are pointed out, and made mention of, we esteem partial and injurious; we know as many whites who were guilty of it; but this is looked over, while the blacks are held up to censure. -Is it a greater crime for a black to pilfer, than for a white to privateer?

We wish not to offend, but when an unprovoked attempt is made, to make us blacker than we are, it becomes less necessary to be over cautious on that account; therefore we shall take the liberty to tell of the conduct of some of the whites.

We know six pounds was demanded by, and paid, to a white woman, for putting a corpse into a coffin; and forty dollars was demanded, and paid, to four white men, for bringing it down the stairs.

Mr. and Mrs. Taylor both died in one night; a white woman had the care of them-, after they were dead she called on Jacob Servoss, esq. for her pay, demanding six pounds for laying them out; upon seeing a bundle with her, he suspected she had pilfered; on searching her, Mr. Taylor's buckles were found in her pocket, with other things.

An elderly lady, Mrs. Malony, was given into the care of a white woman, she died, we were called to remove the corpse, when we came the woman was laying so drunk that she did not know what we were doing, but we know she had one of Mrs. Malony's rings on her finger, and another in her pocket.

Mr. Carey tells us, Bush-hill exhibited as wretched a picture of human misery, as ever existed. A profligate abandoned set of nurses and attendants (hardly any of good character could at that time be procured,) rioted on the provisions and comforts, prepared for the sick, who (unless at the hours when the doctors attended) were left almost entirely destitute of every assistance. The dying and dead were indiscriminately mingled together. The ordure and other evacuations of the sick, were allowed to remain in the most offensive state imaginable. Not the smallest appearance of order or regularity existed. It was in fact a great human slaughter house, where numerous victims were immolated at the altar of intemperance.

It is unpleasant to point out the bad and unfeeling conduct of any colour, yet the defence we have undertaken obliges us to remark, that although "hardly any of good character at that time could be procured" yet only two black women were at this time in the hospital, and they were retained and the others discharged, when it was reduced to order and good government.

The bad consequences many of our colour apprehend from a partial relation of our conduct are, that it will prejudice the minds of the people in general against us-because it is impossible that one individual, can have knowledge of all, therefore at some future day, when some of the most virtuous, that were upon most praise-worthy motives, induced to serve the sick, may fall into the service of a family that are strangers to him, or her, and it is discovered that it is one of those stigmatised wretches, what may we suppose will be the consequence? Is it not reasonable to think the person will be abhored, despised, and perhaps dismissed from employment, to their great disadvantage, would not this be hard? and have we not therefore sufficient reason to seek for redress? We can with certainty assure the public that we have seen more humanity, more real sensibility from the poor blacks, than from the poor whites. When many of the former, of their own accord rendered services where extreme necessity called for it, the general part of the poor white people were so dismayed, that instead of attempting to be useful, they in a manner hid themselves -- a remarkable instance of this -- A poor afflicted dying man, stood at his chamber window, praying and beseeching every one that passed by, to help him to a drink of water; a number of white people passed, and instead of being moved by the poor man's distress, they hurried as fast as they could out of the sound of his cries until at length a gentleman, who seemed to be a foreigner came up, he could not pass by, but had not resolution enough to go into the house, he held eight dollars in his hand, and offered it to several as a reward for giving the poor man a drink of water, but was refused by every one, until a poor black man came up, the gentleman offered the eight dollars to him, if he would relieve the poor man with a little water, "Master" replied the good natured fellow, "I will supply the gentleman with water, but surely I will not take your money for it" nor could he be prevailed upon to accept his bounty: he went in, supplied the poor object with water, and rendered him every service he could.

A poor black man, named Sampson, went constantly from house to house where distress was, and no assistance without fee or reward; he was smote with the disorder, and died, after his death his family were neglected by those he had served.

Sarah Bass, a poor black widow, gave all the assistance she could, in several families, for which she did not receive any thing; and when any thing was offered her, she left it to the option of those she served.

A woman of our colour, nursed Richard Mason and son, when they died, Richard's widow considering the risk the poor woman had run, and from observing the fears that sometimes rested on her mind, expected she would have demanded something considerable, but upon asking what she demanded, her reply was half a dollar per day. Mrs. Mason, intimated it was not sufficient for her attendance, she replied it was enough for what she had done, and would take no more. Mrs. Mason's feelings were such, that she settled an annuity of six pounds a year, on her, for life. Her name is Mary Scott.

An elderly black woman nursed -- with great diligence and attention; when recovered he, asked what he must give for her services -- she replied "a dinner master on a cold winter's day," and thus she went from place to place rendering every service in her power without an eye to reward.

A young black woman, was requested to attend one night upon a white man and his wife, who were very ill, no other person could be had; -- great wages were offered her-she replied, I will not go for money, if I go for money God will see it, and may be make me take the disorder and die, but if I go, and take no money, he may spare my life. She went about nine o'clock, and found them both on the floor; she could procure no candle or other light, but staid with them about two hours, and then left them. They both died that night. She was afterward very ill with the fever -- her life was spared.

Caesar Cranchal, a black man, offered his, services to attend the sick, and said, I will not take your money, I will not sell my life for money. It is said he died with the flux.

A black lad, at the Widow Gilpin's, was intrusted with his young Master's keys, on his leaving the city, and transacted his business, with the greatest honesty, and dispatch, having unloaded a vessel for him in the time, and loaded it again.

A woman, that nursed David Bacon, charged with exemplary moderation, and said she would not have any more.

It may be said, in vindication of the conduct of those, who discovered ignorance or incapacity in nursing, that it is, in itself, a considerable art, derived from experience, as well as the exercise of the finer feelings of humanity -- this experience, nine tenths of those employed, it is probable were wholly strangers to.

We do not recollect such acts of humanity from the poor white people, in all the round we have been engaged in. We could mention many other instances of the like nature, but think it needless.

It is unpleasant for us to make these remarks, but justice to our colour, demands it. Mr. Carey pays William Gray and us a compliment; he says, our services and others of their colour, have been very great &c. By naming us, he leaves these others, in the hazardous state of being classed with those who are called the "vilest." The few that were discovered to merit public censure, were brought to justice, which ought to have sufficed, without being canvassed over in his "Trifle" of a pamphlet -- which causes us to be more particular, and endeavour to recall the esteem of the public for our friends, and the people of colour, as far as they may be found worthy; for we conceive, and experience proves it, that an ill name is easier given than taken away. We have many unprovoked enemies, who begrudge us the liberty we enjoy, and are glad to hear of any complaint against our colour, be it just or unjust; in consequence of which we are more earnestly endeavouring all in our power, to warn, rebuke, and exhort our African friends, to keep a conscience void of offence towards God and man; and, at the same time, would not be backward to interfere, when stigmas or oppression appear pointed at, or attempted against them, unjustly; and, we are confident, we shall stand justified in the sight of the candid and judicious, for such conduct.

Mr. Carey's first, second, and third editions, are gone forth into the world, and in all probability, have been read by thousands that will never read his fourth -- consequently, any alteration he may hereafter make, in the paragraph alluded to, cannot have the desired effect, or atone for the past; therefore we apprehend it necessary to publish our thoughts on the occasion. Had Mr. Carey said, a number of white and black Wretches eagerly seized on the opportunity to extort from the distressed, and some few of both were detected in plundering the sick, it might extenuate, in a great degree, the having made mention of the blacks.

We can assure the public, there were as many white as black people, detected in pilfering, although the number of the latter, employed as nurses, was twenty times as great as the former, and that there is, in our opinion, as great a proportion of white, as of black, inclined to such practices. It is rather to be admired, that so few instances of pilfering and robbery happened, considering the great opportunities there were for such things: we do not know of more than five black people, suspected of any thing clandestine, out of the great number employed; the people were glad to get any person to assist them -- a black was preferred, because it was supposed, they were not so likely to take the disorder, the most worthless were acceptable, so that it would have been no cause of wonder, if twenty causes of complaint occurred, for one that hath. It has been alledged, that many of the sick, were neglected by the nurses; we do not wonder at it, considering their situation, in many instances, up night and day, without any one to relieve them, worn down with fatigue, and want of sleep, they could not in many cases, render that assistance, which was needful: where we visited, the causes of complaint on this score, were not numerous. The case of the nurses, in many instances, were deserving of commiseration, the patient raging and frightful to behold; it has frequently required two persons, to hold them from running away, others have made attempts to jump out of a window, in many chambers they were nailed down, and the door was kept locked, to prevent them from running away, or breaking their necks, others lay vomiting blood, and screaming enough to chill them with horror. Thus were many of the nurses circumstanced, alone, until the patient died, then called away to another scene of distress, and thus have been for a week or ten days left to do the best they could without any sufficient rest, many of them having some of their dearest connections sick at the time, and suffering for want, while their husband, wife, father, mother, &c. have been engaged in the service of the white people. We mention this to shew the difference between this and nursing in common cases, we have suffered equally with the whites, our distress hath been very great, but much unknown to the white people. Few have been the whites that paid attention to us while the black were engaged in the other's service. We can assure the public we have taken four and five black people in a day to be buried. In several instances when they have been seized with the sickness while nursing, they have been turned out of the house, and wandering and destitute until taking shelter wherever they could (as many of them would not be admitted to their former homes) they have languished alone and we know of one who even died in a stable. Others acted with more tenderness, when their nurses were taken sick they had proper care taken of them at their houses. We know of two instances of this.

It is even to this day a generally received opinion in this city, that our colour was not so liable to the sickness as the whites. We hope our friends will pardon us for setting this matter in its true state.

The public were informed that in the West-Indies and other places where this terrible malady had been, it was observed the blacks were not affected with it. Happy would it have been for you, and much more so for us, if this observation had been verified by our experience.

When the people of colour had the sickness and died, we were imposed upon and told it was not with the prevailing sickness, until it became too notorious to be denied, then we were told some few died but not many. Thus were our services extorted *at the peril of our lives,* yet you accuse us of extorting a *little money from you.*

The bill of mortality for the year 1793, published by Matthew Whitehead, and John Ormrod, clerks, and Joseph Dolby, sexton, will convince any reasonable man that will examine it, that as many coloured people died in proportion as others. In 1792, there were 67 of our colour buried, and in 1793 it amounted to 305; thus the burials among us have increased more than fourfold, was not this in a great degree the effects of the services of the unjustly vilified black people?

Perhaps it may be acceptable to the reader to know how we found the sick affected by the sickness; our opportunities of hearing and seeing them have been very great. They were taken with a chill, a headach, a sick stomach, with pains in their limbs and back, this was the way the sickness in general began, but all were not affected alike, some appeared but slightly affected with some of these symptoms, what confirmed us in the opinion of a person being smitten was the colour of their eyes. In some it raged more furiously than in others-some have languished for seven and ten days, and appeared to get better the day, or some hours before they died, while others were cut off in one, two, or three days, but their complaints were similar. Some lost their reason and raged with all the fury madness could produce, and died in strong convulsions. Others retained their reason to the last, and seemed rather to fall asleep than die. We could not help remarking that the former were of strong passions, and the latter of a mild temper. Numbers died in a kind of dejection, they concluded they must go, (so the phrase for dying was) and therefore in a kind of fixed determined state of mind went off.

It struck our minds with awe, to have application made by those in health, to take charge of them in their sickness, and of their funeral. Such applications have been made to us; many appeared as though they thought they must die, and not live; some have lain on the floor, to be measured for their coffin and grave. A gentleman called one evening, to request a good nurse might be got for him, when he was sick, and to superintend his funeral, and gave particular directions how he would have it conducted, it seemed a surprising circumstance, for the man appeared at the time, to be in perfect health, but calling two or three days after to see him, found a woman dead in the house, and the man so far gone, that to adminster any thing for his recovery, was needless-he died that evening. We mention this, as an instance of the dejection and despondence, that took hold on the minds of thousands, and are of opinion, it aggravated the case of many, while others who bore up chearfully, got up again, that probably would otherwise have died.

When the mortality came to its greatest stage, it was impossible to procure sufficient assistance, therefore many whose friends, and relations had left them, died unseen, and unassisted. We have found them in various situations, some laying on the floor, as bloody as if they had been dipt in it, without any appearance of their having had, even a drink of water for their relief; others laying on a bed with their clothes on, as if they had came in fatigued, and lain down to rest; some appeared, as if they had fallen dead on the floor, from the position we found them in.

Truly our task was hard, yet through mercy, we were enabled to go on.

One thing we observed in several instances-when we were called, on the first appearance of the disorder to bleed, the person frequently, on the opening a vein before the operation was near over, felt a change for the better, and expressed a relief in their chief complaints; and we made it a practice to take more blood from them, than is usual in other cases; these in a general way recovered; those who did omit bleeding any considerable time, after being taken by the sickness, rarely expressed any change they felt in the operation.

We feel a great satisfaction in believing, that we have been useful to the sick, and thus publicly thank Doctor Rush, for enabling us to be so. We have bled upwards of eight hundred people, and do declare, we have not received to the value of a dollar and a half, therefor: we were willing to imitate the Doctor's benevolence, who sick or well, kept his house open day and night, to give what assistance he could in this time of trouble.

Several affecting instances occurred, when we were engaged in burying the dead. We have been called to bury some, who when we came, we found alive; at other places we found a parent dead, and none but little innocent babes to be seen, whose ignorance led them to think their parent was asleep; on account of their situation, and their little prattle, we have been so wounded and our feelings so hurt, that we almost concluded to withdraw from our undertaking, but seeing others so backward, we still went on.

An affecting instance -- A woman died, we were sent for to bury her, on our going into the house and taking the coffin in, a dear little innocent accosted us, with, mamma is asleep, don't wake her; but when she saw us put her in the coffin, the distress of the child was so great, that it almost overcame us; when she demanded why we put her mamma in the box? We did not know how to answer her, but committed her to the care of a neighbour, and left her with heavy hearts. In other places where we have been to take the corpse of a parent, and have found a group of little ones alone, some of them in a measure capable of knowing their situation, their cries and the innocent confusion of the little ones, seemed almost too much for human nature to bear. We have picked up little children that were wandering they knew not where, (whose parents were cut off) and taken them to the orphan house, for at this time the dread that prevailed over people's minds was so general, that it was a rare instance to see one neighbour visit another, and even friends when they met in the streets were afraid of each other, much less would they admit into their houses the distressed orphan that had been where the sickness was; this extreme seemed in some instances to have the appearance of barbarity; with reluctance we call to mind the many opportunities there were in the power of individuals to be useful to their fellow men, yet through the terror of the times was omitted. A black man riding through the street, saw a man push a woman out of the house, the woman staggered and fell on her face in the gutter, and was not able to turn herself, the black man thought she was drunk, but observing she was in danger of suffocation alighted, and taking the woman up found her perfectly sober, but so far gone with the disorder that she was not able to help herself; the hard hearted man that threw her down, shut the door and left her -- in such a situation, she might have perished in a few minutes; we heard of it, and took her to Bush-hill. Many of the white people, that ought to be patterns for us to follow after, have acted in a manner that would make humanity shudder. We remember an instance of cruelty, which we trust, no black man would be guilty of: two sisters orderly, decent, white women were sick with the fever, one of them recovered so as to come to the door; a neighbouring white man saw her, and in an angry tone asked her if her sister was dead or not? She answered no, upon which he replied, damn her, if she don't die before morning, I will make her die. The poor woman shocked at such an expression, from this monster of a man, made a modest reply, upon which he snatched up a tub of water, and would have dashed it over her, if he had not been prevented by a black man; he then went and took a couple of fowls out of a coop, (which had been given them for nourishment) and threw them into an open alley; he had his wish, the poor woman that he would make die, died that night. A white man threatened to shoot us, if we passed by his house with a corpse: we buried him three days after.

We have been pained to see the widows come to us, crying and wringing their hands, and in very great distress, on account of their husbands death; having nobody to help them, they were obliged to come to get their husbands buried, their neighbours were afraid to go to their help or to condole with them; we ascribe such unfriendly conduct to the frailty of human nature, and not to wilful unkindness, or hardness of heart.

Notwithstanding the compliment Mr. Carey hath paid us, we have found reports spread, of our taking between one, and two hundred beds, from houses where people died; such slanderers as these, who propagate such wilful lies are dangerous, although unworthy notice. We wish if any person hath the least suspicion of us, they would endeavour to bring us to the punishment which such atrocious conduct must deserve; and by this means, the innocent will be cleared from reproach, and the guilty known.

We shall now conclude with the following old proverb, which we think applicable to those of our colour who exposed their lives in the late afflicting dispensation: --

> God and a soldier, all men do adore,
> In time of war, and not before;
> When the war is over, and all things righted,
> God is forgotten, and the soldier slighted.

"An Address To Those Who Keep Slaves and Uphold the Practice"

The judicious part of mankind will think it unreasonable, that a superior good conduct is looked for, from our race, by those who stigmatize us as men, whose baseness is incurable, and may therefore be held in a state of servitude, that a merciful man would not deem a beast to; yet you try what you can to prevent our rising from the state of barbarism, you represent us to be in, but we can tell you, from a degree of experience, that a black man, although reduced to the most abject state human nature is capable of, short of real madness, can think, reflect, and feel injuries, although it may not be with the same degree of keen resentment and revenge, that you who have been and are our great oppressors, would manifest if reduced to the pitiable condition of a slave. We believe if you would try the experiment of taking a few black children, and cultivate their minds with the same care, and let them have the same prospect in view, as to living in the world, as you would wish for your own children, you would find them upon the trial, they were not inferior in mental endowments.

We do not wish to make you angry, but excite your attention to consider, how hateful slavery is in the sight of that God, who hath destroyed kings and princes, for their oppression of the poor slaves; Pharaoh and his princes with the posterity of King Saul, were destroyed by the protector and avenger of slaves. Would you not suppose the Israelites to be utterly unfit for freedom, and that it was impossible for them to attain to any degree of excellence? Their history shews how slavery had debased their spirits. Men must be willfully blind and extremely partial, that cannot see the contrary effects of liberty and slavery upon the mind of man; we freely confess the vile habits often acquired in a state of servitude, are not easily thrown off; the example of the Israelite shews, who with all that Moses could do to reclaim them from it, still continued in their former habits more or less; and why will you look for better from us? Why will you look for grapes from thorns, or figs from thistles? It is in our posterity enjoying the same privileges with your own, that you ought to look for better things.

When you are pleaded with, do not you reply as Pharaoh did, "wherefore do ye Moses and Aaron, let the people from their work, behold the people of the land, now are many, and you make them rest from their burdens?" We wish you to consider, that God himself was the first pleader of the cause of slaves.

That God who knows the hearts of all men, and the propensity of a slave to hate his oppressor hath strictly forbidden it to his chosen people, "thou shalt not abhor an Egyptian, because thou wast a stranger in his land. Deut. xxiii. 7." The meek and humble Jesus, the great pattern of humanity, and every other virtue that can adorn and dignify men, hath commanded to love our enemies, to do good to them that hate and despitefully use us. We feel the obligations, we wish to impress them on the minds of our black brethren, and that we may all forgive you, as we wish to be forgiven; we think it a great mercy to have all anger and bitterness removed from our minds; we appeal to your own feelings, if it is not very disquieting to feel yourselves under the dominion of a wrathful disposition.

If you love your children, if you love your country, if you love the God of love, clear your hands from slaves, burden not your children or country with them. Our hearts have been sorrowful for the late bloodshed of the oppressors, as well as the oppressed, both appear guilty of each others blood, in the sight of him who said, he that sheddeth man's blood, by man shall his blood be shed.

Will you, because you have reduced us to the unhappy condition our colour is in, plead our incapacity for freedom, and our contented condition under oppression, as a sufficient cause for keeping us under the grievous yoke? We have shewn the cause of our incapacity, we will also shew, why we appear contented; were we to attempt to plead with our masters, it would be deemed insolence, for which cause they appear as contented as they can in your sight, but the dreadful insurrections they have made, when opportunity has offered, is enough to convince a reasonable man, that great uneasiness and not contentment, is the inhabitant of their hearts.

God himself hath pleaded their cause, he hath from time to time raised up instruments for that purpose, sometimes mean and contemptible in your sight; at other times he hath used such as it hath pleased him with whom you have not thought it beneath your dignity to contend, many add to your numbers, until the princes shall come forth from Egypt and Ethiopia stretch out her hand unto God.

Prince Hall

Prince Hall (?–1807) organized one of the first and most prominent African-American societies when he formed the African Masonic Lodge in Boston at the beginning of the Revolutionary era. While Hall and over a dozen others began meeting in 1775, the African Masonic Lodge did not receive formal recognition until 1787—and then, ironically, recognition came from British Masons. Hall was a former slave who gained his freedom in Boston in 1770. Over the next three and a half decades, he became not just a leader of Black Masonry but a revered figure in African-American protest circles as well. As African Masonic lodges formed in other places, particularly New York City and Philadelphia, such was Hall's fame that the African Grand Lodge immortalized the man in 1808 by referring to the national order as the "Prince Hall Masons." Hall's African Masonic Lodge dedicated itself to community-building efforts, education, racial uplift—and protest. Hall himself was black Boston's most outspoken leader during and after the Revolution. In the late 1770s, he petitioned the Massachusetts legislature to end slavery in the Bay State. In the late 1780s, he petitioned the assembly again, this time requesting that the state underwrite voluntary black emigration to Africa. In the late 1790s, he petitioned the local government in Boston to open a school for African-American youth (Hall eventually opened the school in his own home when the white leaders moved too slowly).

Hall also published two seminal tracts in the 1790s, both of which circulated beyond Boston during the next several years. The first "Charge," in 1792, emphasized the duties attending Black Masons as well as the significance of religious piety and racial uplift within the Order of Masons. The second work, published in 1797, addressed more explicitly the plight of black Americans and the need for black unity in the face of a hostile racial climate. Indeed, Hall's pamphlets were issued during a time of tense race relations in Boston. Although the Massachusetts Supreme Court declared slavery in the Bay State null and void in 1783 (freeing roughly three thousand slaves), white citizens were often slow to accept free blacks as equals. In fact, in 1788, the legislature passed a vagrancy law declaring that all out-of-state free blacks leave the polity lest they be incarcerated. Black Masonry offered one way to combat racism because it encouraged mutual protection and community action. Masonry also emphasized a common brotherhood, thereby providing a lesson to society that blacks could live together with whites. Hall depicted for his brethren a just God on the side of the oppressed, and his mastery of religious texts challenged whites to confront their stereotypes and treat blacks as equals in God's eyes. (Hall did have important connections to some of Boston's civic leaders, particularly Jeremy Belknap, a noted man of letters and philanthropist.)

Of particular interest in Hall's second "Charge" is his reference to the Haitian revolution, the most successful slave rebellion in the Western Hemisphere that led to the creation of the Haitian Republic in 1801, the first independent black nation formed by ex-slaves in the West. Because the rebellion was such a shattering event for many American masters, Hall's celebration of it appeared quite bold for the time. A few years after Hall's 1797 address, for example, newly elected President Thomas Jefferson refused to engage in trade with the island of Haiti. If American blacks ever became dejected about their plight, however, Hall encouraged them to remember Haiti.

"A Charge"

(1797)

"My brethren, let us not be cast down under these and many other abuses we
at present labour under . . ."

Beloved Brethren of the African Lodge, "Tis now five years since I deliver'd Charge to you on some parts and points of Masonry. As one branch or superstructure on the foundation; when I endeavoured to shew you the duty of a Mason to a Mason, and charity or love to all mankind, as the mark and image of the great God, and the Father of the human race.

I shall now attempt to shew you that it is our duty to sympathise with our fellow men under their troubles, the families of our brethren who are gone: we hope to the Grand Lodge above, here to return no more. But the cheerfulness that you have ever had to relieve them, and ease their burdens, under their forrows, will never be forgotten by them; and in this manner you will never be weary in doing good.

But my brethren, although we are to begin here, we must not end here; for only look around you and you will see and hear of numbers of our fellow men crying out with holy Job, Have pity on me, O my friends, for the hand of the Lord hath touched me. And this is not to be confined to parties or colours; not to towns or states; not to a kingdom, but to the kingdoms of the whole earth, over whom Christ the king is head and grand master.

Among these numerous sons and daughters of distress, I shall begin with our friends and brethren; and first, let us see them dragg'd from their native country by the iron hand of tyranny and oppression, from their dear friends and connections, with weeping eyes and aching hearts, to a strange land and strange people, whose tender mercies are cruel; and there to bear the iron yoke of slavery & cruelty till death as a friend shall relieve them. And must not the unhappy condition of these our fellow men draw forth our hearty prayer and wishes for their deliverance from these merchants and traders, whose characters you have in the xviii chap. of the Revelations, 11, 12, & 13 verses, and who knows but these same sort of traders may in a short time, in the like manner, bewail the loss of the African traffick, to their shame and confusion: and if I mistake not, it now begins to dawn in some of the West-India islands; which puts me in mind of a nation (that I have somewhere read of) called Ethiopeans, that cannot change their skin: But God can and will change their conditions, and their hearts too; and let Boston and the world know, that He hath no respect of persons; and that that bulwark of envy, pride, scorn, and contempt, which is so visible to be seen in some and felt, shall fall, to rise no more.

When we hear of the bloody wars which are now in the world, and thousands of our fellow men slain; fathers and mothers bewailing the loss of their sons; wives for the loss of their husbands, towns and cities burnt and destroy'd; what must be the heart-felt sorrow and distress of these poor and unhappy people! Though we cannot help them, the distance being so great, yet we may sympathize with them in their troubles, and mingle a tear of sorrow with them, and do as we are exhorted to—weep with those that weep.

Thus my brethren we see what a chequered world we live in. Sometimes happy in having our wives and children like olive branches about our tables; receiving the bounties of our great Benefactor. The next year, or month, or week we may be deprived of some of them, and we go mourning about the streets, so in societies; we are this day to celebrate this Feast of St. John's, and the next week we might be called upon to attend a funeral of some one here, as we have experienced since our last in this Lodge. So in the common affairs of life we sometimes enjoy health and prosperity; at another time sickness and adversity, crosses and disappointments.

So in states and kingdoms; sometimes in tranquility, then wars and tumults; rich today, and poor tomorrow; which shews that there is not an independent mortal on earth, but dependent one upon the other, from the king to the beggar.

The great law-giver, Moses, who instructed by this father-in-law, Jethro, an Ethiopean, how to regulate his courts of justice and what sort of men to choose for the different offices; hear now my words, said he, I will give you counsel, and God shall be with you; be thou for the people to Godward, that thou mayest bring the causes unto God, and thou shall teach them ordinances and laws, and shall shew the way wherein they must walk, and the work that they must do: moreover thou shall provide out of all the people, able men, such as fear God, men of truth, hating covetousness, and place such over them, to be rulers of thousands, of hundreds and of tens.

So Moses hearkened to the voice of his father-in-law, and did all that he said. Exodus xviii. 22–24.

This is the first and grandest lecture that Moses ever received from the mouth of man; for Jethro understood geometry as well as laws, *that* a Mason may plainly see: so a little captive servant maid by whose advice Nomen, the great general of Syria's army, was healed of his leprosy; and by a servant his proud spirit was brought down: 2 Kings v. 3–14. The feelings of this little captive for this great man, her captor, was so great, that she forgot her state of captivity, and felt for the distress of her enemy. Would to Cod (said she to her mistress) my lord were with the prophets in Samaria, he should be healed of his leprosy: So after he went to the prophet, his proud host was so haughty that he not only disdain'd the prophet's direction, but derided the good old prophet; and had it not been for his servant he would have gone to his grave with a double leprosy, the outward and the inward, in the heart, which is the worst of leprosies; a black heart is worse than a white leprosy.

How unlike was this great general's behaviour to that of as grand a character, and as well beloved by his prince as he was; I mean Obadiah, to a like prophet. See for this 1st Kings xviii. from 7 to the 16th.

And as Obadiah was in the way, behold Elijah met him, and he knew him, and fell on his face, and said, Art not thou, my Lord, Elijah, and he told him, Yea, go and tell thy Lord, behold Elijah is here: and so on to the 16th verse. Thus we see that great and good men have, and always will have, a respect for ministers and servants of God. Another instance of this is in Acts viii. 27 to 31, of the European Eunuch, a man of great authority, to Philip, the apostle: here is mutual love and friendship between them. This minister of Jesus Christ did not think himself too good to receive the hand, and ride in a chariot with a black man in the face of day; neither did this great monarch (for so he was) think it beneath him to take a poor servant of the Lord by the hand, and invite him into his carriage, though but with a staff, one coat, and no money in his pocket. So our Grand Master, Solomon, was not asham'd to take the Queen of Sheba by the hand, and lead her into his court, at the hour of high twelve, and there converse with her on points of masonry (for if ever there was a female mason in the world she was one) and other curious matters; and gratified her, by shewing her all his riches and curious pieces of architecture in the temple, and in his house: After some time staying with her, he loaded her with much rich presents: he gave her the right hand of affection and parted in love.

I hope that no one will dare openly (tho' in fact the behaviour of some implies as much) to say, as our Lord said on another occasion, Behold a greater than Solomon is here. But yet let them consider that our Grand Master Solomon did not divide the living child, whatever he might do with the dead one, neither did he pretend to make a law to forbid the parties from having free intercourse with one another without the fear of censure, or be turned out of the synagogue.

Now my brethren, as we see and experience that all things here are frail and changeable and nothing here to be depended upon: Let us seek those things which are above, which are sure, and stedfast, and unchangeable, and at the same time let us pray to Almighty God, while we remain in the tabernacle, that he would give us the grace of patience and strength to bear up under all our troubles, which at this day God knows we have our share. Patience I say, for were we not possess'd of a great measure of it you could not bear up under the daily insults you meet with in the streets of Boston; much more on public days of recreation, how are you shamefully abus'd, and that at such a degree that you may truly be said to carry your lives in your hands, and the arrows of death are flying about your heads; helpless old women have their clothes torn off their backs, even to the exposing of their nakedness; and by whom are these disgraceful and abusive actions committed, not by the men born and bred in Boston, for they are better bred, but by a mob or horde of shameless, low-lived, envious, spiteful persons, some of them not long since, servants in gentlemen's kitchens, scouring knives, tending horses, and driving chaise. 'Twas said by a gentleman who saw that filthy behaviour in the common, that in all the places he had been in, he never saw so cruel behaviour in all his life, and that a slave in the West-Indies, on Sunday or holidays enjoys himself and friends without any molestation. Not only this man, but many in town who hath seen their behaviour to you, and that without any provocation—twenty or thirty cowards fall upon one man—have wonder'd at the patience of the Blacks: 'tis not for want of courage in you, for they know that they dare not face you man for man, but in a mob, which we despise, and had rather suffer wrong than to do wrong, to the disturbance of the community and the disgrace of our reputation: for every good citizen doth honor to the laws of the State where he resides.

My brethren, let us not be cast down under these and many other abuses we at present labour under: for the darkest is before the break of day. My brethren, let us remember what a dark day it was with our African brethren six years ago, in the French West-Indies. Nothing but the snap of the whip was heard from morning to evening; hanging, broken on the wheel, burning, and all manner of tortures inflicted on those unhappy people for nothing else but to gratify their masters pride, wantonness, and cruelty: but blessed be God, the scene is changed; they now confess that God hath no respect of persons, and therefore receive them as their friends, and treat them as brothers. Thus doth Ethiopia begin to stretch forth her hand, from a sink of slavery to freedom and equality.

Although you are deprived of the means of education, yet you are not deprived of the means of meditation; by which I mean thinking, hearing and weighing matters, men, and things in your own mind, and making that judgment of them as you think reasonable to satisfy your minds and give an answer to those who may ask you a question. This nature hath furnished you with, without letter learning, and some have made great progress therein, some of those I have heard repeat psalms and hymns, and a great part of a sermon, only by hearing it read or preached and why not in other things in nature: how many of this class of our brethren that follow the seas can foretell a storm some days before it comes; whether it will be a heavy or light, a long or short one; foretell a hurricane, whether it will be destructive or moderate, without any other means than observation and consideration.

So in the observation of the heavenly bodies, this same class without a telescope or other apparatus have through a smoak'd glass observed the eclipse of the sun: One being ask'd what he saw through his smoaked glass, said, Saw, saw, de clipsey, or de clipseys. And what do you think of it?—Stop, dere be two. Right, and what do they look like?—Look like, why if I tell you, they look like two ships sailing one bigger than tother; so they sail by one another, and make no noise. As simple as the answers are they have a meaning, and shew that God can out o[the mouth of babes and Africans shew forth his glory; let us then love and adore him as the God who defends us and supports us and will support us under our pressures, let them be ever so heavy and pressing. Let us by the blessing of God, in whatsoever state we are, or may be in, to be content; for clouds and darkness are about him; but justice and truth is his habitation; who hath said, Vengeance is mine and I will repay it, therefore let us kiss the rod and be still, and see the works of the Lord.

Another thing I would warn you against, is the slavish fear of man, which bringest a snare, saith Solomon. This passion of fear, like pride and envy, hath slain its thousands.—What but this makes so many perjure themselves; for fear of offending them at home they are a little depending on for some trifles: A man that is under a panic for fear, is afraid to be alone, you cannot hear of a robbery or house broke open or set on fire, but he hath an accomplice with him, who must share the spoil with him, whereas if he was truly bold, and void of fear, he would keep the whole plunder to himself: so when either of them is detected and not the other, he may be call'd to oath to keep it secret, but through fear, (and that passion is so strong) he will not confess, til the fatal cord is put on his neck; then death will deliver him from the fear of man, and he will confess the truth when it will not be of any good to himself or the community: nor is this passion of fear only to be found in this class of men, but among the great.

What was the reason that our African kings and princes have plunged themselves and their peaceable kingdoms into bloody wars, to the destroying of towns and kingdoms, but the fear of the report of a great gun or the glittering of arms and swords, which struck these kings near the seaports with such a panic of fear, as not only to destroy the peace and happiness of their inland brethren, but plung'd millions of their fellow countrymen into slavery and cruel bondage.

So in other countries; see Felix trembling on his throne. How many Emperors and kings have left their kingdoms and best friends at the sight of a handful of men in arms: how many have we seen that have left their estates and their friends and ran over to the stronger side as they thought; all through the fear of men, who is but a worm, and hath no more power to hurt his fellow worm, without the permission of God, than a real worm.

Thus we see, my brethren, what a miserable condition it is to be under the slavish fear of men; it is of such a destructive nature to mankind, that the scriptures every where from Genesis to the Revelations warns us against it; and even our blessed Saviour himself forbids us from this slavish fear of man, in his sermon on the mount; and the only way to avoid it is to be in the fear of God: let a man consider the greatness of his power, as the maker and upholder of all things here below, and that in Him we live, and move, and have our being, the giver of the mercies we enjoy here from day to day, and that our lives are in his hands, and that he made the heavens, the sun, moon and stars to move in their various orders; let us thus view the greatness of God, and then turn our eyes on mortal man, a worm, a shade, a wafer, and see whether he is an object of fear or not; on the contrary, you will think him in his best estate to be but vanity, feeble and a dependent mortal, and stands in need of your help, and cannot do without your assistance, in some way or other; and yet some of these poor mortals will try to make you believe they are Gods, but worship them not. My brethren, let us pay all due respect to all whom God hath put in places of honor over us: do justly and be faithful to them that hire you, and treat them with that respect they may deserve, but worship no man. Worship God, this much is your duty as christians and as masons.

We see then how becoming and necessary it is to have a fellow feeling for our distres'd brethren of the human race, in their troubles, both spiritual and temporal—How refreshing it is to a sick man, to see his sympathising friends around his bed, ready to administer all the relief in their power, although they can't relieve his bodily pain yet they may ease his mind by good instructions and cheer his heart by their company.

How doth it cheer up the heart of a man when his house is on fire, to see a number of friends coming to his relief; he is so transported that he almost forgets his loss and his danger, and fills him with love and gratitude; and their joys and sorrows are mutual.

So a man wreck'd at sea, how must it revive his drooping heart to see a ship bearing down for his relief.

How doth it rejoice the heart of a stranger in a strange land to see the people cheerful and pleasant and are ready to help him.

How did it, think you, cheer the heart of those our poor unhappy African brethren, to see a ship commissioned from God, and from a nation that without flattery faith, that all men are free and are brethren; I say to see them in an instant deliver such a number from their cruel bolts and galling chains, and to be fed like men and treated like brethren. Where is the man that has the least spark of humanity, that will not rejoice with them; and bless a righteous God who knows how and when to relieve the oppressed, as we see he did in the deliverance of the captives among the Algerines; how sudden were they delivered by the sympathising members of the Congress of the United States, who now enjoy the free air of peace and liberty, to their great joy and surprize, to them and their friends. Here we see the hand of God in various ways bringing about his own glory for the good of mankind, by the mutual help of their fellow men, which ought to teach us in all our straits, be they what they may, to put our trust in Him, firmly believing that he is able and will deliver us and defend us against all our enemies, and that no weapon form'd against us shall prosper; only let us be steady and uniform in our walks, speech and behaviour, always doing to all men as we wish and desire they would do to us in the like cases and circumstances.

Live and act as Masons, that you may die as Masons; let those despisers see, altho' many of us cannot read, yet by our searches and researches into men and things, we have supplied that defect; and if they will let us we shall call ourselves a charter'd lodge of just and lawful Masons, be always ready to give an answer to those that ask you a question; give the right hand of affection and fellowship to whom it justly belongs; let their colour and complexion be what it will, let their nation be what it may, for they are your brethren, and it is your indispensable duty so to do; let them as Masons deny this, and we & the world know what to think of them be they ever so grand: for we know this was Solomon's creed, Solomon's creed did I say, it is the decree of the Almighty, and all Masons have learnt it: tis plain market language, and plain and true facts need no apologies.

I shall now conclude with an old poem which I found among some papers:

Let blind admirers handsome faces praise,
And graceful/features *to great honor raise,*
The glories of the red and white express,
I know no beauty but in holiness;
If God of beauty be the uncreate
Perfect *idea, in this* lower *state,*
The greatest beauties of an human mould
Who most *resemble Him we justly hold;*
Whom we resemble not in flesh and blood,
But being sure and holy, just and good:
May such a beauty fall but to my *share,*
For curious *shape* or *face I'll never care.*

3

Daniel Coker

Daniel Coker (1780–1846) wrote one of the most literary pamphlets of the early national period. Indeed, as the historian and literary critic Dorothy Porter once observed, Coker's essay resembles a "scholastic dialogue." As such, it illustrates the flexibility of the pamphleteer's craft. The "Dialogue" does not radically condemn slavery or racism—rather, it subverts the racial stereotypes supporting bondage by logically refuting masters' collective claim to property rights in black human beings. Engaging in a dialogue with a man identified as a Virginia master (that state had the Union's largest slaveholding class in the post-Revolutionary era), Coker's ministerial character takes on every justification of bondage and subtly but persuasively refutes them.

Coker was born to a black mother and a white father. Freeing himself from bondage in Maryland, he eventually became one of the leading black ministers of his day. When the African Methodist church broke free from white control in 1816, Coker was initially offered the bishop's position. He declined the honor (Richard Allen assumed the post), and a few years later Coker left America for the British colony of Sierra Leone on the West African coast.

Coker's "Dialogue" was one of the few pamphlets of protest written and published in the slaveholding South. He thus walked a fine line between projecting his (and other African Americans') views into the mainstream and completely offending white readers— who might have dismissed his pamphlet if they felt Coker were labeling them as evil.

Coker was also writing at a time of trouble for the abolition movement. Although every Northern state had passed a gradual abolition act by the early 1800s (declaring that all persons born after such an act was passed would be freed at a future date), and although Congress had banned the overseas slave trade in 1808, abolitionism stalled in the early decades of the nineteenth century. Southern masters—a large majority of slaveowners— tolerated less and less abolitionists' critiques of bondage. Coker's "Dialogue" tried to reinvigorate the debate over slavery in the South. "I am full of matter," his pamphlet opens. By wielding his pen, Coker would be heard.

"A Dialogue Between a Virginian and an African Minister"

(1810)

"Now, does the property belong to him, who claims it from the legislature that had it not to give, or to the original owner who has never forfeited, nor alienated his right?"

"I said, I will answer also my part; I also will
show mine opinion, for I am full of matter;
the spirit within me constraineth me. JOB
   xxxii. 17, 18.
(Therefore) " Suffer me that I may speak ; and
after that I have spoken, mock on JOB '=
   xxi. 3.

Virginian. GOOD morning sir. As I had some business in town this morning, I thought that I would call on you for the purpose of holding a little conversation.

Minister. Sir, I am happy to see you; pray take a seat.

Virginian. Sir, I have heard of you in the place of my residence, and having understood that you have had a greater opportunity of acquiring information, than those of your colour generally have; and being informed at the same time, that you are a mere person professing the Christian religion; I thought it would afford me some degree of satisfaction to have an interview with you.

Minister. Sir, I can assure you, that I feel my heart to glow with gratitude to that God, who has his ways in the whirlwind, and his paths through the great deep; and whose foot-steps are not known; for putting it into your mind, to condescend so low, as to visit one of the descendants of the African race. And since you have done me this great honour, it will be with infinite pleasure that I shall banish every other concern in order to spend a few hours in your company.

Virginian. Sir, your civility gives me much pleasure, and I am already convinced of the good that results from religion, and literary improvements; and I flatter myself that my visit will be somewhat advantageous to me. But (that I may no longer keep you in suspense) I will hasten to inform you that I have been told you have imbibed a strange opinion, which, I think is repugnant to reason and justice.

Minister. Sir, I perceive by your conversation, that there is something on your mind, of importance, and in order that no advantage be taken of me, for conversing freely with you on the subject, whatever it may be, there is a gentleman in the next room whom I will till, if you have no objection, and we will make a re-capitulation of what has passed in conversation, so that he may pen it down.

Virginian. Yes sir, by all means.

Minister. Mr. C. will you be so good as to walk into this room ?

(Mr. C. being seated, and having received pen, ink, and paper, began to write.)

Virginian. Sir, I have understood that you, have advanced an opinion that it would be just in our legislature to enact a law, for the emancipation of our slaves that we hold as our property; and I think I can convince you, that it would be wrong in the highest degree.

Minister. Sir, I will hear you with pleasure. .

Virginian. You will observe sir, in the first place, that negroes were made slaves by law; they were converted into property by an act of the legislature, and under the sanction of that law, I purchased them; they therefore become my property, and I have a legal right to them. To repeal that law in order to annihilate slavery, would be, violently to destroy, what I legally purchased with my money or inherited from my father. It would be equally unjust with dispossessing me of my horses, cattle or any other species of property. To dispossess me of their children, would be equally unjust with dispossessing me of the annual profits of my estate.

Minister. That is an important objection, and it calls for a serious answer. The matter seems to stand thus. Many years ago, men being deprived of their natural rights to freedom, and made slaves, were by law converted to property. This law, it is true, was wrong; it established iniquity; it was against the law of humanity-, common sense, reason and conscience. It was, however, a law, and under the sanction of it, a number of men, regardless of it's iniquity, purchased these slaves, and made their fellow men their property. But the question is concerning the liberty of a man. The man himself claims it as his own property. He pleads, (and I think in truth) that it was originally his own; that he has never forfeited, nor alienated it; and therefore, by the common laws of justice and humanity, it is still his own. The purchaser of the slave claims the same property. He pleads that he purchased it under the sanction of a law, enacted by the legislature, and therefore it became his. Now, the question is, who has the best claim? Did the property in question belong to the legislature? Was it vested in them? I answer, no; it was not in them collectively; and therefore they could not convey it to those they represent.

Now, does the property belong to him, who claims it from the legislature that had it not to give, or to the original owner who has never forfeited, nor alienated his right? For instance; should a law pass to sell a man's head, -and should I purchase it, have I, in consequence of this law and this purchase, a better claim to this man's head than himself? Therefore, freeing men, in my opinion, is not depriving any one of their property, but restoring it to the right owner; it is suffering the unlawful captive to escape." Turn again our captivity O Lord, as the streams in the south." PSAL. cxxvi. 4, It is not wronging the master, but doing justice to the slave, restoring him to himself. The master, it is true, is wronged, he may suffer, and that greatly; but this is his own fault, and -the fault of the enslaving law, and not of the law that does justice to the oppressed. You say, a law of emancipation would be unjust, because it would deprive men of their property; but is there no injustice on the other side? Let us consider the injustice on both sides, and weigh them in an even balance. On one hand, we see a man deprived of all property; of all capacity to possess property; of his own free agency; of the means of instruction; of his wife and children; and, of almost every thing dear to him; on the other, a man deprived of eighty or one hundred pounds. Shall we hesitate a moment to determine who is the greatest sufferer, and who is treated with the greatest injustice? The matter appears quite glaring, when we consider that "neither this man nor his parents had sinned." JOHN, ix. 3. that he was born to these sufferings; but the other suffers altogether for his own sin, and that of his parents or predecessor.

Virginian. You astonish me? and I am ready to say with one of old " Thou hast hid these thing from the wise and prudent, and hast revealed them unto babes." MATT. xi. 29. But, sir, I have another objection, and that is this. You say that the legislature made them slaves. I say not so, for the Africans enslave one another, and we only purchased those who they made prisoners of war, and reduced to slavery. Pray what will you say to this objection.

Minister. Making prisoners of war slaves, though practised by the Romans and other ancient nations, and though still practised by some barbarous tribes, can, by no means, be justified; it is unreasonable and cruel. Whatever may be said of the chief authors and promoters-of an unjust war, the common soldier, who is under command and obliged to obey, and (as is often the case) deprived of the means of information as to the ground of the war, certainly cannot be thought guilty of a crime so heinous, that for it, himself and posterity, deserve the dreadful punishment of perpetual servitude. It is a cruelty that the present practice of all civilized nations, bears testimony against. Allow the objection to be true; yet, it will not justify you in the practice of enslaving the Africans; but the matter contained in your objection, is only true in part. The history of the slave trade is too tragical to be read with-out a bleeding heart, and weeping eyes. A few of these unhappy Africans, comparatively very few, are criminals, whose servitude is inflicted as a punishment for their crimes. The main body are innocent, unsuspecting creatures; free, living in peace, doing nothing to forfeit the common privileges of men; they are taken or violently borne away, by armed force, from their tender connections; treated with an indignity, and indecency shameful to mention; and a cruelty, shocking to all the tender feelings of humanity, and they and their posterity, forced into a state of servitude and wretchedness for ever. It is true they are commonly taken prisoners by Africans; but it is the encouragement given by Europeans that tempts them to carry on the unprovoked wars. They furnish them with the means, and hold out to them a reward for their plunder. If the Africans are thieves, the Europeans stand ready to receive the stolen goods; if the former are robbers, the latter furnish them with arms, and purchase the spoil. In this case, who is the most criminal, the civilized European or the untutored African? The European merchants know, that they themselves are the great encouragers of these wars, as they are the principal gainers by the event; they know that they purchase these slaves of those, who have no just pretence to claim them as theirs. The African can give the European no better claim than he himself has; the European can give a second purchaser no better claim than is tested in him; and that is, a claim founded only on violence or fraud. In confirmation of this account, might be produced many substantial vouchers, and some who have spent much of their time in this nefarious trafffick: but such as are accustomed to listen to the melancholy tales of this unfortunate race, cannot want sufficient evidence: those I&O have seen multitudes of poor innocent children driven to market and sold like beasts, have it demonstrated before their eyes.

Virginian. Stop sir, you have said enough; I am convinced by the cogency of your argument that we are more in fault (as you have justly observed) than the uncivilized Africans. But why do we spend time in talking about the injustice of the slave trade, when we know that it is, by an act of congress abolished.

Minister. Yes sir, and it is with gratitude I speak it, yea, to the great honour of Mr. Jefferson, late president of these United States, and also the congress that passed it, who shall ever be remembered in my prayers, for the blessing of God on them, and their families; and I hope that a grateful remembrance of their humanity in passing that law, will engrave their names on every heart that is warmed with the least drop of African blood, to latest posterity.

Virginian. I am glad to find that you are not tainted with ingratitude.

Minister. But there is a species of the slave trade still carried on in some parts of the United States, which is equally cruel. A class of men, whose minds seem to have become almost Callous to every tender feeling; who (having agents in various places, suited to their purpose) trade through different states, and by purchase or otherwise, procure a considerable number of this people; Which consequently occasions a separation of the nearest relations in life. Husbands taken from wives, parents from children; they are taken in droves through the country, like herds of cattle, but with less commiseration; for being chained or otherwise fettered, the weight and friction of the shackles, naturally produces much soreness and pain. Sir I perceive you weep (and well you may) but in addition to this, they are greatly incommoded in their travel. Jailes designed for security as such have forfeited their liberty by a breach of the laws, are made reciprocals for this kind of mechanic; when opportunity presents for moving them further, it is generally performed in the dead of the night, that their cries might not be heard, nor legal means used to restore the rights of such as have been kidnapped. Others are chained in the garrets or cellars of private houses, until the number be-coming nearly equal to the success which might have been expected, they are then conveyed on board, and crouded under the hatches of vessels secretly stationed for that purpose, and thus transported to Petersburg in Virginia or such other parts that will ensure the best market; and many others are marched by land to unknown destined places. " Is it not" says Mr. John Parrish "a melancholy circumstance that such an abominable trade should be suffered in a land boasting of liberty?" for, says the same author "while I was waiting, with other friends, on the legislature of Maryland, at their session in 1803, it was well known, that a vessel lay in the river, below Baltimore, to take in slaves; a practice common on the waters of Maryland, Delaware, and some other places. On our presentation" says he "of friends memorial a committee being appointed, reported: one, that it was reasonable, an act should pass to, prevent husbands being separated from wives, and parents from children, under ten years of age; the other, to prevent persons set free, at a given time, by will or otherwise, from being sold and carried out of the state; but neither of these objects could be obtained." The flagrant violation of the rights of humanity was set forth in an humble manner, by the Rev. Absalom Jones, and Mr. James Forten of Philadelphia, in their petition to congress at one of their sessions, held in Philadelphia, in behalf of their suffering brethren in captivity; but were their petitions granted? NO. But as I believe you feel the force of my argument, and consent to the awful truths, I will stop to hear, if you have any other objection to offer against a law of emancipation.

Virginian. Sir, I must confess that there is such a trade existing in the United States, and must also acknowledge that it is a cruel one; but still, I have objections to a law of emancipation.

Minister. Pray sir, what are your objections? Bring them forward, and I will try to answer them.

Virginian. I said I had objections to offer against a law of emancipation, but that is not all; I have something to offer in favour of slavery.

Minister. Sir. I am astonished to hear you say, that you have something to offer in favour of slavery.

Virginian. You are astonished, ah, but I think you will be more surprised when I tell you that I shall draw my argument from the scriptures, and I suppose you will not call them in question, or rail against what they tolerate. Pray have you ever studied divinity?

Minister. No sir, I have never studied it in the way which I expect you mean, that is so as (by the common method of a collegiate education) to be titled Rev. D. C-, D. D. but, let this be as it may, God can teach me by his spirit to understand his word. Pray let me hear, or rather let me see the scripture that tolerates this worst of evils

Virginian. By all means. Have you a bible?

Minister. Yes sir, I should be sorry if I had not, for I live on " the sincere milk of the word" 1 PET. ii. 2. Here is the Bible sir.

Virginian. Well sir, will you please to find it? for I seldom read the bible; but I think I have heard our minister quote a passage of scripture to prove that slavery was just. But I know the ministers of your denomination will not allow that slavery is consistent with justice; indeed I am told that your bishop preaches against it, and for that reason I don't like him, nor indeed any of the methodist society; for they have made a law in their discipline against it, and to tell the truth, I think they are almost as bad as the quakers, only they do not send SO many memorials to the different legislatures in behalf of the freedom of the negroes; but they are forever preaching against slavery (as I understand) and have been instrumental in bringing about the freedom of some thousands in the United Sates. However, all clergymen don't think as they do.

Minister. Sir, as to that, I have but little to say, and that is, they will, no doubt, have their influence. But you wished I would find the text that supported slavery; and how I shall do that I cannot tell, unless I should add a little; and you know that is strictly forbidden; (Bev.xxii.18.) for I don't think that there is any scripture to support it. Can you think of any part of it? for I have a very excellent Concordance which I think will enable you to find it, if it is within the lids of the bible.

Virginian. I think it is something about Abraham's having slaves. I wish you would look, for I don't know what you mean by having a concordance.

Minister. Well sir, I expect I know what you refer to. If I read it, will you know weather it is the same you mean!

Virginian. Yes Sir.

Minister. Well sir, the scripture to Which I think you refer, reads thus, "He that is born in thy house, and he that is bought with thy money, must needs be circumcised." &c. GEN. xvii. 13. Now, I suppose your minister undertook to infer from this, that as Abraham had slaves, and as he bought them with money, therefore to make slaves of the Africans must be right.

Virginian. Yes sir. That is the scripture and that was the inference (and I think a just one,) but that was not the only text that he quoted

Minster. Pray sir, what is the other?

Virginian. Why sir, it is, where Paul says, "Servants obey your masters" or words to that effect.

Minister. You have not quoted the text right, sir. Here is the bible; read COL. iii.22

Virginian. I see my mistake. It reads "Servants obey in all things your masters."

Minister. Well; we will attend to the first text referred to, concerning Abraham's having bought servants in his house.

Virginian. Stop sir. Let me tell you what our minister inferred from it. From the passage in Genesis, he argued, that since Abraham had servants born in his house, and bought with money, they must have served for life, like our negroes; and hence he concluded that it was lawful for us to purchase heathens for servants; and if they had children born in our houses, to make them servants also. From the Law of Moses, he argued that the Israelites were authorized to leave the children of their servants, as an inheritance to their own children forever; he said also, that if this was immoral in itself, a just God would never have given it the sanction of his authority; and if lawful in itself, said he, we may safely follow the example of faithful Abraham, or act according to the law of Moses.

Minister. You will grant the scriptures to be of Divine authority; you will also grant, that they are consistent with themselves, and that one passage may help to explain another: grant me this, and then I reply to your argument in favour of slavery.

Virginian. By all means.

Minister. In the thirteenth verse of the seventeenth chapter of Genesis, we find that Abraham was commanded to circumcise all that were born in his house or bought with money: we find in the sequel of the chapter, that he obeyed the command without delay, and actually circumcised every male in his family who came under this description. This law of circumcision continued in force, it was not abrogated, but confirmed by the law of Moses. Now, to the circumcised, were committed the oracles of God; and circumcision was a token of that covenant, by which (among other things) the land of Canaan, and the various privileges in it, were promised to Abraham and his seed, and to all that were included in that covenant. All were included, 20 whom circumcision (which was the token of the covenant) was administered, agreeably to God's command.   By Divine appointment, not only Abraham, and his natural seed, but he that was bought with money, of any stranger that was not of his seed, was circumcised. Since the seed of the stranger received the token of this covenant, we must believe that he was included and interested in it; that the benefits promised, were to be conferred on him. These persons bought with money, were no longer looked upon as uncircumcised and unclean; as aliens and strangers; but were incorporated with the church and nation of the Israelites, and became one people with them; became God's covenant people.   Whence it appears, that suitable provision was made by the divine law, that they should be properly educated, made free, and enjoy all the common privileges of citizens. It was, by the divine law enjoined upon the Israelites, thus to circumcise all the males born 'in their houses; then, if the purchased servants in question, had any children, their masters were bound by law to incorporate them into their church and nation. The children then were the servants of the Lord, in the same sense as the natural descendants of Abraham were; and therefore, according to the law, LEV. xxv. 42. 54. they could not be made slaves.

" For they are my servants, which I brought forth out of the land of Egypt: they shall not be sold as bondmen. And if he be not redeemed in these years, then he shall go out in the year of Jubilee, both he, and his children with him." The passage of scripture under consideration was so far from authorizing the Israelites to make slaves of their servants children, that they evidently forbid it; and therefore, are so far from proving the lawfulness of your enslaving the children of the Africans, that they clearly condemn the practice as criminal. These passages of sacred writ have been wickedly pressed into the service of mammon perhaps more frequently than any others. But does it not now appear, that these weighty pieces of artillery may be fairly wrested from your minister, and turned upon the hosts of the mammonites, with very good effect? The minister you speak of, who plead for slavery from this passage of scripture, should have observed, that in the law of Moses referred to, there is not the least mention made of the children of these servants; it is not said they should be servants or any thing about them. No doubt some of them had children; but it was unnecessary to mention them, because they were already provided for, by the law of circumcision. To extend the law of Moses to the children of these servants, is arbitrary and presumptuous; it is making them to include much more than is expressed or necessarily implied in the text. And, it is not binding on me to prove how these persons were made servants at first; nor is it necessary we should know whether they were persons who had forfeited their liberty by capital crimes; or whether they had involved themselves in debt by folly or extravagance, and submitted to serve during their lives, in order to avoid a greater calamity; or whether they were driven to that necessity in their younger days, for want of friends to take care of them. We are not informed, whatever may be conjectured.   This, however, we may be certain of, that the Israelites were not sent by a divine mandate, to nations three hundred miles distant, who were neither doing, nor meditating any thing against them, and to whom they had no right whatever, in order to captivate them by fraud or force; tare them away from their native country, and all their tender connections; bind them in chains and fetters; croud them into ships, and there murder them by thousands, for want of air and proper exercise; and then doom the survivors and their posterity to bondage and misery forever-

Virginian. Hold sir, you have said sufficient. I am sorry I mentioned the text: but I had no idea of your being able to give such an explanation of it. Pray sir, where did YOU study divinity!

Minister. In the School of Christ. And that is the best place for a gospel minister to take his degrees. But sir, I think you said something about saint Paul.

Virginian. Yes sir. But, I am quite easy about bringing it forward; for you explain scripture so different from our minister, that I am afraid it will be of but little use to me, that is, in favour of holding the Africans in unconditional bondage. However, the text that I alluded to, is, where saint Paul says, "Servants obey in all things your masters."

Minister. Sir, in order, rightly to understand the matter, we should recollect the situation of Christians at that time. They were under the Roman yoke; the government at that time was in the bands of the heathens who were watching for every opportunity to charge them with designs against it, in order to justify their bloody persecution. But ours is not a heathen, but is called a Christian government, so that the Christians are not, by it, persecuted unto death. In such circumstances, therefore, had the apostle proclaimed liberty to the slaves, it would probably have exposed many of them to certain destruction, and injured the cause he loved so well, and that without the prospect of freeing one single individual; which would have been the height of madness and cruelty. Therefore it was wisdom in him, not to say a single word about freedom, more than he did.

Virginian. More than he did, you say! But did he say any thing about it yea or nay?

Minister. Yes sir, he said, "If thou mayest be made free, use it rather."

Virginian. Show me that sir.

Minister. Here it is; 1 COR. vii. 21.

Virginian. I see it is so, and I wonder that our minister never quoted this text in favour of freedom! It appears, that like Ananias and Saphira, ACTS v. 5,-10, he kept some part back. But I hope God will not make such an example of him.

Minister. I hope not, sir. You say that you wonder, but you need not, for it is likely your minister thought, that if you should free your slaves, you could not afford to pay him so large a salary.

Virginian. Well, perhaps that was it. But, although what you have said appears to be the height of reason, yet I have several objections more to make.

Minister. Stop sir, if you please, and let me finish.

Virginian. By all means; I thought you was done.

Minister. No sir; for I would observe, that though the apostle acted with this prudent reserve, the unreasonableness of perpetual unconditional slavery, may be easily inferred from the righteous and benevolent doctrines and duties, taught in the New Testament. It is very evident, that slavery is contrary to the spirit and nature of the Christian religion. It is contrary to that most excellent precept, laid down by the Divine Author of the Christian establishment, viz. "Whatsoever ye would that men should do to you, do ye even so to them; for this is the law and the prophets." MATT. vii. 13.

Virginian. That is a hard saying, although I know it is a divine precept.

Minister. Hard as it may appear, yet it is a precept that is finely calculated to teach the duties of justice; to enforce their obligations, and persuade the mind to obedience, so that nothing can excel it. No man, when he views the hardships and misery, the boundless labours, the unreasonable punishments, the separation between loving husbands and wives, between affectionate parents and children, can say, in truth, were I in their place, I should be contented; that would say, I so far approve of such usage, as to believe, the law that subjects me to it, is perfectly right; that I and my offspring should be denied the protection of law, and yet by the same law to be bound to suffer all these calamities, though I never forfeited my freedom, nor merited such cruel treatment more than others.—No sir. There is a vicegerent in our breast that bears testimony against this, as unreason able and wicked. " He hath shewed thee, O man, what is good; and what doth the Lord require of thee, but to do justly, and love mercy, and to walk humbly with thy God." MICAH vi. 8.

Virginian. Sir, you have said sufficient. I am convinced that slavery is a great evil; but I think that greater evils would arise from a law of emancipation.

Minister. Sir, I am surprised! but my astonishment is not argument, therefore, let me hear those evils that you think would result from a law of emancipation, that I may answer them.

Virginian. Well sir; in the first place, slaves are unacquainted with the arts of life, being used to act only under the direction of others; they have never acquired the habits of industry; have not that sense of propriety, and spirit of emulation, necessary to make them useful members of civil society. Many have been so accustomed to the meaner vices; habituated to lying, pilfering, and stealing, so that when pinched with want, they would commit these crimes, become pests to society, or end their days on the gallows. Here are evils on both sides, and of two evils we should take the least.

Minister. Sir, I agree that when there are two natural evils before us, we should choose the least; but when two moral evils are before us we should choose neither. To hold men in perpetual bondage is a moral evil. And here I must do as David did, SAM. xvii. 51. that is, take your weapon to destroy this mighty Goliath. For you have very justly observed, that holding these men in slavery is the cause of their plunging into such vicious habits as lying, pilfering, and stealing; then I say, remove the cause, that the effects may cease. That for free men, whether white or black, to steal, lie or pilfer, is evidently a dreadful thing, and for this reason, the path which necessarily leads directly to it, should the more speedily be obstructed. For, "A prudent man foreseeth the evil, and hideth himself: but the simple pass on, and are punished" PROV. xxii. 3. But are these evils confined to a people of a sable countenance? No sir, experience tells us otherwise. Therefor to reason consistently, you should say, that every man, whether white or black, that lies, steals or pilfers, should be made slaves. Now sir, what say you to this?

Virginian. I am sorry I mentioned what I did, for I confess that it is an argument more against slavery than for it: but I have still another objection to offer against a plan of emancipation.

Minister. What is your other objection! for I think you are beginning to glean.

Virginian. Should we set our slaves free, it would lay a foundation for intermarriages, and an unnatural mixture of blood, and OUR posterity at length would all be mulattoes.

Minister. This, I confess, would be a very alarming circumstance, but I think your conclusion is entirely wrong; for it is a rare thing indeed, to see black men with white wives; and when such instances occur, those men are generally of the lowest class, and are despised by their own people. For Divine Providence (as if in order to perpetuate the distinction of color) has not only placed those different nations at a great distance from each other; but a natural aversion and disgust seems to be implanted in the breast of each. For captain, Philip Beavor, in his African memoranda, relates, that "one of the white women of the company of adventurers to the island of Bulama, being taken captive by the natives, no violation of her chastity was offered, owing probably, to the extreme antipathy they have to a white skin, which they fully evidence on several occasions." But sir, is it not surprising, that some of high rank, and who profess abhorrence to such connections, have been first in the transgression? But suppose it should be the cause of intermarriages, (which I am far from believing,) and the number of mulattoes augmented, you should recollect that it is too late to prevent this evil; the matter is already gone beyond recovery; for it may be proved with mathematical certainty, that if things go on in the present course, the future inhabitants of America will be much checkered. For instance, visit some of the gentleman's seats that abound with slaves, and see how children of different complexions, swarm on every side: for all the children of mulattoes, will be mulattoes, and the whites are daily enhancing the number; which you know is an undeniable truth. Thus this realized evil is coming about in a way, truly disgraceful to both colour. Fathers will have their own children for slaves; men will possess their own brothers and sisters for property, and leave them to their heirs, or bell them to strangers for life; and youths will have their old grey headed uncles and aunts, for slaves. This is not imagination or falsehood: it has been, and (I fear) is still the case. O that this, sir, which calls aloud for vengeance, were exterminated from the face of the earth. For, hear what the Lord saith by the mouth of his prophet, "Ah sinful nation, a people laden with iniquity, a seed of evil doers, children that are corrupters! They have forsaken the Lord, thy have provoked the Holy One of Israel unto anger, they are gone away backward." ISAIAH i. 4

Virginian. Sir, I have not another objection to offer, but at the same time, I am of the opinion, that if I was to make my slaves an offer of their liberty, they would not accept of it.

Minister. I know that I have heard some of my colour talk in this strange way, but I Know of no better way for you to clear your skirts of their blood, than to take the scripture for your guide.

Virginian. Why sir, does the scripture say any thing on this subject?

Minister. Yes sir. And I think, something much to the purpose.

Virginian. Pray sir, show me it, or let me hear it.

Minister. My son, hand father the bible.-Well sir, it reads thus; "And if the servant shall plainly say, I love my master, my wife and my children; I will not go out free: then his master shall bring him unto the judges; he shall also bring him to the door, or unto the door post: and his master shall bore his ear through with an awl; and he shall serve him forever." EXODUS XXi. 5, 6

Virginian. Well sir, I have fifty-five negroes; and I will return home, and make them all (that are of age) an offer of their freedom; and those that will not go, according to that passage you have now read, I shall be justified in keeping as slaves.

Minister. Yes sir. But let me tell you how you ought (in my opinion) to use those that will not go (though I don't think there will be many) that is, to treat them well, and consider them as men providentially placed under your care; and show yourself a faithful guardian by giving them a Christian education, and providing them a sufficiency of the necessaries of life; and do not (for God's sake) follow the example of many slave holders in Virginia, who, allow their slaves but one peck of meal for a whole week. How despotically are they ruled! instead of receiving kind and gentle treatment, they are subjected to cruelty and oppression; by masters, mistresses, and hard hearted overseers. It is shocking to the feelings of humanity, in travelling through some parts of the state of Virginia, to see the poor objects (especially in the inclement season) in rags, and many of the females in a manner naked, and trembling with the cold. And yet some of these masters will have the face to say, they treat their slaves well. Custom may have reconciled it to them, but it strikes the feeling minds of strangers with horror and sympathy.

A chief of the Seneca Indians, who had been at the seat of government and beheld the oppression these people laboured under, afterwards inquired whether the quakers kept slaves; on being informed they did not he ex-pressed great satisfaction: mentioned he had been at the City of Washington, and found many white people kept blacks in slavery, and used them no better than horses. That pious man Richard Baxter, treating on the subject, says, that "it is enough to make the heathen hate Christianity," which was verified by a late well authenticated fact: several missionaries being sent out professedly to propagate the gospel among the aborigines of the wilderness, on informing them of their mission, the Indians held a council for upwards of ten days; and at length advised them to return home-that the white people made slaves of the black people, and if they had it in their power, they would make slaves of the Indians; they therefore wanted no such religion. If professors of Christianity would pay more attention to de exhortation of the apostle, "Giving no offence in any thing, that the ministry be not blamed " 2 COR. vi. 3. then would the prejudice of the heathens to the Christian religion, fail to rise no more. Another dreadful consequence of slavery, is this, although the slave is a moral agent, and an accountable creature, and is a capable subject of religion and morality; yet many of them, are by their wicked master (so called) deprived of instruction in the doctrine, and duties of religion; and some masters have actually had recourse to the lash, to effect the same. Some, I said, for thank God, all masters are not so abominably wicked; for, I remember hearing dear old Bishop Asbury the last time he preached in the African church in the city of Baltimore, say, that in some parts of the southern states, there are some owners of slaves who take pleasure in seeing their servants get religion. And is it not too obvious, that those masters who try to keep their slaves from the means of instruction, do it in order to keep them in a state of ignorance, lest they should become too wise to answer their selfish purposes and too knowing to rest easy, and satisfied in their degraded situation? and now sir, if you will have a little patience I will give you a relation of the experience of one of those sufferers, that I have been speaking of and I will give it in his own words. "First," says he "I am chained, and kept back from my public meetings; secondly, I am chained in and out of the house for thirty and some times forty hours together, without the least nourishment, under the sun; thirdly, I am tied and stretched on the ground, as my blessed master was, and suffer the owner of my body to cut my flesh, until pounds of blood, which came from my body, would congeal and cling to the soles of my shoes, and pave my way for several yards. When he would have satisfied his thirst in spilling my blood, he would turn from me to refresh himself with his bottle."

Virginian. Stop sir. Let that be concealed from a Christian nation.

Minister. No sir, I cannot stop, for I have not done with my suffering brother's experience: but I will read you a passage of scripture that strikes my mind. "For behold, the Lord cometh out of his place, to punish the inhabitants of the earth for their iniquity: the earth also shall disclose her blood, and shall no more cover her skin." ISAIAH xxvi; 21.

Virginian. Well sir, go on to finish the experience of this negro, since I find from that scripture, it will ere long, be known.

Minister. Well, and said my poor brother, "He would then leave me to renounce my religion, and the God that made me. But all in vain. When 1 looked and saw my blood running so free, my heart could not help praising my Saviour, and thanking God that he had given me the privilege, and endowed me with fortitude sufficient to bear it without murmuring. My master finding this a great means to make me more fervent in prayer, bethought himself of another diabolical stratagem to put me to shame, which he put into execution, viz. carried me like a malefactor to a neighbouring blacksmith, and there had an iron collar riveted around my neck as though I was a deserter or was about to make an elopement; and then with kicks and cuffs, I was led away and clapt in a field to labour, although scarce able: but thank God Almighty, when I recollected that my dear Lord and Master had commanded me to bear my cross, and take his yoke upon me, my soul, my heart, was elevated. I thought I could have flown, and I went to work with more submission, and with more apparent love than I had done heretofore."

Virginian. Sir, I give you my word, that, if any should think proper to stay with me, I will use them as well as my own children.

Minister. Well, thank God for such a determination.   But there is one thing more that I would request of you, and that is, before you die, make it in your will, that at your death, those slaves who may wish to continue with you shall be free; for your children, or heirs, A, B, or C, may not be of your humane disposition, for very profligate, and cruel children sometimes spring from very pious and benevolent parents.

Virginian. I am glad you mentioned that, for I might not have thought of it. And now let me remind you of what I first said, that is, perhaps my interviews with you would not be in vain, and so I have found it, and I do assure you, if I had my will, there should not be a slave in the United States. But how this could be brought about, I cannot see. Pray let me hear your ideas on this matter.

Minister. Sir, that is an important question, and has been asked more than once, and therefore, I think it will be best for me to read you a piece out of Mr. Parrish's remarks, which I think is much to the purpose.

Virginian. Sir, I should like to hear it.

Minister. Well sir, it reads as follows. "It has been frequently asked, 'How can the United States get rid of slavery?' This is an important question. The immediate liberation of all the slaves, may be attended with some difficulty; but surely something towards & now may be done. In the first place, let the president's plan, (inserted in his notes on Virginia,) be adopted, fixing a period, after which None should be born slaves in the United States; and the coloured children to be free at a certain age. This would tend to quiet the minds of the aged, affording the consoling prospect that their offspring, in a future day will enjoy the blessings of liberty: and let no legal barrier remain to prevent individuals freeing their slaves at pleasure; and thus, in due time, a gradual emancipation would take place, and be fully completed. The Spanish mode for the gradual abolition of slavery, is praise-worthy. They are registered in a book provided for that purpose, and one day in each week allowed them as their own : when they have earned a stipulated sum, another day in the week is added; thus going on, they have an opportunity of acquiring as much as will purchase their entire freedom ; which, at the same time that it accomplishes the desired end, inures them to habits of industry, and prompts to commendable economy.

Virginian. Sir, I am satisfied that that might, and in my opinion, ought to be done.

Minister. Well sir, I am happy that I have made a proselyte of you, to humanity, and not such a one as is delineated in MATT. xxiii. 15.

Virginian. Well my dear friend, I should be happy to spend more time with you, about the salvation of my poor soul, but I hope to see you again before it be long. Farewell

Minister. And the Lord be with you.

Mr.C. Well sir, I am highly gratified with the conversation that I have witnessed, although I have not been able to pay that attention that I could have wished, in consequence of my having to make a memorandum of the same.

Minister. Well sir, for our satisfaction, please to read it over.

Mr. C. With pleasure sir. It reads as follows. I think you had better have it published.

Minister. I think I will, although I am persuaded at the same time, that in SO doing I shall expose my own imbecility.

         ***   ***   ***   ***   ***

The following will show what God is doing for Ethiopia's sons in the United States of America.

"But ye are a chosen generation, a royal priesthood, and an holy nation, a peculiar people; that ye should shew forth the praise of him who hath called you out of darkness into his marvellous light: which in time past were not a people, but are now the people of God: which had not obtained mercy, but now have obtained mercy." 1 PETER ii. 9, 10.

A LIST OF THE NAMES OF THE AFRICAN MINISTERS WHO ARE IN HOLY ORDERS, OF THE AUTHOR'S ACQUALNTANCE.

Rev. Richard Allen, Pastor of the African Methodist Episcopal church.-Philidalphia.

Rev. Absalom Jones, Rector of St. Thomas's Protestent church.-Philadelphia.

Rev. Mr. Tapsicho, Methodist, Philadelphia
Reu. James Champin, do. do.
Rev. Jeffrey Buley, do.   do.
Rev. Abraham Ticompson, do.   New York.
Rev. James Varrick, do.   do.
Rev. William Miller   do.   do.
Rev. June Scott   do.   do.
Rev. Benjamin Paul, Baptist   do.
Rev. Mr. Paul,   do.   Boston
Rev. Paul Cuffe, Presbyterian, Long Island, State of New York
Rev. Jacob Bishop, Baptist, vicinity of Baltimore

A LIST

OF THE NAMES OF THE AFRICAN LOCAL PREACHERS OF THE AUTHORS ACQUAINTANCE

Mr. Thomas Miller, sen. Methodist, New York
Mr. Jacob Matthews,   do.   do.
Mr. George White, Methodist, New York
Mr. Hanibal Moore, do, Baltimore
Mr. Thomas Doublin,   do.   do.
Mr. Richard Williams,   do.   do.
Mr. James Coal,   do.   do.

Mr. Thomas Hall   do. do.
Mr. John Wagh,   do. do.
Mr. Abner Coker,   do. do.
Mr. George Martin, do.Annapolis, New York. B&i mRor&
do. do. do. do. do. do.
Annapolk

A LIST OF AFRICAN CHURCHES

1 Methodist, in Pbiladelphia
1 Protestant, in do. 1 Methodist, in New York.
1 Baptist, in   do. 1 Methodist, on Long IAd in the state of New York
1 Presbyterian, in New York.
1 Baptist, in Boston. I Methodist in Salem, New Jersey~~
1   do.   in West Chester near Philadelphia
2   do.   in Baltimore. 1   do.   in Wilmington, Delaware.
1   do.   in Annapolis, Maryland. 1   do. in Charleston, South Carolina.

Source: Rev. Daniel Coker, *A Dialogue Between A Virginian and an African Minister, A descendant of Africa. . .Minister of the African Methodist Episcopal Church in Baltimore.* Humbly Dedicated to the People of Colour in the United States of America. (Baltimore: Printed by Benjamin Edes, For Joseph James, 1810.)

4

James Forten

James Forten (1767–1842) was a prince, as one black newspaper later referred to him. His was also an archetypal American rags-to-riches story—except for his race. Forten was born to a free black family in Philadelphia and learned his father's sail-making trade. While still in his teens, he enlisted in the colonial Navy during the American Revolution, refusing British offers of education in exchange for his service. After the Revolution, Forten worked at, and then acquired, the sail-making business of Robert Bridges. Until his death in the 1840s, Forten garnered a fortune which made him one of the wealthiest people in Philadelphia, not to mention a leading member of the nation's so-called black elite. Yet no matter how far he traveled economically, Forten hit the obstacle of race. No matter how much he pledged to the American nation, often it refused to embrace him.

In 1813, Forten was reminded of the American racial caste to which he belonged when the Pennsylvania legislature considered a bill restricting black emigration to, and around, the state. Pennsylvania promised blacks much in early national society: it boasted the world's first gradual abolition law in 1780, which slowly sought to drain slavery from the state (nearly seven thousand people remained enslaved in the Quaker State following the Revolution); its constitution did not distinguish black from white rights; and it had the most active abolition group in the world, the Pennsylvania Abolition Society. Nevertheless, white Pennsylvanians complained about black settlers, particularly those former slaves who traveled to the Quaker State from Southern areas. Thus the legislature's proposed bill required black emigrants to register with local officials upon entering Pennsylvania, lest they be subject to fine, explusion, or worse.

While white abolitonists worked behind the scenes to quash the bill, a furious Forten unleashed his pen. Although his motto would remain "America, with thy faults, I love thee still," Forten chided white Americans for restricting black liberties. Citing the Declaration of Independence and the state's constitution, Forten proclaimed that the proposed law violated America's heritage of freedom and justice for all. White citizens would never be subjected to such law; neither should blacks. The law never passed.

Few copies of Forten's original pamphlet exist. One edition is in the American Antiquarian Society's archives in Worcester, Massachusetts. The version below is reprinted from *Freedom's Journal*, February and March 1827, with the following note:

We invite the attention of our readers to a perusal of the following essays (the first number of which we republish this week) from the pen of one of our most intelligent and respectable citizens of Colour in the U. States. They were originally published in the year 1813, in Philadelphia at a time of considerable excitement, when a proposition came before the Legislature of Pennsylvania, to register all free persons of Colour within the state, and also to prevent others from the different states settling within her borders. For ourselves we are so pleased with them, that we are anxious they should circulate far and near, and be perused by friend and foe. We hope every one will judge for himself.

"Series of Letters by a Man of Colour"
(1813)

"This is almost the only state in the Union wherein the African race have justly boasted of rational liberty and the protection of the laws, and shall it now be said they have been deprived of that liberty, and publicly exposed for sale to the highest bidder?"

LETTERS From a MAN OF COLOUR, on a late Bill before the Senate of Pennsylvania.

LETTER I. O Liberty! thou power supremely bright,
    Profuse of bliss and pregnant with delight,
    Perpetual pleasures in thy presence reign,
    And smiling Plenty leads thy wanton train
          Addison.

We hold this truth to be self-evident, that GOD created all men equal, and is one of the most prominent features in the Declaration of Independence, and in that glorious fabric of collected wisdom, our noble Constitution. This idea embraces the Indian and the European, the Savage and the Saint, the Peruvian and the Laplander, the white Man and the African, and whatever measures are adopted subversive of this inestimable privilege, are in direct violation of the letter and spirit of our Constitution, and become subject to the animadversion of all, particularly those who are deeply interested in the measure.

These thoughts were suggested by the promulgation of a late bill, before the Senate of Pennsylvania, to prevent the emigration of people of colour into this state. It was not passed into a law at this session and must in consequence lay over until the next, before when we sincerely hope, the white men, whom we should look upon as our protectors, will have become convinced of the inhumanity and impolicy of such a measure, and forbear to deprive us of those inestimable treasures, Liberty and Independence. This is almost the only state in the Union wherein the African have justly boasted of rational liberty and the protection of the laws, and shall it now be said they have been deprived of that liberty, and publicly exposed for sale to the highest bidder? Shall colonial inhumanity that has marked many of us with shameful stripes, become the practice of the people of Pennsylvania, while Mercy stands weeping at the miserable spectacle? People of Pennsylvania, descendants of the immortal Penn, doom us not to the unhappy fate of thousands of our countrymen in the Southern States and the West Indies; despise the traffic in blood, and the blessing of the African will forever be around you. Many of us are men of property, for the security of which, we have hitherto looked to the laws of our blessed state, but should this become a law, our property is jeopardized, since the same power which can expose to sale an unfortunate fellow creature, can wrest from him those estates which years of honest industry have accumulated. Where shall the poor African look for protection, should the people of Pennsylvania consent to oppress him? We grant there are a number of worthless men belonging to our colour, but there are laws of sufficient rigour for their punishment, if properly and duly enforced. We wish not to screen the guilty do not permit the innocent to suffer. If there are worthless men, there also men of merit among the African race, who are useful members of Society. The truth of this let their benevolent institutions and the numbers clothed and fed by them witness. Punish the guilty man of colour to the utmost limit of the laws, but sell him not to slavery! If he is in danger of becoming a public charge prevent him! If he is too indolent to labour for his own subsistence, compel him to do so; but sell him not slavery. By selling him you do not make him better, but commit a wrong, without benefiting the object of it or society at large. Many of our ancestors were brought here more than one hundred years ago; many of our fathers, many of ourselves, have fought and bled for the independence of our country. Do not then expose us to sale. Let not the spirit of the father behold the son robbed of that liberty which he died to establish, but let the motto of our legislators, be – "The Law knows no distinction."

These are only a few desultory remarks on the subject and intend to succeed this effervescence of feeling, by a series of essays, tending to prove the impolicy and unconstitutionality of the law in question.

For the present, I leave the public to the consideration of the above observations, in which I hope they will see so much truth, that they will never consent to sell to slavery.

LETTER II.

Those patriotic citizens, who, after resting from the toils of an arduous war, which achieved our independence and laid the foundation of the only reasonable Republic upon earth, associated together, and for the protection of those inestimable rights for the establishment of which they had exhausted their blood and treasure, framed the Constitution of Pennsylvania, have by the ninth article declared, "that all men are born equally free and independent, and have certain inherent and indefeasible rights, among which are those of enjoying life and liberty." Under the restraint of wise and well administered laws, we cordially unite in the above glorious sentiment, but by the bill upon which we have been remarking, it appears as if the committee who drew it up mistook the sentiment expressed in this article, and do not consider us as men, or that those enlightened statesmen who formed the constitution upon the basis of experience intended to exclude us from its blessings and protection. If the former, why are we not to be considered as men. Has the God who made the white man and the black, left any record declaring us a different species. Are we not sustained by the same power, supported by the same food, hurt by the same wounds, pleased with the same delights, and propagated by the same means. And should we not then enjoy the same liberty, and be protected by the same laws. – We would wish not to legislate, for our means of information and the acquisition of knowledge are, in the nature of things, so circumscribed, that we must consider ourselves incompetent to the task: but let us, in legislation be considered men. It cannot be that the authors of our Constitution intended to exclude us from its benefits, for just emerging from unjust and cruel emancipation, their souls were too much affected with their own deprivations to commence the reign of terrour over others. They knew we were deeper skinned than they were, but they acknowledged us as men, and found that many an honest heart beat beneath a dusky bosom. They felt that they had no more authority to enslave us, than England had to tyranize over them. They were convinced that if amenable to the same laws in our actions, we should be protected by the same laws in our rights and privileges. Actuated by these sentiments they adopted the glorious fabric of our liberties, and declaring "all men" free, they did not particularize white and black, because they never supposed it would be made a question whether we were men or not. Sacred be the ashes, and deathless be the memory of those heroes who are dead; and revered be the persons and the characters of those who still exist and lift the thunders of admonition against the traffic in blood. And here my brethren in colour, let the tear of gratitude and the sigh of regret break forth for that great and good man, who lately fell a victim to the promiscuous fury of death, in whom you have lost a zealous friend, a powerful, an herculean advocate, a sincere adviser, and one who spent many an hour of his life to break your fetters, and ameliorate your condition – I mean the ever to be lamented Dr. Benjamin Rush.

It seems almost incredible that the advocates of liberty, should conceive the idea of selling a fellow creature to slavery. It is like the heroes of "Vive la Republic," while the decapitated Nun was precipitate into the general reservoir of death, and the palpitating embryo decorated the point of the bayonet. Ye, who should be our protectors, do not destroy. – We will cheerfully submit to the laws, and aid in bringing offenders against them of every colour to justice; but do not let the laws operate so severely, so degradingly, so unjustly against us alone.

Let us put a case, in which the law in question operates peculiarly hard and unjust – I have a brother, perhaps, who, resides in a distant part of the Union, and after a separation of years, actuated by the same fraternal affection which beats in the bosom of a white man, he comes to visit me. Unless that brother be registered in twenty four hours after, and be able to produce a certificate to that effect, he is liable, according to the second and third sections of the bill, to a fine of twenty dollars, to arrest, imprisonment and sale. Let the unprejudiced mind ponder upon this, and then pronounce it the justifiable act of a free people, if he can. To this we trust our cause, without fear of the issue. The unprejudiced must pronounce any act tending to deprive a free man of his right, freedom and immunities, as not only cruel in the extreme, but decidedly unconstitutional both as regards the letter and spirit of that glorious instrument. The same power which protects the white man, should protect the black.

LETTER III.

THE evils arising from the bill before the Legislature, so fatal to the rights of freemen, and so characteristic of European despotism, are so numerous, that to consider them all, would extend these numbers further than time or my talent will permit me to carry them. The concluding paragraph of my last number, states a case of peculiar hardship, arising from the second section of this bill, upon which I cannot refrain from making a few more remarks. The man of colour receiving as a visiter any other person of colour, is bound to turn informer, and rudely report to the Register, that a friend and a brother has come to visit him for a few days, whose name he must take within twenty four hours, or forfeit a sum which the iron hand of the law is authorized to rend from him, partly for the benefit of the Register. Who is this Register? A man, and exercising an office, where ten dollars is the fee for each delinquent, will probably be a cruel man and find delinquents where they really do not exist. The poor black is left to the merciless gripe of an avaricious Register, without an appeal, in the event, from his tyranny or oppression! O miserable race, born to the same hopes, created with the same feeling, and destined for the same goal, you are reduced by your fellow creatures below the brute. The dog is protected and pampered at the board of his master, while the poor African and his descendant, whether a Saint or a felon, is branded with infamy, registered as a slave, and we may expect shortly to find a law to prevent their increase, by taxing them according to numbers, and authorizing the Constables to seize and confine everyone who dare to walk the streets without a collar on his neck – what have the people of colour been guilty of, that they more than others, should be compelled to register their houses, lands, servants and children. Yes, ye rulers of the black man's destiny, reflect upon this; our children must be registered, and bear about them a certificate, or be subject to imprisonment and fine. You, who are perusing this effusion of feeling, are you a parent? Have you children around whom your affections are bound, by those delightful bonds which none but a parent can know? Are they the delight of your prosperity, and the solace of your afflictions? If all this be true, to you we submit our cause. The parent's feelings cannot err. By your verdict will we stand or fall – by your verdict, live slaves or freemen. It is said, that the bill does not extend to children, but the words of the bill are, 'Whether as an inmate, visiter, hireling, or tenant, in his or her house or room.' Whether this does not embrace every soul that can be in a house, the reader is left to judge; and whether the father should be bound to register his child, even within the twenty-four hours after it is brought into the world, let the father's feelings determine. This is the fact, and our children sent on our lawful business, not having sense enough to understand the meaning of such proceedings, must show their certificate of registry or be borne to prison. The bill specifies neither age nor sex – designates neither the honest man or the vagabond – but like the fretted porcupine, his quills aim its deadly shafts promiscuously at all.

For the honour and dignity of our native state, we wish not to see this bill pass into a law, as well as for its degrading tendency towards us; for although oppressed by those to whom we look for protection, our grievances are light compared with the load of reproach that must be heaped upon our commonwealth. The story will fly from the north to the south, and the advocates of slavery, the traders in human blood, will smile contemptuously at the once boasted moderation and humanity of Pennsylvania. What, that place, whose institutions for the prevention of Slavery, are the admiration of surrounding states and of Europe, become the advocates of mancipation and wrong, and the oppressor of the free and innocent – Tell it not in Gath! Publish it not in the streets of Askelon! lest the daughters of the Philistines rejoice! lest the children of the uncircumcised triumph.

It is to be hoped that in our legislature there is a patriotism, humanity, and mercy sufficient to crush this attempt upon the civil liberty of freemen, and to prove that the enlightened body who have hitherto guarded their fellow creatures, without regard to the colour of the skin, will stretch forth the wings of protection to that race, whose persons have been the scorn, and whose calamities have been the jest of the world for ages. We trust the time is at hand when this obnoxious bill will receive its death warrant, and freedom still remain to cheer the bosom of a man of color.

LETTER IV.

I proceed again to the consideration of the bill of unalienable rights belonging to black men, the passage of which will only tend to show, that the advocates of emancipation can enact laws more degrading to the free man, and more injurious to his feelings, than all the tyranny of slavery, or the shackles of infatuated despotism. And let me here remark, that this unfortunate race of humanity, although protected by our laws, are already subject to the fury and caprice of a certain set of men, who regard neither humanity, law nor privilege. They are already considered as a different species, and little above the brute creation. They are thought to be objects fit for nothing else than lordly men to vent the effervescence of their spleen upon, and to tyrannize over, like the bearded Musselman over his horde of slaves. Nay, the Musselman, thinks more of his horse, than the generality of people do of the despised black! – Are not men of colour sufficiently degraded? Why then increase their degradation. It is a well known fact, that black people, upon certain days of public jubilee, dare not to be seen after twelve o'clock in the day, upon the field to enjoy the times; for no sooner do the fumes of that potent devil, Liquor, mount into the brain, than the poor black is assailed like the destroying Hyena or the avaricious Wolf! I allude particularly to the Fourth of July – Is it not wonderful, that the day set apart for the festival of Liberty, should be bused by the advocates of Freedom, in endeavouring to sully what they profess to adore. If men, though they know that the law protects all, will dare, in defiance of law, to execute their hatred upon the defenceless black, will they not by the passage of this bill, believe him still more a mark for their venom and spleen – Will they not believe him completely deserted by authority, and subject to every outrage brutality can inflict – too surely they will, and the poor wretch will turn his eyes around to look in vain for protection. Pause, ye rulers of a free people, before you give us over to despair and violation – we implore you, for the sake of humanity, to snatch us from the pinnacle of ruin, from that gulf, which will swallow our rights, as fellow creatures; our privileges, as citizens; and our liberties, as men!

There are men among us of reputation and property, as good citizens as any men can be, and who, for their property, pay as heavy taxes as any citizens are compelled to pay. All taxes, except personal, fall upon them, and still even they are not exempted from this degrading bill. The villainous part of the community, of all colours, we wish to see punished and retrieved as much as any people can. Enact laws to punish them severely, but do not let them operate against the innocent as well as the guilty. Can there be any generosity in this? Can there be any semblance of justice, or of that enlightened conduct which is ever the boasted pole star of freedom? By no means. This bill is nothing but the ignus fatuus of mistaken policy.

I could write for ages on the subject of this unrighteous bill, but as I think enough has already been said, to convince every unprejudiced mind, of its unjust, degrading, undeserved tendency, one more number shall conclude the letters from A MAN OF COLOUR.

LETTER V.

A few more remarks upon the bill which has been the subject of my preceding numbers, shall conclude these Letters, which have been written in my own cause as an individual, and my brethren as a part of the community. They are the simple dictates of nature and need no apology. They are not written in the gorgeous style of a scholar, nor dressed in the garments of literary perfection. They are the impulse of a mind formed, I trust, for feeling, and smarting under all the rigours which the bill is calculated to produce.

By the third section of this bill, which is its peculiar hardship, the police officers are authorized to apprehend any black, whether a vagrant or a man of reputable character, who cannot produce a Certificate that he has been registered. He is to be arrayed before a justice, who thereupon is to commit him to prison! The jailor is to advertise a Freeman, and at the expiration of six months, if no owner appears for this degraded black, he is to be exposed to sale, and if not sold to be confined at hard labour for seven years! – Man of feeling, read this! – No matter who, no matter where. The Constable, whose antipathy generally against the black is very great, will take every opportunity of hurting his feelings! Perhaps, he sees him at a distance and having a mind to raise the boys in hue and cry against him, exclaims, "Halloa! Stop the Negro?" – The boys, delighting in the sport, immediately begin to hunt him, and immediately from a hundred tongues, is heard the cry – "Hoa, Negro, where is your Certificate!" – Can any thing be conceived more degrading to humanity! Can any thing be done more shocking to the principal of Civil Liberty! – A person arriving from another state, ignorant of the existence of such a law, may fall a victim to its cruel oppression. But he is to be advertised, and if no owner appears – How can an owner appear for a man who is free and belongs to no one! – If no owner appears, he is exposed for sale! – Oh, inhuman spectacle: found in no unjust act, convicted of no crime, he is barbarously sold like the produce of the soil, to the highest bidder, or what is still worse, for no crimes, without the inestimable privilege of a trial by his peers, doomed to the dreary walls of a prison for the term of seven tedious years! My God, what a situation is his. Search the legends of tyranny and find no precedent. No example can be found in all the reigns of violence and oppression, which have marked the lapse of time. It stands alone. It has been left for Pennsylvania, to raise her ponderous arm against liberties of the blacks, whose greatest boast has been, that he resided in a State where Civil Liberty, and sacred Justice were administered alike to all. – What must be his reflections now, that the asylum he left for mancipation has been destroyed, and he is left to suffer like Daniel of old, with no one but his God, to help him! Where is the bosom that does not have a sigh for his fall, unless it be callous to every sentiment of humanity and mercy?

The fifth section of this bill, is also peculiarly bare, inasmuch as it prevents freemen from living where they please – Pennsylvania has always been a refuge from slavery, and to this state the Southern black, when freed, has flown for safety. Why does he this! When masters in many of the Southern states, which they frequently do, free a particular black, unless the black leaves the state in so many hours any person resident of the said state, can have him arrested and again sold to Slavery: – The hunted black is obliged to flee or remain and be again a slave. I have known persons of this discription sold three times after being first emancipated. Where shall he go? Shut every state against him, and, like Pharoah's kine, drive him into the sea. – Is there no spot on earth that will protect him! Against their inclination, his ancestors were forced from their homes by trades in human flesh, and even under such circumstances, the wretched offspring are denied the protection you afforded to brutes.

It is in vain that we are forming societies of different kinds to ameliorate the condition of our unfortunate brethren, to correct their morals and to render them not only honest but useful members to society. All our efforts by this bill, are despised and we are doomed to feel the lash of oppression: – As well may we be outlawed, as well may the glorious privileges of the Gospel, be denied us, and all endeavours used to cut us off from happiness hereafter as well as here! – The case is similar, and I am much deceived if this bill does not destroy the morals it is intended to produce.

I have done. My feelings are acute, and I have ventured to express them without intending either accusation or insult to any one. An appeal to the heart is my intention, and if I have failed, it is my great misfortune, not to have laid a power of eloquence sufficient to convince. But I trust the eloquence of nature will succeed, and the law-givers of this happy Commonwealth will yet remain the Black's friend, and the advocates of Freemen, is the sincere wish of every freeman.

5

Russell Parrott

American participation in the African slave trade ended, by law, on January 1, 1808. The day immediately became an African-American holiday and the first African-American festival to generate its own printed literature. The several January 1st Day sermons, ranging from 1808 through the 1820s, are an important genre of early African-American writing in which orators—largely clergymen—hail the end of the overseas slave trade, consider their own role in American society, and ponder the meaning of Africa in their American lives.

Russell Parrott (1791–1824) was different from most of the January 1st sermonizers. He was just twenty-two years old, a lay reader at the historic African Church of St. Thomas, a protégé of its noted minister Absalom Jones and such community leaders as James Forten. This was Parrott's second January 1st Day sermon, following his appearance at St. Thomas in 1812. He would speak again in 1816. In his brief career Parrott helped mobilize blacks for the defense of the city against the British in 1814. He helped promote the commercial ventures of the black seaman and merchant Paul Cuffee; worked with church leaders in the Augustinian Society to provide higher education for the black clergy; and, with James Forten, authored the Philadelphia black community's famous denunciations of the American Colonization Society in 1817 and 1819. He died in 1824, aged thirty-three. At the time of his death he headed the African Literary Society.

This second sermon is the most vigorous of Parrott's three efforts, a blend of censure and celebration. With historical sweep, he describes Africa and America as inexorably linked since the discovery of the New World, the one to grow and prosper by feeding upon the other. Like most such sermonizers, his depiction of the slave trade condemns its willful cruelty and dissects the arguments of its supporters. Parrott celebrates abolitionist champions, particularly the recently deceased white activist and Revolutionary founder Benjamin Rush, and hails emancipation in Pennsylvania and other Northern states.

His sermon, delivered before a population that would soon utterly reject the program of the colonizationists, affirms the American identity and identification of Philadelphia's free black population.

"An Oration on the Abolition
of the Slave Trade"

(1814)

"The slave trade, the partial abolition of which, we this day meet to celebrate, has filled this earth with more moral turpitude, than any other event that has ever occurred."

AGAIN selected, to bear a conspicuous part in the celebration of the abolition of the slave trade, I should do injustice to my feelings, did I let the present opportunity escape, without expressing my warmest thanks, for the undeserved honour. Though poor in talent, and one of that unfortunate portion of mankind, that unrelenting prejudice has cast in the back ground of society, my most strenuous effort shall be to portray, in language of unadorned truth, the wrongs and sufferings of unhappy Africa, by that traffic which has long disgraced the civilized world.

The discovery of America, opened a new era in the affairs of Europe: the immense treasures that inundated the mother country, the highly coloured descriptions of its soil, climate and resources, spread such an universal desire of gain, that it pervaded all ranks of society, from the peasant to the king. It is from this period, that we may date the commencement of the sufferings of the Africans, and the discovery of the new world; which, to one portion of the human family, has afforded such advantages, to the unfortunate African, has been the source of the greatest misery; it was the precursor of his sufferings, his misery; and it removed him many ages from that state of civilization, which his natural genius entitled him to enjoy.

The infamous barbarities, committed by the Spaniards, in their newly discovered possessions, upon the unoffending inhabitants, caused some few pious men to lay their sufferings before the government, who, to save the aborigines from slavery, cast the shackles upon the African. The magnanimous prince although, he suffered this horrid traffic to disgrace for a short time, an otherwise splendid reign, he formally declared, that within his dominions, slavery should not exist. On the abdication of the throne by Charles, avarice again triumphed over justice, and the piratical Portuguese, who were the first violators of the rights of 'the African,' again could find a market, to vend him and his posterity, to perpetual bondage. England, too at this time, had acquired large possessions in America; and it was proposed to Elizabeth, the then reigning sovereign, to populate her newly acquired domains, by the introduction of Africans: it is said, she expressly forbade any force to be used; but, such was the profligacy of the times, that the calls, of humanity and justice, were totally disregarded, man assumed the nature of the savage; plucked from his bosom every sentiment of pity; and, to gratify his accursed avarice, devoted to lasting bondage his equal, man.

The slave trade, the partial abolition of which, we this day meet to celebrate, has filled this earth with more moral turpitude, than any other event that has ever occurred.

Its iniquity was great, but the heart-rending sufferings, of the unfortunates, who fell within its vortex, are beyond my feeble description. Fancy yourself on the fertile plains of Africa-see, reposing beneath the luxuriant foliage of the palm, the child of her soil-say he is a father, surrounded by a flock of innocents, whose endearing, artless prattle, has bound him to his paternal home, with ties stronger than adamant-providence has blessed him with a competency, and to make that blessing sure, has made him contented- here, is the land of his nativity-here dwells his father, his mother, the partner of his affection, and the friend of his heart; when in the midst of his domestic enjoyment, a fiend steals in and mars all his happiness; the slave merchant, whose steps are marked by desolation and dismay, at one stroke destroys all his sublunary joys; tears from the bosom of his family, the poor African! No tears, no entreaties, will avail; in vain he tells him that a numerous offspring depend upon him for sustenance; that an affectionate wife looks with anxious solicitude for his return; he shrieks with all the violence of desperate anguish-all, all, is lost! he is hurried to the bark, prepared for his reception, where begins the career of his ignomy, and his sufferings. Here, with himself, he finds immured, hundreds of his unfortunate countrymen, whose agonizing groans, and the terrific sound of whose chains, adds fresh fuel to his grief. Hope, delusive hope, amidst all his sombre prospects, holds out one faint, one glimmering ray, that an opportunity to escape may occur; -how vain, how illusory. The signal for departure is made; he sees the home of his affections, recede from his sight-mute and immoveable, he stands,-the transition, from joy most perfect, to woe, is so sudden, that reason is banished, and wild despair usurps her seat. What language can tell the feelings of his soul? what pen portray the intenseness of his grief. The bustle of departure over, these worse than free-booters, have time to turn their attention to their prey. The cruelties perpetrated on board of the slave ship, are such, that to the superficial observer of human nature, it would appear as the effusion of romance, that within the small compass of a vessel, enormities are committed that would make "angels weep." There decrepit age, bending beneath the wright of years, 'and new afflictions; there dejected youth, with all his glowing prospects blasted, while yet in his morning-some emaciated with disease, contracted by inhaling an unhealthy atmosphere, rendered so by the multitude that are confined in these receptacles of misery; some suffering from the, effects of torture, a mutilated limb, or a lacerated body; some driven to desperation by famine, make an attempt to sacrifice their tyrants. Armed but by frenzy, they are soon driven from the deck, with slaughter and death. Some, impelled by the hope of revisiting; their native land, seek a passage to her shores through the yielding waves.-The passage is one continued scene of suffering and barbarity. A cargo, (if I must so term it) of slaves, who on account of the badness of the food, and the number that were crowded together, many were daily emancipated from their chains by the kind hand of death, when these monsters in human shape, to recover the insurance from the underwriters, cast into the sea the sick and the disabled. To what lengths will not the love of lucre drive mankind; what crimes will it not cause them to commit.

Instances of individual sufferings are so numerous that their recital would extort a tear from hearts that never wept before. They, whose fortitude, or whose constitution bear them through the middle passage, ate on the arrival of the ship, exposed for sale. It is now that the bond of relationship, the ties of friendship and affection, more closely cemented by a reciprocity of sufferings, are for a second time to be rent asunder.

With the purchaser, it is not whether he separates parents and children, or husband and wife; a thought of this kind, never enters his cold, calculating soul; but if such or such a one, will suit him best.

The sale ended, conceive the affliction of separation, for my imperfect language cannot tell it—In spite of all the calls of humanity, they are forced from each other's embrace, and doomed to disgrace and labour. The slave is now placed under a code of laws (if laws they can be called,) he is considered as a part of the brute creation; the master is invested with a complete control over him; can either sell or kill him; let his oppressions be what they may, there is no tribunal for the slave to apply to for redress; he is entirely at the mercy of his tyrant, for whom he is compelled to spend the remainder of his wretched existence, in ceaseless toil. If labouring under a meridian sun, he should faint, the lash is his restorative. If, after suffering with heroic fortitude, an accumulation of-wrong and contumelies, that would have laid his persecutors in the dust, he should survive, it is called barbarous in sensibility. If he celebrates in uncouth strains, the departure of some dear friend, from scenes of persecution and distress, it is called inhumanity. His mental faculties are depressed, and ignorance inculcated with the most studious assiduity, and then he is represented as being incapable of receiving instruction; ingenuity is tortured to assimilate him to the brute, as a justification for his inhuman treatment. Thus depressed, it excites wonder that the least ray of rationality should expand itself. What inducement, has the unfortunate slave, to call into action, those talents which only impart lustre to the character of the freeman; no prospects of reward or honour, open to his view; to him, all is hopeless misery. By what right does man thus compel his fellow creature to suffer? my bosom burns with indignation, while I make the inquiry. The religion which we profess, does not sanction it-the plea that they are principally prisoners taken in war, and who would, according to the custom of savage nations," be put to death, if not sold into captivity, will not justify the slave merchant, when it is known, that to their corruptive influence, are owing most of the wars that have desolated unhappy Africa for more than a century. What right has the conqueror to dispose of the liberties of the captive, whom the fortune of war has thrown in his power? that he has the power, we acknowledge, but power and right are terms quite dissimilar in their signification; and as man receives his liberty with his existence, from God, no earthly power has the right to take it from him. Again it is asserted, that many of them are criminals, who have forfeited their lives to the offended laws of their country. They who violate the social compact, deserve punishment; but that punishment should be commensurate with the crime committed. The unhappy culprit, who is doomed to suffer perpetual servitude, and whose guiltless posterity are included in the unhappy number, is punished beyond the measure of his crimes.

They say the slave's situation is more happy, he is better fed and clad than the poor of civilized Europe. Can he claim the proud privilege of being a citizen of the country in which he which he resides, can he lay his hand on his heart, and with honest confidence say, her law is no respector of persons, and in her eye I enjoy equal privileges the rich and powerful? No! The baneful effects of the slave trade were diffused through all the mass of society engaged in it. The generous sailor, whose bosom glows with all the social virtues, engaged in the slave trade, becomes quite a different being, loses those traits of generosity that characterize him when engaged in more honourable employment. The man surrounded by an hundred human creatures, whose lives are at his disposal, subject to his caprice, is in miniature, what Nero was in magnitude, the tyrant an oppressor of his species.

The oppression of the Africans, called down the interposition of Providence, and among the names whom the Deity selected, as the accomplishers of the great work of abolition, stand preeminent those of Sharp, Clarkson, Gregoire, Wilberforce; with our own countrymen, Sewel, Bennezett, Delwin* and tho' last mentioned, yet first in our affection, Rush, the philosopher and the Philanthropist, in whom the cause of humanity has found one of the most indefatigable friends. The sphere of his usefulness was confined to no particular science, nor to any particular virtue, he was familiar with all; he, with true philanthropy, viewed the whole human family as his brethren! and that vast stock of information which he possessed, as the peculiar gift of heaven, for their good. When pestilence hovered over this fair city, shaking from her wings, pale disease; when every avenue was filled with scenes of horror and distress, when the bonds of consanguinity were not strong enough to bind together families; when the child forsook his parent, the parent its partner, it was then, that with unshaken firmness he stood, when all, whose circumstances would permit, had fled, struck with fear; even then, in the abodes of penury and sickness, without prospect of fee or reward, he was found, acting in the double capacity of physician and priest, and while his skilful hand baffled the power of disease, he poured the balm of heavenly consolation upon the wounded heart.-In truth, we may say, that he was commissioned from on high, to be thy guardian angel, Philadelphia, in the darkest hours of peril and affliction. Early in life, he stepped forward as a friend of the abolition of slavery; and during a period of thirty 'years, he was the true friend of the people of colour. The melioration of their situation, was a subject nigh to his heart. The abolition of the slave trade, he knew, to be an act of justice due to the cause of humanity; and the emancipation of those held in slavery, absolutely necessary, to secure from the imputation of inconsistency, the character of his country. To a man of his enlarged and generous mind, these were sufficient excitements, to call into action his talents and his virtues. The claims of the black to the privileges of freedom, he ably and successfully contended for. That they were a portion of the great human family, was a truth that he assisted in establishing on a firm basis. The loss of this great and good man, is sensibly felt by us; he was our father, our counsellor, and our protector: long shall his name and his services, be remembered with gratitude, by the African and his descendants. With such a constellation of talents and virtue, opposed to that mass of corruption, the slave trade, we are not surprised that the monster fell, after rioting for more than a century, in the blood and tears of millions of the human species.

How diminutive are the glories of the greatest potentates, when compared with the achievements of that host of worthies, who accomplished the abolition. They contended, not to enslave, but to liberate: not to depress, but to exalt.

The abolition of the slave trade, is one of the greatest events that mark the present age. It was a sacrifice that virtue compelled avarice to make, at the shrine of justice, as her first oblation. And, when to this is added the emancipation of those already in bondage, the triumph of philanthropy will be complete; when man shall no longer be stigmatised by the name of slave, and heavens first, best gift, be universally enjoyed. That freedom is the natural inheritance of man, is a truth that neither sophistry-nor interest can shake; and the being that exists from under her benign rays, can neither be exhilarated by the influence of learning, nor warmed into a proper knowledge of himself, by religion.

If the security of a country should rest within her bosom, then it is necessary that each citizen should be a freeman.

Pennsylvania, first in virtue, first in patriotism, to the wisdom of thy councils, and the firmness of thy magistrates, we are indebted for the privileges we now enjoy. By this act of justice, you have secured to yourself a band of citizens, who will not forsake you in the hour of danger, whose bosoms are ready to be bared in your service, and whose blood will cheerfully flow in your defence. May you ever remain the sanctuary of liberty, and may your sacred portals never be polluted by the violators of the rights of man.

That we are faithful to our country, we have abundantly proved: where her Hull, her Decatur, and her Bainbridge, fought and conquered, the black bore his part, stimulated by the pure love of country, which neither contempt nor persecution can eradicate from his generous heart. With a jewel of such inestimable value within her bosom, the cheering smiles of that country should not be withheld by narrow-minded prejudice.

Abolition! already are thy blessings diffusing themselves; already Africa experiences its blessed effects; confidence is again restored between man and man; whole villages are no longer depopulated, to glut that insatiable monster, avarice; mild religion begins to unfold her heavenly truth, through this former land of paganism and error-and over the ruins of the altars that idolatry had reared, the sacred temple points its spire towards heaven. Civilization, with her attending handmaids, agriculture and industry, infuses cheerfulness over the face of nature, and inspires the husbandman with gratitude and joy.

Liberty! thou exhilarating soother of human hearts, may thy presence, like the sun, illuminate every soil, and brighten every countenance; may thy animating smiles enliven the humble dwelling of the negro of Africa, as well as the courts and cottages of more favoured climes; may neither the tide of time obliterate, nor the combination of avarice, inhumanity, and injustice, be ever able to eradicate from the human breast, this heaven-born truth, that man was formed for the enjoyments of thy influence, and that without thee, creation is a cheerless blank.

Source: Russell Parrott, *An Oration On The Abolition Of The Slave Trade; Delivered on the First Of January, 1814. At the African Church of St. Thomas.* (Philidelphia: Printed for the Different Societies, by Thomas T. Stiles)

6

Prince Saunders

In 1780, in the wake of Revolutionary War fervor, Pennsylvania legally abolished the institution of slavery. Among the first activities of freed African Americans was the
establishment of a wide variety of social institutions, from churches to insurance agencies
to fraternal lodges. This speech by Prince Saunders (1784–1839), a leading light among
Philadelphia's black elite, heralded the birth of another type of organization: the literary
society. The concern for education Saunders expresses here was representative of an
expanding middle-class urban world with ever-increasing access to classical learning, faith
in progress, and optimism for the capacities of the human mind. That African Americans,
who by and large were denied equal access to education, might express such attitudes may
easily trouble the modern reader. But education was of particular importance to African
Americans arguing for their rights. Many white Americans justified their support of slavery and restrictions on free black life on the basis that black intellects were irredeemably
inferior. Black leaders, in turn, sought to demonstrate the ability of the race to measure up
to contemporary standards of civilization, presuming that displays of black intellect would
cause white prejudice, and eventually slavery itself, to yield. Saunders's speech also evinces
elements of the doctrine of the Fortunate Fall, which stated that God had compensated for
the evil of Africans' enslavement by bringing them under the benign influences of Christian civilization. The troubling implications of such arguments were not lost on the
antebellum generation of black leaders, who would come to treat the strategy implicit
here with considerable suspicion.

"An Address before the
Pennsylvania Augustine Society"

(1818)

"Perhaps there never was a period, when the attention of so many enlightened men was so vigorously awakened to a sense of the importance of a universal dissemination of the blessings of instruction, as at this enlightened age . . ."

AN ADDRESS, etc.:

THE human heart is a parti-coloured piece of Mosaic. But notwithstanding its veriagated appearances, the whited inlaying of those genuine excellencies, and of those enobling affections, which encompass humanity with glory and honour, are but seldom to be found its innate, or, as it were, its spontaneous ornaments.

We hence descry some of the grounds for that invaluable importance which has uniformly been given to education, in supplying the mind with intellectual acquisitions, and for adorning it with those elevated accomplishments which have generally been considered as its peculiar fruits, by the virtuous and contemplative of every age and nation; where the genial influences of the Sun of Science have been experienced, and where the blessings of civilized society have been enjoyed. If by investigating the historic page of antiquity, we take a retrospective view of the numerous votaries of literature and the useful arts, who flourished at those early periods, when the improving influences of knowledge and civilization were wholly confined to the oriental regions, we shall then discover some traces of their views of the intrinsic utility of mutually associating, to aid the progress of those who were aspiring to taste the Castilian spring, while ascending the towering heights of Parnassus, that there they might behold the magnificent temple of the Ruler of the Muses, and hear his venerated oracle.

We have heard of the early distinguishing attainments of the celebrated Aristotle, who improved so much at seventeen years of age, that the immortal Plato, (his preceptor,) gave him the appellation of a Lover of the Truth. He soon afterwards became tutor to Alexander the great, and founder of the sublime researches of the ancient Peripotetici. The accomplished and eloquent youth, Antonius Gripho, a native of Gaul, came to Rome, and taught rhetoric and poetry at the house of Julius Caesar, when a mere boy; and historians tell us, that his school was frequented by Cicero and others of the most eminent literati of the age.

Many, in different periods, by cultivating the arts and sciences, have contributed to human happiness and improvement, by that invincible zeal for moral virtue and intellectual excellence, which their example has inspired in other minds and hearts, as well as by the sublimity of those traces of truth with which they have illuminated the world, and dignified the intercourse of civilized society.

Perhaps there never was a period, when the attention of so many enlightened men was so vigorously awakened to a sense of the importance of a universal dissemination of the blessings of instruction, as at this enlightened age, in this, in the northern and eastern sections of our country, in some portions of Europe, and in the island of Hayti.

The hope is encouraged, that in the above-mentioned portions of the world, the means of acquiring knowledge sufficient to read and understand the sacred Scriptures, and to manage with propriety, the ordinary concerns of domestic and social life, will soon be within the reach of every individual. Then, we trust, that we shall see a practical exemplification of the beauty and excellence of those celestial precepts and commandments which came from heaven, and which are equally applicable to all descriptions of men. They address themselves to the king upon the throne; they visit the obscurity of the humblest dwelling; they call upon the poor man to cultivate every good principle of action, as well as the man of a more elevated rank, and to aim at a life of purity, innocence, elevated virtue, and moral excellence, with the assurance that he too, shall reap his reward in that better scene of human destination, to which Christianity has called all those who fear God and work righteousness.

Wherever these lofty and commanding views of piety and virtue have been encouraged, a high sense of the social, moral, and practical obligations and duties of life, have been cherished and cultivated with an elevated and an invincible spirit.

Under the influence of this spirit, this benevolent spirit, practical Christians, of every denomination, have elevated their views far beyond the circumscribed boundaries of selfishness, sectarianism, and party zeal; and, being bound together by the indissoluble links of that golden chain of charity and kind affection, with which Christianity invariably connects its sincere votaries, and standing upon the common ground of Christian equality, they encircle the great community of those who profess the religion of our divine Master, in the arms of their charity and love, and become co-workers and fellow-labourers in the illumination, the improvement, and the ultimate felicity of those who will, undoubtedly, eventually belong to the commonwealth of the Israel of our God.

In such improved sections of the world, the gardens of the Academy are thronged with youth, whose ardour to reap its fairest flowers, would even vie with that evinced by the hazardous enterprize of the intrepid Jason of antiquity, when he cast the watchful Dragon, and seized that invaluable prize, the Golden Fleece.

We have reason to be grateful, my friends, that it has pleased God to permit us to witness a period when those unjust prejudices, and those hitherto insuperable barriers to the instruction, and, consequently, to the intellectual, the moral, and the religious improvement and elevation of the people of colour, under which our fathers groaned, are beginning to subside.

And now, in the true spirit of the religion of that beneficent Parent, who has made of one blood all nations of men who dwell upon the face of the whole earth, many persons of different regions and various nations, have been led to the contemplation of the interesting relations in which the human race stand to each other. They have seen that man, as a solitary individual, is a very wretched being. As long as he stands detached from his kind, he is possessed neither of happiness nor of strength. We are formed by nature to unite; we are impelled towards each other by the benevolent instincts in our frames; we are linked by a thousand connexions, founded on common wants.

Benevolent affection therefore, or, as it is very properly termed, humanity, is what man, as such in every station, owes to man. To be inaccessible, contemptuous, avaricious, and hard hearted, is to revolt against our very reason and nature; it is, according to the language of inspiration, to "hide ourselves from our own flesh."

The genuine kind affections, and the elevated sensibilities of Christianity, as they are exhibited to us in the conduct and character of our blessed Saviour, during his residence in this scene of our pilgrimage, are suited to call forth into vigorous exercise, the best sentiments, feelings and dispositions of the human heart; while they disclose to the admiring view of his obedient followers, those indissoluble and enobling moral ties, which connect earth with heaven, and which assimilate man to the benevolent Author of his being.

Wherever Christianity is considered as a religion of the affections, every well instructed, practical Christian, habitually aspires at an entire imitation of the example, and to yield a cheerful and unreserved obedience to the precepts and instructions of its heavenly founder. So peculiar is the adaptation of Christianity to become a universal religion; for wherever its spirit enters into the councils of nations, we find it unbinding the chains of corporeal and mental captivity, and diffusing over the whole world, the maxims of impartial justice, and of enlightened benevolence.

Such, and so sublimely excellent, are the fruits of a spirit of Christian charity and practical beneficence; for to it alone the glory is due, of having placed the weak under the protection of their stronger brethren; for she unceasingly labours to improve all the varying circumstances and conditions of mankind: so that, among those who profess her true spirit, the love of our neighbour is not an inactive principle, but it is real beneficence; and they, like the good Samaritan in the gospel, evince their sincerity by ministering to the necessities, and in labouring for the welfare, improvement and happiness of mankind.

Mess'rs Vice-Presidents, and Gentlemen of the Pennsylvania Augustine Education Society.

ALTHOUGH the seat of your respected President is vacant on this intersecting occasion, on account of the severe indisposition with which he is visited, still we trust that his heart is with you, and that you have his best wishes and his prayers, for the prosperity of this excellent establishment. The hope is encouraged, that you will never be weary in labouring for the promotion of the cause and interests of science and literature among the rising generation of the people of colour. For upon their intellectual, moral and religious improvements, depend the future elevation of their standing, in the social, civil and ecclesiastical community. Surely then, my friends, you are associated for the most laudable, interesting, and invaluable purposes.

Therefore, let it be the unceasing labour, the undeviating and the inflexibly firm purpose of the members of this Association, individually and collectively, to inspire all within the sphere of their influence, with a sense of the value and importance of giving their children a good education. Hear the words of revelation, calling upon you who profess to be Christians, to "train up your children in the way they should go," and to "bring them up in the nurture and admonition of the Lord." And if you believe this high authority, how can you be excused, if you neglect to give them the means of acquiring a knowledge of their duty to that divine instructor who came to call them to glory, to virtue, and to immortality.

Permit me to again entreat you, duly to appreciate the importance of religiously educating your children. For, a Christian education is not only of great utility while sojourning in this scene of discipline and probation, but it is more transcendently excellent in that more elevated scene of human destination to which we are hastening. For even the ruthless hand of death itself, cannot disrobe the soul of those virtuous principles, which are sometimes acquired through the medium of a virtuous education, and "which, when transplanted to the skies, in heaven's immortal garden bloom."

Source: Prince Saunders, *An Address; Delivered at Bethel Church, Philadelphia; on the 30th of September, 1818. Before the Pennsylvania Augustine Society, for the Education of People of Colour* (Philadelphia: Printed by Joseph Rakestraw, 1818).

7

Robert Alexander Young

In 1829, Robert Alexander Young self-published one of the most interesting and unusual pamphlets by an African American to appear in the antebellum North. Little is known of Young, though he may have been a working-class preacher of mixed racial heritage who plied his trade on the streets of New York City. In its focus on the spirit of liberty inherent in all men, the "Ethiopian Manifesto" contains strong overtones of the Enlightenment's natural rights philosophy, which undergirded the American Revolution. At the same time, it professed an almost mystical messianism quite out of keeping with the well-reasoned logic of the African-American pamphlet tradition. Instead, Young's writing appears as an African-American counterpart to two important American religious traditions. The first was millennialism, which foresaw the imminent return of Christ and the imposition of his just rule. The tradition of the Puritan jeremiad, which warned against the dangers of apostasy and thus unified the community of the faithful, constituted the second. Young's jeremiad admonished slaveholders for their sins and predicted their imminent downfall. At the same time, though it did not ask African Americans to actively resist their oppression, it challenged them to retain their faith in God despite their misfortune.

"Ethiopian Manifesto"

(1829)

"Know, then, in your present state or standing, in your sphere of government in any nation within which you reside, we hold and contend you enjoy but a few of your rights of government within them."

Southern District of New-York, s s.

BE IT REMEBERED, That on the 18th day of February, A.D. 1829, in the 53d year of the Independence of the United States of America, Robert Alexander Young, of the said district, hath deposited in this office the title of a book the right whereof he claims as author, in the words following, to wit:

"The Ethiopian Manifesto, issued in defence of the Black Man's Rights, in the scale of Universal Freedom."

In conformity to the Act of Congress of the United States, entitled "An Act for the Encouragement of Learning, by securing the copies of Maps, Charts, and Books, to the author and proprietors of such copies, during the time therein mentioned." And also to an Act, entitled "An Act supplementary to an act, entitled an act for the encouragement of learning, by securing the copies of Maps, Charts, and Books, to the authors and proprietors of such copies, during the times therein mentioned, and extending the benefits thereof to the arts of designing, engraving, and etching historical and other prints."

FRED I. BETTS,
Clerk of the Southern District of New-York.

ETHIOPIAN MANIFESTO

By the Omnipotent will of God, we, Rednaxela, sage, and asserter to the Ethiopian of his rights, do hereby declare, and make known, as follows: -

Ethiopians! the power of Divinity having within us, as man, implanted a sense of the due and prerogatives belonging to you, a people, of whom we were of your race, in part born, as a mirror we trust, to reflect to you from a review of ourselves, the dread condition in which you do at this day stand. We do, therefore, to the accomplishment of our purpose, issue this but a brief of our grand manifesto, herefrom requiring the attention towards us of every native, or those proceeding in descent from the Ethiopian or African people; a regard to your welfare being the great and inspiring motive which leads us to this our undertaking. We do therefore strictly enjoin your attention to these the dictates from our sense of justice, held forth and produced to your notice, but with the most pure intention.

Ethiopians! open your minds to reason; let therein weigh the effects of truth, wisdom, and justice (and a regard to your individual as a general good), and the spirit of these our words we know full well, cannot but produce the effect for which they are by us herefrom intended. –Know, then, in your present state or standing, in your sphere of government in any nation within which you reside, we hold and contend you enjoy but a few of your rights of government within them. We here speak of the whole of the Ethiopian people, as we admit not even those in their state of native simplicity, to be in an enjoyment of their rights, as bestowed to them of the great bequest of God to man.

The impositions practised to their state, not being known to them from the heavy and darksome clouds of ignorance which so woefully obscures their reason, we do, therefore, for the recovering of them, as well as establishing to you your rights, proclaim, that duty— imperious duty, exacts the convocation of ourselves in a body politic; that we do, for the promotion and welfare of our order, establish to ourselves a people framed unto the likeness of that order, which from our mind's eye we do evidently discern governs the universal creation. Beholding but one sole power, supremacy, or head, we do of that head, but hope and look forward for succour in the accomplishment of the great design which he hath, in his wisdom, promoted us to its undertaking.

We find we possess in ourselves an understanding; of this we are taught to know the ends of right and wrong, that depression should come upon us or any of our race of the wrongs inflicted on us of men. We know in ourselves we possess a right to see ourselves justified therefrom, of the right of God; knowing, but of his power hath he decreed to man, that either in himself he stands, or by himself he falls. Fallen, sadly, sadly low indeed, hath become our race, when we behold it reduced but to an enslaved state, to raise it from its degenerate sphere, and instill into it the rights of men, are the ends intended of these our words; here we are met in ourselves, we constitute but one, aided as we trust, by the effulgent light of wisdom to a discernment of the path which shall lead us to the collecting together of a people, rendered disobedient to the great dictates of nature, by the barbarity that hath been practised upon them from generation to generation of the will of their more cruel fellow-men. Am I, because I am a descendant of a mixed race of men, whose shade hath stamped them with the hue of black, to deem myself less eligible to the attainment of the great gift allotted of God to man, than are any other of whatsoever cast you please, deemed from being white as being more exalted than the black?

These words, which carry to the view of others the dictates of my mind. I borrow not from the sense of white men or of black: learn, my brother and fellow-Ethiopian, it is but the invigorating power of Deity instills them to my discernment. Of him do I know I derive my right; of him was I on the conception of a mother's womb created free; who then in the shape of man shall dare to rob me of my birthright as bestowed to me in my existence from God? No, I am in myself a man, and as a man will live, or as a man will die; for as I was born free of the will allotted me of the freedom of God, so do I claim and purport to establish an alike universal freedom to every son and daughter descending from the black; though however mixed in grades of colour through an intercourse of white with black; still as I am in myself, but a mixture of like, I call to witness, if the power of my mind hath not a right to claim an allegiance with all descendants of a race, for the justification of whose rights reason hath established within me the ends for their obtainment? God, an almighty, sole, and governing God, can alone direct me to the ends I have, but of his will to fulfill, be they here to the view of the universal world from him established; for as I do in myself stand upright, and claim in myself, as outwardly from myself, all my rights and prerogatives as pertaining to me in my birthright of man, so do I equally claim to the untutored black of every denomination, be he in bondage or free, an alike right; and do hereby publicly protest against the infringement of his rights, as is at this day practised by the fiendish cast of men who dare, contrary to the knowledge of justice, as hath been implanted of God in the soul of man, to hold him in bondage, adducing from his servitude a gorgeous maintenance. Accursed and damned be he in mind, soul and body, who dare after this my protest, to claim the slightest alleged right to hold a man, as regards manly visage, shape, and bearing, equal in all points, though ignorant and untaught with himself, and in intrinsic worth to the view of Deity; by far in his sacred presence, must he appear the better man, the calm submission to his fate, pointing him to the view of justice at the throne of God, as being more worthy of the rights of man, than the wretch who would claim from him his rights as a man.

I pause. Custom here points to me her accursed practises, if founded in error, as base injustice; shall they stand? nay, aught they to be allowed or sanctioned, for so to do by the cognizance of the just, the wise, the great, the good, and sound men of discretion of this world? I speak for no man, understanding but in myself my rights, that from myself shall be made known to a people, rights, which I, of the divine will of God, to them establish. Man—white man—black man—or, more properly, ye monsters incarnate, in human shape, who claim the horrid right to hold nature's untutored son, the Ethiopian, in bondage, to you I do herefrom speak. Mark me, and regard well these my words; be assured, they convey the voice of reason, dictated to you through a prophetic sense of truth. The time is at hand when many signs shall appear to you, to denote that Almighty God regards the affairs of afflicted men:- for know, the cries of bitter servitude, from those unhappy sons of men, whom ye have so long unjustly oppressed with the goading shafts of an accursed slavery, hath descended to Deity. Your God, the great and mighty God, hath seen your degradation of your fellow brother, and mortal man; he hath long looked down with mercy on your suffering slave; his cries have called for a vindication of his rights, and know ye they have been heard of the Majesty of Heaven, whose dignity have you not offended by deeming a mortal man, in your own likeness, as but worthy of being your slave, degraded to your brute? The voice of intuitive justice speaks aloud to you, and bids you to release your slave; otherwise stings, eternal stings, of an outraged and goading conscience will, ere long, hold all them in subjection who pay not due attention to this, its admonition. Beware! know thyselves to be but mortal men, doomed to the good or evil, as your works shall merit from you. Pride ye not yourselves in the greatness of your worldly standing, since all things are but moth when contrasted with the invisible spirit, which in yourself maintains within you your course of action. That within you will, to the presence of your God, be at all times your sole accuser. Weigh well these my words in the balance of your conscientious reason, and abide the judgement thereof to your own standing, for we tell you of a surety, the decree hath already passed the judgement seat of an undeviating God, wherein he hath said, "surely hath the cries of the black, a most persecuted people, ascended to my throne and craved my mercy; now, behold! I will stretch forth mine hand and gather them to the palm, that they become unto me a people, and I unto them their God." Hearken, therefore, oh! slaveholder, thou task inflicter against the rights of men, the day is at hand, nay the hour draweth nigh, when poverty shall appear to thee a blessing, if it but restore to thy fellow-man his rights; all worldly riches shall be known to thee then but as a curse, and in thine heart's desire to obtain contentment, when sad reverses come upon thee, then shalt thou linger for a renewal of days, that in thine end thou might not curse the spirit which called thee forth to life. Take warning, again we say, for of a surety from this, God will give you signs to know, in his decrees he regards the fallen state of the sons of men. Think not that wisdom descries not from here your vanity. We behold it, thou vain bloated upstart worldling of a slaveholder, laugh in derision of thy earthly taught and worldly sneer; but know, on thee we pronounce our judgment, and as fitting thee, point out to thy notice this our sign. Of the degraded of this earth, shall be exalted, one who shall draw from thee, as though gifted of power divine, all attachment and regard of thy slave toward thee. Death shall he prefer to a continuance of his race:—being doomed to thy vile servitude, no cohabitation shall be known between the sexes, while suffering under thy slavery; but should ungovernable passion attain over the untaught mind an ascendancy, abortion shall destroy the birth. We command it, the voice of imperative justice, though however harsh, must be obeyed. Ah! doth your expanding judgement, base slaveholder, not from here descry that the shackles which have been by you so undeservingly forged upon a wretched Ethiopian's frame, are about to be forever from him unlinked. Say ye, this can never be accomplished? If so, must indeed the power and decrees of Infinity become subservient to the will of depraved man. But learn, slaveholder, thine will rests not in thine hand: God decrees to thy slave his rights as man. This we issue forth as the spirit of the black man or Ethiopian's rights, established from the Ethiopian's Rock, the foundation of his civil and religious rights, which hereafter will be exemplified in the order of its course. Ethiopians, throughout the world in general, receive this as but a lesson presented to you from an instructive Book, in which many, many therein are contained, to the vindication of its purpose. As came John the Baptist, of old, to spread abroad the forthcoming of his master, so alike are intended these our words, to denote to the black African or Ethiopian people, that God has prepared them for a leader, who awaits but for his season to proclaim to them his birthright. How shall you know this man? By indubitable signs which cannot be controverted by the power of mortal, his marks being stamped in open visage, as equally so upon his frame, which constitutes him to have been particularly regarded in the infinite work of God to man.

Know ye, then, if a white man ever appeared on earth, bearing in himself the semblance of his former race, the man we proclaim ordained of God, to call together the black people as a nation in themselves. We say, in him will be seen, in appearance a white man, although having been born of a black woman, his mother. The proof is strong, and in Granada's Island, Grand Anta Estate, there, some time ago, did dwell his mother—his father then owner of the said estate. The church books of St. Georgestown, the capital of Grenada, can truly prove his birth. As another instance wherein providence decreed he should appear peculiar in his make, the two middle toes on each of his feet were, in his conception, webbed and bearded. Now, after the custom of the ancient order of men, with long and flowing hair, by like appearances may he be known; none other man, but the one bearing alike marks, and proving his identity from the island on which he was born, can be the man of whom we speak. To him, thou poor black Ethiopian or African slave, do thou, from henceforth, place a firm reliance thereon, as trusting in him to prove thy liberator from the infernal state of bondage, under which you have been so long and so unjustly laboring. To thee he pledges himself, in life to death, not to desert thee, his trust being in the power of the Almighty, who giveth not the race to the swift nor the battle to the strong, but decrees to all men the justice he establishes. As such, we draw from him the conception of your rights, and to its obtainment we issue this to you, our first pledge of faith, binding ourselves herefrom to render to you, at all times, such services as shall tend most to your advantage in effecting a speedy deliverance from your mortal and most deadly foe, the monster of a slaveholder. We would most particularly direct you to such government of yourselves as should be responsible but to God, your maker, for the duty exacted of you to your fellow-men; but, under goading situations, where power and might is but the construction of law, it then behooves the depressed and vilely injured to bear his burthen with the firmness of his manhood:—So at this time, we particularly recommend to you, degraded sons of Africa, to submit with fortitude to your present state of suffering, relying in yourselves, from the justice of a God, that the time is at hand, when, with but the power of words and the divine will of our God, the vile shackles of slavery shall be broken asunder from you, and no man known who shall dare to own or proclaim you as his bondsman. We say it, and assert it as though by an oracle given and delivered to you on high. God, in his holy keeping, direct thee, thou poor untaught and degraded African slave, to a full conception of these the words we have written for your express benefit. Our care and regard of you will be that of a fostering parent toward a beloved offspring. The hatred of your oppressor we fear not, nor do we his power, or any vile machinations that may be resorted to by incendiaries towards us. We hold ourself, with the aid of our God therewith, at all times ready to encounter, trusting but in God, our Creator, and not in ourselves, for a deliverance from all worldly evil.

Peace and Liberty to the Ethiopian first, as also all other grades of men, is the invocation we offer to the throne of our God.

REDNAXELA

DATED FROM THE
ETHIOPIAN'S ROCK,
IN THE
THIRTY-SEVENTH YEAR
FROM ITS
FOUNDATION,
THIS THIRTEENTH DAY OF FEBRUARY, A.D.
1829

Source: Robert Alexander Young, *The Ethiopian Manifesto, Issued in Defence of the Black Man's Rights in the Scale of Universal Freedom* (New York: Printed for the author, 1829)

David Walker

David Walker (1784–1830) wrote probably the most important pamphlet of the antebellum era. It energized countless black activists, from Maria Stewart to Henry Highland Garnet. It struck fear in white authorities, North and South. It just might have cost him his life. Why?

On first glimpse, Walker's "Appeal" may appear to be as straightforward a challenge to white power and slavery as could have been written. Walker calls on Americans to institute racial justice (by ending slavery and treating African Americans equally) lest black rebels take matters into their own hands. But the "Appeal" is also a complex document which belies easy categorization. For one thing, it is both strongly worded and yet vague on details. It is written for black as well as white eyes. Stylistically, it integrates reasoned argument with sections of bombast and folk wisdom (Walker criticizes members of the black community who fail publicly to condemn white racism yet he also challenges the race to strive for education and uplift). Finally, Walker's ultimate message about violence is ambiguous. Did he really encourage a mass uprising of the black masses or did he say an uprising would occur only if slavery persisted?

Walker wrote his "Appeal" during a lull in the broader abolitionist movement. The American Colonization Society (ACS) was one of the fastest-growing reform organizations of the 1820s. Longstanding abolition societies often refused to condemn the ACS, whose members (such as James Madison) were national political leaders. Walker rebuked the ACS in no uncertain terms, and condemned the entire plan to "repatriate" free blacks to Africa. Slavery would grow only stronger, he argued, once free black leaders had been removed and silenced.

Walker was born free in North Carolina, moved to Boston, and ran a used-clothing shop in the Fisherman's Wharf section of the city. He worked on the nation's first independent black newspaper, *Freedom's Journal* (based in New York), and was a leader of Boston's General Colored Association. He died mysteriously in 1830. His work remained a vivid presence.

The selection below comes from Article IV of Walker's "Appeal," subtitled "Our Wretchedness in Consequence of the Colonizing Plan." It contains Walker's bracketed editorial comments and notes. The original text of this third edition of the "Appeal" first appeared in 1830.

"Appeal to the Colored Citizens of the World"
(1829, 1830)

When God Almighty commences his battle on the continent of America, for the oppression of his people, tyrants will wish they were never born."

The following selection comes from section four of Walker's lengthy "Appeal," "Our Wretchedness In Consequence of the Colonizing Plan."

OUR WRETCHEDNESS IN CONSEQUENCE OF THE COLONIZING PLAN.

My dearly beloved brethren:—This is a scheme on which so many able writers, together with that very judicious coloured Baltimorean, have commented, that I feel my delicacy about touching it. But as I am compelled to do the will of my Master, I declare, I will give you my sentiments upon it.—Previous, how-ever, to giving my sentiments, either for or against it, I shall give that of Mr. Henry Clay, together with that of Mr. Elias B. Caldwell, Esq. of the District of Columbia, as extracted from the National Intelligence, by Dr. Torrey, author of a series of "Essays on Morals, and the Diffusion of Useful Knowledge."

At a meeting which was convened in the District of Columbia, for the express purpose of agitating the subject of colonizing us in some part of the world, Mr. Clay was called to the chair, and having been seated a little while, he rose and spoke, in substance, as follows: says he—"That class of the mixt population of our country [coloured people] was peculiarly situated; they neither enjoyed the immunities of freemen, nor were they subjected to the incapacity of slaves, but partook, in some degree, of the qualities of both. From their condition, and the unconquerable prejudices resulting from their colour, they never could amalgamate with the free whites of this country. It was desirable, therefore, as it respected them, and the residue of the population of the country, to drain them off. Various schemes of colonization had been thought of, and a part of our continent, it was supposed by some, might furnish a suitable establishment for them. But, for his part, Mr. C. said, he had a decided preference for some part of the Coast of Africa. There ample provision might be made for the colony itself, and it might be rendered instrumental to the introduction into that extensive quarter of the globe, of the arts, civilization, and Christianity." [Here I ask Mr. Clay, what kind of Christianity? Did he mean such as they have among the Americans—distinction, whip, blood and oppression? I pray the Lord Jesus Christ to forbid it.] "There," said he, "was a peculiar, a moral fitness, in restoring them to the land of their

---

* See Dr. Torrey's Portraiture of Domestic Slavery in the United States, pages 85, 86.

fathers, and if instead of the evils and sufferings which we had been the innocent cause of inflicting upon the inhabitants of Africa, we can transmit to her the blessings of our arts, our civilization, and our religion. May we not hope that America will extinguish a great portion of that moral debt which she has contracted to that unfortunate continent? Can there be a nobler cause than that which, whilst it proposes," &c. * * * * * * * [you know what this means.] "contemplates the spreading of the arts of civilized life, and the possible redemption from ignorance and barbarism of a benighted quarter of the globe?"

Before I proceed any further, I solicit your notice, brethren, to the foregoing part of Mr. Clay's speech, in which he says, (➔ look above) "and if, instead of the evils and sufferings, which we had been the innocent cause of inflicting," &C.—What this very learned statesman could have been thinking about, when he said in his speech, "we had been the innocent cause of inflicting," &c., I have never been able to conceive. Are Mr. Clay and the rest of the Americans, innocent of the blood and groans of our fathers and us, their children?— Every individual may plead innocence, if he pleases, but God will, before long, separate the innocent from the guilty, unless something is speedily done which I suppose will hardly be, so that their destruction may be sure. Oh Americans! let me tell you, in the name of the Lord, it will be good for you, if you listen to the voice of the Holy Ghost, but if you do not, you are ruined! ! ! Some of you are good men; but the will of my God must be done. Those avaricious and ungodly tyrants among you, I am awfully afraid will drag down the vengeance of God upon you. When God Almighty commences his battle on the continent of America, for the oppression of his people, tyrants will wish they never were born.

But to return to Mr. Clay, whence I digressed. He says, "It was proper and necessary distinctly to state, that he understood it constituted no part of the object of this meeting, to touch or agitate in the slightest degree, a delicate question, connected with another portion of the coloured population of our country. It was not proposed to deliberate upon or consider at all, any question of emancipation, or that which was connected with the abolition of slavery. It was upon that condition alone, he was sure, that many gentlemen from the South and the West, whom he saw present, had attended, or could be expected to co-operate. It was upon that condition only, that he himself had attended."

That is to say, to fix a plan to get those of the coloured people, who are said to be free, away from among those of our brethren whom they unjustly hold in bondage, so that they may be enabled to keep them the more secure in ignorance and wretchedness, to support them and their children, and consequently they would have the more obedient slaves. For if the free are allowed to stay among the slaves, they will have intercourse together, and, of course, the free will learn the slaves *bad habits*, by teaching them that they are MEN, as well as other people, and certainly *ought* and *must* be FREE.

I presume, that every intelligent man of colour must have some idea of Mr. Henry Clay, originally of Virginia, but now of Kentucky; they know too, perhaps, whether he is a friend, or a foe to the coloured citizens of this country, and of the world. This gentleman, according to his own words, had been highly favoured and blessed of the Lord, though he did not acknowledge it; but, to the contrary, he acknowledged men, for all the blessings with which God had favoured him. At a public dinner, given him at Fowler's Garden, Lexington, Kentucky, he delivered a public speech to a very large concourse of people— in the concluding clause of which, he says, "And now, my friends and fellow citizens, I cannot part from you, on possibly the last occasion of my ever publicly addressing you, without reiterating the expression of my thanks, from a heart overflowing with gratitude. I came among you, now more than thirty years ago, an orphan boy, pennyless, a stranger to you all, without friends, without the favour of the great, you took me up, cherished me, protected me, honoured me, you have constantly poured upon me a bold and unabated stream of innumerable favours, time which wears out every thing has increased and strengthened your affection for me. When I seemed deserted by almost the whole world, and assailed by almost every tongue, and pen, and press, you have fearlessly and manfully stood by me, with unsurpassed zeal and undiminished friendship. When I felt as if I should sink beneath the storm of abuse and detraction, which was violently raging around me, I have found myself upheld and sustained by your encouraging voices and approving smiles. I have doubtless, committed many faults and indiscretions, over which you have thrown the broad mantle of your charity. But I can say, and in the presence of God and in this assembled multitude, I will say, that I have honestly and faithfully served my country—that I have never wronged it—and that, however unprepared, I lament that I am to appear in the Divine presence on other accounts, I invoke the stern justice of his judgment on my public conduct, without the slightest apprehension of his displeasure."

Hearken to this Statesman indeed, but no philanthropist, whom God sent into Kentucky, an orphan boy, penniless, and friendless, where he not only gave him a plenty of friends and the comforts of life, but raised him almost to the very highest honour in the nation, where his great talents, with which the Lord has been pleased to bless him, has gained for him the affection of a great portion of the people with whom he had to do. But what has this gentleman done for the Lord, after having done so much for him? The Lord has a suffering people, whose moans and groans at his feet for deliverance from oppression and wretchedness, pierce the very throne of Heaven, and call loudly on the God of Justice, to be revenged. Now, what this gentleman who is so highly favoured of the Lord, has done to liberate those miserable victims of oppression, shall appear before the world by his letters to Mr. Gallatin, Envoy Extraordinary and Minister Plenipotentiary to Great Britain, dated June 19, 1826.—Though Mr. Clay was writing for the States, yet neverthe-less, it appears from the very face of his letters to that gentleman, that he was as anxious, if not more so, to get those free people and sink them into wretchedness, as his constituents, for whom he wrote.

The Americans of North and of South America including the West India Islands—no trifling portion of whom were, for stealing, murdering, &c. compelled to flee from Europe, to save their necks or banishment, have effected their escape to this continent, where God blessed them with all the comforts of life—He gave them a plenty of every thing calculated to do them good—not satisfied with this, however, they wanted slaves and wanted us for their slaves, who belong to the Holy Ghost, and no other, who we shall have to serve instead of tyrants.—I say, the Americans want us, the property of the Holy Ghost to serve them. But there is a day fast approaching, when (unless there is a univer-sal repentance on the part of the whites, which will scarcely take place, they have got to be so hardened in consequence of our blood, and so wise in their own conceit.) To be plain and candid with you, Americans! I say that the day is fast approaching, when there will be a greater time on the continent of America, than ever was witnessed upon this earth since it came from the hand of its Creator. Some of you have done us so much injury, that you will never be able to repent.—Your cup must be filled.—You want us for your slaves, and shall have enough of us—God is just, *who will give you your fill of us*. But Mr. Henry Clay, speaking to Mr. Gallatin, respecting coloured people, who had effected their escape from the U. States (or to them *hell upon earth! ! !*) to the hospitable shores of Canada,* from whence it would cause more than the lives of the Americans to get them, to plunge into wretchedness—he says: "The General Assembly of Kentucky, one of the states which is most affected by the escape of slaves into Upper Canada has again, at their session which

---

*Among the English, our real friends and benefactors.

has just terminated, invoked the interposition of the General Government. In the treaty which has been recently concluded with the United Mexican States, and which is now under the consideration of the Senate, provision is made for the restoration of fugitive slaves. As it appears from your statements of what passed on that subject, with the British Plenipotentiaries, that they admitted the correctness of the principle of restoration, it is hoped that you will be able to succeed in making satisfactory arrangements."

There are a series of these letters, all of which are to the same amount; some however, presenting a face more of his own responsibility. I wonder what would this gentleman think, if the Lord should give him among the rest of his blessings enough of slaves? Could he blame any other being but himself? Do we not belong to the Holy Ghost? What business has he or any body else, to be sending letters about the world respecting us? Can we not go where we want to, as well as other people, only if we obey the voice of the Holy Ghost? This gentleman, (Mr. Henry Clay) not only took an active part in this colonizing plan, but was absolutely chairman of a meeting held at Washington, the twenty-first day of December 1816, to agitate the subject of colonizing us in Africa.—Now I appeal and ask every citizen of these United States and of the world, both *white* and *black*, who has any knowledge of Mr. Clay's public labor for these States—I want you candidly to answer the Lord, who sees the secrets of our hearts.—Do you believe that Mr. Henry Clay, late Secretary of State, and now in Kentucky, is a friend to the blacks, further, than his personal interest extends? Is it not his greatest object and glory upon earth, to sink us into miseries and wretchedness by making slaves of us, to work his plantation to enrich him and his family? Does he care a pinch of snuff about Africa—whether it remains a land of Pagans and of blood, or of Christians, so long as he gets enough of her sons and daughters to dig up gold and silver for him? If he had no slaves, and could obtain them in no other way if it were not, repugnant to the laws of his country, which prohibit the importation of slaves (which act was, indeed, more through apprehension than humanity) would he not try to import a few from Africa, to work his farm? Would he work in the hot sun to earn his bread, if he could make an African work for nothing, particularly, if he could keep him in ignorance and make him believe that God made him for nothing else but to work for him? Is not Mr. Clay a white man, and too delicate to work in the hot sun! ! Was he not made by his Creator to sit in the shade, and make the blacks work without remuneration for their services, to support him and his family! ! ! I have been for some time taking notice of this man's speeches and public writings, but never to my knowledge have I seen any thing in his writings which insisted on the emancipation of slavery, which has almost ruined his country. Thus we see the depravity of men's hearts, when in pursuit only of gain—particularly when they oppress their fellow creatures to obtain that gain—God suffers some to go on until they are lost forever. This same Mr. Clay, wants to know, what he has done, to merit the disapprobation of the American people. In a public speech delivered by him, he asked: "Did I involve my country in an unnecessary war?" to merit the censure of the Americans—"Did I bring obliquy upon the nation, or the people whom I represented? —did I ever lose any opportunity to advance the fame, honor and prosperity of this State and the Union?" How astonishing it is, for a man who knows so much about God and his ways, as Mr. Clay, to ask such frivolous questions? Does he believe that a man of his talents and standing in the midst of a people, will get along unnoticed by the penetrating and all seeing eye of God, who is continually taking cognizance of the hearts of men? Is not God against him, for advocating the murderous cause of slavery? If God is against him, what can the Americans, together with the whole world do for him? Can they save him from the hand of the Lord Jesus Christ?

I shall now pass in review the speech of Mr. Elias B. Caldwell Esq. of the District of Columbia, extracted from the same page on which Mr. Clay's will be found. Mr. Caldwell, giving his opinion respecting us, at that ever memorable meeting, he says: "The more you improve the condition of these people, the more you cultivate their minds, the more miserable you make them in their present state. You give them a higher relish for those privileges which they can never attain, and turn what we intend for a blessing into a curse." Let me ask this benevolent man, what he means by a blessing intended for us? Did he mean sinking us and our children into ignorance and wretchedness, to support him and his family? What he meant will appear evident and obvious to the most ignorant in the world (See Mr. Caldwell's intended blessings for us, O! my Lord ! ! "No," said he, "if they must remain in their present situation, keep them in the *lowest state of degradation and ignorance.* The nearer you bring them to the condition of brutes, the better chance do you give them of possessing their *apathy.*" Here I pause to get breath, having labored to extract the above clause of this gentleman's speech, at that colonizing meeting. I presume that everybody knows the meaning of the word "*apathy,*" —if any do not, let him get Sheridan's Dictionary, in which he will find it explained in full. I solicit the attention of the world, to the foregoing part of Mr. Caldwell's speech, that they may see what man will do with his fellow men, when he has them under his feet. To what length will not man go in iniquity when given up to a hard heart, and reprobate mind, in consequence of blood and oppression? The last clause of this speech, which was written in a very artful manner, and which will be taken for the speech of a friend, without close examination and deep penetration, I shall now present. He says, "surely, Americans ought to be the last people on earth, to advocate such slavish doctrines, to cry peace and contentment to those who are deprived of the privileges of civil liberty, they who have so largely partaken of its blessings, who know so well how to estimate its value, ought to be among the foremost to extend it to others." The real sense and meaning of the last part of Mr. Caldwell's speech is, get the free people of colour away to Africa, from among the slaves, where they may at once be blessed and happy, and those who we hold in slavery, will be contented to rest in ignorance and wretchedness, to dig up gold and silver for us and our children. Men have indeed got to be so cunning, these days, that it would take the eye of a Solomon to penetrate and find them out.

→ ADDITION.—OUR dear Redeemer said, "Therefore, whatsoever ye have spoken in darkness, shall be heard in the light; and that which ye have spoken in the ear in closets, shall be pro-claimed upon the house tops."

How obviously this declaration of our Lord has been shown among the Americans of the United States. They have hitherto passed among some nations, who do not know any thing about their internal concerns, for the most enlightened, humane charitable, and merciful people upon earth, when at the same time they treat us, the (coloured people) secretly more cruel and unmerciful than any other nation upon earth.—It is a fact that in our Southern and Western States, there are millions who hold us in chains or in slavery, whose greatest object and glory, is centered in keeping us sunk in the most profound ignorance and stupidity, to make us work without remunerations for our services. Many of whom if they catch a coloured person, whom they hold in unjust ignorance, slavery and degradation, to them and their children, with a book in his hand, will beat him nearly to death. I heard a wretch in the state of North Carolina said that if any man would teach a black person whom he held in slavery, to spell, read or write, he would prosecute him to the very extent of the law.—Said the ignorant wretch,* "a Nigar, ought not to have any

---

*It is a fact, that in all our Slave-holding States (in the countries) there are thousands of the whites, who are almost as ignorant in comparison as horses, the most they know, is to beat the coloured people, which some of them shall have their hearts full of yet.

more sense than enough to work for his master." May I not ask to fatten the wretch and his family?—These and similar cruelties these *Christians* have been for hundreds of years inflicting on our fathers and us in the dark God has however, very recently published some of their secret crimes on the house top, that the world may gaze on their Christianity and see of what kind it is composed.—Georgia for instance, God has completely shown to the world, the *Christianity* among its white *inhabitants*. A law has recently passed the Legislature of this *republican* State (Georgia) prohibiting all free or slave persons of colour, from learning to read or write; another law has passed the *republican* House of Delegates, (but not the Senate) in Virginia, to prohibit all persons of colour, (free and slave) from learning to read or write, and even to hinder them from meeting together in order to worship our Maker! ! ! ! ! !—Now I solemnly appeal, to the most skilful historians in the world, and all those who are mostly acquainted with the histories of the Antideluvians and of Sodom and Gomorrah, to show me a parallel of barbarity. *Christians! ! Christians! ! !* I dare you to show me a parallel of cruelties in the annals of Heathens or of Devils, with those of Ohio, Virginia and of Georgia—know the world that these things were before done in the dark, or in a corner under a garb of humanity and religion. God has however, taken of the fig-leaf covering, and made them expose them-selves on the house top. I tell you that God works in many ways his wonders to perform, he will unless they repent, make them expose themselves enough more yet to the world.—See the acts of the *Christians* in FLORIDA, SOUTH CAROLINA, and KENTUCKY—was it not for the reputation of the house of my Lord and Master, I would mention here, an act of cruelty inflicted a few days since on a black man, by the white *Christians* in the PARK STREET CHURCH, in this (CITY) which is almost enough to make Demons themselves quake and tremble in their FIREY HABITATIONS.—Oh! my Lord how refined in iniquity the whites have got to be in consequence of our blood*—what kind! ! Oh ! what kind! ! ! of Christianity can be found this day in all the earth! ! ! ! ! !

I write without the fear of man, I am writing for my God, and fear none but himself; they may put me to death if they choose—(I fear and esteem a good man however, let him be black or white.) I forbear to comment on the cruelties inflicted on this Black Man by the Whites, in the Park Street MEETING HOUSE, I will leave it in the dark! ! ! ! ! But I declare that the atrocity is really to Heaven daring and infernal, that I must say that God has commenced a course of exposition among the Americans, and the glorious and heavenly work will continue to progress until they learn to do justice.←

Extract from the Speech of Mr. John Randolph, of Roanoke.

Said he:—"It had been properly observed by the Chairman, as well as by the gentleman from this District (meaning Messrs. Clay and Caldwell) that there was nothing in the proposition submitted to consideration which in the smallest degree touches * The Blood of our fathers who have been murdered by the whites, and the groans of our Brethren, who

---

* "Niger," is a word derived from the Latin, which was used by the old Romans, to designate inanimate beings, which were black: such as soot pot wood, house, &c. Also, animals which they considered inferior to the human species, as a black horse, cow, hog, bird, dog, &c. The white Americans have applied this term to Africans, by way of reproach for our colour, to aggravate and heighten our miseries, because they have their feet on our throats, prejudice-what have we to do with it? Their prejudices will be obliged to fall like lightning to the ground, in succeeding generations; not, however, with the will and consent of all the whites, for some will be obliged to hold on to the old adage, viz: the blacks are not men, but were made to be an inheritance to us and our children for ever! ! ! ! ! ! I hope the residue of the coloured people, will stand still and see the salvation of God and the miracle which he will work for our delivery from wretchedness under the Christians ! ! ! ! ! !

are now held in cruel ignorance, wretchedness and slavery by them, cry aloud to the Maker of Heaven and of earth, against the whole continent of America, for redresses. Another very important and delicate question, which ought to be left as much out of view as possible, is Negro Slavery. "There is no fear," Mr. R. said, "that this proposition would alarm the slave-holders; they had been accustomed to think seriously of the subject.—There was a popular work on agriculture by John Taylor of Caroline, which was widely circulated, and much confided in, in Virginia. In that book, much read because coming from a practical man, this description of people, [referring to us half free ones] were pointed out as a great evil. They had indeed been held up as the greater bug-bear to every man who feels an inclination to emancipate his slaves, not to create in the bosom of his country so great a nuisance. If a place could be provided for their reception, and a mode of sending them hence, there were hundreds, nay thousands of citizens who would, by manumitting their slaves, relieve themselves from the cares attendant on their possession. The great slave-holder," Mr. R. said, "was frequently a mere sentry at his own door-bound to stay on his plantation to see that his slaves were properly treated, &c." Mr. R. concluded by saying, that he had thought it necessary to make these remarks being a slave-holder himself, to shew that, "so far from being connected with abolition of slavery, the measure proposed would prove one of the greatest securities to enable the master to keep in possession his own property."

Here is a demonstrative proof, of a plan got up, by a gang of slave-holders to select the free people of colour from among the slaves, that our more miserable brethren may be the better secured in ignorance and wretchedness, to work their farms and dig their mines, and thus go on enriching the Christians with their blood and groans. What our brethren could have been thinking about, who have left their native land and home and gone away to Africa, I am unable to say. This country is as much ours as it is the whites, whether they will admit it now or not, they will see and believe it by and by. . . .

→ ADDITION.—If any of us see fit to go away, go to those who have been for many years, and are now our greatest earthly friends and benefactors—the English. If not so, go to our brethren, the Haytians, who, according to their word, are bound to protect and comfort us. The Americans say, that we are ungrateful—but I ask them for heaven's sake, what should we be grateful to them for—for murdering our fathers and mothers?—Or do they wish us to return thanks to them for chaining and hand-cuffing us, branding us, cramming fire down our throats, or for keeping us in slavery, and beating us nearly or quite to death to make us work in ignorance and miseries, to support them and their families. They certainly think that we are a gang of fools. Those among them, who have volunteered their services for our redemption, though we are unable to compensate them for their labours, we nevertheless thank them from the bottom of our hearts, and have our eyes steadfastly fixed upon them, and their labours of love for God and man.—But do slave-holders think that we thank them for keeping us in miseries, and taking our lives by the inches?

Before I proceed further with this scheme, I shall give an extract from the letter of that truly Reverend Divine, (Bishop Allen,) of Philadelphia, respecting this trick. At the instance of the editor of the Freedom's Journal, he says, "Dear Sir, I have been for several years trying to reconcile my mind to the Colonizing of Africans in Liberia, but there have always been, and there still remain great and insurmountable objections against the scheme. We are an unlettered people, brought up in ignorance, not one in a hundred can read or write, not one in a thousand has a liberal education; is there any fitness for such to be sent into a far country, among heathens, to convert or civilize them when they themselves are neither civilized or Christianized? Se: the great bulk of the poor, ignorant

Africans in this country, exposed to every temptation before them: all for the want of their morals being refined by education and proper attendance paid unto them by their owners, or those who had the charge of them. It is said by the Southern slave-holders, that the more ignorant they can bring up the Africans, the better slaves they make, ('go and come.') Is there any fitness for such people to be colonized in a far country to be their own rulers? Can we not discern the project of sending the free people of colour away from their country? Is it not for the interest of the slave-holders to select the free people of colour out of the different states, and send them to Liberia? Will it not make their slaves uneasy to see free men of colour enjoying liberty? It is against the law in some of the Southern States, that a person of colour should receive an education, under a severe penalty. Colonizationists speak of America being first colonized; but is there any comparison between the two ? America was colonized by as *wise, judicious and educated* men as the world afforded. WILLIAM PENN did not want for *learning, wisdom, or intelligence*. If all the people in Europe and America were as ignorant and in the same situation as our brethren, what would become of the world? Where would be the principle or piety that would govern the people? We were stolen from our mother country, and brought *here*. We have *tilled* the ground and made fortunes for thousands, and still they are not weary of our services. *But they who stay to till the ground must be slaves*. Is there not land enough in America, or 'corn enough in Egypt?' Why should they send us into a far country to die? See the thousands of foreigners emigrating to America every year: and if there be ground sufficient for them to cultivate, and bread for them to eat, why would they wish to send the *first tillers* of the land away? Africans have made fortunes for thousands, who are yet unwilling to part with their services; but the free must be sent away, and those who remain, must be *slaves*. I have no doubt that there are many good men who do not see as I do, and who are for sending us to Liberia; but they have not duly considered the subject—they are not men of colour.— This land which we have watered with our *tears* and *our blood*, is now our *mother country*, and we are well satisfied to stay where wisdom abounds and the gospel is free."

"RICHARD ALLEN,

"Bishop of the African Methodist Episcopal

"Church in the United States."

I have given you, my brethren, an extract verbatim, from the letter of that godly man, as you may find it on the aforementioned page of Freedom's Journal. I know that thousands, and perhaps millions of my brethren in these States, have never heard of such a man as Bishop Allen—a man whom God many years ago raised up among his ignorant and degraded brethren, to preach Jesus Christ and him crucified to them—who notwithstanding, had to wrestle against principalities and the powers of darkness to diffuse that gospel with which he was endowed among his brethren—but who having overcome the combined powers of devils and wicked men, has under God planted a Church among us which will be as durable as the foundation of the earth on which it stands. Richard Allen! O my God! The bare recollection of the labours of this man, and his ministers among his deplorably wretched brethren, (rendered so by the whites) to bring them to a knowledge of the God of Heaven, fills my soul with all those very high emotions which would take the pen of an Addison to portray. It is impossible my brethren for me to say much in this work respecting that man of God. When the Lord shall raise up coloured historians in succeeding generations, to present the crimes of this nation, to the then gazing world, the Holy Ghost will make them do justice to the name of Bishop Allen, of Philadelphia. Suffice it for me to say, that, the name of this very man (Richard Allen) though now in obscurity and degradation, will notwithstanding, stand on the pages of history among the greatest divines who have lived since the apostolic age, and among the Africans, Bishop Allen's will be entirely preeminent. My brethren, search after the character and exploits of this godly man among his ignorant and miserable brethren to bring them to a knowledge of the truth as it is in our Master. Consider upon the tyrants and false Christians against whom he had to contend in order to get access to his brethren. See him and his ministers in the States of New York, New Jersey, Pennsylvania, Delaware and Maryland, carrying the gladsome tidings of free and full salvation to the coloured people. Tyrants and false Christians however, would not allow him to penetrate far into the South, for fear that he would awaken some of his ignorant brethren, whom they held in wretchedness and misery—for fear, I say it, that he would awaken and bring them to a knowledge of their Maker. O my Master! my Master! I can-not but think upon Christian Americans! ! !—What kind of people can they be? Will not those who were burnt up in Sodom and Gomorrah rise up in judgment against Christian Americans with the Bible in their hands, and condemn them? Will not the Scribes and Pharisees of Jerusalem, who had nothing but the laws of Moses and the Prophets to go by, rise up in judgment against Christian Americans, and condemn them,* who, in addition to these have a revelation from Jesus Christ the Son of the living God? In fine, will not the Antideluvians, together with the whole heathen world of antiquity, rise up in judgment against Christian Americans and condemn them? The Christians of Europe and America go to Africa, bring us away, and throw us into the seas, and in other ways murder us, as they would wild beast. The Antideluvians and heathens never dreamed of such barbarities.—Now the Christians believe, because they have a name to live, while they are dead, that God will overlook such things. But if he does not deceive them, it will be because he has over-looked it sure enough. But to return to this godly man, Bishop Allen. I do hereby openly affirm it to the world, that he has done more in a spiritual sense for his ignorant and wretched brethren than any other man of colour has, since the world began. And as for the greater part of the whites, it has hitherto been their greatest object and glory to keep us ignorant of our Maker, so as to make us believe that we were made to be slaves to them and their children, to dig up gold and silver for them.

It is notorious that not a few professing Christians among the whites, who profess to love our Lord and Saviour Jesus Christ, have assailed this man and laid all the obstacles in his way they possibly could, consistent with their profession—and what for? Why, their course of proceeding and his, clashed exactly together—they trying their best to keep us ignorant, that we might be the better and more obedient slaves—while he, on the other hand, doing his very best to enlighten us and teach us a knowledge of the Lord. And I am sorry that I have it to say, that many of our brethren have joined in with our oppressors, whose dearest objects are only to keep us ignorant and miserable against this man to stay his hand.— However, they have kept us in so much ignorance, that many of us know no better than to fight against ourselves, and by that means strengthen the hands of our natural enemies, to rivet their infernal chains of slavery upon us and our children. I have several times called the white Americans our *natural enemies*—I shall here define my meaning of the phrase. Shem, Ham and Japheth, together with their father Noah and wives, I believe were not natural enemies to each other. When the ark rested after the flood upon Mount Arrarat, in Asia, they (eight) were all the people which could be found alive in all the earth—in fact if Scriptures be true, (which I believe are) there were no other living men in all the earth,

---

* I mean those whose labours for the good, or rather destruction of Jerusalem and the Jews ceased before our Lord entered the Temple, and overturned the tables of the Money Changers.

notwithstanding some ignorant creatures hesitate not to tell us that we, (the blacks) are the seed of Cain the murderer of his brother Abel. But where or of whom those ignorant and avaricious wretches could have got their information, I am unable to declare. Did they receive it from the Bible? I have searched the Bible as well as they, if I am not as well learned as they are, and have never seen a verse which testifies whether we are the seed of Cain or of Abel. Yet those men tell us that we are the seed of Cain, and that God put a dark stain upon us, that we might be known as their slaves! ! ! Now, I ask those avaricious and ignorant wretches, who act more like the seed of Cain, by murdering the whites or the blacks? How many vessel loads of human beings have the blacks thrown into the seas? How many thousand souls have the blacks murdered in cold blood, to make them work in wretchedness and ignorance, to support them and their families ? * —However, let us be the seed of *Cain, Harry, Dick, or Tom*! !! God will show the whites what we are, yet. I say, from the beginning, I do not think that we were natural enemies to each other. But the whites having made us so wretched, by subjecting us to slavery, and having murdered so many millions of us, in order to make us work for them, and out of devilishness—and they taking our wives, whom we love as we do ourselves—our mothers who bore the pains of death to give us birth—our fathers and dear little children, and ourselves, and strip and beat us one before the other—chain, hand-cuff, and drag us about like rattle-snakes—shoot us down like wild bears, before each other's faces to make us submissive to, and work to support them and their families. They (the whites) know well, if we are *men*—and there is a secret monitor in their hearts which tells them we are—they know, I say, if we *are* men, and see them treating us in the manner they do, that there can be nothing in our hearts but death alone, for them, notwithstanding we may appear cheerful, when we see them murdering our dear mothers and wives because we cannot help ourselves. Man, in all ages and all nations of the earth, is the same. Man is a peculiar creature—he is the image of his God, though he may be subjected to the most wretched condition upon earth, yet the spirit and feeling which constitute the creature, man, can never be entirely erased from his breast, because the God who made him after his own image planted it in his heart; he cannot get rid of it.

The whites knowing this, they do not know what to do; they know that they have done us so much injury, they are afraid that we, being men and not brutes, will retaliate, and woe will be to them; therefore, that dreadful fear, together with an avaricious spirit, and the natural love in them, to be called masters, (which term will yet honour them with to their sorrow) bring them to the resolve that they will keep us in ignorance and wretchedness, as long as they possibly can,** and make the best of their time, while it lasts.

---

*How many millions souls of the human family have the blacks beat nearly to death, to keep them from learning to read the Word of God and from writing. And telling lies about them, by holding them up to the world as a tribe of TALKING APES, void of INTELLECT! ! ! ! ! incapable of LEARNING, &c.

** And still holds us up with indignity as being incapable of acquiring knowledge! ! ! See the inconsistency of the assertions of those wretches—they beat us inhumanely, sometimes almost to death, for attempting to inform ourselves, by reading the Word of our Maker, and at the same time tell us, that we are beings void of intellect! How admirably their practices agree with their professions in this case. Let me cry shame upon you Americans, for such out-rages upon human nature! ! ! If it were possible for the whites always to keep us ignorant and miserable, and make us work to enrich them and their children, and insult our feelings by representing us as talking Apes, what would they do? But glory, honour and praise to Heaven's King, that the sons and daughters of Africa, will, in spite of all the opposition of their enemies, stand forth in all the dignity and glory that is granted by the Lord to his creature man.

Consequently they, themselves, (and not us) render them-selves our natural enemies, by treating us so cruel. They keep us miserable now, and call us their property, but some of them will have enough of us by and by—their stomachs shall run over with us; they want us for their slaves, and shall have us to their fill. We are all in the world together! !—I said above, because we cannot help ourselves, (viz. we cannot help the whites murdering our mothers and our wives) but this statement is incorrect—for we can help ourselves; for, if we lay aside abject servility, and be determined to act like men, and not brutes—the murderers among the whites would be afraid to show their cruel heads. But O, my God! —in sorrow I must say it, that my colour, all over the world, have a mean, servile spirit. They yield in a moment to the whites, let them be right or wrong—the reason they are able to keep their feet on our throats. Oh ! my coloured brethren, all over the world, when shall we arise from this death-like apathy?—And be men! ! You will notice, if ever we become men, (I mean *respectable* men, such as other people are,) we must exert ourselves to the full. For remember, that it is the greatest desire and object of the greater part of the whites, to keep us ignorant, and make us work to support them and their families.—Here now, in the Southern and Western sections of this country, there are at least three coloured persons for one white, why is it, that those few weak, good-for-nothing whites, are able to keep so many able men, one of whom, can put to flight a dozen whites, in wretchedness and misery? It shows at once, what the blacks are, we are ignorant, abject, servile and mean—and the whites know it—they know that we are too servile to assert our rights as men—or they would not fool with us as they do. Would they fool with any other peoples as they do with us? No, they know too well, that they would get themselves ruined. Why do they not bring the inhabitants of Asia to be body servants to them? They know they would get their bodies rent and torn from head to foot. Why do they not get the Aborigines of this country to be slaves to them and their children, to work their farms and dig their mines? They know well that the Aborigines of this country, or (Indians) would tear them from the earth. The Indians would not rest day or night, they would be up all times of night, cutting their cruel throats. But my colour, (some, not all,) are willing to stand still and be murdered by the cruel whites. In some of the West-Indies Islands, and over a large part of South America, there are six or eight coloured persons for one white.*

Why do they not take possession of those places? Who hinders them? It is not the avaricious whites—for they are too busily engaged in laying up money—derived from the blood and tears of the blacks. The fact is, they are too servile, they love to have Masters too well! ! Some of our brethren, too, who seeking more after self aggrandizement, than the glory of God, and the welfare of their brethren, join in with our oppressors, to ridicule and say all manner of evils falsely against our Bishop. They think, that they are doing great things, when they can get in company with the whites, to ridicule and make sport of those who are labouring for their good. Poor ignorant creatures, they do not know that the

---

*For instance in the two States of Georgia, and South Carolina, there are, perhaps, not much short of six or seven hundred thousand persons of colour; and if I was a gambling character, I would not be afraid to stake down upon the board FIVE CENTS against TEN, that there are in the single State of Virginia, five or six hundred thousand Coloured persons. Four hundred and fifty thousand of whom (let them be well equipt for war) I would put against every white person on the whole continent of America. (Why? why because I know that the Blacks, once they get involved in a war, had rather die than to live, they either kill or be killed.) The whites know this too, which make them quake and tremble. To show the world further, how servile the coloured people are, I will only hold up to view, the one Island of Jamaica, as a specimen of our meanness. *(continues)*

sole aim and object of the whites, are only to make fools and slaves of them, and put the whip to them, and make them work to support them and their families. But I do say, that no man, can well be a despiser of Bishop Allen, for his public labours among us, unless he is a despiser of God and of Righteousness. Thus, we see, my brethren, the two very opposite positions of those great men, who have written respecting this "Colonizing Plan." (Mr. Clay and his slave-holding party,) men who are resolved to keep us in eternal wretchedness, are also bent upon sending us to Liberia. While the Reverend Bishop Allen, and his party, men who have the fear of God, and the wellfare of their brethren at heart. The Bishop, in particular, whose labours for the salvation of his brethren, are well known to a large part of those, who dwell in the United States, are completely opposed to the plan—and advise us to stay where we are. Now we have to determine whose advice we will take respecting this all important matter, whether we will adhere to Mr. Clay and his slave holding party, who have always been our oppressors and murderers, and who are for colonizing us, more through apprehension than humanity, or to this godly man who has done so much for our benefit, together with the advice of all the good and wise among us and the whites. Will any of us leave our homes and go to Africa? I hope not.**

Let them commence their attack upon us as they did on our brethren in Ohio, driving and beating us from our country, and my soul for theirs they will have enough of it. Let no man of us budge one step: and let slave-holders come to beat us from our country. America is more our country, than it is the whites—we have enriched it with our *blood and tears*. The greatest riches in all America have arisen from our blood and tears:—and will they drive us from our property and homes, which we have earned with our *blood*? They must look sharp or this very thing will bring swift destruction upon them. The Americans have got so fat on our blood and groans, that they have almost forgotten the God of armies. But let them go on.

→ADDITION.—I will give here a very imperfect list of the cruelties inflicted on us by the enlightened Christians of America. —First, no trifling portion of them will beat us nearly to death if they find us on our knees praying to God,—They hinder us from going to hear the word of God—they keep us sunk in ignorance, and will not let us learn to read the word of God, nor write—If they find us with a book of any description in our hand

---

* *(continued)* In that Island, there are three hundred and fifty thousand souls-of whom fifteen thousand are whites, the remainder, three hundred and thirty-five thousand are coloured people ! and this Island is ruled by the white people ! ! !! ! ! ! ! (15,000) ruling and tyranizing over 335,000 persons! ! ! ! ! ! ! !-O! coloured men!! O! coloured men!!! O! coloured men!!!! Look!! look!!! at this!!!! and, tell me if we are not abject and servile enough, how long, O! how long my colour shall we be dupes and dogs to the cruel whites?-I only passed Jamaica, and its inhabitants, in review as a specimen to show the world, the condition of the Blacks at this time, now coloured people of the whole world, I beg you to look at the (15000 white,) and (Three Hundred and Thirty-five Thousand coloured people) in that Island, and tell me how can the white tyrants of the world but say that we are not men, hut were made to be slaves and Dogs to them and their children forever!! !! ! !-why my friend only look at the thing ! ! ! ! (15000) whites keeping in wretchedness and degradation (335000) viz. 22 coloured persons for one white !! !!!!! when at the same time, an equal number (15000) Blacks, would almost take the whole of South America, because where they go as soldiers to fight death follows in their tram.

** Those who are ignorant enough to go to Africa, the coloured people ought to be glad to have them go, for if they are ignorant enough to let the whites fool them off to Africa, they would be no small injury to us if they reside in this country.

they will beat us nearly to death—they are so afraid we will learn to read, and enlighten our dark and benighted minds—They will not suffer us to meet together to worship the God who made us—they brand us with hot iron—they cram bolts of fire down our throats—they cut us as they do horses, bulls, or hogs—they crop our ears and sometimes cut off bits of our tongues—they chain and hand-cuff us, and while in that miserable and wretched condition, beat us with cow-hides and clubs—they keep us half naked and starve us sometimes nearly to death under their infernal whips or lashes (which some of them shall have enough of yet)—They put on us fifty-sixes and chains, and make us work in that cruel situation, and in sickness, under lashes to support them and their families.—They keep us three or four hundred feet under ground working in their mines, night and day to dig up gold and silver to enrich them and their children.—They keep us in the most death-like ignorance by keeping us from all source of information, and call us, who are free men and next to the Angels of God, their property! ! ! ! ! They make us fight and murder each other, many of us being ignorant, not knowing any better.—They take us, (being ignorant,) and put us as drivers one over the other, and make us afflict each other as bad as they themselves afflict us—and to crown the whole of this catalogue of cruelties, they tell us that we the (blacks) are an inferior race of beings! incapable of self government! !—We would be injurious to society and ourselves, if tyrants should loose their unjust hold on us ! ! ! That if we were free we would not work, but would live on plunder or theft! ! ! ! that we are the meanest and laziest set of beings in the world! ! ! ! ! That they are obliged to keep us in bondage to do us good ! ! ! ! ! !—That we are satisfied to rest in slavery to them and their children ! ! ! ! ! !—That we ought not to be set free in America, but ought to be sent away to Africa ! ! ! ! ! ! ! !—That if we were set free in America, we would involve the country in a civil war, which assertion is altogether at variance with our feeling or design, for we ask them for nothing but the rights of man, viz. for them to set us free, and treat us like men, and there will be no danger, for we will love and respect them, and protect our country—but cannot conscientiously do these things until they treat us like men.←

How cunning slave-holders think they are!!!—How much like the king of Egypt who, after he saw plainly that God was determined to bring out his people, in spite of him and his, as powerful as they were. He was willing that Moses, Aaron and the Elders of Israel, but not all the people should go and serve the Lord. But God deceived him as he will Christian Americans, unless they are very cautious how they move. What would have become of the United States of America, was it not for those among the whites, who not in words barely, but in truth and in deed, love and fear the Lord ?—Our Lord and Master said : "[But] Whose shall offend one of these little ones which believe in me, it were better for him that a millstone were hanged about his neck, and that he were drowned in the depth of the sea."

But the Americans with this very threatening of the Lord's, not only beat his little ones among the Africans, but many of them they put to death or murder. Now the avaricious Americans, think that the Lord Jesus Christ will let them off, because his words are no more than the words of a man! ! ! In fact, many of them are so avaricious and ignorant, that they do not believe in our Lord and Saviour Jesus Christ. Tyrants may think they are so skillful in State affairs is the reason that the government is preserved. But I tell you, that this country would have been given up long ago, was it not for the lovers of the Lord. They are indeed, the salt of the earth. Remove the people of God among the whites, from this land of blood, and it will stand until they cleverly get out of the way.

I adopt the language of the Rev. Mr. S. E. Cornish, of New York, editor of the Rights of All, and say: "Any coloured man of common intelligence, who gives his countenance and influence to that colony, further than its missionary object and interest extend, should be considered as a traitor to his brethren, and discarded by every respectable man of colour. And every member of that society, however pure his motive, whatever may be his religious character and moral worth, should in his efforts to remove the coloured population from their rightful soil, the land of their birth and nativity, be considered as acting gratuitously unrighteous and cruel."

Let me make an appeal brethren, to your hearts, for your cordial co-operation in the circulation of "The Rights of All", among us. The utility of such a vehicle conducted, cannot be estimated. I hope that the well informed among us, may see the absolute necessity of their co-operation in its universal spread among us. If we should let it go down, never let us undertake any thing of the kind again, but give up at once and say that we are really so ignorant and wretched that we cannot do any thing at all! !—As far as I have seen the writings of its editor, I believe he is not seeking to till his pockets with money, but has the welfare of his brethren truly at heart. Such men, brethren, ought to be supported by us.

But to return to the colonizing trick. It will be well for me to notice here at once, that I do not mean indiscriminately to condemn all the members and advocates of this scheme, for I believe that there are some friends to the sons of Africa, who are laboring for our salvation, not in words—only but in truth and in deed, who have been drawn into this plan—Some, more by persuasion than any thing else; while others, with humane feelings and lively zeal for our good, seeing how much we suffer from the afflictions poured upon us by unmerciful tyrants, are willing to enroll their names in any thing which they think has for its ultimate end our redemption from wretchedness and miseries; such men, with a heart truly overflowing with gratitude for their past services and zeal in our cause, I humbly beg to examine this plot minutely, and see if the end which they have in view will be completely consummated by such a course of procedure. Our friends who have been imperceptibly drawn into this plot I view with tenderness, and would not for the world injure their feelings, and I have only to hope for the future, that they will withdraw themselves from it;—for I declare to them, that the plot is not for the glory of God, but on the contrary the perpetuation of slavery in this country, which will ruin them and the country forever, unless something is immediately done.

Do the colonizationists think to send us off without first being reconciled to us? Do they think to bundle us up like brutes and send us off, as they did our brethren of the State of Ohio? * Have they not to be reconciled to us, or reconcile us to them, for the cruelties with which they have afflicted our fathers and us?

Methinks colonizationists think they have a set of brutes to deal with, sure enough. Do they think to drive us from our country and homes, after having enriched it with our blood and tears, and keep back millions of our dear brethren, sunk in the most barbarous wretchedness, to dig up gold and silver for them and their children? Surely, the Americans must think that we are brutes, as some of them have represented us to be. They think that we do not feel for our brethren, whom they are murdering by the inches, but they are dreadfully deceived. I acknowledge that there are some deceitful and hypocritical wretches

---

*The great slave holder, Mr. John Randolph, of Virginia, intimated in one of his great, happy and eloquent HARRANGUES, before the Virginia Convention, that Ohio is a slave State, by ranking it among other Slave-holding States. This probably was done by the HONORABLE Slave-holder to deter the minds of the ignorant; to such I would say, that Ohio always was and is now a free State, that it never was and I do not believe it ever will be a slave-holding State; the people I believe, though some of them are hard hearted enough, detest Slavery too much to admit an evil into their bosom, which gnaws into the very vitals, and sinews of those who are now in possession of it.

among us, who will tell us one thing while they mean another, and thus they go on aiding our enemies to oppress themselves and us. But I declare this day before my Lord and Master, that I believe there are some true-hearted sons of Africa, in this land of oppression, but pretended *liberty*! ! ! !—who do in reality feel for their suffering brethren, who are held in bondage by tyrants. Some of the advocates of this cunningly devised plot of Satan represent us to be the greatest set of cut-throats in the world, as though God wants us to take his work out of his hand before he is ready. Does not vengeance belong to the Lord ? Is he not able to repay the Americans for their cruelties, with which they have afflicted Africa's sons and daughters, without our interference, unless we are ordered ? It is surprising to think that the Americans, having the Bible in their hands, do not believe it. Are not the hearts of all men in the hands of the God of battles? And does he not suffer some, in consequence of cruelties, to go on until they are irrecoverably lost? Now, what can be more aggravating, than for the Americans, after having treated us so bad, to hold us up to the world as such great throat-cutters? It appears to me as though they are resolved to assail us with every species of affliction that their ingenuity can invent. !--→See the African Repository and Colonial Journal, from its commencement to the present day—see how we are through the medium of that periodical, abused and held up by the Americans, as the greatest nuisance to society, and throat-cutters in the world.) But the Lord sees their actions. Americans! notwithstanding you have and do continue to treat us more cruel than any heathen nation ever did a people it had subjected to the same condition that you have us. Now let us reason—I mean you of the United States, whom I believe God designs to save from destruction, if you will hear. For I declare to you, whether you believe it or not, that there are some on the continent of America, who will never be able to repent. God will surely destroy them, to show you his disapprobation of the murders they and you have inflicted on us. I say, let us reason; had you not better take our body, while you have it in your power, and while we are yet ignorant and wretched, not knowing but a little, give us education, and teach us the pure religion of our Lord and Master, which is calculated to make the lion lay down in peace with the lamb, and which millions of you have beaten us nearly to death for trying to obtain since we have been among you, and thus at once, gain our affection while we are ignorant? Remember Americans, that we must and shall be free and enlightened as you are, will you wait until we shall, under God, obtain our liberty by the crushing arm of power? Will it not be dreadful for you? I speak Americans for your good. We must and shall be free I say, in spite of you. You may do your best to keep us in wretchedness and misery, to enrich you and your children; but God will deliver us from under you. And wo, wo, will be to you if we have to obtain our freedom by fighting. Throw away your fears and prejudices then, and enlighten us and treat us like men, and we will like you more than we do now hate you,* and tell us now no more about colonization, for America is as much our country, as it is yours.—Treat us like men, and there is no danger but we will all live in peace and happiness together.

For we are not like you, hard hearted, unmerciful, and unforgiving. What a happy country this will be, if the whites will listen. What nation under heaven, will be able to do any thing with us, unless God gives us up into its hand? But Americans, I declare to you, while you keep us and our children in bondage, and treat us like brutes, to make us support you and your families, we can-not be your friends. You do not look for it, do you? Treat us then like men, and we will be your friends. And there is not a doubt in my mind, but that the whole of the past will be sunk into oblivion, and we yet, under God, will become a

---

*You are not astonished at my saying we hate you, for if we are men, we cannot but hate you, while you are treating us like dogs.

united and happy people. The whites may say it is impossible, but remember that nothing is impossible with God.

The Americans may say or do as they please, but they have to raise us from the condition of brutes to that of respectable men, and to make a national acknowledgement to us for the wrongs they have inflicted on us. As unexpected, strange, and wild as these propositions may to some appear, it is no less a fact, that unless they are complied with, the Americans of the United States, though they may for a little while escape, God will yet weigh them in a balance, and if they are not superior to other men, as they have represented themselves to be, he will give them wretchedness to their very heart's content.

And now brethren, having concluded these four Articles, I submit them, together with my Preamble, dedicated to the Lord, for your inspection, in language so very simple, that the most ignorant, who can read at all, may easily understand—of which you may make the best you possibly can.* Should tyrants take it into their heads to emancipate any of you, remember that your freedom is your natural right.

You are men, as well as they and instead of returning thanks to them for your freedom, return it to the Holy Ghost, who is our rightful owner. If they do not want to part with your labours, which have enriched them, let them keep you, and my word for it, that God Almighty, will break their strong band. Do you believe this, my brethren ?—See my Address, delivered before the General Coloured Association of Massachusetts, which may be found in Freedom's Journal, for Dec. 20, 1828.~See the last clause of that Address. Whether you believe it or not, I tell you that God will dash tyrants, in combination with devils, into atoms, and will bring you out from your wretchedness and miseries under these *Christian People! ! ! ! !*

Those philanthropists and lovers of the human family, who have volunteered their services for our redemption from wretchedness, have a high claim on our gratitude, and we should always view them as our greatest earthly benefactors.

If any are anxious to ascertain who I am, know the world that I am one of the oppressed, degraded and wretched sons of Africa rendered so by the avaricious and unmerciful, among the whites. —If any wish to plunge me into the wretched incapacity of a slave, or murder me for the truth, know ye, that I am in the hand of God, and at your disposal. I count my life not dear unto me, but I am ready to be offered at any moment. For what is the use of living, when in fact I am dead. But remember, Americans, that as miserable, wretched, degraded and abject as you have made us in preceding, and in this generation, to support you and your families, that some of you, (whites) on the continent of America, will yet curse the day that you ever were born. You want slaves, and want us for your slaves ! ! ! My colour will yet, root some of you out of the very face of the earth! ! ! ! ! ! You may doubt it

---

*Some of my brethren, who are sensible, do not take an interest in enlightening the minds of our more ignorant brethren respecting this BOOK and in reading it to them, just as though they will not have either to stand or fall by what is written in this book. Do they believe that I would be so foolish as to put out a book of this kind without strict-ah! very strict commandments of the Lord?-Surely the blacks and whites must think that I am ignorant enough.-Do they think that I would have the audacious wickedness to take the name of my God in vain?

Notice, I said in the concluding clause of Article 3-I call God, I call Angels I call men to witness, that the destruction of the Americans is at hand and will be speedily consummated unless they repent. Now I wonder if the world think that I would take the name of God in this way in vain? What do they think I take God to be? Do they suppose that I would trifle with that God who will not have his Holy name taken in vain?-He will show you and the world, in due time, whether this book is for his glory, or written by me through envy to the whites, as some have represented.

if you please. I know that thousands will doubt—they think they have us so well secured in wretchedness, to them and their children, that it is impossible for such things to occur.*

So did the antideluvians doubt Noah, until the day in which the flood came and swept them away. So did the Sodomites doubt until Lot had got out of the city, and God rained down fire and brimstone from Heaven upon them, and burnt them up. So did the king of Egypt doubt the very existence of a God; he said, "who is the Lord, that I should let Israel go?" Did he not find to his sorrow, who the Lord was, when he and all his mighty men of war, were smothered to death in the Red Sea? So did the Romans doubt, many of them were really so ignorant, that they thought the whole of mankind were made to be slaves to them; just as many of the Americans think now, of my colour. But they got dreadfully deceived. When men got their eyes opened, they made the murderers scamper. The way in which they cut their tyrannical throats, was not much inferior to the way the Romans

---

* Why do the Slave-holders or Tyrants of America and their advocates fight so hard to keep my brethren from receiving and reading my Book of Appeal to them?-Is it because they treat us so well?-Is it because we are satisfied to rest in Slavery to them and their children?-Is it because they are treating us like men, by compensating us all over this free country!! for our labours? -But why are the Americans so very fearfully terrified respecting my Book? -Why do they search vessels, &c. when entering the harbours of tyrannical States, to see if any of my Books can be found, for fear that my brethren will get them to read. Why, I thought the Americans proclaimed to the world that they are a happy, enlightened, humane and Christian people, all the in-habitants of the country enjoy equal Rights! ! America is the Asylum for the oppressed of all nations! ! !

Now I ask the Americans to see the fearful terror they labor under for fear that my brethren will get my Book and read it-and tell me if their declaration is true-viz, if the United States of America is a Republican Government?-Is this not the most tyrannical, unmerciful, and cruel government under Heaven-not excepting the Algerines, Turks and Arabs?-I believe if any candid person would take the trouble to go through the Southern and Western sections of this country, and could have the heart to see the cruelties inflicted by these Christians on us, he would say, that the Algerines, Turks and Arabs treat their dogs a thousand times better than we are treated by the Christians.-But perhaps the Americans do their very best to keep my Brethren from receiving and reading my "Appeal" for fear they will find in it an extract which I made from their Declaration of Independence, which says, "we hold these truths to be self-evident, that all men are created equal," &c. &c. &c.-If the above are not the causes of the alarm among the Americans, respecting my Book, I do not know what to impute it to, unless they are possessed of the same spirit with which Demetrius the Silversmith was possessed-however, that they may judge whether they are of the same avaricious and ungodly spirit with that man, I will give here an extract from the Acts of the Apostles, chapter xix,-verses 23, 24, 25, 26, 27.

"And the same time there arose no small stir about that way. For a certain man named Demetrius, a silversmith, which made silver shrines for Diana, brought no small gain unto the craftsmen; whom he called together with the workmen of like occupation, and said, Sirs, ye know that by this craft we have our wealth: moreover, ye see and hear, that not alone at Ephesus, but almost throughout all Asia, this Paul hath persuaded and turned away much people, saying, that they be no gods which are made with hands: so that not only this our craft is in danger to be set at nought; but also that the temple of the great goddess Diana should be despised, and her magnificence should be destroyed, whom all Asia and the world worshippeth."

I pray you Americans of North and South America, together with the whole European inhabitants of the world, (I mean Slave-holders and their advocates) to read and ponder over the above verses in your minds, and judge whether or not you are of the infernal spirit with that Heathen Demetrius, the Silversmith: In fine I beg you to read the whole chapter through carefully.

or murderers, served them, when they held them in wretchedness and degradation under their feet. So would Christian Americans doubt, if God should send an Angel from Heaven to preach their funeral sermon. The fact is, the Christians having a name to live, while they are dead, think that God will screen them on that ground.

See the hundreds and thousands of us that are thrown into the seas by Christians, and murdered by them in other ways. They cram us into their vessel holds in chains and in hand-cuffs-men, women and children, all together ! ! O ! save us, we pray thee, thou God of Heaven and of earth, from the devouring hands of the white Christians! ! !

Oh ! thou Alpha and Omega !
The beginning and the end,
Enthron'd thou art, in Heaven above,
Surrounded by Angels there.

From Whence thou seest the miseries
To which we are subject;
The whites have murder'd us, O God
And kept us ignorant of thee.

Not satisfied with this, my Lord!
They throw us in the seas:
Be pleas'd, we pray, for Jesus' sake,
To save us from their grasp.

We believe that, for thy glory's sake,
Thou wilt deliver us;
But that thou may'st effect these things,
Thy glory must be sought.

In conclusion, I ask the candid and unprejudiced of the whole world, to search the pages of historians diligently, and see if the Antideluvians—the Sodomites—the Egyptians—the Babylonians—the Ninevites—the Carthagenians—the Persians—the Macedonians—the Greeks—the Romans—the Mahometans—the Jews—or devils, ever treated a set of human beings, as the white Christians of America do us, the blacks, or Africans. I also ask the attention of the world of mankind to the declaration of these very American people, of the United States.

A declaration made July 4, 1776.

It says,* "When in the course of human events, it becomes necessary for one people to dissolve the political bands which have connected them with another, and to assume among the Powers of the earth, the separate and equal station to which the laws of nature and of nature's God entitle them. A decent respect for the opinions of mankind requires, that they should declare the causes which impel them to the separation.—We hold these truths to be self evident—that all men are created equal, that they are endowed by their Creator with certain unalienable rights: that among these, are life, liberty, and the pursuit of happiness that, to secure these rights, governments are instituted among men, deriving their just powers from the consent of the governed; that when ever any form of govern-

---

* See the Declaration of Independence of the United States.

ment becomes destructive of these ends, it is the right of the people to alter or to abolish it, and to institute a new government laying its foundation on such principles, and organizing its powers in such form, as to them shall seem most likely to effect their safety and happiness. Prudence, indeed, will dictate, that governments long established should not be changed for light and transient causes; and accordingly all experience hath shewn, that mankind are more disposed to suffer, while evils are sufferable, than to right themselves by abolishing the forms to which they are accustomed. But when a long train of abuses and usurpations, pursuing invariably the same object, evinces a design to reduce them under absolute despotism, it is their right it is their duty to throw off such government, and to provide new guards for their future security." See your Declaration Americans! ! !

Do you understand your own language? Hear your language, proclaimed to the world, July 4th, 1776 → "We hold these truths to be self evident—that ALL MEN ARE CREATED EQUAL! ! that they *are endowed by their Creator with certain unalienable rights*; that among these are life, *liberty*, and the pursuit of happiness! ! " Compare your own language above, extracted from your Declaration of Independence, with your cruelties and murders inflicted by your cruel and unmerciful fathers and yourselves on our fathers and on us—men who have never given your fathers or you the least provocation! ! ! ! !

Hear your language further! → "But when a long train of abuses and usurpation, pursuing invariably the same object, evinces a design to reduce them under absolute despotism, it is their *right*, it is their *duty*, to throw off such government, and to provide new guards for their future security."

Now, Americans! I ask you candidly, was your sufferings under Great Britain, one hundredth part as cruel and tyranical as you have rendered ours under you? Some of you, no doubt, believe that we will never throw off your murderous government and "provide new guards for our future security." If Satan has made you believe it, will he not deceive you? * Do the whites say, I being a black man, ought to be humble, which I readily admit?

I ask them, ought they not to be as humble as I? or do they think that they can measure arms with Jehovah? Will not the Lord yet humble them? or will not these very coloured people whom they now treat worse than brutes, yet under God, humble them low down enough? Some of the whites are ignorant enough to tell us, that we ought to be submissive to them, that they may keep their feet on our throats. And if we do not submit to be beaten to death by them, we are bad creatures and of course must be damned, &c. If any man wishes to hear this doctrine openly preached to us by the American preachers, let him go into the Southern and Western sections of this country—I do not speak from hear say—what I have written, is what I have seen and heard myself. No man may think that my book is made up of conjecture—I have travelled and observed nearly the whole of those things myself, and what little I did not get by my own observation, I received from those among the whites and blacks, in whom the greatest confidence may be placed.

The Americans may be as vigilant as they please, but they cannot be vigilant enough for the Lord, neither can they hide themselves, where he will not find and bring them out.

---

*The Lord has not taught the Americans that we will not some day or other throw off their chains and hand-cuffs, from our hands and feet, and their devilish lashes (which some of them shall have enough of yet) from off our backs.

9

William Hamilton

In 1830, in indirect response to a brutal race riot in Cincinnati in 1829, free black leaders throughout the North met in Philadelphia at the first of many national conventions. The movement they began continued throughout the antebellum period, into the Civil War and the early period of Reconstruction, and resumed again in the late nineteenth century. Largely denied access to the mechanisms of formal politics, free black Northerners instead organized themselves into these quasi-political bodies, where they debated the problems they confronted, considered options for their remedy, and addressed a broader public with their concerns. The proceedings, reports, and addresses of these conventions were printed in pamphlet form, where they could circulate throughout black communities and easily be reprinted in the black and abolitionist press. William Hamilton (1773–1836), a prominent black New Yorker, presided over the 1834 convention. Instrumental in forming independent African-American educational and benevolent institutions in New York City (including the African Society for Mutual Relief, the Phoenix Society, and the Philomathean Society), Hamilton also worked on behalf of William Lloyd Garrison's *Liberator*. He was a celebrated speaker and wrote several pamphlets between the early 1800s and the 1830s. His introductory address to the 1834 convention wonderfully embodied important tensions developing in antebellum black protest thought. On the one hand, Hamilton espoused an Enlightenment vision of the color-blind society, united in a single community of interests and free of "caste" prejudices. On the other, he called for exclusive and united action among blacks to act for their own liberation. The apparent contradiction he explained as a temporary expedient, necessary only so long as the "strong combination" of hostile interests—namely, the American Colonization Society—continued to oppose blacks' liberties.

"Address to the National Convention of 1834"

(1834)

"That society must be the most happy, where the good of one is the common good of the whole."

GENTLEMEN,

It is with the most pleasing sensations, that I, in behalf of my coloured fellow citizens of New-York, tender you of the Delegation to this Convention, a hearty welcome to our city. And, gentlemen, with regard to myself, my full vibrates the felicitation.

You have convened to take into consideration what may be the best means for the promotion of the best interest of the people of colour of these United States, particularly of the free people thereof. And that such Convention is highly necessary, I think a few considerations will amply show.

First, the present form of society divides the interest of the community into several parts. Of these, there is that of the white man, that of the slave, and that of the free coloured man. How lamentable, how very lamentable, it is that there should be, any where on earth, a community of castes, with separate interests! That society must be the most happy, where the good of one is the common good of the whole. Civilization is not perfect, nor has reason full sway, until the community shall see that a wrong done to one is a wrong done to the whole; that the interest of one is or ought to be the common interest of the whole. Surely that must be a happy state of society where the sympathies of all are to all alike.

How pleasing, what a compliment to the nation, is the expression of Mons. Vallier, a celebrated traveller in Africa, where, speaking of the Hottentots, he says "There none need to offer themselves as objects of the compassion, for all are compassionate." Whatever our early-tutored prejudice may say to the contrary, such a people must be happy. Give me a residence in such a society, and I shall fancy myself in a community the most refined.

But alas for the people of colour in this community! their interest is not identified with that of other man. From them, white men stand aloof. For them the eye of pity hath scarcely a tear.

To them the hand of kindness is palsied, to them the dregs of mercy scarcely are given. To them the finger of scorn is pointed; contumely and reproach is continually theirs. They are a taunt, a hissing, and a by-word. They must cringe, and crouch, and crawl, and succumb to their peers. Long, long, long has the demon of prejudice and persecution beset their path. And must they make no effort to throw off the evils by which they are beset? Ought they not to meet to spread out their wrongs before one another? Ought they not to meet to consult on the best means of relief? Ought they not to make one weak effort; nay, one strong, one mighty moral effort, to roll off the burden that crushes them?

Under present circumstances it is highly necessary the free people of colour should combine, and closely attend to their own particular interest. All kinds of jealousy should be swept away from among them, and their whole eye fixed, on their own peculiar welfare. And can they do better than to meet thus; to take into consideration what are the best means to promote their elevation, and after having decided, to pursue those means with unabating zeal until their end is obtained.

Another reason why this Convention is necessary, is, that there is formed a strong combination against the people of colour, by some who are the master spirits of the day, by men whose influence is of the strongest character, to whom this nation bow in humble submission, and submit to their superior judgement, who turn public sentiment whichever way they please.

You cannot but perceive that I allude to the Colonization Society. However pure the motives of some of the members of that society may be, yet the master spirits thereof are evil minded towards us. They have put on the garb of angels of light. Fold back their covering, and you have in full array those of darkness.

I need not spread before you the proofs of their evil purposes. Of that you have had a quantity sufficient; and were there no other good reason for this Convention, the bare circumstance of the existence of such an institution would be a sufficient one. I do hope, confidently hope, that the time will arrive, and is near at hand, when we shall be in full possession of all the rights of men.

But as long at least as the Colonization Society exists, will a Convention of coloured people be highly necessary. This society is the great Dragon of the land, before whom the people bow and cry, Great Jehovah, and to whom they would sacrifice the free people of colour. That society has spread itself over this whole land; it is artful, it suits itself to all places. It is one thing at the south, and another at the north; it blows hot and cold; it sends forth bitter and sweet; it sometimes represents us as the most corrupt, vicious, and abandoned of any class of men in the community. Then again we are kind, meek, and gentle. Here we are ignorant, idle, a nuisance, and a drawback on the resources of the country. But as abandoned as we are, in Africa we shall civilize and christianize all that heathen country. And by thus preaching continually, they have distilled into the minds of the community a desire to see us removed.

They have resorted to every artifice to effect their purposes, by exciting in the minds of the white community, the fears of insurrection and amalgamation; by petitioning State legislatures to grant us no favors; by petitioning Congress to aid in sending us away; by using their influence to prevent the establishment of seminaries for our instruction in the higher branches of education.

And such are the men of that society that the community are blind to their absurdities, contradictions and paradoxes. They are well acquainted with the ground and the wiles by which to beguile the people.

It is therefore highly necessary we should meet, in order that we may confer on the best means to frustrate the purpose of so awful a foe.

I would beg leave to recommend an attentive consideration to this matter. Already you have done much toward the enervation of this giant: he begins to grow feeble; indeed he seems to be making his last struggle, if we may judge from his recent movements. Hang around him; assail him quickly. He is vulnerable. Well pointed darts will fetch him down, and soon he breathes no more.

Cheer up my friends! Already has your protest against the Colonization Society shown to the world that the people of colour are not willing to be expatriated. Cheer up. Already a right feeling begins to prevail. The friends of justice, of humanity, and the rights of man are drawing rapidly together, and are forming a moral phalanx in your defence.

That hitherto strong-footed, but sore-eyed vixen, prejudice, is limping off, seeking the shade. The Anti-Slavery Society and the friends of immediate abolition, are taking a noble, bold and manly stand, in the cause of universal liberty. It is true that they are assailed the faster they recruit. From present appearances the prospect is cheering, in a high degree. Anti-Slavery Societies are forming in every direction. Next August proclaims the British dominions free from slaves.

These United States are her children, they will soon follow so good an example. Slavery, that Satanic monster, that beast whose mark has been so long stamped on the forehead of the nations, shall be chained and cast down into blackness and darkness forever.

Soon, my brethren, shall the judgement be set. Then shall rise in glory and triumph, reason, virtue, kindness and liberty, and take a high exalted stand among the sons of men. Then shall tyranny, cruelty, prejudice, and slavery be cast down to the lowest depths of oblivion; yea, be banished from the presence of God, and the glory of his power for ever. Oh blessed consummation, and devoutly to be desired!

It is for you, my brethren, to help on in this work of moral improvement. Man is capable of high advances in his reasoning and moral faculties. Man is the pursuit of happiness. And reason, or experience, which is the parent of reason, tells us that the highest state of morality is the highest state of happiness. Aside from a future day of judgement and retribution, there is always a day of retribution at hand. That society is most miserable that is most immoral—that most happy that is most virtuous. Let me therefore recommend earnestly that you press upon our people the necessity and advantage of a moral reformation. It may not produce an excess of riches, but it will produce a higher state of happiness, and render our circumstances easier.

You, gentlemen, can begin here. By managing this conference in a spirit of good will and true politeness; by constantly keeping in view and cultivating a spirit of peace, order and harmony, rather than satire, wit, and eloquence; by putting the best possible construction on each other's language, rather than charging each other with improper motives. These dispositions will bespeak our character more or less virtuous and refined, and render our setting more or less pleasant. I will only now add, that the report of the Conventional Board will be submitted at your call; and my earnest hope is that you may have a peaceful, pleasant sitting.

Source: Minutes of the Fourth Annual Convention for the Improvement of the Free People of Colour, in the United States Held by Adjournments in the Asbury Church, New-york, from the 2d to the 12th of June Inclusive, 1834 (New York: Published by Order of the Convention, 1834).

10

Elizabeth Wicks

Among the rarest published documents of African Americans are the proceedings and reports of the many women's groups that proliferated in free black communities before the Civil War. Few were ever printed, and few of those survive. In big cities, black women might have belonged to several such groups, a reading society, a literary society, a mutual benefit and insurance society. In Troy, New York, with a population of about four hundred blacks and nearly twelve thousand whites, the African Female Benevolent Society (AFBS) combined several of these functions. It was a mutual aid society, providing some financial help for sick and stricken members. It was also a literary society, where members' writings were shared with the group. And, judging from Ms. Wicks's stirring affirmation of black education, it was quite likely a reading society, promoting study among its members.

Many such groups were church-based, but the AFBS appears to be an independent organization. Sectarian, political, or personal conflicts were not uncommon in African-American communities, and Mrs. Dungy's comments on another Troy black women's group, the Female Union Society, suggest one or more of these conflicts was the reason at least two such groups existed in this smallish African-American community. The AFBS is also of interest because it was one of the very few racially integrated societies. Eliza Dungy's remarks eulogize a recently deceased member, Jane Lansing, who was a white woman, although Dungy's remarks suggest Lansing was likely the only white member.

The pamphlet presented here is a combination annual report and eulogy, probably printed primarily for distribution among members and contributors. Thus, the text was not directed to a larger public, but rather spoke to the feelings and concerns of a couple of dozen reformers.

"Address Delivered Before the African Female Benevolent Society of Troy"

(1834)

"I trust to that feeling which is ever planted in the female heart, to make allowances for the feeble attempts I am about to make."

ADDRESS

My Dear Sisters,

I rise with unfeigned pleasure to address you, in compliance with your request, although my abilities are small compared with many others: yet I trust to that feeling which is ever planted in the female heart, to make allowances for the feeble efforts I am about to make. My friends, amidst the many changes and scenes which have hurried us to and fro in this unfeeling world, not a few difficulties have obstructed our way; but our heavenly Father has removed them all, and been-pleased to spare our lives, and bring us together to hail the birth day of our anniversary. This day closes our year, and the same we would celebrate by the help of Divine assistance as we know we can do nothing of ourselves. And though there is no time which we ought not to feel all happiness for our friends, yet let this be a day in which each heart goes forth with peculiar wishes for the welfare of all societies, wherever they may be formed by the descendants of the sons and daughters of -Ethiopia; and looking around me I feel a deep sensation of happiness arise in my heart, almost beyond expression, to see the well known faces of our friends from the different societies, manifest the name they bear by coming hither also, and uniting with us on this occasion. We are brought to see and hear that the joyful tidings are spreading far and wide; the colored population are exerting themselves in every direction for the improvement and cultivation of their minds whenever they are allowed the privilege of so doing; and, my friends, I think I see an opening in behalf of our oppressed race. The dark and stormy cloud that has forever been hanging over us appears in some measure to be gradually breaking away, and unfolds to our view a scene of pleasing and encouraging prospects; and with the Divine works with which we are blessed and surrounded, we can cast our eyes no where without discerning the hand of him who formed them. Let me invite you my friends, to catch with me some reflection, some serious moment for looking with thoughtful eye on all around us. Let us lift our view to that immense arch of heaven which encompasses US above, and behold the sun in all its splendor rolling over our heads by day, and the moon by night, in her mild and serene majesty, surrounded by that host of stars which presents to our imaginations innumerable worlds: survey the wonders that fill the earth which we inhabit; contemplate a steady and powerful hand that has brought around spring and summer, autumn and winter, in regular course, and at this time showered his manifold blessings upon us. We are therefore assured that we are not overlooked by that Supreme Being who is no respecter of persons or colour.

I would address myself to that class of friends who yet remain divided from us, and who have not felt interested enough to take an active part in the measures which lay before them. I would say to them, wherever they are, if they are not all within the sound of my voice, my friends take no offence, for it is not my wish to offend you: No, I hope I shall not be guilty of inflicting the slightest wound on any; but permit me to say I hope you will awake to a sense of your welfare, and see the duty that IS incumbent upon you. Take resolution and persevere I would not be partial and say, join here or there; nor yet yonder; but let your minds lead somewhere: It matters not where, if it is only employed in a noble act.

Let me invite you to put your shoulder to the wheel and press forward without delay; and if we are not bound by the same title, let our heart and minds be engaged in the same work; and let us all strive, with one accord, to raise ourselves from that humble state which we have ever, from our earliest existence, been groveling under, and keep our eyes fixed steadfast on that being who has promised a blessing to all who truly call on him; for, by so doing, my friends, we shall find a friend who will never forsake us, even if all others look upon us with contempt.

While we are enjoying all these privileges, and are endowed with all the blessings that a bountiful Providence can shower upon us, let our minds travel south and sympathize with the present state of the two millions of our brethren who are yet in bondage, and denied the smallest privilege we enjoy. We would ask, is their state growing better? Alas, what circumstance can arise; what event take place that shall change their condition. They have nothing to invite a conqueror, for they lie beyond his reach; and the most of them even beyond the journeys of fame. Shall the native force of their genius break their fetters? Or will any ever arise and lead them to fame, freedom, and happiness? Or shall they rise to that state by the slow and gradual progress of art and science? Alas, the flight for centuries past has extinguished all hopes of any change for the better, Their mental degradation has given their destiny a gloom as deep as that which the scorching heavens has spread over our complexion. And from whom, then, shall they look for relief? If they knew the God whom we are taught to worship, they might call on him; but Lord, they know thee not. They are not allowed to worship the true God, as we are taught to do; and, abandoned to themselves they seem doomed forever to trace the dreary road which leads toward the extinction of intelligence, virtue and happiness. It is often alleged, in defense of the slave trade, that our fore parents, Who were stolen from their own country, brought here and Sold among Christian people, had thereby a chance given them to learn and embrace religion. Hapless lot. The father of spirits could, indeed, break through all their prejudices and force conviction upon them.

Their enslavers, however, will be allowed but little merit, if any, in the day of judgment, upon the grounds of affecting their conversion by forcing them from their native country into cruel slavery. Much indeed can be said in praise of the noble and benevolent exertions of many individuals to promote humanity, order and civility, among our unhappy nation. They have spared no pains or expense. In this Godlike work their will has been blessed. They were found doing a duty, and they will not loose their reward Whether our brethren are now at the point of depression, or are to sink still deeper, is only known to the Ruler of providence, yet it is impossible for us to reflect upon their condition but with sensations of grief and sorrow. Unhappy sons and daughters of affliction, when shall light and order pervade the cheerless regions whence you dwell?

What power shall heave the adamantine bars which secure the gates of your dungeon, and bring you forth? When shall the cherub hope smile on you from heaven, and with a compassionate voice call you to the pleasures of reason, to the delights of immortality? In the natural course of events your destiny seems hopeless. No force of words can suitably describe or deplore your case; and your only hope of relief is in Omnipotence itself. Your deliverer must be a being of Almighty power, wisdom and goodness. To that being, then, we will commend you and ourselves-to his favor, to his grace, and to his everlasting mercy.

Furthermore, my friends, we who live in a Christian land can have no such excuse to offer, when we must stand before the searcher of all hearts, as our brethren who have never heard of God and eternity; therefore let us no longer plot on through life, thinking only of the present and scarce ever send forward a thought into futurity until we come upon the brink of the precipice; for it will then be too late to make preparations. Let us not complain that we have no time, and that we are pressed with business; for time, says the poet, is the stuff that life is made of, and to waste time is to squander the main ingredients of life, one of Heaven's richest blessings. Oh, righteous heaven, remember it not against us in the great day of trial, lest it swell the catalogue of our crimes beyond forgiveness.

We who are in possession of liberty, and this day hold in our hands the banner of union, benevolence and freewill. The time may come when the face of the moral and of course the natural world shall be changed; when the wilderness and solitary places shall blossom like the rose; when all the families and nations of the earth shall be of one mind, and shall allay their thirst at the same pure fountain of heavenly wisdom. Then shall the Indian no more adore the sun, nor think to wash away his moral pollution in the streams; but all nations shall adore one God. Then, my friends, let us begin to know and to prize our true interests and be convinced that nothing is more certain than that envy, malice and prejudice add infinitely to the number and weight of our sins. and bring upon us-the curse and wrath of -heaven. Then why not let love, friendship and cordial affection become universal. Let peace wave her banner among us; let our institutions be founded on friendship, and permanent as the eternal laws of justice, let there be a ground of hope as firm as a rock on which truth and reason may build a fabric that shall never fall; and let us all go on our way in friendship the coming year. And may the sun, each day of the year, when It rises, find us at peace with our friends, and at its sitting happy with ourselves. May we from day to day increase in knowledge and improve some good exercise, that when we have finished our course on earth and our flesh shall fail and our hearts shall break, God may be our portion and strength forever; and may all fall asleep with the image of the blessed redeemer.

The rising generation is rapidly advancing towards the stage of action and must soon fill the places we now occupy; and their advantages are greater and their prospects fairer than ours were at their age in consequence of our population being more enlightened at this time.

I would say to you children let not your days and years of childhood and youth be wasted away without improvement and utterly lost to every valuable and noble purpose; for, remember my little friends that time once past never returns. The moments which are lost are lost forever, and we seldom any of us begin to think until we are incapable of action, and the whole season of youth, in the greatest number of instances, is so passed away as to drag after it an age barren of knowledge and virtue; a bleak and comfortless season of care, decrepitude and sorrow; for such is the perverseness of many, that they will not be Instructed by the experience of others.

Although you are young and in the full enjoyment of health, and the fair promise of many years to come yet remember what many are to day you may be tomorrow. For the world is full of snares and temptations. They lie in every path and assume every form. The road to destruction is often strewed with roses, and pointed flints are seen to pave the way to honor. Vice will assume the semblance of virtue, and falsehood by a thousand seducing arts deceive the incautious heart to receive it as truth: but at the same time, my little friends, I would not flatter you with the hope that life-can be passed without actions or that the most consummate virtue will not meet with difficulties and trials; nay without them there would be no virtue. It is the contest with our infirmities and sorrows which gives its nature and its name; and it is the victory over them which ensures its reward on earth and in heaven, but in the hour of extreme difficulty and danger though I hope that the rude and boisterous storm of adversity and affliction may never blast the prospects of your promising youth, or that censure and reproach those cruel destroyers of youth should ever cross your path; but if such an hour should ever come to any of you when your best powers seem to give way, and your trembling virtue shrinks from the conflict. I would direct you then to that sure and saving power which is promised to those who ask it. And now, my dear children, as your friend and instructor, although feeling the necessity of being more qualified, and also the incapability of discharging to you the duties in a religious point of view, yet let me beg of you, as I love you, and value -your interests, to lay hold on the means of instruction which are set before you, and ever hold in remembrance that gratitude, which is due to that kind and benevolent friend who for the past year has stood in our defense, and when others found fault would always find an excuse; she has been a pillar to our cause and all the recompense she requires is that-we may profit thereby. And will you treasure up these few broken hints from one who loves you, and go on your way rejoicing and remember your Creator in the days of your youth.

AN EULOGY
ON THE DEATH OF MRS. JANE LANSING,
WITH AN
ADDRESS,
AS DELIVERED BY ELIZA A. T. DUNG.Y, BEFORE THE
AFRICAN FEMALE BENEVOLENT SOCIETY OF
TROY, AT THE FIRST ANNIVERSARY,
FEB. 19, 1834.

I did not mention, in reading the annual report, neither -as it forgotten, that I wish to make a few remarks upon the subject of our having received the decided approbation of two ladies in this city, by donations. One of the ladies we thought to have had the pleasure of seeing with us to day; but as she is not here may she receive, wherever she may be, the thanks of this society for the interest she has taken in their behalf and in the improvement of the people of color in general. The other lady, who Was a member of this institution, is not with us to day. No, we will presume to say she has Joined a never ending anniversary above. The lady to whom we here allude, is MRS. JANE LANSING, who departed this life Dec. 8,1833. In her the city has lost one of the brightest ornaments in the female hemisphere. From a large circle of relatives and friends a beloved tie is broken: and from that class of people who are necessiated to solicit assistance, a sympathizing friend: yes, one that allowed none to leave her door with a sad heart because their wants were not supplied. Last in name, but not in paying that just tribute of respect which her beloved memory deserves, comes the sable daughter of benevolence!

Sisters of Benevolence, is there one among you that amidst the pleasures which this world affords, would not be willing to pause a moment: but methinks if you do, the tears can scarcely be restrained; and be not ashamed if a few do escape. Surely you would not shed them in a more mournful cause than over the memory of a departed friend, yes, and one of our members; for our belonging to a despised race did not operate in her heart against US. No! no sooner did she hear that we were endeavoring to raise an institution for the benefit of each other and the extricating ourselves from that degradation to which we have been so long subject, than her benevolent hand was stretched out towards us. She sent to see the constitution by which we were to be governed; and the next meeting that was held, her name was received as a member and a sum remitted better deserving the name of a donation than that of an initiation fee; and as she always remembered US, even to the last, so had we ought to remember her. Know I should not wish YOU to think me partial, my friends, in addressing my own society, by any means; for I believe that MRS. LANSING: had the general good of the people of color at heart, and that the endeavors they have been making, as has been the case through the year that is past, to improve, has given her infinite satisfaction.   But if you will consider the relation she bore to us as one of our members, you will no doubt pardon me if in addressing myself to the Female Benevolent Society, I intrude upon your time a little while longer.

Having, my dear friends, endeavored in an imperfect manner, to give you a faint idea of the respect which this institution feels due to their highly valued member and true friend, I will make a few remarks on the objects of this society. The cultivation of the youthful mind is one of the greatest; but as the compositions which have been read in your hearing will give you a better idea of the improvement they have made through the past year, than a discussion upon the subject, I will forbear. Ask why they wrote them, and methinks they would tell, because the elder members of the society told us youth was the time to cultivate the mind: that while we had it in our power we ought to store our minds with such knowledge as is within our grasp; and a wish to excel each other in the excellency of their productions. I expect there has been a general anxiety to see who would hark the best piece for this occasion; but I will leave you to judge that have heard them read in your hearing. Relieving the sick and assisting the destitute, is another object in which each and every one who is united with this institution is engaged; but as the limited rules of our constitution admit of no drafts on the bank, under one year, we have been under the necessity of postponing the report of our finances; but should this society be permitted to appear before you again, I think they will be able to rehearse to you some instances that will give you heartfelt satisfaction. You will now allow me to pause, and take a view of this interesting assembly. What do I see; three societies, three institutions for the benefit of the people of colour. What an interesting sight. Who can view them but with emotions of pleasure. I will take the liberty of addressing each individually. For this purpose I will commence with the African Female Benevolent Society of Troy. There, see them, what a company, united to assist each other and help those who may be in need. Does not your heart overflow with gratitude to the Great Being who hath protected and enabled you to commence this excellent work? Do you not feel in a degree repaid this day for the anxiety and fiendlike trials with which you have been assailed through the past year? The superstitions of some and the prophecies of others have continually crossed your path; but with a brave heart you have persevered; neither turning to the right nor left; allowing no impediment to stop your progress, until you have reached a rest beyond the difficulties that beset us; and the sisters that have run with you; there see them: what a sight. And now allow me to address myself to the Female Union Society for a few moments. Have you too stemmed the current that has run so strongly against any efforts that might be made for the improvement of the people of color; and have you reached a rest? I congratulate you on your success; and your managers I would recommend to those who daily address an omnipotent being; that they would ask his grace to assist them in their arduous task: and may He grant his newer to enable the females of colour in this city to banish from among them those fiends, discord, contention and jealousy; and in their place rear the banner of love, unity and friendship; that we may all rally around it. And to those of the members that I have the pleasure of addressing I would say, may you be as firmly united as the initials of the title you bear.

The Male Free-Will Benevolent Society have an excellent title indeed. I think, if you will permit me to have a few thoughts upon the subject, none that unite with you can say they were forced so to do; if they read their title more than once. You too have had a rough road to travel; various and many were the windings and turnings but under the guidance Of your experienced officers, actuated as they were by a feeling for the welfare of their brethren of colour in this city, you have almost reached a rest as I take the liberty of terming the end of the year. Continue to preserve and you may be in action what you are in word; a free will band. Now to those who as yet have taken no active part with these institutions, I must say, can you remain any longer idle and listless after the scene that presents itself before you? Surely not. I should not express so much surprise at your unwillingness to unite with us were there but one Society; but here are three; and yet a spectator no longer than now, I hope, to you that have favored us with your company this afternoon: may you be gratified with all you have seen and heard and be doubly rewarded by our Heavenly Father for the trouble you have taken to come hither; and may you all be rewarded, encouraged and prospered.

Pardon me my friends if a mistake,
or rude expression from my lips escape.
Whilst I've been speaking it was not my design
To wound your feelings or prejudice your minds.

Before I close, to all I'd say,
Have you remark'd the joy thats here to day:
I'll tell the cause, if you will hear,:
We've clos'd the first and commenced the second year.

Should God protect and bring you here,
To hail the anniversary of another year,
The pleasing sight I fear I shall not view;
Oh no! my friends I now bid you a long adieu.

Sisters of Benevolence our motto I'll recall
United we stand but divided we fall.
E. A. T. DUNGY.

CONSTITUTION
OF THE
AFRICAN
FEMALE BENEVOLENT SOCIETY
OF TROY
FORMED FEBRUARY 12, 1883

Conscious that among the various pursuits that have engaged the attention of mankind in the different eras of the world, none have been considered, by persons of judgment and penetration, as superior to the cultivation of the intellectual powers bestowed upon us by the God of nature, it therefore becomes a duty incumbent upon us as daughters of a despised race, to use our utmost endeavors to enlighten the understanding and cultivate the talents entrusted to our keeping; that by so doing we may, in a great measure, break down the strong barrier of prejudice, and raise ourselves to an equality with those of our fellow beings who differ from us in complexion alone, but with ourselves are children of one Eternal Parent, by whose immutable law we are entitled to the same rights and privileges; and actuated by a natural feeling for the welfare of our friends, and cherishing such virtues as will render us happy and useful to society, we trust by the blessing of God we shall be able to accomplish the object of our union. We have therefore associated ourselves under the name of the African Female Benevolent Society of Troy, and have adopted the following Constitution.

ANNUAL REPORT.

This Society was formed under the most discouraging circumstances, and at the first meeting, held February 12th, 1833, there were but ten persons present who were willing to unite heart and hand in a work which, if the Almighty continues to smile upon it, will prove beneficial to those that faint not. At present we have 65 members; but by this I should wish you to understand that we have only added more names to our roll; for why call those members who run well for a while and then turn back, alleging as a reason, that the Society funds will never do them any good; particularly the youth, who think, we presume to say, that they have the greatest of blessings, health; and also all things that are necessary for the present. I would address those persons,- Think ye the rough hand of sickness will ever visit you ? Why not then prepare for the worst? For I believe that as sure as this institution has been formed, and has met here today, to celebrate this anniversary, so sure it will prove a source of joy and a relief to those who may continue to uphold it by their united endeavors. When the hour of trouble comes upon those, then, who have neglected to act according to the constitution by which they have pledged themselves, we shall have to enforce that clause which cuts them off from any relief. In this case we shall mourn over the condemned persons as a household mourneth after a kinsman: For are we not a company of sisters united to support and assist each other? If one is afflicted do we not feel for her, and endeavor to assist her; and if in trouble, lend a hand to her relief? Sisters of Benevolence, for by that title I shall now call you, mourn then if one of our members becoming deluded turneth aside.

As it respects our funds, at the first meeting that was held $15 were received and handed to the treasurer for a deposite. At present we have $100.00 in the funds. All private expenses incurred by the Society have been paid by voluntary contributions for the purpose, not wishing to lay our hands on that entrusted to our keeping.

ELIZA A. T. DUNGY, secretary.

Source: Elizabeth Wicks, *Address Delivered Before the African Female Benevolent Society of Troy on Wednesday, February 12, 1834. To Which is Annexed an Eulogy on the Death of Mrs. Jane Lansing, With an Address by Eliza. A. T. Dungy.* (Troy: Printed By R. Buckley, 1834)

11

Maria W. Stewart

Maria W. Stewart (1803–1879) was a trailblazing pamphleteer and female activist. She was the first woman to address publicly what was considered then a "promiscuous audience" of men and women at Boston's African Masonic Hall in 1833. Her writings—which were brought together in 1835 in an extended pamphlet entitled simply "Productions"—heralded a black female reformer's perspective. Following in the footsteps of David Walker, Stewart called on black communities to organize in newly assertive ways. Women had particularly important roles in a bolder black reform movement, not just as mothers, wives, and sisters but as educators and even activists. In short, black women need not leave the reform work to men of either color.

Stewart's work as a schoolteacher in Boston helped her to reach such conclusions, as did her involvement in that city's vibrant black community. African Americans there formed a rich array of benevolent, religious, literary, and abolitionist groups before the Civil War. Generations of black Bostonians held public speeches and rallies, and they consistently printed memorials protesting such issues as discriminatory educational facilities and the lack of adequate legal protections. When William Lloyd Garrison started his radical abolitionist paper *The Liberator* in 1831, black Bostonians became important contributors and avid readers. Stewart was both.

As this document illustrates, Stewart earned her fame by publishing and speaking at a time when, as she put it, men and women of both colors looked quizzically at black female activists. Did they have a right to speak publicly on matters relating to slavery and racial injustice? "So what if I am a women," she replied. Citing David Walker's influence, Stewart forthrightly challenges both blacks and whites to conquer racial problems. Even more than Walker, however, she promulgates a liberation theology: Religion bolsters reform efforts, Stewart says, because God favors the oppressed. Stewart moved eventually to New York City, where she continued to teach and protest.

"Productions"

(1835)

"Had we as a people received one half the early advantages the whites have received,
I would defy the government of these United States to deprive us any longer of our rights."

AN ADDRESS DELIVERED AT THE AFRICAN MASONIC HALL, BOSTON, FEBRUARY 27, 1833

African rights and liberty is a subject that ought to fire the breast of every free man of color in these United States, and excite in his bosom a lively, deep, decided, and heart-felt interest. When I cast my eyes on the long list of illustrious names that are enrolled on the bright annals of fame among the whites, I turn my eyes within, and ask my thoughts, "Where are the names of *our* illustrious ones?" It must certainly have been for the want of energy on the part of the free people of color, that they have been long willing to bear the yoke of oppression. It must have been the want of ambition and force that has given the whites occasion to say that our natural abilities are not as good, and our capacities by nature inferior to theirs. They boldly assert that, did we possess a natural independence of soul, and feel a love for liberty within our breasts, some one of our sable race long before this would have testified it, notwithstanding the disadvantages under which we labor. We have made our-selves appear altogether unqualified to speak in our own defence, and are therefore looked upon as objects of pity and commiseration. We have been imposed upon, insulted and derided on every side; and now, if we complain, it is considered as the height of impertinence. We have suffered ourselves to be considered as dastards, cowards, mean, faint-hearted wretches; and on this account, (not because of our complexion) many despise us, and would gladly spurn us from their presence.

These things have fired my soul with a holy indignation, and compelled me thus to come forward, and endeavor to turn their attention to knowledge and improvement; for knowledge is power. I would ask, is it blindness of mind, or stupidity of soul, or the want of education, that has caused our men who are 60 or 70 years of age, never to let their voices be heard, nor their hands be raised in behalf of their color? Or has it been for the fear of offending the whites? If it has, O ye fearful ones, throw off your fearfulness, and come forth in the name of the Lord, and in the strength of the God of Justice, and make yourselves useful and active members in society; for they admire a noble and patriotic spirit in others; and should they not admire it in us? If you are men, convince them that you possess the spirit of men; and as your day, so shall your strength be. Have the sons of Africa no souls? Feel they no ambitious desires? Shall the chains of ignorance forever confine them? Shall the insipid appellation of "clever negroes," or "good creatures," any longer con-tent them? Where can we find among ourselves the man of science, or a philosopher, or an able statesman, or a counsellor at law? Show me our fearless and brave, our noble and gallant ones. Where are our lecturers on natural history, and our critics in useful knowledge? There may be a few such men among us, but they are rare. It is true, our fathers bled and died in the revolutionary war, and others fought bravely under the command of Jackson, in defence of liberty. But where is the man that has distinguished himself in these modern days by acting wholly in the defence of African rights and liberty? There was one; although he sleeps, his memory lives.

I am sensible that there are many highly intelligent gentlemen of color in these United States, in the force of whose arguments, doubtless, I should discover my inferiority; but if they are blest with wit and talent, friends and fortune, why have they not made them-selves men of eminence, by striving to take all the reproach that is cast upon the people of color, and in endeavoring to alleviate the woes of their brethren in bondage? Talk, with-out effort, is nothing; you are abundantly capable, gentlemen, of making yourselves men of distinction; and this gross neglect, on your part, causes my blood to boil within me. Here is the grand cause which hinders the rise and progress of the people of color. It is their want of laudable ambition and requisite courage.

Individuals have been distinguished according to their genius and talents, ever since the first formation of man, and will continue to be while the world stands. The different grades rise to honor and respectability as their merits may deserve. History informs us that we sprung from one of the most learned nations of the whole earth; from the seat, if not the parent of science; yes, poor, despised Africa was once the resort of sages and legisla-tors of other nations, was esteemed the school for leaning, and the most illustrious men in Greece flocked thither for instruction, But it was our gross sink and abominations that provoked the Almighty to frown thus heavily upon us, and give our glory unto others. Sin and prodigality have caused the downfall of nations, kings and emperors; and were it not that God in wrath remembers mercy, we might indeed despair; but a promise is left us; "Ethiopia shall again stretch forth her hands unto God."

But it is of no use for us to boast that we sprung from this learned and enlightened nation, for this day a thick mist of moral gloom hangs over millions of our race. Our condition as a people has been law for hundreds of years, and it will continue to be so, unless, by true piety and virtue, we strive to regain that which we have lost. White Amer-icans, by their prudence, economy and exertions, have sprung up and become one of the most flourishing nations in the world, distinguished for their knowledge of the arts and sciences, for their polite literature. While our minds are vacant, and starving for want of knowledge, theirs are filled to overflowing. Most of our color have been taught to stand in fear of the white man, from their earliest infancy, to work as soon as they could walk, and call "master," before they scarce could lisp the name of mother. Continual fear and labo-rious servitude have in some degree lessened in us that natural force and energy which belong to man; or else, in defiance of opposition, our men, before this, would have nobly and boldly contended for their rights. But give the man of color an equal opportunity with the white from the cradle to manhood, and from manhood to the grave, and you would discover the dignified states-man, the man of science, and the philosopher. But there is no such opportunity for the sons of Africa, and I fear that our powerful ones are fully determined that there never shall be. Forbid, ye Powers on high, that it should any longer be said that our men possess no force. O ye sons of Africa, when will your voices be heard in our legislative halls, in defiance of your enemies, contending for equal rights and liberty? How can you, when you reflect from what you have fallen, refrain from crying mightily unto God, to turn away from us the fierceness of his anger, and remember our transgressions against us no more forever. But a God of infinite purity will not regard the prayers of those who hold religion in one hand, and prejudice, sin and pollution in the other; he will not regard the prayers of self-righteousness and hypocrisy. Is it possible, I exclaim, that for the want of knowledge, we have labored for hundreds of years to support others, and been content to receive what they chose to give us in return? Cast your eyes about, look as far as you can see; all, all is owned by the lordly white, except here and there a lowly dwelling which the man of color, midst deprivations, fraud and opposition, has been scarce able to procure. Like king Solomon, who put neither nail nor hammer to the temple, yet received the praise; so also have the white Americans gained themselves a name, like the names of the great men that are in the earth, while in reality we have been their principal foundation and support. We have pursued the shadow, they have obtained the substance; we have performed the labor, they have received the profits; we have planted the vines, they have eaten the fruits of them.

I would implore our men, and especially our rising youth, to flee from the gambling board and the dance-hall; for we are poor, and have no money to throw away. I do not consider dancing as criminal in itself, but it is astonishing to me that our young men are so blind to their own interest and the future welfare of their children, as to spend their hard earnings for this frivolous amusement; for it has been carried on among us to such an unbecoming extent, that it has became absolutely disgusting. "Faithful are the wounds of a friend, but the kisses of an enemy are deceitful." Had those men among us, who have had an opportunity, turned their attention as assiduously to mental and moral improvement as they have to gambling and dancing, I might have remained quietly at home, and they stood contending in my place. These polite accomplishments will never enroll your names on the bright annals of fame, who admire the belle void of intellectual knowledge, or applaud the dandy that talks largely on politics, without striving to assist his fellow in the revolution, when the nerves and muscles of every other man forced him into the field of action, You have a right to rejoice, and to let your hearts cheer you in the days of your youth; yet remember that for all these things, God will bring you into judgment. Then, O ye sons of Africa, turn your mind from these perishable objects, and contend for the cause of God and the rights of man. Form yourselves into temperance societies. There are temperate men among you; then why will you any longer neglect to strive, by your example, to suppress vice in all its abhorrent forms? You have been told repeatedly of the glorious results arising from temperance, and can you bear to see the whites arising in honor and respectability, without endeavoring to grasp after that honor and respectability also?

But I forbear. Let our money, instead of being thrown away as heretofore, be appropriated for schools and seminaries of learning for our children and youth. We ought to follow the example of the whites in this respect. Nothing would raise our respectability, add to our peace and happiness, and reflect so much honor upon us, as to be ourselves the promoters of temperance, and the supporters, as far as we are able, of useful and scientific knowledge. The rays of light and knowledge have been hid from our view; we have been taught to consider ourselves as scarce superior to the brute creation; and have performed the most laborious part of American drudgery. Had we as a people received one half the early advantages the whites have received, I would defy the government of these United States to deprive us any longer of our rights.

I am informed that the agent of the Colonization Society has recently formed an association of young men, for the purpose of influencing those of us to go to Liberia who may feel disposed. The colonizationists are blind to their own interest, for should the nations of the earth make war with America, they would find their forces much weakened by our absence; or should we remain here, can our "brave soldiers," and "fellow-citizens," as they were termed in time of calamity, condescend to defend the rights of the whites, and be again deprived of their own, or sent to Liberia in return? Or, if the colonizationists are real friends to Africa, let them expend the money which they collect, in erecting a college to educate her injured sons in this land of gospel light and liberty; for it would be most thankfully received on our part, and convince us of the truth of their professions, and save time, expense and anxiety. Let them place before us noble objects, worthy of pursuit, and see if we prove ourselves to be those unambitious negroes they term us. But ah! methinks their hearts are so frozen towards us, they had rather their money should be sunk in the ocean than to administer it to our relief; and I fear, if they dared, like Pharaoh, king of Egypt, they would order every male child among us to be drowned. But the most high God is still as able to subdue the lofty pride of these white Americans, as He was the heart of that ancient rebel. They say, though we are looked upon as things, yet we sprang from a scientific people. Had our men the requisite force and energy, they would soon convince them by their efforts both in public and private, that they were men, or things in the shape of men. Well may the colonizationists laugh us to scorn for our negligence; well may they cry, "Shame to the sons of Africa." As the burden of the Israelites was too great for Moses to bear, so also is our burden too great for our noble advocate to bear. You must feel interested, my brethren, in what he undertakes, and hold up his hands by your good works, or in spite of himself, his soul will become discouraged, and his heart will die within him; for he has, as it were, the strong bulls of Bashan to contend with.

It is of no use for us to wait any longer for a generation of well educated men to arise. We have slumbered and slept too long already; the day is far spent; the night of death approaches; and you have sound sense and good judgment sufficient to begin with, if you feel disposed to make a right use of it. Let every man of color throughout the United States, who possesses the spirit and principles of a man, sign a petition to Congress, to abolish slavery in the District of Columbia, and grant you the rights and privileges of common free citizens; for if you had had faith as a grain of mustard seed, long before this the mountains of prejudice might have been removed. We are all sensible that the Anti-Slavery Society has taken hold of the arm of our whole population, in order to raise them out of the mire. Now all we have to do is, by a spirit of virtuous ambition to strive to raise ourselves; and I am happy to have it in my power thus publicly to say, that the colored inhabitants of this city, in some respects, are beginning to improve. Had the free people of color in these United States nobly and boldly con-tended for their rights, and showed a natural genius and talent, although not so brilliant as some; had they held up, encouraged and patronized each other, nothing could have hindered us from being a thriving and flourishing people. There has been a fault among us. The reason why our distinguished men have not made themselves more influential is, because they fear that the strong current of op-position through which they must pass, would cause their downfall and prove their overthrow. And what gives rise to this opposition? Envy. And what has it amounted to? Nothing, And who are the cause of it? Our whited sepulchres, who want to be great, and don't know how; who love to be called of men 'Rabbi, Rabbi, who put on false sanctity, and humble themselves to their brethren, for the sake of acquiring the highest place in the synagogue, and the upper-most seats at the feast. You, dearly beloved, who are the genuine followers of our Lord Jesus Christ, the salt of the earth and the light of the world, are not so culpable. As I told you, in the very first of my writing, I tell you again, I am but as a drop in the bucket-as one particle of the small dust of the earth. God will surely raise up those among us who will plead the cause of virtue, and the pure principles of morality, more eloquently than I am able to do.

It appears to me that America has become like the great city of Babylon, for she has boasted in her heart, "I sit a queen, and am no widow, and shall see no sorrow?" She is indeed a seller of slaves and the souls of men; she has made the Africans drunk with the wine of her fornication; she has put them completely beneath her feet, and she means to keep them there; her right hand supports the reins of government, and her left hand the wheel of power, and she is determined not to let go her grasp. But many powerful sons and daughters of Africa will shortly arise, who will put down vice and immorality among us, and declare by Him that sitteth upon the throne, that they will have their rights; and if refused, I am afraid they will spread horror and devastation around. I believe that the oppression of injured Africa has come up before the Majesty of Heaven; and when our cries shall have reached the ears of the Most High, it will be a tremendous day for the people of this land; for strong is the arm of the Lord God Almighty.

Life has almost lost its charms for me; death has lost its sting and the grave its terrors; and at times I have a strong desire to depart and dwell with Christ, which is far better. Let me entreat my white brethren to awake and save our sons from dissipation, and our daughters from ruin. Lend the hand of assistance to feeble merit, plead the cause of virtue among our sable race; so shall our curses upon you be turned into blessings; and though you should endeavor to drive us from these shores, still we will cling to you the more firmly; nor will we attempt to rise above you: we will presume to be called your equals only.

The unfriendly whites first drove the native American from his much loved home. Then they stole our fathers from their peaceful and quiet dwellings, and brought them hither, and made bond-men and bond-women of them and their little ones; they have obliged our brethren to labor, kept them in utter ignorance, nourished them in vice, and raised them in degradation; and now that we have enriched their soil, and filled their coffers, they say that we are not capable of becoming like white men, and that we never can rise to respectability in this country. They would drive us to a strange land. But before I go, the bayonet shall pierce me through. African rights and liberty is a subject that ought to fire the breast of every free man of color in these United States, and excite in his bosom a lively, deep, decided and heart-felt interest.

A Lecture by Maria W. Stewart, given at Franklin Hall, Boston, September 21, 1832.

Why sit we here and die? If we say we will go to a foreign land, the famine and the pestilence are there, and there we shall die. If we sit here, we shall die. Come, let us plead our cause before the whites: if they save us alive, we shall love-and if they kill us, we shall not die.

Methinks I heard a spiritual interrogation-"Who shall go forward, and take of the reproach that is cast upon the people of color? Shall it be a woman?" And my heart made this reply-"If it is thy will, be it even so, Lord Jesus?"

I have heard much respecting the horrors of slavery; but may Heaven forbid that the generality of my color throughout these United States should experience any more of its horrors than to be a servant of servants, or hewers of wood and drawers of water! Tell us no more of southern slavery; for with few exceptions, although I may be very erroneous in any opinion, yet I consider our condition but little better than that. Yet, after all, methinks there are no chains so galling as the chains of ignorance-no fetters so binding as those that bind the soul, and exclude it from the vast field of useful and scientific knowledge. O, had

I received the advantages of early education, my ideas would, ere now, have expanded far and wide; but, alas! I possess nothing but moral capability-no teachings but the teachings of the Holy Spirit.

I have asked several individuals of my sex, who transact business for themselves, if, providing our girls were to give them the most satisfactory references, they would not be willing to grant them an equal opportunity with others? Their reply has been-for their own part, they had no objection; but as it was not the custom, were they to take them into their employ, they would be in danger of losing the public patronage.

And such is the powerful force of prejudice—Let our girls possess what amiable qualities of soul they may-let their characters be fair and spotless as innocence itself-let their natural taste and ingenuity be what they may-it is impossible for scarce an individual of them to rise above the condition of servants. Ah! why is this cruel and unfeeling distinction? Is it merely because God has made our complexion to vary? If it be, O shame to soft, relenting humanity! "Tell it not in Gath! publish it not in the streets of Askelon!" Yet, after all, methinks were the American free people of color to turn their attention or more assiduously to moral worth and intellectual improvement, this would be the result: -prejudice would gradually diminish, and the whites would be compelled to day,-Unloose those fetters!

Though black their skins as shades of night,

Their hearts are pure-their souls are white.

Few white persons of either sex, who are calculated for anything else, are willing to spend their lives and bury their talents in performing mean, servile labor. And such is the horrible idea that I entertain respecting a life of servitude, that if I conceived of their being no possibility of my rising above the condition of a servant, I would gladly hail death as a welcome messenger. O, horrible idea, indeed! to possess noble souls aspiring after high and honorable acquirements, yet confined by the chains of ignorance and poverty to lives of continual drudgery and toil. Neither do I know of any who have enriched themselves by spending their lives as house-domestics, washing windows, shaking carpets, brushing boots, or tending upon gentlemen's tables. I can but die for expressing my sentiments; and I am as willing to die by the sword as the pestilence-for I am a true born American-your blood flows in my veins, and your spirit fires my breast.

I observed a piece in the Liberator a few months since, stating that the colonizationists had published a work respecting us, asserting that we were lazy and idle. I confute them on that point. Take us generally as a people, we are neither lazy nor idle; and considering how little we have to excite or stimulate us, I am almost astonished that there are so many industrious and ambitious ones to be found-although I acknowledge, with extreme sorrow, that there are some who never were and never will be serviceable to society. And have you not a similar class among yourselves?

Again-It was asserted that we were "a ragged set, crying for liberty." I reply to it, the whites have so long and so loudly pro-claimed the theme of equal rights and privileges, that our souls have caught the flame also, ragged as we are. As far as our merit deserves, we feel a common desire to rise above the condition of servants and drudges. I have learnt, by bitter experience, that continual hard labor deadens the energies of the soul, and benumbs the faculties of the mind: the ideas become confined, the mind barren, and, like the scorching sands of Arabia, produces nothing-or like the uncultivated soil, brings forth thorns and thistles.

Again, continual hard labor irritates our tempers and sours our dispositions; the whole system becomes worn out with toil and fatigue; nature herself becomes almost exhausted, and we care but little whether we live or die. It is true that the free people of color throughout these United States are neither bought nor sold, nor under the lash of the cruel driver; many obtain a comfortable support; but few, if any, have an opportunity of becoming rich and independent; and the employments we most pursue are as unprofitable to us as the spider's web or the floating bubbles that vanish into air. As servants, we are respected; but let us presume to aspire any higher, our employer regards us no longer. And were it not that the King eternal has declared that Ethiopia shall stretch forth her hands unto God, I should indeed despair.

I do not consider it derogatory, my friends, for persons to live out to service. There are many whose inclination leads them to aspire no higher-and I would highly commend the performance of almost anything for an honest livelihood; but where constitutional strength is wanting, labor of this kind, in its mildest form, is painful. And doubtless many are the prayers that have ascended to Heaven from Afric's daughters for strength to perform their work. Oh, many are the tears that have been shed for the want of that strength! Most of our color have dragged out a miserable existence of servitude from the cradle to the grave. And what literary acquirements can be made, or useful knowledge derived, from either maps, books or charts, by those who continually drudge from Monday morning until Sunday noon? O, ye fairer sisters, whose hands are never soiled, whose nerves and muscles are never strained, go learn by experience! Had we had the opportunity that you have had, to improve our moral and mental faculties, what would have hindered our intellects from being as bright, and our manners from being as dignified as yours? Had it been our lot to have been nursed in the lap of affluence and ease, and to have basked beneath the smiles and sunshine of fortune, should we not have naturally supposed that we were never made to toil? And why are not our forms as delicate, and our constitutions as slender, as yours? Is not the workmanship as curious and complete? Have pity upon us-have pity upon us, O ye who have hearts to feel for others' woes; for the hand of God has touched us. Owing to the disadvantages under which we labor, there are many flowers among us that are born to bloom unseen, And waste their fragrance on the desert air.

My beloved brethren, as Christ has died in vain for those who will not accept of offered mercy, so will it be in vain for the advocates of freedom to spend their breath in our behalf, unless with united hearts and souls you make some mighty efforts to raise your sons and daughters from the horrible state of servitude and degradation in which they are placed. It is upon you that woman depends; she can do but little besides using her influence; and it is for her sake and yours that I have come forward and made myself a hissing and a reproach amongst the people; for I am also one of the wretched and miserable daughters of the descendants of fallen Africa. Do you ask-Why are you wretched and miserable? I reply, look at many of the most worthy and interesting of us doomed to spend our lives in gentlemen's kitchens. Look at our young men, smart, active and energetic, with souls filled with ambitious fire; if they look forward, alas! what are their prospects? They can be nothing but the humblest laborers, on account of their dark complexions; hence many of them lose their ambition, and become worthless. Look at our middle-aged men, clad in their rusty plaids and coats-in winter, every cent they earn goes to buy their wood and pay their rents; their poor wives also toil beyond their strength to help support their families. Look at our aged sires, who heads are whitened with the frosts of seventy winters, with their old wood saws on their backs.

Alas, what keeps us so? Prejudice, ignorance and poverty. But ah! methinks our oppression is soon to come to an end; yea, before the majesty of heaven, our groans and cries have reached the ears of the Lord of Sabaoth. As the prayers and tears of Christians will avail the finally impenitent nothing; neither will the prayers and tears of the friends of human-ity avail us anything, unless we possess a spirit of virtuous emulation within our breasts. Did the Pilgrims, when they first landed on these shores, quietly compose themselves, and say, "The Britons have all the money and all the power, and we must continue their servants forever?" Did they sluggishly sigh and say, "Our lot is hard-the Indians own the soil, and we cannot cultivate it?" No-they first made powerful efforts to raise themselves and then God raised up those illustrious patriots, Washington and Lafayette, to assist and defend them. And, my brethren, have you made a powerful effort? Have you prayed the legislature for mercy's sake to grant you all the rights and privileges of free citizens, that your daughters may rise to that degree of respectability which true merit deserves, and your sons above the servile situations which most of them fill?

12

Robert Purvis

In the "Appeal of Forty Thousand Citizens, Threatened with Disfranchisement, to the People of Pennsylvania," leaders of the African-American community protest the recent act of the Pennsylvania Constitutional Convention in adding the word "white" to voting qualifications. The disfranchisement of black voters, reflecting increasing white racial hostility, was a victory for whites who argued that blacks were never intended to be considered citizens and participants in the political process. In response, from a mass meeting of African Americans, is this declaration affirming black citizenship rights and castigating kowtowing to pro-slavery sentiment. The "Appeal" was mainly the work of Robert Purvis (1810–1898), the light-skinned, wealthy antislavery activist deeply involved in black community affairs and a leader of the Vigilance Committee, the black Underground Railroad network in Philadelphia. His co-signers were also among the Philadelphia black elite leadership group.

In this passionate and legalistic appeal, African Americans claim their heritage as Pennsylvanians and Americans and seize for themselves the legacy of the Declaration of Independence, Pennsylvania's early constitution, and the state's 1780 Gradual Emancipation Act. Their opponents, they argue, are capitulating to Southern slaveholder demands reflecting their hatred and fear of the free black population, and by their capitulation threaten the liberty of all. While rooted in an explication of principle and law, the "Appeal" also makes use of statistical information to demonstrate the worth of black citizens. From a recent special census of the black community conducted by black leaders and white abolitionists, Purvis marshals the numbers of black churches, schools, and relief organizations that show the black community as busy, hardworking and productive, deeply involved in taking care of their own.

A Pennsylvania Supreme Court decision discussed at some length is *Fogg v. Hobbs*. In 1838, following ratification of the new constitution with its exclusionary provision, the Court, in convoluted fashion, decided that African Americans were not included in the pale of American citizenship and therefore could be denied the right to vote. The introduction below was printed in the *Colored American* in 1838.

"Appeal of Forty Thousand Citizens, Threatened with Disfranchisement, to the People of Pennsylvania"

(1837)

"When you have taken from an individual his right to vote, you have made the government, in regard to him, a mere despotism; and you have taken a step towards making it a despotism to all."

IMPORTANT DOCUMENT.

WE have received the appeal of forty thousand colored citizens of Pennsylvania, to the freemen of that State, against the unrighteous and illegal decision of the "Reform Convention," and against the partial, immature views of the Judges of the Supreme Court. It is a powerful document. We are delighted with its talent and spirit. Our good brethren have touched the right key. - We must respect our own rights, before we expect others to do so, and we must show to the world that we know our rights, and have keen sensibilities, when they are invaded, or we shall always be subject to unlawful encroachments.

We hope a hundred thousand copies, at least, of the appeal and remonstrance - for it is both - will be circulated in Pennsylvania; and we again suggest the propriety and importance, of sending living agents with these documents. Their presence and personal appeals to the judgment and consciences of the citizens, will be irresistible. It is one thing to read about oppression, but it is quite another thing to hear about it, from the lips of the oppressed. There are among our brethren in Pennsylvania, men, in every way qualified to hold personal conferences with the freemen of the State. - Men, whose talents and personal appearance could not otherwise than interest, favorably, the feelings, and govern the sentiments of the people. This should be done - no measure should be neglected, which might have the least tendency to influence the public. The decision of the Supreme Court should be considered no barrier whatever. Every inspector has a right to decide the constitution for himself, on this point, and if his decision be appealed from, and the election contested, this will bring the subject before the legislature, where it will be acted upon by the representatives of the people. The "Reform Convention," (a misnomer,) has done one good thing - it has stripped the Colonization Society of its sheep's clothing, and shown them out in their true character, as ragged wolves. Who will not henceforth mark the Society and the men, who, with honey upon their lips, and gall in their hearts, would scheme the disfranchisement of forty thousand peaceable, virtuous, enterprising citizens? - some of whom were actors in the revolutionary struggles which achieved the independence of our country; and have ever since been among the most enterprising in carrying forward the interests and prosperity of the Republic. Instead of being disfranchised, such men should be denominated fathers, and respected and honored as patriots of the country.

The Colonization spirit is the spirit of darkness, and the Colonization heart is a den of thieves. In it herd wolves and reptiles. They are skilled in devouring, and are busy seeking to devour. We shall publish the "Appeal" as we have room.

A very numerous and respectable meeting of the colored citizens of Pennsylvania, was held in the Presbyterian Church, Seventh Street, below Shippen, on the evening of the 14th inst. The meeting was organized by calling John P. Burr to the chair, and appointing Thomas Butler and Stephen H. Gloucester Vice-Presidents, and James Cornish and James Forten, Jr., Secretaries. After an appropriate prayer by the Rev. Charles W. Gardner, the Chairman, with some suitable observations, stated the object of the meeting, - which was to receive the report of a Committee consisting of the following gentlemen: Robert Purvis, James Cornish, J. C. Bowers, Robert B. Forten, J. J. C. Bias, James Needham, and John P. Burr - appointed at a public meeting held prior to the above, in St. Paul's Lutheran Church, Quince Street, to prepare an appeal in behalf of forty thousand citizens, threatened with disfranchisement, to their fellow citizens, remonstrating against the late cruel act of the Reform Convention: Robert Purvis, Chairman of Committee, presented and read the appeal; it was accepted, and remarks were then made by James Forten, sr., Robert Purvis, J. C. Bowers, F. A. Hinton, Charles W. Gardner, and several others, after which it was adopted with a unanimity and spirit equalled only by the memorable meeting of 1817.

The following resolutions were unanimously adopted:

1. *Resolved*, That our warm and grateful thanks are due those gentlemen who, on the floor of the Convention, stood by us in the hour of need, in the able assertion and advocacy of our rights, and to others who voted against the insertion of the word "white." Also, that like thanks are due to our Abolition friends for their active though unavailing exertions to prevent the unrighteous act.

2. *Resolved*, That a committee of five be appointed to draw up a remonstrance against the Colonization Society, to be presented to the various Churches, Presbyterys, Conferences, and Conventions. The following persons were appointed: — James Forten, sr., S. H. Gloucester, Robert Douglass, Charles W. Gardner, and Bishop [Morris] Brown.

President: John P. Burr
Vice Presidents: Thomas Butler and S.H. Gloucester
Secretaries: James Cornish and James Forten, Jr.

APPEAL

FELLOW CITIZENS: — We appeal to you from the decision of the "Reform Convention," which has stripped us of a right peaceably enjoyed during forty-seven years under the Constitution of this commonwealth. We honor Pennsylvania and her noble institutions too much to part with our birthright, as her free citizens, without a struggle. To all her citizens the right of suffrage is valuable in proportion as she is free; but surely there are none who can so ill afford to spare it as ourselves.

Was it the intention of the people of this commonwealth that the convention to which the Constitution was committed for revision and amendment, should tear up and cast away its first principles? Was it made the business of the Convention to deny "that all men are born equally free," by making political rights depend upon the skin in which a man is born? Or to divide what our fathers bled to unite, to wit, TAXATION and REPRESENTATION? We will not allow ourselves for one moment to suppose, that the majority of the people of Pennsylvania are not too respectful of the rights and too liberal towards the feelings of others, as well as too much enlightened to their own interests, to deprive of the right of suffrage a single individual who may safely be trusted with it. And we cannot believe that you have found among those who bear the burdens of taxation any who have proved, by their abuse of the right, that it is not safe in their hands. This is a question, fellow-citizens, in which we plead *your* cause as well as our own. It is the safe-guard of the strongest that he lives under a government which is obliged to respect the voice of the weakest. When you have taken from an individual his right to vote, you have made the government, in regard to him, a mere despotism; and you have taken a step towards making it a despotism to all. To your women and children, their inability to vote at the polls may be no evil, because they are united by consanguinity and affection with those who can do it. To foreigners and paupers the want of the right may be tolerable, because a little time or labor will make it theirs. They are candidates for the privilege, and hence substantially enjoy its benefits. But when a distinct class of the community, already sufficiently the objects of prejudice, are wholly, and for ever, disfranchised and excluded, to the remotest posterity, from the possibility of a voice in regard to the laws under which they are to live - it is the same thing as if their abode were transferred to the dominions of the Russian Autocrat, or of the Grand Turk. They have lost their check upon oppression, their wherewith to buy friends, their panoply of manhood; in short, they are thrown upon the mercy of a despotic majority. Like every other despot, this despot majority, will believe in the mildness of its own sway; but who will the more willingly submit to it for that?

To us our right under the Constitution has been more precious, and our deprivation of it will be the more grievous, because our expatriation has come to be a darling project with many of our fellow citizens. Our abhorrence of a scheme which comes to us in the guise of Christian benevolence, and asks us to suffer ourselves to be transplanted to a distant and barbarous land, *because we are a "nuisance" in this*, is not more deep and thorough than it is reasonable. We love our native country, much as it has wronged us; and in the peaceable exercise of our inalienable rights, we will cling to it. The immortal Franklin, and his fellow laborers in the cause of humanity, have bound us to our homes where with chains of grat-itude. We are PENNSYLVANIANS, and we hope to see the day when Pennsylvania will have reason to be proud of us, as we believe she has now none to be ashamed!

Will you starve our patriotism?

Will you cast our hearts out of the treasury of the commonwealth? Do you count our enmity better than our friendship?

Fellow citizens, we entreat you, in the name of fair dealing, to look again at the just and noble charter of Pennsylvania freedom, which you are asked to narrow down to the lines of caste and color. The Constitution reads as follows: —

"Article 3, paragraph 1. In elections by the citizens, every freeman, of the age of twenty-one years, having resided in the state two years next before the election and within that time paid a State or county tax, which shall have been assessed at least six months before the election, shall enjoy the rights of an election."

This clause guarantees the right of suffrage to us as fully as to any of our fellow citizens whatsoever, for

1. Such was the intention of the framers. In the original draft reported by a committee of nine, the word "WHITE" stood before "FREEMAN." On motion of Albert Gallatin it was stricken out, for the express purpose of including colored citizens with the pale of the elective franchise. (See Minutes of the Convention, 1790.)

2. We are CITIZENS. This, we believe, would never have been denied, had it not been for the scheme of expatriation to which we have already referred. But as our citizen-ship has been doubted by some who are not altogether unfriendly to us, we beg leave to submit some proof, which we think you will not hastily set aside.

We were regarded as CITIZENS by those who drew up the articles of confederation between the States, in 1778. The fourth of the said articles contains the following language:—"The free inhabitants of each of these States, paupers, vagabonds, and fugitives from justice excepted, shall be entitled to all privileges and immunities of free *citizens* in the several States." That we were not excluded under the phrase "paupers, vagabonds, and fugitives from justice," any more than our white countrymen, is plain from the debates that preceded the adoption of the article. For, on the 25th of June, 1778, "the delegates from South Carolina moved the following amendment *in behalf of their* State. In article fourth; between the words *free* inhabitants, insert *white*. Decided in the negative; ayes, two States; nays, eight States; one State divided." Such was the solemn decision of the revolutionary Congress, concurred in by the entire delegation from our own commonwealth. On the adoption of the present Constitution of the United States no change was made as to the rights of citizenship. This is explicitly proved by the Journal of Congress. Take, for example, the following resolution passed in the House of Representatives, December 21, 1803: "On motion; *Resolved*, That the Committee appointed to enquire and report whether any further provisions are necessary for the more effectual protection of American seamen, do enquire into the expediency of granting protections to such American seamen, *citizens of the United States*, as *are free persons of color*, and that they report by bill, or otherwise."

… Proofs might be multiplied. In almost every State we have been spoken of, either expressly or by implication; as *citizens*, in the very year before the adoption of the present Constitution, 1789, the "Pennsylvania Society for Promoting the Abolition of Slavery & c," put forth an address, signed by "BENJAMIN FRANKLIN, *President*," in which they stated one of their objects to be, "to *qualify* those who have been restored to freedom, for the exercise and enjoyment of CIVIL LIBERTY." The Convention of 1790, by striking out the word "WHITE," fixed the same standard of *qualification* for all; and, in fact, granted and guaranteed "civil liberty" to all who possessed that qualification. Are we now to be told, that the Convention did not intend to include colored men, and that BENJAMIN FRANKLIN did not know what he was about, forasmuch as it was impossible for a colored man to become a citizen of the commonwealth?

It may here be objected to us, that in point of fact we have lost by the recent decision of the [Pennsylvania] Supreme Court, in the case of *Fogg* vs. *Hobbs*, whatever claim to the right of suffrage we may have had under the Constitution of 1790; and hence have no reason to oppose the amended Constitution. Not so. We hold our rights under the present Constitution none the cheaper for that decision. The section already cited gives us all that we ask—all that we can conceive it in the power of language to convey. Reject, fellow citizens, the partial, disfranchising Constitution offered you by the Reform Convention, and we shall confidently expect that the Supreme Court will do us the justice and itself the honor to retract its decision. Should it not, our appeal will still be open to the conscience and common sense of the people, who through their chief magistrate and a majority of two-thirds of both branches of the Legislature may make way to the bench of the Supreme Court, for expounders of the Constitution who will not do violence to its most sacred and fundamental principles.

We cannot forbear here to refer you to some points in the published opinion of the Court as delivered by Chief Justice Gibson, which we believe will go far to strip it of the weight and authority ordinarily conceded to the decision of the highest tribunal (save the elections) of this commonwealth.

1. The Court relies much on a decision *said to have been had* "ABOUT" forty-three years ago, the claim of which to a place in the repository of Pennsylvania law is thus set forth by the Court itself:—

"About the year 1795, as I have it from James Gibson, Esq., of the Philadelphia bar, the very point before us was ruled by the High Court of Errors and Appeals, against the right of Negro suffrage. Mr. Gibson declined an invitation to be concerned in the argument, and therefore has no memorandum of the cause to direct us to the record. I have had the office searched for it; but the papers had fallen into such disorder as to preclude a hope of its recovery. Most of them were imperfect, and many were lost or misplaced. *But Mr. Gibson's remembrance of the decision is perfect and entitled to full confidence.*"

Now, suppressing doubt, and supposing such a decision actually to have emanated from the then highest tribunal of the commonwealth, does not the fact that it was so utterly forgotten as not to have regulated the polls within the memory of the present generation; nor to have been brought up against us in the Reform Convention; prove that it was virtually retracted? And if retracted, is it now to be revived to the overthrow of rights enjoyed without contradiction during the average life of man?

2. The Court argues that colored men are not *freemen*, and hence not entitled by the present Constitution to vote, because under laws prior to the Constitution there *might be* individuals who were not slaves, and yet were not *freemen!*

3. Since the argument above referred to, such as it is, does not rest upon color, it is not less applicable to the descendants of Irish and German ancestors than to ourselves. If there ever have been within the commonwealth, men, or sets of men, who though personally free were not technically *freemen*, it is unconstitutional, according to the doctrine of the Court, for their descendants to exercise the right of suffrage, pay what taxes they may, till in "the discretion of the judges," their blood has "become so diluted in successive descents as to lose its distinctive character." Is this the doctrine of Pennsylvania freedom?

4. Lastly, the Court openly rests its decision on the authority of a wrong which this commonwealth so long ago as 1780 solemnly acknowledged, and, to the extent of its power, forever repealed. To support the same *wrong* in *other States*, the Constitution of *this*, when it uses the words "every freeman," must be understood to exclude every freeman of a certain color! The Court is of opinion that the people of this commonwealth had no power to confer the rights of citizenship upon one who, were he in another State, *might be* loaded by its laws with "countless disabilities." Now, since in some of the States men may be found in slavery who have not the slightest trace of African blood, it is difficult to see, on the doctrine of the Court, how the Constitution of Pennsylvania could confer the right of citizenship upon any person; and, indeed, how it could have allowed the emancipation of slaves of any color. To such vile dependence on its own ancient *wrongs*, and on the present *wrongs* of other States, is Pennsylvania reduced by this decision!

Are we then presumptuous in the hope that this grave sentence will be as incapable of resurrection fifty years hence, as is that which the Chief Justice assures us was pronounced *"about* the year 1795?" No. The blessings of the broad and impartial charter of Pennsylvania rights can no more be wrested from us by legal subtlety, than the beams of our common sun or the breathing of our common air.

What have we done to forfeit the inestimable benefits of this charter? Why should tax-paying colored men, any more than other tax-payers, be deprived of the right of voting for their representatives? It was said in the Convention, that this government belongs to the *Whites.* We have already shown this to be false, as to the past. Those who established our present government designed it equally for all. It is for you to decide whether it shall be confined to the European complexion in future. Why should you exclude us from a fair participation in the benefits of the republic? Have we oppressed the whites? Have we used our rights to the injury of any class? Have we disgraced it by receiving bribes? Where are the charges written down, and will swear to them? We challenge investigation. We put it to the conscience of every Pennsylvanian, whether there is, or ever has been, in the common wealth, either a political party or religious sect which has less deserved than ourselves to be thus disfranchised. As to the charge of idleness, we fling it back indignantly. Whose brows have sweat for our livelihood but our own? As to vice, if it disqualifies us for civil liberty, why not apply the same rule to the whites, so far as they are vicious? Will you punish the innocent for the crimes of the guilty? The execution of the laws is in the hands of the whites. If we are bad citizens let them apply the proper remedies. We do not ask the right of suffrage for the inmates of our jails and penitentiaries, but for those who honestly and industriously contribute to bear the burdens of the State. As to inferiority to the whites, if indeed we are guilty of it, either by nature or education, we trust our enjoyment of the rights of freemen will on that account be considered the less dangerous. If we are incompetent to fill the offices of State, it will be the fault of the whites only if we are suffered to disgrace them. We are in too feeble a minority to cherish a mischievous ambition. Fair protection is all that we aspire to.

We ask your attention, fellow citizens, to facts and testimonies which go to show that, considering the circumstances in which we have been placed, our country has no reason to be ashamed of us, and that those have the most occasion to blush to whom nature has given the power.

By the careful inquiry of a committee appointed by the "Pennsylvania Society for Promoting the Abolition of Slavery," it has been ascertained that the colored population of Philadelphia and its suburbs, numbering 18,768 souls, possess at the present time, of real and personal estate, not less than $1,350,000. They have paid for taxes during the last year $3,232.83, for house, water, and ground rent, $166,963.50. This committee estimate the income of the holders of real estate occupied by the colored people, to be $7\frac{1}{2}$ per cent on a capital of about $2,000,000. Here is an addition to the wealth of their white brethren. But the rents and taxes are not all; to pay them, the colored people must be employed in labor, and here is another profit to the whites, for no man employs another unless he can make his labor profitable to himself. For a similar reason, a profit is made by all the whites who sell to colored people the necessaries or luxuries of life. Though the aggregate amount of the wealth derived by the whites from our people can only be conjectured, its importance is worthy of consideration by those who would make it less by lessening our motive to accumulate for ourselves.

Nor is the profit derived from us counterbalanced by the sums which we in any way draw from the public treasures. From a statement published by order of the Guardians of the Poor of Philadelphia, in 1830, it appears that out of 549 out-door poor relieved during the year, only 22 were persons of color, being about four per cent of the whole number, while the ratio of our population to that of the city and suburbs exceeds $8\frac{1}{4}$ per cent. By a note appended to the printed report above referred to, it appears that the colored *paupers* admitted into the almshouse for the same period, did not exceed four per cent of the whole. Thus it has been ascertained that they pay more than they receive in the support of their own poor. The various "mutual relief" societies of Philadelphia expend upwards of $7,000 annually for the relief of their members when sick or disabled.

That we are not neglectful of our religious interests, nor of the education of our children, is shown by the fact that there are among us in Philadelphia, Pittsburg, York, West Chester, and Columbia, 22 churches, 48 clergymen, 26 day schools, 20 Sabbath schools, 125 Sabbath school teachers, 4 literary societies, 2 public libraries, consisting of about 800 volumes, besides 8,333 volumes in private libraries, 2 tract societies, 2 Bible societies, and 7 temperance societies.

In other parts of the State we are confident our condition will compare very favorably with that in Philadelphia, although we are not furnished with accurate statistics.

Our fathers shared with yours the trials and perils of the wilderness. Among the facts which illustrate this, it is well known that the founder of your capital, from whom it bears the name of Harrisburg, was rescued by a *colored man*, from a party of Indians, who had captured, and bound him to the stake for execution. In gratitude for this act, he *invited colored persons* to settle in his town, and offered them land on favorable terms. When our common country has been invaded by a foreign foe, colored men have hazarded their lives in its defence. Our fathers fought by the side of yours in the struggle which made us an independent republic . . .

Said the Hon. Charles Miner, of Pennsylvania, in Congress, February 7th, 1828 -"The African race make excellent soldiers. - Large numbers of them were with Perry, and aided to gain the brilliant victory on lake Erie. A whole battalion of them was distinguished for its soldiery appearance." The Hon. Mr. Clark, in the Convention which revised the Constitution of New York, in 1821, said, in regard to the right of suffrage of colored men -"In the war of the revolution these people helped to fight your battles by land and by sea. Some of your states were glad to turn out corps of colored men, and to stand shoulder to shoulder with them. In your late war they contributed largely towards splendid victories. On lakes Erie and Champlain, where your fleets triumphed over a foe superior in numbers and engines of death, they were manned in a large proportion with men of color. And in this very house, in the fall of 1814, a bill passed, receiving the approbation of all the branches of your government, authorizing the governor to accept the services of 2,000 free people of color."

On the 20th of March, 1779, it was recommended by Congress to the States of Georgia and South Carolina to raise 3,000 colored troops who were to be rewarded for their services by their freedom. - The delegations from those States informed Congress that such a body of troops would be not only "formidable to the enemy," but would "lessen the danger of revolts and desertions" among the slaves themselves. (See Secret Journal of the Old Congress, Vol. 1. pages 105–107.)

During the last war, the free people of color were called to the defense of the country by GENERAL JACKSON, and received the following testimony to the value of their services, in which let it be remarked that they are addressed as fellow citizens with the whites: "SOLDIERS! When, on the banks of the Mobile, I called you to take up arms, inviting you to partake the perils and glory of your white fellow citizens, I expected much from you - for I was not ignorant that you possessed qualities most formidable to an invading enemy. I knew with what fortitude you could endure hunger and thirst, and all the fatigues of a campaign. I knew well how you loved your native country, and that you had, as well as ourselves, to defend what man holds most dear, his parents, relations, wife, children, and property. You have done more than I expected. In addition to the qualities which I previously knew you to possess, I find, moreover, among you a noble enthusiasm, which leads you to the performance of great things. SOLDIERS - the President of the United States shall hear how praiseworthy was your conduct in the hour of danger, and the representatives of the American people will, I doubt not, give you the praise which your deeds deserve. Your General anticipates them in applauding your noble ardor, &c.

By order, (Signed) THOMAS BUTLER

"Aid-de-Camp."

Are we to be thus looked to for help in the "hour of danger," be trampled under foot in the time of peace? In which of the battles of the revolution did not our fathers fight as bravely as yours, for American liberty? Was it that their children might be disfranchised and loaded with insult that they endured the famine of Valley Forge, and the horrors of the Jersey Prison Ship? Nay, among those from whom you are asked to wrench the birthright of CIVIL LIBERTY, are those who themselves shed their blood on the snows of Jersey, and faced British bayonets in the most desperate hour of the revolution.

In the hours of danger, too, colored men have shown themselves the friends of their white countrymen. When the yellow fever ravaged Philadelphia in 1793, and the whites fled, and there were not found enough of them in the city to bury their own dead, the colored people volunteered to do that painful and dangerous duty. They appointed two of their own number to superintend the sad work, who afterwards received the following testimonial: -

"Having, during the prevalence of the late malignant disorder, had almost daily opportunities of seeing the conduct of Absalom Jones and Richard Allen, and the people employed by them to bury the dead, I with cheerfulness give this testimony of my approbation of their proceedings, as far as the same came under my notice. Their diligence, attention and decency of deportment, afforded me at the time much satisfaction.

(Signed) MATTHEW CLARKSON, Mayor.

Philadelphia, Jan 23, 1794.

It is notorious that many whites who were forsaken by their own relations and left to the mercy of this fell disease, were nursed gratuitously by the colored people. Does this speak an enmity which would abuse the privileges of civil liberty to the injury of the whites? We have the testimony of a committee of the Senate of this commonwealth, no longer ago than 1830, who were appointed to report upon the expediency of restricting the emigration of colored people into the commonwealth. The following extract from their report, signed by Hon. Mr. Breck, chairman, testifies to our character: "On this subject your committee beg to remark, that by the last census our colored population amounted to about 36,000, or whom 30,000 inhabit the eastern district, and only 6,000 the western. And this number, so small compared with the white population, is scattered among 1,500,000 of our own color, making 1 colored to 42 whites. So few of these, it is believed by your committee, need not at present be an object of uneasiness, and would not seem to require the enactment of any restrictive laws, MORE ESPECIALLY AS THEY ARE FOR THE GREATER PART, INDUSTRIOUS, PEACEABLE, AND USEFUL PEOPLE."

Be it remembered, fellow citizens, that it is only the "industrious, peaceable, and useful" part of the colored people that we plead. We would have the right of suffrage only as the reward of industry and worth. We care not how high the qualification be placed. All we ask, is that no man shall be excluded on account of his color, that the same rule shall be applied to all.

Are we to be disfranchised, lest the purity of the *white* blood should be sullied by an intermixture with ours? It seems to us that our white brethren might well enough reserve their fear, till we seek such alliance with them. We ask no social favors. We would not willingly darken the doors of those to whom the complexion and features, which our Maker has given us, are disagreeable. The territories of the commonwealth are sufficiently ample to afford us a home without doing violence to the delicate nerves of our white brethren, for centuries to come. Besides, we are not intruders here, nor, were our ancestors. Surely you ought to bear as unrepiningly the evil consequences of your fathers' guilt, as we those of our fathers' misfortune. Proscription and disfranchisement are the last things in the world to alleviate these evil consequences. Nothing, as shameful experience has already proved, can so powerfully promote the evil which you profess to deprecate, as the degradation of our race by the oppressive rule of yours. Give us that fair and honorable ground which self-respect requires to stand on, and the dreaded amalgamation, if it take place at all, shall be by your own fault, as indeed it always has been. We dare not give full vent to the indignation we feel on this point, but we will not attempt wholly to conceal it.

We ask a voice in the disposition of those public resources which we ourselves have helped to earn; we claim a right to be heard, according to our numbers, in regard to all those great public measures which involve our lives and fortunes, as well as those of our fellow citizens; we assert our right to vote at the polls as a shield against that strange species of benevolence which seeks legislative aid to banish us—and we are told that our white fellow citizens cannot submit to an *intermixture of the races!* Then let the indentures, title-deeds, contracts, notes of hand, and all other evidences of bargain, in which colored men have been treated as *men*, be torn and scattered on the winds. Consistency is a jewel. Let no white man hereafter ask his colored neighbor's *consent* when he wants his property or his labor; lest he should endanger the Anglo-Saxon purity of his descendants? Why should not the same principle hold good between neighbor and neighbor, which is deemed necessary, as a fundamental principle, in the Constitution itself? Why should you be ashamed to act in private business, as the Reform Convention would have you act in the capacity of a commonwealth? But, no! we do not believe our fellow citizens, while with good faith they hold ourselves bound by their contracts with us, and while they feel bound to deal with us only by fair contract, will ratify the arbitrary principle of the Convention, howmuchsoever they may prefer the complexion in which their Maker has pleased to clothe themselves.

We would not misrepresent the motives of the Convention; but we are constrained to believe that they have laid our rights a sacrifice on the altar of slavery. We do not believe our disfranchisement would have been proposed, but for the desire which is felt by political aspirants to gain the favor of the slave-holding States. This is not the first time that northern statesmen have "bowed the knee to the dark spirit of slavery," but it is the first time that they have bowed so low! Is Pennsylvania, which abolished slavery in 1780, and enfranchised her tax-paying colored citizens in 1790, now, in 1838, to get upon her knees and repent of her humanity, to gratify those who disgrace the very name of American Liberty, by holding our brethren as goods and chattels? We freely acknowledge our brotherhood to the slave, and our interest in his welfare. Is this a crime for which we should be ignominiously punished? The very fact that we are deeply interested for our kindred in bonds, shows that we are the right sort of stuff to make good citizens of. Were we not so, we should better deserve a lodging in your penitentiaries than a franchise at your polls. Doubtless it will be well pleasing to the slaveholders of the South to see us degraded. They regard our freedom from chains as a dangerous example, much more our political freedom. They see in everything which fortifies our rights, an obstacle to the recovery of their fugitive property. Will Pennsylvania go backwards towards slavery, for the better safety of southern slave property? Be assured the South will never be satisfied till the old "Keystone" has returned to the point from which she started in 1780. And since the number of colored men in the commonwealth is so inconsiderable, the safety of slavery may require still more. It may demand that a portion of the white tax-payers should be unmanned and turned into chattels—we mean those whose hands are hardened by daily toil.

Fellow citizens, will you take the first step towards reimposing the chains which have now rusted for more than fifty years? Need we inform you that every colored man in

Pennsylvania is exposed to be arrested as a fugitive from slavery? and that it depends not upon the verdict of a jury of his peers, but upon the decision of a judge on summary process, whether or not he shall be dragged into southern bondage? The Constitution of the United States provides that "no person shall be deprived of life, liberty, or property, without due process of law"—by which is certainly meant a TRIAL BY JURY. Yet the act of Congress of 1793, for the recovery of fugitive slaves, authorizes the claimant to seize his victim without a warrant from any magistrate, and allows him to drag him before "any magistrate of a county, city, or town corporate, where such seizure has been made," and upon proving, by "oral testimony or affidavit," to the satisfaction of such magistrate that the man is his slave, gives him a right to take him into everlasting bondage.

Thus may a free-born citizen of Pennsylvania be arrested, tried without counsel, jury, or power to call witnesses, condemned by a single man, and carried across Mason and Dixon's line, within the compass of a single day. An act of this commonwealth, passed 1820, and enlarged and re-enacted in 1825, it is true, puts some restraint upon the power of the claimant under the act of Congress; but it still leaves the case to the decision of a single judge, without the privilege of a jury! What unspeakably aggravates our loss of the right of suffrage at this moment is, that, while the increased activity of the slave-catchers enhances our danger, the Reform Convention has refused to amend the Constitution so as to protect our liberty by a jury trial! We entreat you to make our case your own—imagine your own wives and children to be trembling at the approach of every stranger, lest their husbands and fathers should be dragged into a slavery worse than Algerine— worse than death! Fellow citizens, if there is one of us who has abused the right of suffrage, let him be tried and punished according to law. But in the name of humanity, in the name of justice, in the name of the God you profess to worship, who has no respect of persons, do not turn into gall and wormwood the friendship we bear to yourselves by ratifying a Constitution which tears from us a privilege dearly earned and, inestimably prized. We lay hold of the principles which Pennsylvania asserted in the hour which tried men's souls— which BENJAMIN FRANKLIN and his eight colleagues, in name of the commonwealth, pledged their lives, their fortunes, and their sacred honor to sustain: We take our stand upon that solemn declaration; that to protect inalienable rights "governments are instituted among men, deriving their JUST POWERS from the CONSENT of the governed," and proclaim that a government which tears away from us and our posterity the very power of CONSENT, is a tyrannical usurpation which we will never cease to oppose. We have seen with amazement and grief the apathy of white Pennsylvanians while the "Reform Convention" has been perpetrating this outrage upon the good old principles of Pennsylvania freedom. But however others may forsake these principles, we promise to maintain them on *Pennsylvania soil*, to the last man. If this disfranchisement is designed to uproot us, it shall jail Pennsylvania's fields, valleys, mountains, and rivers; her canals, railroads, forests, and mines; her domestic altars, and her public, religious and benevolent institutions; her Penn and Franklin, her Rush, Rawle, Wistar, and Vaux; her consecrated past and her brilliant future, are as dear to us as they can be to you. Firm upon our Pennsylvania BILL OF RIGHTS, and trusting in a God of Truth and justice, we lay our claim before you, with the warning that no amendments of the present Constitution can compensate for the loss of its foundation principle of equal rights, nor for the conversion into enemies of 40,000 friends.

13

David Ruggles

David Ruggles (1810–1849) remains an underrated figure among antebellum black writers. Although not the author of a single towering work of literature, such as Douglas's "Narrative" or David Walker's "Appeal," he was, for a time, one of the most active and vociferous pamphleteers in America. Unfortunately for Ruggles, who also gained fame as a preacher, reform lecturer, and would-be politician in New York's Liberty Party during the 1840s, his literary output came during a period when black activism was somewhat overshadowed by a new generation of white abolitionists like William Lloyd Garrison, Amos Phelps, and Samuel J. May. These reformers started new abolition societies in the 1830s and were the first white activists to admit blacks into their ranks. But they also shined the spotlight on themselves.

Ruggles's pamphlet marks the beginning of organized black self-defense groups during the antebellum era. Between the 1830s and 1850s, black communities throughout the North formed Vigilance Societies such as the one in New York, or at least informal associations of activists willing to stand up to slave-catchers who patrolled Northern cities in search of alleged fugitives. As slave-catchers often grabbed free blacks on their patrols in the North, blacks fought back. One of the best examples was the Anthony Burns case of 1854, in which Boston's black community spirited away Burns (an avowed fugitive) before he could be returned to his Virginia master. Ruggles's document illuminates the earlier roots of such activity; New York's Vigilance Committee aided over three hundred blacks to elude slave-catchers.

Ruggles's literary voice was a brash reminder of the autonomy of black protest, even during the 1830s—the heydey of interracial reform. Ruggles produced five pamphlets between 1834 and 1837, some of them running near eighty pages. His style, as represented here, was confident and even confrontational, clearly evoking David Walker's stance. According to Ruggles, free black communities had the power to stand up to racist whites, slaveholding Southerners, and even Northern reformers. Particularly noteworthy is Ruggles's explicit call for Northern African Americans to help Southern slaves. Though such activity already was taking place on the Underground Railroad, Ruggles's public acknowledgment of it certainly was bold. Even radical white reformers refrained from making Ruggles's claim.

"New York Committee of Vigilance for the Year 1837, together with Important Facts Relative to Their Proceedings"

(1837)

"These servants are free by the laws of New York; nor do we hesitate to say, that it is the duty, not only of your committee, but of every citizen, to inform them of that fact, and to aid them in securing their freedom."

PREFACE.

The origin and object of the New York Committee of Vigilance are as follows: At a meeting of The Friends of Human Rights, held in the city of New York, Nov. 20, 1835, for the purpose of adopting measures to ascertain, if possible, the extent to which the cruel practice of kidnapping men, women and children, is carried on in this city, and to aid such unfortunate persons as may be in danger of being *reduced to Slavery*, in maintaining their rights—ROBERT BROWN, Esq. was called to the Chair, and David Ruggles, appointed Secretary.

The meeting being impressed with the alarming *fact* that any colored person within this State is liable to be arrested as a *fugitive from slavery* and put upon his defence to prove his freedom, and that any such person thus arrested is denied the *right of trial by jury*, and, therefore subject to a hurried trial, often without the aid of a friend or a counsellor—We hold ourselves bound by the Golden Rule of our Saviour, to aid them, to *do to others as we would have them do to us*. It is therefore,

Resolved, That William Johnston, David Ruggles, Robert Brown, George R. Barker, J. W. Higgins, be appointed a committee to aid the people of color, legally to obtain their rights.

Resolved, That this Committee be authorized to add to their number and to fill vacancies.

Resolved, That three members shall be a quorum at any meeting regularly called.

Resolved, That this meeting commend the Committee to the confidence of the people of color and to the liberality and support of the friends of Human Rights.

ROBERT BROWN, Chairman.

DAVID RUGGLES, Secretary

ANNUAL MEETING OF THE NEW YORK COMMITTEE OF VIGILANCE. —. A public meeting will be held, in aid of the people of Color, tomorrow evening, January 16th, at the Third Presbyterian Church, corner of Thompson and Houston streets, to commence at seven o'clock precisely. The attendance of the public is respectfully invited.

W. JOHNSTON, Chairman of Committee of Arrangements.

We, the Committee appointed by the said meeting, being deeply impressed with the important and urgent nature of the duties committed to us, earnestly solicit the aid of the friends of humanity for the accomplishment of the following objects

1. To protect unoffending, defenceless, and endangered persons of color, by securing their rights as far as practicable.

2. By obtaining for them when arrested, under the pretext of being *fugitive slaves*, such protection as the law will afford.

These objects are so continually pressing themselves on the notice of the friends of our colored brethren especially in the City of New York, that we feel compelled by the dictates of humanity, and by the authority or God to exert ourselves in their behalf, and therefore we appeal to you, to *aid* in this work of philanthropy and Christian benevolence.

ROBERT BROWN

WILLIAM JOHNSTON,

DAVID RUGGLES,

GEORGE R. BARKER

J. W. HIGGINS

All communications may be addressed to *DAVID RUGGLES*, Secretary for the Committee, New York.

FIRST ANNUAL REPORT

OF THE

COMMITTEE OF VIGILANCE

FOR THE
PROTECTION OF THE PEOPLE OF COLOR.

The Committee, of Vigilance for the protection of the people of color, feel much pleasure and satisfaction in meeting the friends by whom they were appointed to labor in behalf of the oppressed, and would respectfully submit to them the following report of their efforts during the past year.—Your committee commenced their important labors with mingled feelings of deep responsibility and hope of usefulness, encouraged on the one hand by the cordial approbation of many of their friends, and depressed on the other by the fearful apprehensions of those, who while friendly to the interests of our colored brethren, considered our attempt as not only hazardous, but hopeless. —It is with peculiar pleasure, therefore, your committee meet you on this anniversary of their appointment, especially as none of the evils anticipated by our fearful friends, have been realized, while much has been accomplished which will, we trust, not only prove the necessity of such committees but stimulate our friends to a greater zeal in the prosecution of the good work in which they are engaged.

Before entering into a detail of their operations, your committee beg to present to your mind their views of the nature and extent of the field in which they labor, on which subject they believe much error prevails, even among our abolition friends. We have generally believed that much oppression and injustice was practised against our colored brethren; that they labored under the unholy prejudice induced on the minds of the community by the blighting influence of slavery; that they suffered many privations even as freemen, which have kept them in a state of degradation and poverty; that they have been generally a people robbed and spoiled, and trodden under foot, by those, who not only boast of the possession of liberty, but admit it to be the inherent right of every man, and still more by those who as Christians proclaim themselves the freemen of the Lord—but a more intimate acquaintance with the subject has convinced us that the view generally taken is very far short of the truth: we formerly believed that these evils arose principally from, those who might be considered the base and unprincipled part of society, or men who held public opinion in contempt, or who were so accustomed to the feelings and practices of slave holders, that they could not separate a colored skin from a piece of merchandize: but we have been deceived; we find it difficult to name a class of the community, or a department In life where the colored man is not exposed to oppression, and aggravated evils which ought not to be tolerated in civilized society.

So fully convinced are we of the distressing extent of these evils, we feel assured we might have removed a load of human suffering, the existence of which would scarcely be credited by a superficial observer, had we possessed funds, and agents equal to the work. That colored people were often kidnapped from the free states was generally known—but we have found the practice so extensive that no colored man is safe, be his age or condition in life what it may—by sea and land, in slave states, or in those where colored men are considered free, in all the varied occupations of life, they are exposed to the horrors of slavery. The high prices obtained by slaveholders for their fellow men in the markets of the south, tempt the cupidity of those pests of society, the slave agents, who not only track like the blood hound, the poor fugitive through the states, but drag the freeman to bondage for the price of blood; with all the satanic subtlety of their profession they allure by a thousand false pretences their victims, or by brutal violence force them from all the endearments of their homes, to a life of toll and misery; and may not the oppressed and endangered justly claim your sympathy and your aid? Doubtless they may, and hence the necessity of a committee of vigilance to shield them from the deadly influence of slavery, even in a land of boasted liberty, where perpetual watchfulness, prudence, and firmness is required to protect the peaceful citizen from falling a prey to the ruthless grasp of southern tyranny. One class of colored persons to which the attention of your committee has been directed, and where greater facility of affording relief has existed than in most other cases, is that of slaves brought into the free states by their masters: we find them generally ignorant of the fact, that under certain circumstances, they may claim their freedom: we feel it our duty to inform them of this important fact, and by our aid and counsel give them that assistance which may render them not only free, but useful members of society.

From the pro-slavery spirit pervading, the free states, we find innumerable evils continually springing up to embitter the lot of the colored man they are kept in ignorance, being not only excluded from the higher literary institutions, but not only from most common schools, and thus denied the ennobling advantages of science, all the higher professions are closed against them; they are confined as much as possible to mean and unprofitable employments; they are exposed by their unfavorable condition to many temptations to the commission of offences which those more protected by education or property or public opinion, generally avoid, and then branded even by our judges as dangerous members of society, though truth should have preserved them from such unmerited censure, as the numbers charged in our courts bear a less proportion to the white than their comparative population.

Among other prominent evils, we cannot forbear mentioning one of no ordinary character, the fact that the laws enacted for the protection of the colored people, are continually violated, not only by men in private life, but even by our judges. When the laws of a country are equitably administered, without respect of persons, when men may appeal to the tribunal of Justice with confidence of an impartial hearing, every member of the community feels a satisfactory assurance in the possession of that portion of right which the law has assigned him, even though it be less than other men enjoy; but when courts of law are made the rendezvous of oppression, when those who are appointed to the solemn duty of administering justice, not only pander to the vulgar prejudices of society, but pollute their office by betraying the cause of the oppressed, and turn aside the poor from their right when judges wield the power of law to subvert and destroy the welfare of their fellow men, then indeed the foundation on which the social fabric rests trembles and affords no support to the superstructure. Yet such is the state of some of our courts of law, when the colored man appeals for justice; and hence the necessity of a committee of vigilance by which he may be protected, and who may, if need be, bring to public view, and hold up to the contempt and indignation of every honest and virtuous mind, the delinquencies of such unrighteous judges and here we stand on vantage ground. Every man capable of discerning between right and wrong, can perceive the absolute necessity of preserving the fountains of justice pure for the protection of civilized society. A corrupt judge is held in abhorrence throughout the world, and every one, from a principle of self-preservation, unites in condemning him as a traitor to his country, a man whose memory lives but in the execration of his fellow men.

Your committee have felt it their duty to direct their attention in an especial manner to this important subject, in relation to certain trials in this city, to which they will shortly call your attention. The labors of your committee appear to have had a very beneficial effect on the minds of the colored people generally: every one at all acquainted with the condition and feelings of our colored brethren, will admit, that there existed a listlessness, a feeling of indifference, arising perhaps from several causes, but certainly owing in a great degree to the apparently remote connexion between the exertions of their friends, and the urgent claims of their suffering brethren. While they admired and embraced the principles of the American Anti-Slavery Society, while they perceived their measures to be well calculated to diffuse through the community not only a knowledge of those fundamental principles, which constitute the basis of our civil and religious liberty and social welfare, but to stimulate men to act on those just and holy principles; yet they felt the operations of this committee in an especial manner to interest their hearts, and call forth the energy of their hands; while they felt the pressure of the evil under which they had so long suffered, they felt too that hope deferred maketh the heart sick; they saw their friends snatched from them by the merciless hand of the ruffian or gentleman slave holder; they found the judge a ready agent to stamp the villainy with the seal of law; they found the great mass of society look on, if not with approbation, at least with unconcern; they saw their friendless brother of the South, who dared to escape from the grasp of tyranny, seized as a felon, and chained and driven back to torture and hopeless bondage for life; they heard the cry of millions throughout the States go up to heaven, How long, O Lord, wilt thou not avenge our blood, while their cry excited only the scorn and contempt of their oppressors, and they saw on the side of the oppressor the unrighteous statutes of the land, and the powerful prejudices of society, and the iniquitous practices of the church, and the commercial interests of the world; while but few instances of benevolent exertion appeared to relieve the gloom that surrounded them. While there existed no organized body of men who would stand as a refuge for the oppressed, as a rallying point, a centre of action, they found the assistance too uncertain, and their ultimate success too insecure to engage them in those strenuous exertions so requisite to the attainment of any important object. We all know by experience the powerful effects of sincere friendly co-operation in any enterprise, and especially when the mind has been previously depressed by long continued suffering, this friendly co-operation they needed, and never did a people respond more cheerfully, or more promptly to the call of their friends, than our colored brethren in this important work; they feel it to be emphatically their work: every kind and benevolent feeling of their heart is called into exercise, every principle of humanity and honor, and even of self interest is aroused. No man that loves his brother or feels for his suffering fellowman, would stand aloof from this enterprise of benevolence; but what colored man, who knows the peculiar evils to which his brethren are exposed, will not rejoice to bring to their aid every resource within the range of his influence? and thus indeed we have found them efficient coadjutors. To them we have been principally indebted for funds, in them we find steady and uniform agents, and by their exertions, we trust this work will not only spread extensively in this city, but throughout the states. But while we thus commend the liberality of our colored friends, we must beg all others, and especially the abolitionists, to remember that we need their aid, their counsel and their contributions. We have, through the past year, been laboring not only without the assistance of many of our friends, but in the midst of their fears, and under the additional disadvantage that the subscriptions we need are generally supposed to be in behalf of the Anti-Slavery Society, to which our friends already subscribe. Many do not appear to distinguish between the two operations, but imagine if they subscribe to the one it is sufficient; but in no respect do we derive advantage from such contributions, having no connection with the Anti-Slavery Society, and consequently need funds exclusively for this object; and indeed we may confidently appeal to the advocates of immediate emancipation for their aid, on the ground of mutual co-operation. How can the noble principles of the Anti-Slavery Constitution be more consistently brought into operation, than by the exertions of this committee. How often has the taunt of the enemy been thrown what good do you do for the colored man? you talk of his right to freedom, you condemn the prejudice existing in the minds of men against him, you disturb the tranquillity of the slaveholder, and render the lot of the slave more miserable, by your wild speculations; but what relief do you afford him, and what exertions do you make to alleviate his sufferings? In reply to these vain words, we say as cordial adherents to the principles of immediate emancipation, let him come within the reach of our hand, and he shall rise to liberty and peace, and the light of truth, and the blessings of social life. We wish to bring into operation the principles of the Anti-Slavery Constitution in detail, in every individual case that may come within the sphere of our influence. To effect a mighty revolution, such as the general abolition of slavery, requires agents, and funds, and time, and influence, proportioned to the magnitude of the work; but while we long and labor for the accomplishment of this noble cause, let us not lose sight of the minor evils, which tend in the aggregate to make up that monstrous system of iniquity; let us in every case of oppression and wrong, inflicted on our brethren, prove our sincerity, by alleviating their sufferings, affording them protection, giving them counsel, and thus in our individual spheres of action, prove ourselves practical abolitionists.

Since the commencement of their labors, your committee have directed their attention to the following subjects:

1st The arrival of persons (needing their aid and counsel) from the South and other parts.

2nd The arrival and departure of vessels, suspected as slavers, or having persons on board claimed as slaves, or who were in danger of being kidnapped and sold.

3rd The arrival and proceedings of slave agents and kidnappers.

4th The arrest of persons claimed as fugitive slaves.

5th The abduction of persons by kidnappers.

6th The recovery of persons detained in the South.

7th The recovery of property due to colored people by wills, &c.

In the prosecution of these subjects, your committee have had occasion in several instances to appeal to courts of law, although they have determined to avoid as much as possible that course, being conscious, that they labor under many disadvantages in such appeals, and at the same time fully aware, that they can better secure the welfare of those they wish to aid, by their private exertions.

The persons referred to arriving in New York, may be classed as follows: first, persons brought as domestic slaves; second, persons escaping from the oppressive laws of southern States lately enforced against free people of color; third, persons who may have been slaves, and take refuge in the free states from the horrors of slavery. Those brought as domestics, are often kept a long time as slaves in the free states. It is a very prevalent error that there are no slaves in this state. But your committee have found many instances of persons having estates in the South, who reside here, and keep slaves in defiance of the laws of the states. In the city of New York alone, these slaves must be very numerous, and we find it a common practice to remove them after a residence of several years to the South, and dispose of them as slaves in the markets. These servants are free by the laws of New York; nor do we hesitate to say, that it is the duty, not only of your committee, but of every citizen, to inform them of that fact, and to aid them in securing their freedom. Among this class, your committee have happily been the means of effecting much good; in some cases appealing to the slaveholders, and obtaining regular manumission, and in others obtaining the admission of the master that the servant was free by law; and in all the cases which have come under our care, the accomplishment of our object, the liberty of the slaves, and their ultimate protection and safety.

Of the second class persons, fleeing from the oppressive laws of southern states, we would observe, that multitudes are now driven from the South, not only by the outrage of Lynch committees, but by the operation of the acts, passed in Virginia and some other states, for the expulsion of free people of color. These unfortunate refugees are generally unable to secure the little property they possess, are compelled to flee for safety in haste, and often without free papers. The design and tendency of these inhuman laws is, evidently, not only to secure the peaceful tenure of those who are now in bondage, without the dangerous example of freemen of color in a land of slaves, but also to reduce as many of the free as possible to slavery. Why the oppressive haste with which they are driven out? because they are liable by law to be sold as slaves if they do not escape by a given time, and we have proofs of their being thus sold; and not only so, those who flee are not secure. What means the numerous slave agents prowling over the free states? To find fugitive slaves? Aye, and to find fugitive freemen. These friendless strangers are well known to their ruthless pursuers who drove them out; they know their former place of residence, their circumstances, the names and ages of their family, the time of their removal, and every item necessary to substantiate their claim to them as slaves before our pliant judges; and as these poor people can obtain no trial by jury, can appeal to no higher tribunal, they may fall victims to the cruelty of the slaveholder, by the fiat of a single judge on exparte evidence, a process that could not in common law secure the recovery of a dog. Many cases of this description have come to the knowledge of your committee, but as it is desirable to give a few facts in proof, we will cite a case lately before the public. We refer to the kidnapping of Peter John Lee, of Westchester, by a southern slave agent, aided by several officers of the city of New York. It is true they did not condescend to bring their victim before a judge, fearing probably the production of free papers; but it appears by the account given by his distressed wife, now residing in this city, that they were driven from Northampton, Va., some years ago, by the violence of the slaveholders of that place, who were determined to expel all free colored persons. The following facts go to establish the truth of our assertion, respecting the operation of law and Lynch outrage against the free people of color at the South:

FREE BLACKS AT THE SOUTH. –We are informed by a person from the South, that measures are spoken of there, to expel the free colored population, by the imposition of such heavy taxes upon them, that they will be obliged to remove. Should this policy be adopted, it will operate to the great disadvantage of those who may be driven away by it, and who will be obliged to seek in other States a domicile that will hardly be allowed to them. –*Philad Gazette.*

And in the item which follows, our readers will see the work of extermination is now begun. What are we coming to? Where are these things to end?

REPUBLICANISM. –A public meeting held in Brinkley's District, Somerset County, Md., on the 2d inst., adopted, among others, the following resolution:

Resolved, That all *free negroes* who shall not leave the said District on or before the 1st day of September next, shall be considered as *insurgents, and as opposed to the good order and well being of the white citizens thereof.*

THE THREAT ABOUT TO BE EXECUTED. –The Cambridge (Md.) Chronicle, of August 27, referring to the meeting at which the above resolution was passed says:

We noticed the meeting at the time; but supposing it owed its origin to an excitement resulting a from an exaggerated view of things, thought to hear no more of it. We were mistaken, however it is the subject of an advertisement in Tuesday's Village Herald, setting forth that the resolutions adopted at the meeting will be carried into effect that the free negroes remaining in the district will be expelled. Both the tone and the style of the advertisement seem somewhat calculated to excite surprise. We certainly did not expect such an emanation from any part of Somerset, knowing the deferential regard she has uniformly paid to the laws; and we would be slow to believe that the publication in question, which concludes in the following exceptionable manner, could receive the sanction of any considerable number of citizens.

"Judge Lynch will be in the district on the last day of this month (August) in order to commence his judicial services–we trust his associates will not be far behind him, as we presume his Judgeship will be crowded with business: we sincerely wish, however, that the free negroes (poor human Creatures!) will not trust their cause to the venerable Judge, but make their escape before he, arrives; for he will be compelled to do his duty, notwithstanding any law, custom, or usage heretofore practised in any of the courts of this state to the contrary."

THE EFFECTS OF SLAVERY ON THE FREE COLORED PEOPLE OF THE SOUTH. – Mary Morgan, of No. 59 *King street, New York, widow* of James Morgan, who died in the spring of 1834, with the small pox, says that she and her husband owned a farm of 250 acres of land in Pasquotank County, about five or six miles from Elizabeth City, North Carolina; that they had hogs, cattle, and horses, and were well to live; that they were both born free, as were both their parents; that as many as six or seven years ago [before they had been provoked to it by northern abolition] a number of the lower class of the whites went about the country to disturb the free colored people; that they frequently came into their dwelling, broke their table, and cups, and saucers, and beat James Morgan a number of times, sometimes with a club, at other times with a cowhide, and at one time so severely that his life was despaired of.

Some of the better class of whites called at the house, and said they thought he was so badly hurt he could not live. For a fortnight after, he was not able to cut a stick of wood. Seven places on his head were shaved to put on plasters, and his back and legs were also much bruised. So frequently were they attacked, that they had to leave their dwelling more than *one hundred* times, often in showers of rain. At one time, Mary was put on horseback, behind one of the ruffians, who rode off violently for about a mile, took her off, and placed her in a mud puddle up to her waist, in a dark night, and there left her to get out as she could. These things happened so frequently that the Friends, Commonly called Quakers, (who were really friends to them,) advised them to sell their property and come to the North. Those who caused them to suffer, gave no other reason for their conduct, than that they were free negroes, and ought to go to the North, and that there was no law for free negroes in Carolina. Joseph Elliott, Thomas Elliott, and Aaron Elliott, of the society of Friends, were their near neighbors, and were often very kind to them, and did their best to prevent the abuse. Miles White, a merchant of Elizabeth city, knows this statement to be true; other free colored people of that neighborhood suffered pretty much in the same way. They came to New-York, where her husband was taken sick, and died; Mary and the children were taken to the Almshouse, where they staid about seven weeks, and were then turned out, penniless, and had it not been for the charity of some humane persons, they might have perished from want.

The farm in Carolina was sold for the small sum of $350, which was soon eaten up by the expense of coming to New York, and the maintenance of the family while here.

Mary Morgan has to support, by *day's* works, five small children. The friends of the oppressed, who have any sympathy to spare, will do well to render her some assistance–at least, by furnishing her with work. *No. 59* King-street is her residence.

Of the third class, those who escape from slavery, we have had numerous instances. As the individuals we refer to had not been claimed or proven slaves by legal process, we have felt it our duty to aid them, by securing them the means of support by their own industry, and thus rendering themselves useful members of society. And here we would take an opportunity to express our decided approbation of that feeling so generally prevalent in the free states; a feeling of disgust at the inhumanity of those who would send back the fugitive slave to the chains and scourgings of the task-master. There are few men so hardened against the claims of our common humanity, so utterly lost to the sympathy of nature, as to aid the slave agent in his work of blood. It requires those extraordinary samples of human depravity, which have lately disgraced our city, as police officers and judges, to accomplish such deeds, at which the mind naturally revolts. We find few men, even among those who would tolerate slavery, so destitute of feeling as to justify such acts, much less to aid in the perpetration of them.

• • •

The following account of the trial of Abraham Goslee, an alleged slave, will illustrate the nature of the justice and impartiality with which the Recorder of New York treats the colored man when charged with the crime of stealing himself:

Important Decision.—The Philadelphia, "Friend," states that a recent trial of a negro man and his family, arrested as fugitive slaves, before the Supreme Court of New Jersey, has resulted in the discharge of the prisoners, and the establishment of some important principles in relation to the arrest of slaves in free States. The trial was a long and deeply interesting one. David Paul Brown, the eminent abolition lawyer of Philadelphian, and Theodore Frelinghuysen, were counsel for the fugitives. 1. Chief Justice Hornblower expressed it as his decided opinion, that the law of Congress regulating the arrest of fugitive slaves is unconstitutional, because no power is given by the Constitution to Congress for legislating on this subject. 2. That every person, white or black, free or slave, was entitled to a trial by jury in New Jersey.— 3. That the color of a person should no longer be considered as a presumptive evidence of slavery in that state. — [Essex Gazette.]

That many vessels arrive in the port of New York, with slaves illegally held, by captains and passengers, is fully established by the experience of your committee. These slaves are quite ignorant of the laws of the United States in their favor, and equally unable to avail themselves of the benefit of these statutes, if apprised of them; some of these slaves are brought direct from the coast of Africa, others from the West Indies, South America, and other foreign ports, and many from the Southern States. The ordinary course adopted by foreign captains and others, is to re-ship them for the South, where they obtain a ready market for them as slaves. In several manifest violations of the laws of the States, your committee have commenced suits in the United States' Courts, but by the influence of pro-slavery sentiments, they have failed in obtaining a verdict against the parties. Some of the more prominent cases are the following: Capt. Shallitoe, against whom a suit is still pending, has, at various times, brought Africans direct from the coast to this country, and held them as slaves. The present prosecution of this individual, by your committee, is for wages and compensation to Quasele, a native of Africa, brought by the Captain to this country, where he held him as a slave till he came under the notice of your committee, being found nearly frozen in the street last winter: this case is confidently expected to terminate in obtaining a remuneration for his services.

About two years ago, a passenger brought a young man from Martinique and held his as a slave in N. York. A few months since, he was about to sail for N. Orleans and ordered the young man to prepare to go with him, but he being fearful that his master intended to sell him, applied to your committee for advice. On learning the facts of this case, they assured him he was free, and immediately took a writ of replevy to recover his clothes, and commenced a suit for his wages, which his master evaded, by secreting himself till the vessel sailed.

The brig Brilliante, now lying in this port, is a renewed proof in point. This vessel according to the testimony of several of the crew, and the evidence of several other persons acquainted with her, here in other ports, is a regular slaver, although of smaller dimensions than usual. She brought slaves on a late trip from Africa to Rio Janeiro, and had on board five native Africans, when she was admitted to an entry port, the laws of the United States expressly prohibiting the introduction of these men; forbidding the vessel an entry, and rendering the captain and owners liable to a penalty and the confiscation of the vessel; your committee commended a process against the captain, and held him to bail for the offence; he was, however, released, after an exparte hearing before judges. The following statement will fully illustrate the case:

THE FOREIGN SLAVE TRADE REVIVED, AND NEW YORK A SLAVE PORT.—
We have now to call the attention of our readers to one of the most atrocious perversions of justice and law, we have ever known. Corrupt as we know our courts to be, especially where the rights and interests of colored men were at issue, we had not supposed them to utterly regardless of law and of right, as they have now proved themselves to be, in the case we are about to detail.

Before entering on this case, however, we deem it important to state the following facts:
1. Within a few months, the St. Nicholas, a suspicious looking vessel, came into this

port. One circumstance after another, soon made it manifest, that she was a slaver. Complaint was lodged, in due form, with Mr. Price, the District Attorney. Process was issued. The evidence was deemed insufficient, and the Captain and vessel were discharged. The vessel obtained her outfit, left the port, colors flying, and in a few weeks was captured, on her return voyage from Africa, *with slaves on board!*

2. Still more recently, the "Brig Governor Temple," came into this port, from the coast of Gambia, with thirteen native Africans on board. Again complaint was made to the District Attorney. He was informed that there was reason to fear they would be smuggled away to the South as slaves; that three of them, on some pretence, had already been sent there, and some action was sought to secure the liberty of the others. The heartless reply was, "Well, if they have gone to the South, that's their misfortune," and *no action was taken!*

3. A gentleman in this city, whose name we are not at liberty to mention, an owner of Texan lands, informed a member of our Executive Committee, a few months since, that another gentleman, in this city also an owner of Texan lands, had, a short time previous, formally proposed to him to invest funds in a ship to go into the slave trade from Africa to Texas, assuring him that an *immense profit would be realized on the investment!*

4. The New Orleans Bulletin of Dec. 10, declares "on high authority, that the Texan government intends entering a formal complaint to the Cabinet at Washington, against the practice, pursued by *American Citizens*, of introducing into their territory, in *vessels belonging to the United States*, negroes, coming from *other quarters* than this Union.

• • •

The efforts made by your committee to recover property due to colored persons, has been the means of developing some of the odious effects of slavery in the free states. We select the two following cases as specimens of the existence of slavery in New York. Mr. Joshua Pell, of New Rochelle, hired from Pumpton, New Jersey, a man named James Trebout, whom he held as a slave four years; he also bought the man's wife for seventy dollars, from his master in New Jersey, and kept her as slave, till the facts came to the knowledge of your committee; we then endeavored to obtain wages for these poor people, but the slave holders had craftily caused them to put their mark to a paper as a receipt in full, specifying some supply of clothing, and small sums of money which prevented the prosecution of a suit against him.

In a more recent case, a slave, now residing in this city, applied to your committee for advice; he stated he belonged to a man at the Ponds, Morris county, New Jersey; his master sold him for ten years for two hundred dollars, to be remitted by monthly installments; his master, after receiving these payments several months, wished to have his money in larger sums, and told the man to meet him at Hoboken and he would get him better employment, to enable him to pay his sooner; he met him accordingly, when he was thrown into prison, and ultimately sold to another man for two hundred dollars; from this man he effected his escape, and now lives in New York, determined to resist the fraudulent claims of his taskmasters. The persons were hired from Jersey to a free state, and were there fore comparatively safe, but in very many instances we find they are sold from New Jersey, to persons travelling to the South, where they become slaves for life. The great extent to which kidnapping and slave dealing is carried on in the state of New Jersey, calls for the prompt and energetic exertions of the friends of abolition. It has been ascertained by your committee that considerable sums of money have been frequently bequeathed to colored persons by their deceased masters: in innumerable instances, they are defrauded of these legacies. Several of these bequests have been discovered by your committee, and information given to the parties necessary for their recovery.

Thus far have we advanced.

The events of the past year should stimulate us to a more earnest pursuit of the objects we have in view. While our gratitude and praise is due to God for the signal interpositions of his providence, we take courage, and confide in divine aid and guidance for the lash, or the endangered freeman fears the sound of the ruffian kidnapper, or the friendless wanderer seeks a shelter and a home, or the widow and orphan need a friend, or the captive prisoner an advocate to plead his cause; while we have hearts to feel or hands to work, the command of our Master shall be our counsellor and guide. "Remember them that are in bonds as being bound with them, and those that adversity as being yourselves also in the body."

14

Henry Highland Garnet

The national conventions African Americans held in the antebellum period offered important opportunities for black leaders to consider the nature of their plight and to debate
strategies and tactics of resistance. They were not without their challenges. Conventions
were public meetings, reported upon by both the black press and white critics. Vigorous
debate threatened to present America the image of a disunited black leadership, which
might feed stereotypes—already rampant in popular media—of African Americans as incapable of acting politically or even properly policing themselves. On the other hand,
debates on the convention floor revealed a wide range of opinion among black leaders,
which was both healthy and completely natural. One of the deepest cleavages to beset a
black national convention arose in Buffalo in 1843, when Henry Highland Garnet, a
young New York clergyman, requested the convention's endorsement of an address calling for enslaved African Americans to demand freedom from their masters. If they were
rebuffed, Garnet demanded that slaves take their freedom, even if it cost them their lives.
Frederick Douglass led the opposition to publishing Garnet's call. The ensuing debate
revealed important tensions in the movement over the proper role of violence in the freedom struggle. It also underscored the significance of pamphleteering—Garnet's address
was *not* published in the official Buffalo minutes for fear it would ignite a rebellion blacks
could not win. It might also provoke a bloody white backlash, some of the Garnet's opponents feared.

Although Garnet would publish his "Address" in 1848 (together with Walker's
"Appeal"), the editors have placed it here for clarity. Garnet (1815–1881) was one of the
most outspoken black leaders of the antebellum era. Like his sometimes tactical adversary
Frederick Douglass, Garnet had escaped bondage in Maryland and became a celebrated
orator and (later) an American diplomat. Unlike Douglass, he encouraged slaves to rebel
and defended black emigration schemes before the Civil War.

Garnet was about ten when his parents staged a daring flight from their master. After
getting a pass to attend a funeral, the Garnets headed north, eventually settling in New
York City. Young Henry grew up in a vibrant community of black activists and was
educated at an abolitionist-sponsored school by African-American teachers. Garnet stud-
ied at Oneida Institute in upstate New York, became the minister of a congregation in
Troy, and worked in the Liberty Party. After leaving America for the Caribbean and
Britain, Garnet returned to the United States and helped recruit black soldiers during the
Civil War. He died just after assuming a post as minister to Liberia.

Many scholars cite Garnet as a standard-bearer of black nationalism—a fierce advocate
of black autonomy and militant action. When William Whipper called for blacks to view
white reformers as brothers-in-arms, Garnet replied, "They are our allies. *Ours* is the
battle!"

Garnet's "Address" in Buffalo exemplified his activist beliefs. Too hot to handle in 1843,
it would become a touchstone for generations of black reformers.

Debate over Garnet's
"Address to the Slaves of the United States
of America"
(1843)

"Mr. Douglas remarked, that there was too much physical force,
both in the address and the remarks of the speaker last up."

[Tuesday August 15th, 1843.]

Afternoon Session.—The Convention met as per adjournment. The President in the chair. Prayer by the Rev. Mr. Davis, of Canada. The Convention united in singing a liberty song.

The roll was then called and the minutes of the previous meeting were read and approved. . . .

The business committee reported, by their chairman, H.H. Garnit, an address to the slaves of this land, prepared for the occasion, which was read and accepted.

C.B. Ray moved its reference to a select committee of five, of which he hoped Mr. Garnit, whose production the address was, would be the chairman. Mr. Ray remarked, that his object in moving its reference to a committee was, that it might pass through a close and critical examination, and perceiving some points in it that might in print appear objectionable, to have it somewhat modified, and also that it might proceed forth from a special committee, of which the author should be the chairman, and thus receive the usual credit due to chairmen of committees presenting documents to public bodies.

H.H. Garnit arose to oppose the motion of reference, and anticipating more than was contemplated by the mover, and fearing the fate of the address, if the motion prevailed, proceeded to give his reasons why the motion should not prevail, and why the address should be adopted by the Convention, and sent out with its sanction; in doing which Mr. Garnit went into the whole merits of the case. He reviewed the abominable system of slavery, showed its mighty workings, its deeds of darkness and death—how it robbed parents of children, and children of parents, husbands of wives; how it porstituted the daughters of the slaves; how it murdered the colored man. He referred to the fate of Denmark Vesey and his accomplices—of Nat Turner; to the burning of McIntosh, to the case of Madison Washington, as well as to many other cases—to what had been done to move the slaveholders to let go their grasp, and asked what more could be done—if we have not waited long enough—if it were not time to speak louder and longer—to take higher ground and other steps. Mr. Garnit, in this speech occupied nearly an hour and a half, the rule having been suspended to allow him to proceed. It was a masterly effort, and the whole Convention, full as it was, was literally infused with tears. Mr. Garnit concluded amidst great applause.

Frederic Douglass, not concurring with certain points in the address, nor with the sentiments advanced by Mr. Garnit, arose to advocate its reference to the committee, and also to reply to Mr. Garnit. Mr. Douglass remarked, that there was too much physical force, both in the address and the remarks of the speaker last up. He was for trying the moral means a little longer; that the address, could it reach the slaves, and the advice, either of the address or the gentleman, be followed, while it might not lead the slaves to rise in insurrection for liberty, would, nevertheless, and necessarily be the occasion of an insurrection; and that was what he wished in no way to have an agency in bringing about, and what we were called upon to avoid; and therefore, he hoped the motion to refer would prevail.

Mr. Garnit arose to reply, and said that the most address said in sentiment, with what the gentleman excepted to, was, that it advised the slaves to go to their masters and tell them they wanted their liberty, and had come to ask for it; and if the master refused it, to tell them, then we shall take it, let the consequence be what it may.

Mr. Douglass said, that would lead to an insurrection, and we were called upon to avoid such a catastrophy. He wanted emancipation in a better way, as he expected to have it.

The question of reference was further discussed by James N. Gloucester, taking the same view of the case with Mr. Douglass; and by Wm. C. Munro, who opposed its reference, concurring fully in the views expressed by Mr. Garnit.

The hour for adjournment, as fixed upon by the rules, having come, the Convention adjourned to meet at 9 o'clock Thursday morning.

Thursday August, 17th, 1843.

Morning Session.—The Convention met pursuant to adjournment—the President in the chair—prayer by the Rev. James Sharpe of Rochester, N.Y. The members then united in singing a liberty song—the roll of the Convention was called—the minutes of the previous meeting were read and approved.

The address to the slaves and its reference, being the subject of discussion at the hour of adjournment, the discussion was resumed, and Mr. Sharpe of Rochester, having obtained the floor, proceeded to speak in opposition to the address—the discussion under the motion having taken this wide range, Mr. Sharpe having occupied the time prescribed by the rules, asked for a suspension of them to allow him to proceed—the rules were not suspended. E.B. Dunlap of Niagara, rose to reply to Mr. Sharpe, but from the ground he took in the debate was pronounced out of order. C.B. Ray having obtained the floor, pressed his motion of reference, giving his reasons for so doing. The question was called for and put, and the motion prevailed by a large majority. The chair announced the following as the committee on the address. H.H.Garnit, chairman, F.Douglas, A.M. Sumner, S.N. Davis, and R. Banks. . . .

[Friday, August 18th, 1843.]

On motion of Mr. A. M. Sumner, it was Resolved, That the order of the day be suspended that we may proceed to consider the address to the slaves, and the resolution attached. Mr. Sumner proceeded to oppose the address. He remarked that the adoption of that address by the Convention would be fatal to the safety of the free people of color of the slave States, but especially so to those who lived on the borders of the free States; and living in Cincinnati as he did he thought he was fully prepared to anticipate very properly what might be the result thereabouts, and he felt bound on behalf of himself and his constituents, to oppose its passage. Mr. Sumner said, that we of Cincinnati were prepared to meet any thing that may come upon us unprovoked, but we were not ready injudiciously to provoke difficulty; he entreated the Convention to pause before they adopted the address.

Mr. Munro moved that no person who had before spoken on this subject, be permitted to speak more than ten minutes—it was carried.

Messrs. Watson of Cincinnati, and Jenkins of Columbus, O., and Malvin of Cleceland, O., took the same view of the question with Mr. Sumner. The subject was futher opposed by Messrs. Outley of Lockport, N.Y., Remond of Salem, Mass., and Brown of Buffalo. The subject was advocated by Messrs. Johnson of Rochester, and Lewis of Toledo O.; they concurred with Mr. Garnit, and thought it was time to speak the sentiments of this address.

Mr. Garnit then rose and spoke at length, he being allowed by vote an additional ten minutes, urging the adoption of this address. He took much the same view of the subject that he had before taken, excepting that he reviewed the objections of the brethren who thought it would be fatal to the free people of the slave states and to those also on the borders of the free states.

C.B. Ray, chairman of the committee to whom had been referred the subject of the Press, announced on behalf of the committee, that they were ready to report—the report was accepted and laid on the table to be called up at the next session. The hour for adjournment having arrived, the Convention adjourned.

Afternoon Session.—The Convention must pursuant to adjournment-the president in the chair—prayer by the Rev. Mr. Watson of O. The members united in singing a liberty song. The roll of the Convention was called—the minutes of the previous meeting were read and approved.

The committee to whom had been referred the subject of the Mechanic Arts, reported by their chairman Robert Banks—the report was accepted and on motion adopted. For the report see page 26.

The address to the slaves now being the order of the day, Frederic Douglass rose and made some forcible remarks against its adoption. Mr. Townsend of Albany, moved that the question upon the address be now taken—it was carried. Mr. Remond moved that the question be taken by the yeas and nays—carried. Mr. Remond moved that the question be taken was lost by the following vote. *Yeas*—Theo. S. Wright, J.H. Townsend, W.P. McIntire, H.H.Garnit, John Wandall, T. Woodson, James Fountain, Jason Jeffrey, H.W. Johnson, A. Peek, R.H. Johnson, S. Talbot, E.B. Dunlap, U.Lett, D.Lewis, W.C. Munro, R. Banks, R. Allen—18. *Nays*—C.Lennox Remond, F. Douglass, James Sharpe, J.P. Morris, R. Francis, W. Johnson, A. Outley, J.F. Platt, G. Weir, W.W. Brown, S.H. Davis, A.M. Sumner, W. Watson, W.H. Yancy, D. Jenkins, G.W. Tucker, H. Jackson, N.W. Jones, Joseph Roxbury—19.

"Address to the Slaves of the United States"
(1848)

Brethren and Fellow Citizens:—Your brethren of the North, East, and West have been accustomed to meet together in National Conventions, to sympathize with each other, and to weep over your unhappy condition. In these meetings we have addressed all classes of the free, but we have never, until this time, sent a word of consolation and advice to you. We have been contented in sitting still and mourning over your sorrows, earnestly hoping that before this day your sacred liberty would have been restored. But, we have hoped in vain. Years have rolled on, and tens of thousands have been borne on streams of blood and tears, to the shores of eternity. While you have been oppressed, we have also been partakers with you; nor can we be free while you are enslaved. We, therefore, write to you as being bound with you.

Many of you are bound to us, not only by the ties of a common humanity, but we are connected by the more tender relations of parents, wives, husbands, children, brothers, and sisters, and friends. As such we most affectionately address you.

Slavery has fixed a deep gulf between you and us, and while it shuts out from you the relief and consolation which your friends would willingly render, it affects and persecutes you with a fierceness which we might not expect to see in the fiends of hell. But still the Almighty Father of mercies has left to us a glimmering ray of hope, which shines out like a lone star in a cloudy sky. Mankind are becoming wiser, and better—the oppressor's power is fading, and you, every day, are becoming better informed, and more numerous. Your grievances, brethren, are many. We shall not attempt, in this short address, to present to the world all the dark catalogue of this nation's sins, which have been committed upon an innocent people. Nor is it indeed necessary, for you feel, them from day to day, and all the civilized world look upon them with amazement.

Two hundred and twenty-seven years ago, the first of our injured race were brought to the shores of America. They came not with glad spirits to select their homes in the New World. They came not with their own consent, to find an unmolested enjoyment of the blessings of this fruitful soil. The first dealings they had with men calling themselves Christians, exhibited to them the worst features of corrupt and sordid hearts; and convinced them that no cruelty is too great, no villainy and no robbery too abhorrent for even enlightened men to perform, when influenced by avarice and lust. Neither did they come flying upon the wings of Liberty, to a land of freedom. But they came with broken hearts, from their beloved native land, and were doomed to unrequited toil and deep degradation. Nor did the evil of their bondage end at their emancipation by death. Succeeding generations inherited their chains, and millions have come from eternity into time, and have returned again to the world of spirits, cursed and ruined by American slavery.

The propagators of the system, or their immediate ancestors, very soon discovered its growing evil, and its tremendous wickedness, and secret promises were made to destroy it. The gross inconsistency of a people holding slaves, who had themselves "ferried o'er the wave" for freedom's sake, was too apparent to be entirely overlooked. The voice of Freedom cried, "Emancipate yourselves." Humanity supplicated with tears for the deliverance of the children of Africa. Wisdom urged her solemn plea. The bleeding captive plead his innocence, and pointed to Christianity who stood weeping at the cross. Jehovah frowned upon the nefarious institution, and thunderbolts, red with vengeance, struggled to leap forth to blast the guilty wretches who maintained it. But all was in vain. Slavery had stretched its dark wings of death over the land, the Church stood silently by—the priests prophesied falsely, and the people loved to have it so. Its throne is established, and now it reigns triumphant.

Nearly three millions of your fellow-citizens are prohibited by law and public opinion, (which in this country is stronger than law,) from reading the Book of Life. Your intellect has been destroyed as much as possible, and every ray of light they have attempted to shut out from your minds. The oppressors themselves have become involved in the ruin. They have become weak, sensual, and rapacious-they have cursed you—they have cursed themselves—they have cursed the earth which they have trod.

The colonists threw the blame upon England. They said that the mother country entailed the evil upon them, and that they would rid themselves of it if they could. The world thought they were sincere, and the philanthropic pitied them. But time soon tested their sincerity.

In a few years the colonists grew strong, and severed themselves from the British Government. Their independence was declared, and they took their station among the sovereign powers .of the earth. The declaration was a glorious document. Sages admired it, and the patriotic of every nation reverenced the God-like sentiments which it contained. When the power of Government returned to their hands, did they emancipate the slaves? No; they rather added new links to our chains. Were they ignorant of the principles of Liberty? Certainly they were not. The sentiments of their revolutionary orators fell in burning eloquence upon their hearts, and with one voice they cried, Liberty or Death. Oh what a sentence was that! It ran from soul to soul like electric fire, and nerved the arm of thousands to fight in the holy cause of Freedom. Among the diversity of opinions that are entertained in regard to physical resistance, there are but a few found to gainsay that stern declaration. We are among those who do not. Slavery! How much misery is comprehended in that single word. What mind is there that does not shrink from its direful effects? Unless the image of God be obliterated from the soul, all men cherish the love of Liberty. The nice discerning political economist does not regard the sacred right more than the untutored African who roams in the wilds of Congo. Nor has the one more right to the full enjoyment of his freedom than the other. In every man's mind the good seeds of liberty are planted, and he who brings his fellow down so low, as to make him contented with a condition of slavery, commits the highest crime against God and man. Brethren, your oppressors aim to do this. They endeavor to make you as much like brutes as possible. When they have blinded the eyes of your mind—when they have embittered the sweet waters of life—then, and not till then, has American slavery done its perfect work.

TO SUCH DEGRADATION IT IS SINFUL IN THE EXTREME FOR YOU TO MAKE VOLUNTARY SUBMISSION. The divine commandments you are in duty bound to reverence and obey. If you do not obey them, you will surely meet with the displeasure of the Almighty. He requires you to love him supremely, and your neighbor as yourself—to keep the Sabbath day holy—to search the Scriptures—and bring up your children with respect for his laws, and to worship no other God but him. But slavery sets all these at nought, and hurls defiance in the face of Jehovah. The forlorn condition in which you are placed, does not destroy your moral obligation to God. You are not certain of heaven, because you suffer yourselves to remain in a state of slavery, where you cannot obey the command-ments of the Sovereign of the universe. If the ignorance of slavery is a passport to heaven, then it is a blessing, and no curse, and you should rather desire its perpetuity than its abolition. God will not receive slavery, nor ignorance, nor any other state of mind, for love and obedience to him. Your condition does not absolve you from your moral obligation. The diabolical injustice by which your liberties are cloven down, NEITHER GOD, NOR ANGELS, OR JUST MEN, COMMAND YOU TO SUFFER FOR A SINGLE MOMENT. THEREFORE IT IS YOUR SOLEMN AND IMPERATIVE DUTY TO USE EVERY MEANS, BOTH MORAL, INTELLECTUAL, AND PHYSICAL THAT PROMISES SUCCESS. If a band of heathen men should attempt to enslave a race of Christians, and to place their children under the influence of some false religion, surely Heaven would frown upon the men who would not resist such aggression, even to death. If, on the other hand, a band of Christians should attempt to enslave a race of heathen men, and to entail slavery upon them, and to keep them in heathenism in the midst of Christianity, the God of heaven would smile upon every effort which the injured might make to disenthral themselves.

Brethren, it is as wrong for your lordly oppressors to keep you in slavery, as it was for the man thief to steal our ancestors from the coast of Africa. You should therefore now use the same manner of resistance, as would have been just in our ancestors when the bloody foot-prints of the first remorseless soul-thief was placed upon the shores of our fatherland. The humblest peasant is as free in the sight of God as the proudest monarch that ever swayed a sceptre. Liberty is a spirit sent out from God, and like its great Author, is no respecter of persons.

Brethren, the time has come when you must act for yourselves. It is an old and true saying that, "if hereditary bondmen would be free, they must themselves strike the blow." You can plead your own cause, and do the work of emancipation better than any others. The nations of the world are moving in the great cause of universal freedom, and some of them at least will, ere long, do you justice. The combined powers of Europe have placed their broad seal of disapprobation upon the African slave-trade. But in the slaveholding parts of the United States, the trade is as brisk as ever. They buy and sell you as though you were brute beasts. The North has done much—her opinion of slavery in the abstract is known. But in regard to the South, we adopt the opinion of *the New York Evangelist*— We have advanced so far, that the cause apparently waits for a more effectual door to be thrown open than has been yet. We are about to point out that more effectual door. Look around you, and behold the bosoms of your loving wives heaving with untold agonies! Hear the cries of your poor children! Remember the stripes your fathers bore. Think of the torture and disgrace of your noble mothers. Think of your wretched sisters, loving virtue and purity, as they are driven into concubinage and are exposed to the unbridled lusts of incar-nate devils. Think of the undying glory that hangs around the ancient name of Africa—and forget not that you are native born American citizens, and as such, you are justly entitled to all the rights that are granted to the freest. Think how many tears you have poured out upon the soil which you have cultivated with unrequited toil and enriched with your blood; and then go to your lordly enslavers and tell them plainly, that you *are determined to be free.* Appeal to their sense of justice, and tell them that they have no more right to oppress you, than you have to enslave them. Entreat them to remove the grievous burdens which they have imposed upon you, and to remunerate you for your labor. Promise them renewed diligence in. the cultivation of the soil, if they will render to you an equivalent for your services. Point them to the increase of happiness and prosperity in the British West Indies since the Act of Emancipation.

Tell them in language which they cannot misunderstand, of the exceeding sinfulness of slavery, and of a future judgment, and of the righteous retributions of an indignant God. Inform them that all you desire is FREEDOM, and that nothing else will suffice. Do this, and for ever after cease to toil for the heartless tyrants, who give you no other reward but stripes and abuse. If they then commence the work of death, they, and not you, will be responsible for the consequences. You had better all *die—die immediately*, than live slaves and entail your wretchedness upon your posterity. If you would be free in this generation, here is your only hope. However much you and all of us may desire it, there is not much hope of redemption without the shedding of blood. If you must bleed, let it all come at once—rather *die freemen, than live to be slaves*. It is impossible like the children of Israel, to make a grand exodus from the land of bondage. The Pharaohs are on both sides of the blood-red waters! You cannot move *en masse*, to the dominions of the British Queen—nor can you pass through Florida and overrun Texas, and at last find peace in Mexico. The propagators of American slavery are spending their blood and treasure, that they may plant the black flag in the heart of Mexico and riot in the halls of the Montezumas. In the language of the Rev. Robert Hall, when addressing the volunteers of Bristol, who were rushing forth to repel the invasion of Napoleon, who threatened to lay waste the fair homes of England, "Religion is too much interested in your behalf, not to shed over you her most gracious influences."

You will not be compelled to spend much time in order to become inured to hardships. From the first moment that you breathed the air of heaven, you have been accustomed to nothing else but hardships. The heroes of the American Revolution were never put upon harder fare than a peck of corn and a few herrings per week. You have not become enervated by the luxuries of life. Your sternest energies have been beaten out upon the anvil of severe trial. Slavery has done this, to make you subservient, to its own purposes; but it has done more than this, it has prepared you for any emergency. If you receive good treatment, it is what you could hardly expect; if you meet with pain, sorrow, and even death, these are the common lot of slaves.

Fellow men! Patient sufferers! behold your dearest rights crushed to the earth! See your sons murdered, and your wives, mothers and sisters doomed to prostitution. In the name of the merciful God, and by all that life is worth, let it no longer be a debatable question whether it is better to choose *Liberty or death*.

In 1822, Denmark Veazie [Vesey], of South Carolina, formed a plan for the liberation of his fellow men. In the whole history of human efforts to overthrow slavery, a more complicated and tremendous plan was never formed. He was betrayed by the treachery of his own people, and died a martyr to freedom. Many a brave hero fell, but history, faithful to her high trust, will transcribe his name on the same monument with Moses, Hampden, Tell, Bruce and Wallace, Toussaint L'Ouverture, Lafayette and Washington. That tremendous movement shook the whole empire of slavery. The guilty soul-thieves were overwhelmed with fear. It is a matter of fact, that at that time, and in consequence of the threatened revolution, the slave States talked strongly of emancipation. But they blew but one blast of the trumpet of freedom and then laid it aside. As these men became quiet, the slaveholders ceased to talk about emancipation; and flow behold your condition today! Angels sigh over it, and humanity has long since exhausted her tears in weeping on your account!

The patriotic Nathaniel Turner followed Denmark Veazie [Vesey]. He was goaded to desperation by wrong and injustice. By despotism, his name has been recorded on the list of infamy, and future generations will remember him among the noble and brave.

Next arose the immortal Joseph Cinque, the hero of the *Amistad*. He was a native African, and by the help of God he emancipated a whole ship-load of his fellow men on the high seas. And he now sings of liberty on the sunny hills of Africa and beneath his native palm-trees, where he hears the lion roar and feels himself as free as that king of the forest.

Next arose Madison Washington that bright star of freedom, and took his station in the constellation of true heroism. He was a slave on board the brig *Creole*, of Richmond, bound to New Orleans, that great slave mart, with a hundred and four [sic] others. Nineteen struck for liberty or death. But one life was taken, and the whole were emancipated, and the vessel was carried into Nassau, New Providence.

Noble men! Those who' have fallen in freedom's conflict, their memories will be cherished by the true-hearted and the God-fearing in all future generations; those who are living, their names are surrounded by a halo of glory.

Brethren, arise, arise[Strike for your lives and liberties. Now is the day and the hour. Let every slave throughout the land do this, and the days of slavery are numbered. You cannot be more oppressed than you have been-you cannot suffer greater cruelties than you have already. *Rather die freemen than live to be slaves*. Remember that you are FOUR MILLIONS!

It is in your power so to torment the God-cursed slaveholders that they will be glad to let you go free. If the scale was turned, and black men were the masters and white men the slaves, every destructive agent and element would be employed to lay the oppressor low. Danger and death would hang over their heads day and night. Yes, the tyrants would meet with plagues more terrible than those of Pharaoh. But you are a patient people. You act as though, you were made for the special use of these devils. You act as though your daughters were born to pamper the lusts of your masters and overseers. And worse than all, you tamely submit while your lords tear your wives from your embraces and defile them before your eyes. In the name of God, we ask, are you men? Where is the blood of your fathers? Has it all run out of your veins? Awake, awake; millions of voices are calling you! Your dead fathers speak to you from their graves. Heaven, as with a voice of thunder, calls on you to arise from the dust.

Let your motto be resistance! *resistance!* RESISTANCE! No oppressed people have ever secured their liberty without resistance. What kind of resistance you had better make, you must decide by the circumstances that surround you, and according to the suggestion of expediency. Brethren, adieu! Trust in the living God. Labor for the peace of the human race, and remember that you are FOUR MILLIONS.

15

The National Convention of Colored People

When African-American conventions met, these quasi-political bodies followed standard parliamentary procedure by organizing themselves into various subcommittees, each of which addressed one element of black people's plight in America. Most were not the fact-finding ventures typical of legislative committees. Instead, they served as pulpits from which black activists might bolster various approaches to elevation, or pursue particular arguments against the obstacles confronting black uplift. The committee reports appended to the proceedings of the National Convention of 1847 (meeting in Troy, New York) best exemplify this aspect of the convention tradition. From advocating black control of the press to lauding the virtues of the independent yeoman farmer, committee reports highlighted a variety of approaches to black activism. Often, they became subjects of intense debate on the convention floor. As examples of black activists thoughtfully confronting individual issues, they are without peer.

One agenda item requires explanation. In 1846 white antislavery activist and philanthropist Gerrit Smith offered a portion of his considerable land holdings to African Americans in an effort to encourage black migration from urban to rural areas. Smith hoped that as many as several thousand individuals would be resettled on his upstate New York lands. He began by donating forty acres each to Frederick Douglass, William Wells Brown, and Charles Lenox Remond (of Boston). Because New York limited black suffrage (by requiring African Americans to own a certain amount of land or to have attained $250 in wealth), Smith hoped his plan would be one avenue to attaining black voting rights.

Smith's proposal compelled the Troy convention to think anew of the connections between black and white reform (Gerrit Smith was well respected by many black activists). And it prompted debate on the potential of uplift strategies via agricultural endeavors.

Proceedings of the National Convention
of Colored People

(1847)

"Of the means for the advancement of a people placed as we are,
none are more available than a Press."

REPORT OF THE COMMITTEE ON A NATIONAL PRESS.

The Committee on a "National Press and Printing Establishment for the People of Color" made the following

REPORT,

on the importance and practicability of such an undertaking:

"It being admitted that the Colored People of the United States are pledged, before the world and in the face of Heaven, to struggle manfully for advancement in civil and social life, it is clear that our own efforts must mainly, if not entirely, produce such advancement. And if we are to advance by our own efforts, (under the Divine blessing,) we must use the means which will direct such efforts to a successful issue.

Of the means for the advancement of a people placed as we are, none are more available than a Press. We struggle against opinions. Our warfare lies in the field of thought. Glorious struggle! God-like warfare! In training our soldiers for the field, in marshaling our hosts for the fight, in leading the onset, and through the conflict, we need a Printing Press, because a printing press is the vehicle of thought—is a ruler of opinions.

Among ourselves we need a Press that shall keep us steadily alive to our responsibilities, which shall constantly point out the principles which should guide our conduct and our labors, which shall cheer us from one end of the land to the other, by recording our acts, our sufferings, our temporary defeats and our steadily approaching triumph—or rather the triumph of the glorious truth "Human Equality," whose servants and soldiers we are.

If a Press be not the most powerful means for our elevation, it is the most immediately necessary. Education of the intellect, of the will, and of character, is, doubtless, a powerful, perhaps the most powerful means for our advancement: yet a Press is needed to keep this very fact before the whole people, in order that all may constantly and unitedly labor in this, the right direction. It may be that some other means might seem even more effectual than education; even then a Press will be the more necessary, inasmuch as it will afford a field in which the relative importance of the various means may be discussed and settled in the hearing of the whole people, and to the profit of all.

The first step which will mark our certain advancement as a People, will be our Declaration of Independence from all aid except from God and our own souls. This step can only be taken when the minds of our people are thoroughly convinced of its necessity and importance. And such conviction can only be produced through a Press, which shall show that although we have labored long and earnestly, we have labored in too many directions and with too little concert of action; and that we must, as one man, bend our united efforts in the one right direction in order to advance.

We need a Press also as our Banner on the outer wall, that all who pass by may read why we struggle, how we struggle, and what we struggle for. If we convince the world that we are earnestly and resolutely striving for our own advancement, one half the battle will already be won, because well and rightly begun. Our friends will the more willingly help us; our foes will quail, because they will have lost their best allies—our own inertness, carelessness, strifes and dependence upon others. And there is no way except through a Press—a National Press—that we can tell the world of our position in the path of Human Progress.

Let there be, then, in these United States, a Printing Press, a copious supply of type, a full and complete establishment, wholly controled by colored men; let the thinking writing-man, the compositors, pressman, printers' help, all, all be men of color;—let this establishment be so well endowed as to be beyond the chances of temporary patronage; and then there will be a fixed fact, a rallying point, towards which the strong and the weak amongst us would look with confidence and hope; from which would flow a steady stream of comfort and exhortation to the weary strugglers, and of burning rebuke and overwhelming argument upon those who dare impede our way.

The time was when a great statesman exclaimed, "Give me the song-making of a people and I will rule that people." That time has passed away from our land, wherein the reason of the people must be assaulted and overcome: this can only be done through the Press. We have felt, and bitterly, the weight of odium and malignity wrought upon us by one or two prominent presses in this land: we have felt also the favorable feeling wrought in our behalf by the Anti-Slavery Press. But the amount of the hatred against us has been conventional antipathy, and of the favorable feeling has been human sympathy. Or friends sorrow with us, because, they say are unfortunate! We must batter down those antipathies, we must command something manlier than sympathies. We must command the respect and admiration due men, who, against fearful odds, are struggling steadfastly for their rights. This can only be done through a Press of our own. It is needless to support these views with a glance at what the Press has done for the down-trodden among men; let us rather look forward with the determination of accomplishing, through this engine, an achievement more glorious than any yet accomplished. We lead the forlorn hope of Human Equality, let us tell of its onslaught on the battlements of hate and caste, let us record its triumph in a Press of our own.

In making these remarks, your Committee do not forget or underrate the good service done by the newspapers which have been, or are now, edited and published by our colored bretheren. We are deeply alive to the talent, the energy and perseverance, which these papers manifest on the part of their self-sacrificing conductors. But these papers have been, and are, a matter of serious pecuniary loss to their proprietors; and as the proprietors are always poor men, their papers have been jeoparded, or stopped for the want of capital. The history of *our* newspapers is the strongest argument in favor of the establishment of a Press. These papers abundantly prove that we have all the talent and industry requisite to conduct a paper such as we need; and they prove also, that among 500,000 free people of color no one man is yet set apart with a competence for the purposed of advocating with the pen our cause and the cause of our brethren in chains. It is an imposition upon the noble-minded colored editors, it is a libel upon us as a free and thinking people, that we have hitherto made no effort to establish a Press on a foundation so broad and national that it may support one literary man of color and an office of colored compositors.

The importance and necessity of a National Press, your Committee trust, are abundantly manifest.

The following plan, adopted by the Committee of seven, appointed by the Convention with full power, is in the place of the Propositions proposed by the Committee of three.

1st. There shall be an Executive of eleven persons, to be denominated the Executive Committee on the National Press for the Free Colored People of the United States, viz:

2nd. *Massachusetts*—Leonard Collins, James Mars; *Connecticut*—Amos G. Beman, James W.C. Pennington; *Kentucky*—Andrew Jackson; *New York*—J.McCune Smith, Chas. B. Ray, Alex Crummell; *New Jersey*—E.P.Rogers; *Pennsylvania*—Andrew Purnell, George B. Vachon; of which Committee James McCune Smith, of New York, shall be Chairman, and Amos G. Beman, of Connecticut, Secretary.

3d. The members of this Committee residing in the city of New York shall be a Financial Committee, who shall deposit, in trust for the Executive Committee, in the "New York Seaman's Bank for Savinngs," all the funds received by them from the Agents.

4th. No disposition shall be made of the funds by any less than a two-thirds majority of the whole Committee.

5th. The Committee shall hold stated meetings once in six months, and shall then publish an account of their proceedings, the receipts, and from whom all sums are sent to them by Agents.

6th. The Rev. J.W.C. Pennington, of Connecticut, shall be the Foreign Agent of the National Press; and the Agents shall always be ex-officio members of the Committee.

7th. The remuneration of the Home Agent shall be 20 per cent.; of the Foreign Agent 30 per cent., on collections made.

8th. The meetings of the Committee shall take place in the city of New York.

9th. The Agents shall report and remit to the Committee, at least once a month for the Home, and once in two months for the Foreign Agent.

10th. Member of the Committee, from any two States, may call an extra meeting thereof by giving the Chairman and Secretary thirty days notice.

Respectfully submitted,

J. McCUNE SMITH,
G.B. WILSON
WM. H. TOPP.

REPORT OF THE COMMITTEE ON COMMERCE.

The Committee on Commerce, on meeting to take into consideration the subject assigned them, found in the possession of one of their number a document which seems to them to be so immediately connected with the subject, that they agree to have it read.

By the mysterious providence of God, we find the captivity has dispersed our race far and wide. Long years of darkness, imbecility and slavery, have been our portion. But God hath appointed us unto restoration. For princes shall come out of Egypt, and Ethiopia shall soon stretch forth her hands unto God. We bless and praise Jehovah's name that he ever liveth to carry out his own counsels of judgment and mercy. To this island of Jamaica, he hath been especially gracious. He hath brought to our shores the inestimable boon of Freedom, and opened before us a career of glory that is sufficient to animate and inspire most apathetic and deadened soul. What hath the Eternal here wrought? He hath conferred upon us the blessings of free institutions, and the gift of a country, in the most endearing sense of that term. We are the great body of the people. We have a climate which seems made for us, and we for the climate. Surely, "the lines have fallen unto us in pleasant places, and we have a goodly heritage." The price by which great things may be obtained in our hands, and our only desire is that it may be used wisely and for the best of purposes. But to make our advantages of the best possible avail, we need encouragement and co-operation from our brethren and friends throughout the world. Lend us your prayers and your sympathies, and we *stipulate on our part, that the great experiment which is now in progress for the elevation of our long injured race, shall be thoroughly successful and satisfactory in its results*. It is our blessing, notwithstanding hitherto it has not been in our power to turn it to the best account, that we are surrounded by similar moral and political institutions, and speak a language the same as that spoken by the great body of our brethren in America, and friends in other parts of the world. In this we are afforded great facilities for correspondence. We also possess a goodly number of churches and chapels and schools, such as our present circumstances might be thought to admit of. In these institutions no caste distinctions are tolerated. Our civil and political advancement is, upon the whole, encouraging. In the jury box, in the magistracy, in the municipal corporations and the Legislature, we are rapidly filling our places. But in one respect our progress does not keep pace with our general advancement. In the Commerce of the country we have no proportionate share. Now the relation existing between us and our brethren of North America, is one of mutual sympathy and co-operation in all that pertains to the general welfare of the race, and your co-operation with us, is in nothing more demanded than in *Commercial enterprise*. In this island our people constitute practically the market, and in America abound those commodities which are in the greatest demand amongst us. There is already commercial intercourse, existing to some extent, between the two countries. But in whose hands, whether in America, or on this island, is this important department of national prosperity? In the hands of the friends, or the foes, of the advancement of the African race? Is the influence which it gives, exerted for, or against us? We fear that with few exceptions these interrogaties must be answered in the negative. This state of things ought no longer to continue. Did we possess a body of merchants in America, and a correspondent body in Jamaica, impressed with that indelible type which is the peculiar characteristic of the African race, we cannot mistake the vast amount of good that would be accomplished on all sides. White Americans visiting our ports, and having to transact business, for the most part, with men of our hue, would be found ere long to have acquired more humane and rational views of our race. They would stand rebuked as regards the prejudice and oppression which evil minded men are ever disposed to invoke against us and to inflict upon us.—They would return from our shores with more favorable impressions, and the re-action upon North American slavery would be irresistibly great. Unite the most repulsive of mankind in enlightened commercial intercourse, and their antagonism will be found to lose its edge, and the feelings of civility and politeness succeed to its place.

Commerce is the great lever by which modern Europe has been elevated from a state of barbarism and social degradation, whose parallel is only to be found in the present condition of the African race—to the position which she now so proudly occupies. Commerce ever has been the great means by which the Jews, her ancient people, have been able to preserve their national existence. To Commerce, America owes her present importance, and we, too, if we would acquire any very great influence for good, must join in the march of Commerce. With the means which Commerce supplies, enlightenment can be carried forward, religious and philanthropic institutions sustained, and the natural resources which God has caused to be buried in the bosom of the soil, may be successfully developed, and made to contribute their quota to universal happiness, which is calculated to bind all mankind in one common brotherhood.

To our white Anti-slavery friends, we would convey our deep and abiding sense of the cordial interests which they have manifested in our advancement. We would at the same time express our regret that in their cursory visits among us, they seem to have quite over-looked the absence of commercial engagements among our class. We solicit their co-operation in rendering us at once an intelligent community, and the West Indies shall become the great nursery from which may be obtained those best suited, from their pecu-liar constitution, to carry the blessings of Religion, Agriculture and Commerce to the very heart of Africa. We believe the Niger Expedition to have been perfectly feasible, and failed only from the want of associating with it a sufficient number of intelligent and God-fearing men of the African race. May our Anti-slavery friends then feel the importance of engaging our people, both here and in America, in the pursuit of a healthy and vigorous Commerce. This will give us energy of character, and fit us for embarking in the most arduous enterprises for the rescue of suffering humanity. May God move their hearts to assist us in such a manner as we may best assist ourselves.

To carry out these views we have availed ourselves of the opportunity which is presented in the visit of Mr. Pennington to our island, to organize a society to be called the Jamaica Hamie Association. The object of this Society is to effect a correspondence with our brethren in America, and friends throughout the world. We solicit your hearty concur-rence with us in these measures as we are anxious to engage our race, and friends, universally, in some common effort for the extinction of slavery and the elevation of our people, and engage them in Commerce throughout the wide range of our dispersion; and Agriculture in our fatherland will place within our reach the means of successfully compet-ing with slavery on the one hand, of disarming prejudice on the other, and at the same time of promoting that charitable feeling which everywhere and under all circumstances char-acterize the christian. A movement of this kind would be indeed the harbinger of better times, and a dawn of that glorious day when the lion shall lie down with the lamb, and they shall no more hurt nor harm in all the holy mountain of the Lord.

Committee—EDWARD VICARS, President; PETER CONSTANTINE, George Ennis, Vice Presidents; Peter Jallep, James Millington, Secretaries; George Reily, Trea-surer; Robert Duaney, Teller, &c., c.

Kingston, Jamaica, April 28th, 1846.

Resolved, That we hail with great pleasure the courteous proposal from our brethren in the island of Jamaica to open a friendly correspondence with us.

Resolved, That we cordially respond to the sentiments contained in the address of the Jamaica Hamic Association, believing as we do that a more intimate acquaintance with our brethren in those islands will be a mutual benefit and advantage.

Resolved, That a committee of thirteen be appointed to reply to the address of the Jamaica Hamic Association, and that said committee be instructed to express to our brethren our cordial sympathy and readiness to unite with them in any proper measures for the advancement of our common cause.

Signed—J.W.C. Pennington, Randall D. Kenney, W.C. Nell, P. Harris, Charles Seth.

Resolved, That the committee of West India Correspondence be, and they are hereby, instructed to report their correspondence to the next Annual Convention.

The following committee was appointed by the Convention, in accordance with the recommendation of the Report: *Connecticut*, J.W.C. Pennington, A.G. Beman; *New York*, R. D. Kenney, T. Van Rensselaer, George Hogarth, Peyton Harris, Henry H. Garnet, Nathan Johnson; *Massachusetts*, Moses Jacdson, Wm. C. Nell; *Ohio*, A.M. Sumner; *Michigan*, Robt. Banks; *Nassau*, N.P., Alex. Theuy.

REPORT OF THE COMMITTEE ON AGRICULTURE.

Your committee to whom was referred the subject of Agriculture, regret that they have not had time so fully to consider the subject as its importance demands; they beg leave, however, to submit the following reflections.

By Agriculture, is meant the cultivation and improvement of the soil, with everything intimately connected therewith, such as the cultivation of fruit, the raising of flocks, herds, &c.

This subject is beginning now to take its proper rank among the great questions of the civilized world. More than formerly, it is receiving a portion, at least, of the attention it demands, as well in Europe as in this country, from men in the first conditions of life, both as respects literature and wealth. And well it may, for it was the primitive pursuit of life, the calling of earth's first born ones, the mode of subsistence and happiness prescribed by God himself, therefore the true mode by which to live, the best mode. When God made this earth, he intended to people it with man, as well as to make it the abode of beast. It was, therefore, as necessary to provide some thing, as well as some place, upon which to subsist. God, therefore, who understood the wants of man and beast, and best how to supply them, made the earth of the composition of which it is, that it might yield food for man and food for beast. And when he said, "In the sweat of thy face shalt thou eat bread," he meant, that by man's labor should he eat bread. And it is equally evident, that that labor was to be expended in procuring from the earth a subsistence. Your Committee have made these remarks, from their convictions that an Agricultural life was *the* life intended for man to pursue. If so, then it is among the most happy and honorable of pursuits.

The great aim of the masses of mankind, in this life, is to be placed in easy circumstances, or beyond want, prospective as well as present. Towards this point they bend all their efforts, it is the great absorbing theme that engrosses all their thoughts and attention. Or if to be placed beyond want for the future, as well as the present, be not the absorbing theme with man, then what we shall we eat, or what shall we drink, and wherewithal shall we be clothed, is the question. When man is thus provided for, or has the means by which, in ordinary cases, he is certain thus to be provided for; if he does not regard himself in easy circumstances, all his anxieties and cares for the future, vanish away.

The question now is, what pursuit in life is best adapted to place man in the circumstances in which it is his highest aim to the placed, viz: freedom from undue care and anxiety about the necessaries and comforts of life. Your committee, without hesitation, reply, that the cultivation of the soil, of which man is himself the owner, is the very pursuit best adapted to accomplish this end. For the man who owns his farm and devotes his time to cultivate it, to planting and sowing, to the raising of fruits and flocks and herds, with a congenial sun and refreshing showers, will, after a few months, when cometh the harvest reap, and gather into barns, food for the supply of his own wants and the wants of his beasts. And if, at seed time, he has laid his plans accordingly, he will, in ordinary cases, have something to dispose of to meet such wants, as the products of his farm, directly do not meet. If the earth should yield but sparingly, the producer thereof will have the first supply; if any be in want, it must be him who produces not.

The wants of man, in most cases, are more of the imaginary than real. The imaginary wants, what men would have if they could, occupy the thoughts and the attention, much more than they pain the heart. It is the real wants that cause solicitude, anxieties and pain. Now, the pursuit of Agriculture, will, in all ordinary cases, produce wherewith to meet the real wants of life, and in most cases do even more. In fact, it is the only pursuit in which a man has so many reasons to expect that the reward of his hands will be given him. For harvest, as well as seed time, is sure to come. The liabilities also, to a failure, in this pursuit, are less than in others. The pursuit of Agriculture, then, is the surest road for man to place himself in easy circumstances, or beyond want.

The farmer is an *independent man*; the man of no other pursuit, is so much so. He may do without what men of trade and traffic have to dispose of, and upon the disposal of which, depends their very living; but they cannot do without what he produces. To him they must come for the very things upon which human existence, under God, is absolutely dependent. Without him, they have neither house, home, food, nor clothing. They must have the bread he produces, the cotton, the flax, and the wool he grows. They must have the timber from this forest, the clay from his bed for brick, the sugar from his grove, his beet, or his cane. They must have the silk from the worm he nurses, and the covering for the feet even, from the back of the herds and the flocks he raises. Yea, the very articles in which they trade and traffic, are the fruit of the farmer's toil. If he toil not, then they trade and traffic not. The great staples of the commerce of the world, are either directly or indirectly the products of the farm. Let the farmer cease his toil, or toil only to supply his own wants; let him produce for himself alone, and not for others, and our merchants must close their shops; our ships must lie moored at their respective docks; our manufactories must cease the hum of the spindle, and the loom, and the millions of operatives must scatter themselves whither they will. Our cities, too must become desolate, and the capital of the world of nothing worth. The converse of this, it is true, is the state of the civilized world; but it is because the agriculturalist toils on, producing what he can, and the earth yields sufficiently, through his skill, for him who toils, and for him who toils not. The surplus beyond the wants of the producer is converted into articles of trade, and the merchant buys, sells, ships and gets gain, and commerce and trade flourish.

An agricultural life is productive of moral, mental and physical culture. The farmer levels the forest, shatters and cleaves the rock in sunder, and tills the soil, which God's own hands have made; and when he climbs the mountain, even to the clouds, or enters the forest, or surveys the plain; when his eye glances upon the waving grass and grain, upon the thrifty corn, he sees the order, the variety, the beauty, and the wonders of nature, and must be led to look from nature up to nature's God, to love and admire the wisdom, the goodness, and the power of God, as thus displayed, and be made a better man.

But an agricultural life is evidently the employment designed by God for man; it must be adapted to his whole nature, mental and physical, as well as moral, and conduce therefore to the growth of the mind. An agricultural pursuit is peculiarly adapted to, and promotive or, scientific pursuits. It may very naturally lead to the study of the structure and composition of the various earths, rocks, and minerals, of which the earth is composed, and of the vegetables which she produces. The Agriculturist may then become the better geologist, mineralogist and botanist, because aided in the study of these sciences by the very employment he follows, and that too, without interfering scarcely at all with that employment. It must, then, produce mental culture. And the very nature of the employment calls into exercise the muscles and the physical powers of the body, and must conduce to physical culture and to health.

But an Agricultural life is open to all, and the things that obstruct other modes of life do not obstruct this. And if it be the road to competency, to independence and to easy circumstances, and if, in addition thereto, it is conducive to moral, mental, and physical culture, then ought it to be restored to by our own people. For them all, or nearly all, the other pursuits in life, which lead to easy circumstances, we are deprived, or have not the means to embark therein, to compete with those long skilled in these pursuits and having capital adapted thereto. But we live in a country yet comparatively in its infancy, and most of which is an unbroken wilderness, with a temperate climate, and where land is both cheap and productive. And there is no barrier to the purchase of the soil by our people in any part of the country where it is desirable to seek a home. And if we may not, from the peculiar circumstances in our case, be men of other pursuits, we may become, if we will, Agriculturalists, and be independent and happy. Besides, the farmer's life is adapted to our pecuniary circumstances and condition. To commence a business, in the business part of the country, which would yield, in ordinary cases, a competency, would require a capital much larger than the most of us possess. But a few dollars, comparatively, will purchase a farm sufficiently large to afford a comfortable subsistence, at the outset; will provide the necessary implements of husbandry, and at the same time be the most productive investment that can be made of small sums of money. For every stroke of the ax, every furrow of the plow, and every rod that is cultivated, while it meets the current wants, will be adding improvements and increasing the value of the farm. He may not have money as men in other pursuits have, he does not need it as they do; they are dependent upon their money for the necessaries of life, he has them without money and without price. But though he has not the money they have, the very means by which he lives adds annually to the value of his farm, and he is becoming every year a wealthier man.

An Agricultural life also tends to equality in life. The community is a community of farmers. Their occupations are the same; their hopes and interests the same; they occupy a similar position in society; the one is not above the other, whether of the proscribed or any other class, they are all alike farmers. And as it is by placing men in the same position in society that all castes fade away, all castes in this case will be forgotten, and an equality of rights, interests and privileges only exist. An Agricultural life then is the life for a proscribed class to pursue, because it tends to break down all proscriptions.

Your Committee cannot close these suggestions without referring to the beneficent act of Gerrit Smith, Esq., which has opened the way to our people to the farmer's life. They refer to it also because they wish to urge those possessed of these advantages to use them, as well from the influence it will exert upon others as for the benefit that will result to themselves. You Committee think they see in this beneficent act of Mr. Smith's, a Divine Providence directing our people to this mode of life as well as opening the way to it. They regard this as a God-send, which, like other gifts of God, is not to be slighted, but used and not abused; and which, if used, will give to us a character, a name and a place among the people of earth, useful to ourselves, gratifying to the donor and honorable to God. For here we have put into our hands, without money and without price, the means to place us in independent and happy circumstances. And we believe that the destiny of our people now hangs upon the use to be made of this gift by those to whom it is given, as much as upon any one thing that presents itself to our consideration. That, if this land shall be settled and improved, and the wilderness made to bud and blossom as the rose, as bud and blossom it may, by its now present owners, that they will work for themselves a character and create an influence that shall command the respect for themselves and their brethren, of those who now very little respect us; that will stop the mouths of those who speak slightly of us, and will exert an influence upon our brethren who have not shared in those gifts, to turn their attention to and engage in the pursuit of Agricultural life.

Your Committee, aware that this gift of land by Mr. Smith concerns the people of the State of New York directly, have, nevertheless, referred to it here, with the hope that the Convention will pass the Resolutions in reference to this matter herewith submitted, both to evince our appreciation of those gifts, and to express our high regard for the donor, as well as to exert some influence upon those in possession of these lands to go and cultivate them. We also submit a resolution recommending our people generally to become Agriculturalists, as the life easiest of access to them.

Whereas, GERRIT SMITH, of Peterboro, has made a donation of One Hundred and Forty Thousand acres of land, to Three Thousand Colored Citizens of New York: and,

Whereas, This Convention regards the above donation as a manifestation of love on the part of the donor; a love for God in carrying out the Divine intention to grant to all a share in the means of subsistence and happiness; a love for humanity, in seeking the down-trodden and oppressed among men as the objects of this donation, and a love of human progress in placing in the hands of the oppressed the means of self-elevation; and,

Whereas, The freedom, independence and steadiness of the farmer's life will throw among the colored people elements of character essential to happiness and progress; Therefore,

Resolved, That this Convention do express its deep thanks to Gerrit Smith, of Peterboro, for his splendid donation to the cause of God and humanity.

Resolved, That this Convention do call upon the Grantees of this land to forsake the cities and towns and settle upon this land and cultivate it, and hereby build a tower of strength for themselves.

Resolved, That we recommend to our people, also throughout the country, to forsake the cities and their employments of dependency therein, and emigrate to those parts of the country where land is cheap, and become cultivators of the soil, as the surest road to respectability and influence.

Resolved, That a copy of the preamble and these resolutions that refer to the gift of Mr. Smith, be signed by the President and Secretary of this Convention, and transmitted to him at Peterboro.

All which is respectfully submitted,

CHARLES B. RAY

WILLIS A. HODGES

REPORT OF THE COMMITTEE ON ABOLITION.

The Committee appointed to draft a Report respecting the best means of abolishing Slavery and destroying Caste in the United States, beg leave most respectfully to Report: That they have had the important subjects referred to them, under consideration, and have carefully endeavored to examine all their points and bearings to the best of their ability; and from every view they have been able to take they have arrived at the conclusion that the best means of abolishing slavery is proclamation of truth, and that the best means of destroying caste is the mental, moral and industrial improvement of our people.

First, as respects Slavery. Your Committee find this monstrous crime, this stupendous iniquity, closely interwoven with all the great interests, institutions and organizations of the country; pervading and influencing every class and grade of society, securing their support, obtaining their approbation and commanding their homage. Availing itself of the advantage which age gives to crime, it has perverted the judgment, blunted the moral sense, blasted the sympathies, and created in the great mass, —the overwhelming majority of the people—a moral sentiment altogether favorable to its own character, and its own continuance. Press and pulpit are alike prostituted and made to serve the end of this infernal institution. The power of the government and the sanctity of religion, church and state, are joined with the guilty oppressor against the oppressed—and the voice of this great nation is thundering in the ear of our enslaved fellow countrymen the terrible that, *you shall be slaves or die!* The slave is in the minority, a small minority. The oppressors are an overwhelming majority. The oppressed are three millions, their oppressors are seventeen millions. The one is weak, the other is strong; the one is without arms, without means of concert, and without arms, without means of concert, and without government; the other possess every advantage in these respects; and the deadly din of their million of musketry, and loud-mouthed cannon tells the down-trodden slave in unmistakable language, *he must be a slave or die.* In these circumstances, your committee are called upon to report as to best means of abolishing slavery. And without pretending to discuss all the ways which have been suggested from time to time by various parties and factions, though did time permit, they would gladly do so, they beg at once to state their entire disapprobation of any plan of emancipation involving a resort to bloodshed. With the facts of our condition before us, it is impossible for us to contemplate any appeal to the slave to take vengence on his guilty master, but with the utmost reprobation. Your Committee regard any counsel of this sort as the perfection of folly, suicidal in the extreme, and abominable wicked. We should utterly frown down and wholly discountenance any attempt to lead our people to confide in brute force as a reformatory instrumentality. All argument put forth in favor of insurrection and bloodshed, however well intended, is either the result of an unpardonable impatience or an atheistic want of faith in the power of truth as a means of regenerating and reforming the world. Again we repeat, let us set our faces against all such absurd, unavailing, dangerous and mischievous ravings, emanating from what source they may. The voice of God and of common sense, equally point out a more excellent way, and that way is a faithful earnest, and persevering enforcement of the great principles of justice and morality, religion and humanity. These are the only invincible and infallible means within our reach with which to overthrow this foul system of blood and ruin. Your Committee deem it susceptible of the clearest demonstration, that slavery exists in this country, because the people of this country WILL its existence. And they deem it equally clear, that no system or institution can exist for an hour against the earnestly-expressed WILL of the people. IT were quite easy to bring to the support of the foregoing proposition powerful and conclusive illustrations from the history of reform in all ages, and especially in our own. But the palpable truths of the propositions, as well as the familiarity of the facts illustrating them, entirely obviate such a necessity.

Our age is an age of great discoveries; and one of the greatest is that which revealed that this world is to be ruled, shaped and guided by the *marvelous might of wind.* The human voice must supersede the roar of cannon. Truth alone is the legitimate antidote of falsehood. Liberty is always sufficient to grapple with tyranny. Free speech- -free discussion- -peaceful agitation, —-the foolishness of preaching these, under God, will subvert this giant crime, and send it reeling to its grave, as if smitten by a voice from the throne of God. Slavery exists because it is popular. It will cease to exist when it is made unpopular. Whatever therefore tends to make Slavery unpopular tends to its destruction. This every Slaveholder knows full well, and hence his opposition to all discussion of the subject. It is an evidence of intense feeling of alarm, when John C. Calhoun calls upon the North to put down what he is pleased to term "this plundering agitation." Let us give the Slaveholder what he most dislikes. Let us expose his crimes and his foul abominations. He is reputable and must be made disreputable. He must be regarded as a moral lepor—— shammed as a loathsome wretch—-as enemy of God and man, to be excerated by the community till he shall repent of his foul crimes, and give proof of his sincerity by breaking every chain and letting the oppressed go free. Let us invoke the Press and appeal to the pulpit to deal out the righteous denunciations of heaven against oppression, fraud and wrong, and the desire of our hearts will soon be given us in the triumph of Liberty throughout all the land.

As to the second topic upon which the Committee have been instructed to report, the Committee think the subject worthy of a far wider range of discussion than the limited time at present allotted to them will allow. The importance of the subject, the peculiar position of our people, the variety of interests involved with questions growing out of it, all serve to make this subject one of great complexity as well as solemn interest.

Your Committee would therefore respectfully recommend the appointment of a Committee of one, whose duty it shall be to draft a full Report on this subject, and report at the next National Convention.

Your Committee would further recommend the adoption of the following Resolutions as embodying the sentiments of the foregoing Report:

Resolved, That our only hope for peaceful Emancipation in this land is based on a firm, devoted, and unceasing assertion of our rights, and a full, free and determined exposure of our multiplied wrongs.

Resolved, That, in the language of inspired wisdom, there shall be no peace to the wicked, and that this guilty nation shall have no peace, and that we will do all that we can to *agitate!* AGITATE!! AGITATE!! Till our rights are restored and our Brethren are redeemed from their cruel chains.

All of which is respectfully submitted,

FREDERICK DOUGLASS

ALEXANDER CRUMMELL

JOHN LYLE

THOS. VAN RENSSELAER

Source: Proceedings of the National Convention of Colored People and Their Friends, Held in Troy, N.Y., on the 6th, 7th, 8th, and 9th October, 1847 (Troy, NY: Steam Press of J.C. Kneeland and Co., 1847).

16.

The Colored National Convention of 1848

As the convention movement matured, it increasingly revealed cleavages among African-American activists that had never appeared in earlier conventions. The exchange evident in the proceedings of the Cleveland National Convention of 1848, which are here reprinted in their entirety, demonstrated important differences of opinion among Northern blacks of different social class and community status. One of the tenderest of these concerned the respectability of manual labor. Prominent leaders lambasted their working-class brethren for perpetuating stereotypes of blacks as menial by undertaking low-status employments. Many among the black nonelite reminded them that none *chose* degrading labor and that national leaders ought not forget the struggles of everyday African Americans against a society bent on maintaining their inferiority. Perhaps the presence of these debates indicated growing rifts among leaders and the rank and file within the movement. It is likely, however, that the public airing of contention was possible only within a movement increasingly confident in its own strength and security.

The Cleveland Convention considered a range of other topics, including who blacks should support politically. "Mr. Van Buren" in the minutes refers to the former president Martin Van Buren of New York. In 1848, he became the Free Soil Party's presidential candidate. This new party had recently met in Buffalo, and its platform called for preventing slavery's expansion in the West. But abolitionists wondered about Van Buren—who never had been a friend of their cause. He was Andrew Jackson's vice-president between 1828 and 1836, and Jackson (a Tennessee slaveholder) made clear his disdain of the abolitionist movement. Should free blacks vote for Van Buren where they could (most states still disenfranchised free black citizens) or at least work for the Free Soil cause? Those questions prompted considerable debate in 1848.

One last item of note distinguished the Cleveland meeting: delegates accepted an address from a woman appearing on the convention floor—one of the few speeches by a woman transcribed in any convention's meeting.

"Report of the Proceedings of the Colored National Convention . . . held in Cleveland"

(1848)

*"Resolved, That holding liberty paramount to all earthly considerations,
we pledge ourselves, to resist properly, every attempt to infringe upon our rights."*

REPORT:

The Delegates of the National Convention of Colored Freemen, met in the Court House, Cleveland, O., Wednesday, September 6th, 1848, 10 o'clock, A. M.

On motion of D. Jenkins of Ohio, Abner H. Francis of N. Y., was called to the chair, and William H. Burnham, of Ohio, appointed Secretary.

The enrolling of Delegates was here gone through with, and on motion, a committee of five on organization was appointed by the Chair, viz:—J. Jones, of Ill., F. Douglass, of N. Y., Henry Bibb, of Mich., C. H. Langston and J. L. Watson, of Ohio. The Committee Reported:

> For President,
> Frederick Douglass, of New York.
> For Vice-President,
> J. Jones, of Illinois.
> For Secretary,
> WILLIAM H. DAY, of Ohio.

The report of the Committee was adopted, and the Convention added as Vice Presidents, one from each State represented, viz:—Allen Jones, of Ohio, Thomas Johnson, of Michigan, and Abner H. Francis, of New York.

> For Assistant Secretaries,
> William H. Burnham and Justin Holland, of Ohio.

A Business Committee of seven was then appointed. A point of order was here raised by A. H. Francis, of N. Y., as to the appointing and rejecting gentlemen from the Committee who were not regular delegates, which was settled by passing a resolution, saying, that all colored persons present or who might be present were delegates, and were expected to participate as such.

The Business Committee, consisted of the following persons:—Chairman, M. R. Delany, M. D., of New York; C. H. Langston, and D. Jenkins, Ohio; H. Bibb, and G. W. Tucker, Mich; W. H. Topp, New York, and Thomas Brown, Ohio; and on motion two were added to that Committee, viz:—J. L. Watson, and J. Malvin, of Ohio.

On motion, a Committee on Rules for the government of the Convention was appointed—D. Jenkins, of Ohio, Chairman.

Also, Committee on Finance, G. W. Tucker, of Michigan, Chairman.

The President was conducted to the chair by A. H. Francis, and after an able address from the President and the appointing of the above Committees, the Convention adjourned to 2 1–2 o'clock, P. M.

Wednesday, 2 1–2 o'clock, P. M., Second Session.

The Convention met, President in the Chair. After some remarks of the President as to the requisites to good order, the Business Committee not being ready to report, opportunity was given for a volunteer speech or song. The time not being taken up, the President sang with applause, a liberty song.—Mr. Allen Jones, of Ohio, spoke of the object of the Convention, and followed with a narrative of his slave-life. He said he had earned for his master $10,000, and after he had paid for his liberty, $360, and yet some people would say he was "not able to take care of himself."

The Committee on Rules here reported, and after the discussion of the proposed amendment, the Report as a whole was adopted. Messrs. Cox and Day, were here called out to sing a Liberty song.

F. Douglass then offered the following resolution:—That this Convention commends the conduct of Capt. Sayres and Mr. Dayton, in their noble attempt to rescue from cruel bondage 76 of our brethren in the Capital of this Republic, and that atrocious imprisonment. F. Douglass made a few remarks in its support. A. H. Francis, of N. Y., made a few remarks on an article in the "Cleveland Plaindealer," abusive of Bibb and the Buffalo Convention, asserting that the article was false in fact and cringing to prejudice in principle. Henry Lott supported the resolution. Frederick Douglass followed, speaking of the principle involved, namely, the morality of running away. After remarks in accordance with the invitation of the President by Messrs. Patterson, Fitzgerald, Lewis, J. M. Langston, Wastson, of Oberlin, and Jones, of Ill., the Business Committee reported a portion of the Declaration of Principles. [See Resolutions 1, 5.]

The Pledge to sustain, was changed in its position so as to come after the Resolutions, and the Preamble laid on the table for the purpose of first considering the Resolutions, of which the 1st was passed. The 2nd was taken up and earnestly sustained by Dr. Delaney. W. H. Day, here obtained the floor, when the President announced that the hour of adjournment had arrived, whereupon the Convention adjourned.

A crowded public meeting was held in the evening at the Court House. The exercises were conducted by Messrs. Douglass, Bibb, and Delany, and the enthusiastic cheering showed how well the sentiments were received.

Thursday, 9 o'clock, A. M. Third Session.

Convention was called to order by the President. Prayer by the Rev. John Lyle of N. Y.

The names of the Delegates not present and who had not been present in person but by credentials, were on motion struck out from the Roll. The minutes of the previous Session were then approved.

William H. Day having the floor, offered an amendment to the 2nd Resolution, namely, to insert the words, "and professional"—which amendment was adopted.

J. D. Patterson, here obtained the floor to object to some expressions used by M. R. Delany in discussing the 2nd, Resolution. He argued that those who were in the editorial chair and others, not in places of servants, must not cast slurs upon those, who were in such places from necessity. He said, we know our position and feel it; but when he heard the Doctor say, that he would rather receive a telegraphic despatch that his wife and two children had fallen victims to a loathsome disease, than to hear that they had become the servants of any man, he thought that he must speak.

Dr. Delany replied: He meant not, nor did the Resolution mean to cast a slur upon any individual, and presenting in a strong light the Resolution and its reasonableness, closed with a hope, that his brother (Patterson,) had been convinced, as he took him to be a minister, or student for the ministry—and ministers exert great influence.

John L. Watson, of Cleveland, O., remarked that we were aiming at the same thing, but he had a different way of getting at it. He understood Dr. Delany, as having, the day before, said, that if we became the boot-blacks, the white mechanics would look down on us, but if we became mechanics, etc., they would respect us. To this he took exceptions.

The President suggested that the discussion had taken a desultory turn, and that it would be best to keep to the question.

After remarks by several gentlemen, D. Jenkins moved the previous question, was sustained, and the 2nd Resolution adopted. The 3rd Resolution adopted also.

The 4th Resolution was read, and J. L. Watson remarked upon it. A. H. Francis, of N. Y., heartily supported the Resolution. He might, he said, relate an experience. He had been in nearly all the avocations named in the Resolution; he had been waiter, etc., and he had been in a mercantile business of $20,000 or $30,000 a year, and was in mercantile business now. He felt that we ought to take a stand in favor of the Resolutions.

David Jenkins, of Ohio, was in favor of the Resolution.—He was a painter in the city of Columbus, and although, when first he went there he was not employed by others, he went to work and employed himself, and was there yet. He had succeeded in obtaining contracts from the State and County in which he resides.

Frederick Douglass took the floor. He thought that as far as speakers intimated that any useful labor was degrading, they were wrong. He would suggest a Resolution so as to suit both parties, which he though might be done. He had been a chimney-sweep, and was probably the first that had ever made the announcement from the public stand. He had been a wood-sawyer. He wished not that it should stand thus:—White Lawyer—Black Chimney-sweep; but White Lawyer, Black Lawyer, as in Massachusetts; White Domestic, Black Domestic. He said: Let us say what is necessary to be done, is honorable to do; and leave situations in which we are considered degraded, as soon as necessity ceases.

He was followed by several gentlemen, when Messrs. Patterson, Copeland, and Douglass, severally proposed amendments, which were on motion rejected.

The 4th Resolution was adopted with but one dissenting vote.

The Business Committee reported the remainder of the Declaration of Principles. [See Resolutions 6, 10.] The 5th Resolution unanimously adopted.

The 6th Resolution was referred to a Committee of five—Henry Bibb, Chairman. The 7th Resolution was adopted. The 8th Resolution was under discussion when the Convention's hours of adjournment arrived.

Thursday, 2 1–2 o'clock P. M. Fourth Session.

Convention met, President Douglass in the Chair. Prayer by J. D. Patterson. Report of morning session read, corrected and approved, and Convention resumed the consideration of the 8th Resolution.

William H. Topp, of N. Y., was opposed to this Resolution passing, for the reason, first, that he wished to do nothing that would commit himself against the Buffalo nomination, for he intended to give his support and influence to Mr. Van Buren, but all who voted in favor of the Resolution would, to be consistent, be compelled to oppose the Buffalo nominees.

Henry Bibb defended the entire equality position of the Buffalo Convention. J. D. Patterson agreed with Mr. Bibb.

Mr. Day, of Ohio, rose to a point of order, as to the propriety of discussing the merits of the Buffalo Platform, under this Resolution.

The President decided that strictly the point of order would obtain, but as he supposed gentlemen to be giving reasons for not supporting the Resolution, as they were in favor of the Van Buren Platform, he thought they might proceed. Mr. Patterson proceeded, and was soon called to order by the President for not speaking to the Resolution under consideration.

While this was pending, and after earnest remarks by various gentlemen, the Business Committee presented Resolutions 13–23 for the consideration of the Convention.

Resolution No. 8 was then adopted; Nos. 9 and 10 adopted.

A Committee of five was here appointed to prepare an Address to the Colored People of the United States—that Committee to report to this Convention.

Eleventh resolution taken up and adopted. F. Douglass was appointed to the Committee to carry out the spirit of the 11th resolution. Resolution No. 21, with reference to time of final adjournment, was on motion here taken up and adopted.

Twelfth resolution taken up, and after earnest remarks in its favor, adopted.

The 13th Resolution, referring to the Buffalo nominations, was on motion laid over till morning. 14th adopted. Resolution 15th was read, and the word "necessary" was substituted for the word "justifiable," and the Resolution as amended was adopted; when the Convention adjourned.

Thursday evening, the Public Meeting was held in the Tabernacle, which was more than filled at an early hour; and when at the close the audience joined in singing "Come join the Abolitionists," and sent up three hearty cheers for "Liberty—Equality—Fraternity," the slaveocrat must have trembled.

Friday, 9 o'clock A. M. Fifth Session.

Convention was called to order by Vice-President Jones, of Illinois. Prayer by Rev. Mr. Kenyon, of Cleveland.

The 13th Resolution was then taken up. Messrs. Francis, of N. Y., Brown and Jenkins, of Ohio, and Lightfoot, of Mich., spoke in its favor. C. H. Langston thought the 8th and 13th Resolutions conflicted, and was opposed to this Convention's saying that the Buffalo Convention had for its object entire equality. He was in favor of the new movement, but would not be so inconsistent as to pass this while the other was on the records. The 13th, on motion, was laid on the table, for the sake of rescinding the 8th. The 8th was rescinded, and the 13th again taken up. After remarks by many gentlemen, the Committee on the Address reported that they had met, and each had proposed a written abstract of what such an address should be, and that the Committee had appointed one of their number from the various abstracts to put together an address. F. Douglass here read the substance of the different abstracts, that the Convention might know the substance of the address. The action of the Committee was approved.

M. R. Delany here proposed a substitute for the 8th Resolution, as follows:

> Resolved, That we recommend to our brethren throughout the several States, to support such persons and parties alone as have a tendency to enhance the liberty of the colored people of the United States.

This substitute was adopted, and on motion the 13th Resolution was adopted also.

William H. Day, Frederick Douglass, John Lyle, Sabram Cox, Richard Copeland, and W. B. Depp, asked permission to enter their dissent from the vote endorsing the 13th Resolution on the minutes.

The 14th resolution was so amended as to read, "to obtain their liberty," instead of the words, "effecting their escape," as it was thought that the slave *might* need to use some other means for liberty than running away.

Resolution 16 adopted. The 17th Resolution was read, when F. Douglass took the floor in opposition to the preamble, inasmuch as it intimated that slavery could not be abolished by moral means alone. Henry Bibb sustained the preamble and resolutions at length. Frederick Douglass replied.

J. Jones, of Ill., here proposed an amendment to the preamble, as follows:

whereas, American slavery is politically, as well as morally, an evil of which this country stands guilty; and whereas, the two great political parties of the Union have, by their acts and nominations, betrayed the sacred cause of human freedom; and "whereas a Convention," etc., which was accepted, and the preamble, as amended, prefixed to the 13th Resolution.

The Secretaries were instructed to prepare a synopsis of the proceedings of the Convention, and forward it to Mr. Harris, Editor of the Cleveland Herald, and to the Editors of the North Star, as they had said they would be happy to publish them free of charge. H. G. Turner, editor of the Cleveland True Democrat made a similar proposal.

It was also resolved to print 500 copies of the proceedings in pamphlet form, and the Secretaries were appointed a Committee of publication.

Convention then adjourned.

Friday, P. M., 2 1–2 o'clock. Sixth Session.

Convention assembled. Vice-President Jones in the Chair.

Prayer by Rev. William Ruth, of Colchester, C. W.

The 11th Rule was suspended, and 5 minutes voted as the allotted time for speakers. No. 19 was called up for reading.

When Frederick Douglass appeared and Dr. Delany asked that the President might now have the attention of the Convention as he was to leave at three o'clock, and had a few parting words to give.

The President's valedictory was able, eloquent, and earnest, and a vote of thanks was passed by acclamation. [See Resolution, No. 20.]

No. 49, on motion, was recommended to the consideration of the people of the United States.

22nd Resolution being the next in order, was on motion laid on the table. The 23rd Resolution was about to be amended so as to pass a vote of thanks to the Sheriff having charge of the Court House, and to all the citizens of Cleveland for their hospitality, etc., as well as to Judge Andrews and the Cleveland Bar, when A. H. Francis, who with his lady had just returned from Steamboat Saratoga, and had brought back with him Frederick Douglass, proposed that the resolution should read, "to all the citizens of Cleveland *excepting one!*" He proceeded to state a fact. He went on the steamboat Saratoga, was asking for a cabin passage, was refused by the Clerk, when a gentleman, (God forbid, he would not say gentlemen,) a —— some one in the audience said —— thing ———— in the shape of a colored man, interfered, telling him that it was of no use for him to try to obtain a cabin passage on those boats, and intimating that colored men had no business in the cabin.

The Resolution as amended was adopted, and another as follows:

That Alexander Bowman of the Steamboat Saratoga, and resident of Cleveland, receive the burning reprobation of this Convention, until he repents.

And he did receive it, if a unanimous shout against him is any evidence of it. He was fairly ostracized.

Messrs. J. L. Watson, J. Malvin and J. Lott, were appointed committee to inform the parties in each resolution, of the action of the Convention.

Dr. Delany, from the Business Committee reported on Nos. 23, 24, 25, 26, 28, and 29. Nos. 24 and 25 passed.

The Rules were then suspended, to hear two resolutions presented by Elder Kenyon in behalf of the citizens of Cleveland, and moved their adoption by O. D. O'Brien. They were adopted, as follows, the citizens of Cleveland only voting on them:

Resolved, That we hail as an omen of vast good to the colored people of this entire nation, the present Convention held in this city; and that with such examples of intelligence, eloquence, wit, and power of argument, as have been presented before us in the sentiments and speeches of the various members of said Convention, we are confident of the ultimate elevation of the colored population, to all the social, intellectual, civil and religious rights and immunities, of a republican and Christian country.

Resolved, That we bid a hearty God-speed to these our brethren, the sons of Africa, and citizens of America, in all well-directed and legitimate efforts to secure for themselves an honorable and elevated position amongst men.

No. 26, as amended, adopted; 27 adopted also. No. 28 taken up, but was almost immediately laid on the table. No. 30 adopted.

No. 29 as amended was adopted, as also Nos. 31 and 32.—The preamble to the Declaration of Principles was here taken from the table and adopted.

On motion of G. W. Tucker, No. 22 was taken up, and after earnest discussion indefinitely postponed. No. 3 was here presented by M. R. Delany, as it had been rejected by the committee. G. W. Tucker moved its indefinite postponement. The Rule was here suspended, and the time of adjournment extended to 7 o'clock. After an animated discussion upon the indefinite postponement, the Rules were suspended to hear remarks from a lady who wished to say something on the subject of the Rights of Woman. The President then introduced to the audience, Mrs. Sanford, who made some eloquent remarks, of which the following is a specimen:

"From the birth-day of Eve, the then prototype of woman's destiny, to the flash of the star of Bethlehem, she had been the slave of power and passion. If raised by courage and ambition to the proud trial of heroism, she was still the marred model of her first innocence; if thrown by beauty into the ordeal of temptation, man lost his own dignity in contemning her intellectual weight, and refusing the right to exercise her moral powers; if led by inclination to the penitential life of a recluse, the celestial effulgence of a virtuous innocence was lost, and she only lived out woman's degradation!

"But the day of her regeneration dawned. The Son of God had chosen a mother from among the daughters of Eve! A Saviour, who could have come into this a God-man, ready to act, to suffer, and to be crucified, came in the helplessness of infancy, for woman to cherish and direct. Her *exaltation was consummated!*

"True, we ask for the Elective Franchise; for the right of property in the marriage covenant, whether earned or bequeathed. True, we pray to co-operate in making the laws we obey; but it is not to domineer, to dictate or assume. We ask it, for it is a right guaranteed by a higher disposer of human events than man. We pray for it now, for there are duties around us, and we weep at our inability.

"And to the delegates, officers, people and spirit of this Convention, I would say, God speed you in your efforts for elevation and freedom; stop not; shrink not; look not back, till you have justly secured an *unqualified citizenship of the United States, and those inalienable rights granted you by an impartial Creator.*"

Convention passed a vote of thanks to Mrs. Sanford, and also requested a synopsis of her, from which the above are extracts.

A vote of thanks was here passed to John M. Sterling, Esq., of Cleveland, for the presentation of a bundle of books entitled "Slavery as it is."

Discussion was resumed on the indefinite postponement of the Resolution as to Woman's Right. Objection was made to the resolution, and in favor of its postponement, by Messrs. Langston and Day, on the ground that we had passed one similar, making all colored persons present, delegates to this Convention, and they considered *women persons.*

Frederick Douglass moved to amend the 33rd Resolution, by saying that the word persons used in the resolution designation delegates, be understood to include *woman.* On the call for the previous question, the Resolution was not indefinitely postponed. Mr. Douglass' amendment was seconded and carried, with three cheers for woman's rights.

No. 34 was passed.

The whole of the 6th Resolution was referred to the next National Convention.

The National Central Committee appointed was—

Frederick Douglass, N. Y.	Charles H. Langston, O.
J. Jones, Illinois.	Henry Bibb, Michigan.
J. G. Britton, Indiana.	John Peck, Pennsylvania.
George Day, Wisconsin.	J. P. Hilton, Mass.
Josiah Conville, New Jersey.	

On inquiry, it was found that the Convention was composed of Printers, Carpenters, Blacksmiths, Shoemakers, Engineer, Dentist, Gunsmiths, Editors, Tailors, Merchants, Wheelwrights, Painters, Farmers, Physicians, Plasterers, Masons, Students, Clergymen, Barbers and Hair Dressers, Laborers, Coopers, Livery Stable Keepers, Bath House Keepers, Grocery Keepers.

At 7 o'clock, the Convention adjourned *sin dic,* with three cheers for Elevation—Liberty—Equality, and Fraternity.

Resolutions, etc., presented to the National Convention of Colored Freemen by the Business Committee.

Declaration of Sentiments.

Whereas, in the present position of the Colored people in the United States of North America, they, as a class, are known to the country and the intelligent world as menials and domestics or servants; and

Whereas, it is apparent, as the history of the world, both ancient and modern, will testify, that no people thus conditioned, from the Conventional order of society, can attain an equality with the dominant class; and

Whereas, an equality of persons cannot be claimed, where there is not an equality of attainments,—attainments establishing character, and character being that which is essentially necessary to make us equal to our white fellow-countrymen;—

Resolved, That the following Declaration of Principles we pledge ourselves to maintain and carry out among the colored people of the United States to the best of our ability.

1. Resolved, That we shall forever oppose every action, emanating from what source it may, whether civil, political, social or religious, in any manner derogatory to the universal equality of man.—Adopted.

2. Resolved, That whatever is necessary for the elevation of one class is necessary for the elevation of another; the respectable industrial occupations, as mechanical trades, farming or agriculture, mercantile and professional business, wealth and education, being necessary for the elevation of the whites; therefore those attainments are necessary for the elevation of us. Adopted.

3. Resolved, That we impressively recommend to our brethren throughout the country, the necessity of obtaining a knowledge of mechanical trade, farming, mercantile business, the learned professions, as well as the accumulation of wealth,—as the essential means of elevating us as a class.—Adopted.

4. Resolved, That the occupation of domestics and servants among our people is degrading to us as a class, and we deem it our bounden duty to discountenance such pursuits, except where necessity compels the person to resort thereto as a means of livelihood.

5. Resolved, That as Education is necessary in all departments, we recommend to our people, as far as in their power lies, to give their children especially, a business Education.

6. Resolved, That the better to unite and concentrate our efforts as a people, we recommend the formation of an association, to be known as the——. [Referred to a Committee, and subsequently the whole Resolution referred to the next Convention.]

7. Resolved, That while our efforts shall be entirely moral in their tendency, it is no less the duty of this Convention to take Congnizance of the Political action of our brethren, and recommend to them that course which shall best promote the cause of Liberty and Humanity.

8. Resolved, That we recommend to our brethren throughout the several states, to support no person or party, let the name or pretensions be what they may, that shall not have for their object the establishment of equal rights and privileges, without distinction of color, clime or condition.

9. Resolved, That holding Liberty paramount to all earthly considerations, we pledge ourselves, to resist properly, every attempt to infringe upon our rights.

10. Resolved, That Slavery is the greatest curse ever inflicted on man, being of hellish origin, the legitimate offspring of the Devil, and we therefore pledge ourselves, individually, to use all justifiable means for its speedy and immediate overthrow.

11. Whereas a knowledge of the real moral, social, and political condition of our people is not only desirable but absolutely essential to the intelligent prosecution of measures for our elevation and improvement, and whereas our present isolated condition makes the attainment of such knowledge exceedingly difficult, Therefore

Resolved, That this National Convention does hereby request the colored ministers and other persons throughout the Northern States, to collect, or cause to be collected accurate statistics of the condition of our people, during the coming year, in the various stations and circuits in which they may find themselves located, and that they be, and hereby are requested to prepare lists, stating—

1st. The number of colored persons in the localities where they may be stationed; their general moral and social condition; and especially how many are farmers and mechanics, how many are merchants or storekeepers, how many are teachers, lawyers, doctors, ministers, and editors; how many are known to take an pay for newspapers; how many literary, debating, and other societies, for moral, mental, and social improvement; and that said ministers be, and hereby are, respectfully requested to forward all such information to a Committee of one, who shall be appointed for this purpose, and that the said Committee of one be requested to make out a synopsis of such information and to report the same to the next colored National Convention.

1. Resolved, That Temperance is another great lever for Elevation, which we would urge upon our people and all others to use, and earnestly recommend the formation of societies for its promotion.

2. Resolved, That while we heartily engage in recommending to our people the Free Soil movement, and the support of the Buffalo Convention, nevertheless we claim and are determined to maintain the higher standard and more liberal views which have heretofore characterized us as abolitionists.

3. Resolved, That as Liberty is a right inherent in man, and cannot be arrested without the most flagrant outrage, we recommend to our brethren in bonds, to embrace every favorable opportunity of effecting their escape.

4. Resolved, that we pledge ourselves individually, to use all justifiable means in aiding our enslaved brethren in escaping from the Southern Prison House of Bondage.

5. Resolved, that we recommend to the colored people every where, to use every just effort in getting their children into schools, in common with others in their several locations.

6. Whereas, American Slavery is politically and morally an evil of which this country stands guilty, and cannot be abolished alone through the instrumentality of moral suasion and whereas the two great political parties of the Union have by their acts and nominations betrayed the sacred cause of human freedom, and

Whereas, a Convention recently assembled in the city of Buffalo having for its object the establishment of a party in support of free soil for a free people, and Whereas said Convention adopted for its platform the following noble expression, viz; "Free Soil, Free Speech, Free Labor and Free Men," and believing these expressions well calculated to increase the interest now felt in behalf of the down-trodden and oppressed of this land; therefore,

Resolved, That we recommend to all colored persons in possession of the right of the elective Franchise, the nominees of that body for their suffrages, and earnestly request all good citizens to use their united efforts to secure their election to the chief offences in the gift of the people.

Resolved, that the great Free Soil Party of the United States, is bound together by a common sentiment expressing the wish of a large portion of the people of this Union, and that we hail with delight this great movement as the dawn of a bright and more auspicious day. [The Resolutions were rejected, but the Preamble prefixed to the 13th Resolution.]

7. Resolved, That Love to God and man, and Fidelity to ourselves ought to be the great motto which we will urge upon our people.

8. To the honorable members of the Convention of citizens of color of the United States of America, greeting. I beg leave to report for your consideration the result of my labors as an Agent to promote a project of home emigration to the State of Michigan. * * * * I was appointed on October the 24th, in the year 1845 by an organization of gentlemen of color in the Vicinity of Lewis, Ohio. * * The object of my agency was to explore wild unsettled territory. * * I found large and fertile tracts of government land, in Kent and other counties, but in Oceana and Mason counties there are peculiar facilities, which do

not present themselves in any of the other parts of the State which I have visited. Oceana and Mason are lake counties, with about sixty miles seaboard. There are navigable rivers emptying into Lake Michigan and affording at their mouths good harbors, delightful sites for cities and villages, also with hydraulic powers of every magnitude. Plenty of land ready for the plow at $1.25 per acre. Valuable Timber may be had here in abundance. Grass is now to be found from knee-high to the height of a man. The surface of the meadows is a deep vegetable mould, below which in many places are found beds of Lime. Fruit, Fish, and Game in abundance. Also, Salt Springs. Plaster of Paris has been discovered there. During the last spring a constant trade was kept up between these lands and Chicago, Milwaukee, and the ports on Lake Michigan. There are four sawmills in the two counties. Lumber is wanted at $7 per thousand on the lake shore. Shingles, shingle-bolts, staves, tan-bark, cedar posts, etc, all bring a liberal price, and demand Gold and Silver, and provisions during the season of navigation. I now submit the subject, etc., hoping that you will adopt some feasible plan to arouse our people to consider the importance of the same.

Jefferson Fitzgerald."

9. Resolved, That the thanks of this Convention be tendered to the President for the able and impartial manner in which he has presided over its deliberations.

10. Resolved, That this Convention adjourn *sine die* on Friday, Sept. 8th, 6 o'clock P. M.

11. Whereas, we find ourselves far behind the military tactics of the civilized world, therefore,

Resolved, That this Convention recommend to the Colored Freemen of North America to use every means in their power to obtain that science, so as to enable them to measure arms with assailants *without* and invaders within; therefore,

Resolved, That this Convention appoint Committees in the different States as Vigilant Committees, to organize as such where the same may be deemed practicable.

12. Resolved, That this Convention return their sincere thanks to Judge Andrews and the Bar of Cleveland, in adjourning the Court and tendering to us the use of the Court House for the sittings of the Convention. [See minutes.]

Resolved, That among the means instrumental in the elevation of a people there is none more effectual than a well-conducted and efficient newspaper; and believing the North Star, published and edited by Frederick Douglass and M. R. Delany at Rochester, fully to answer all the ends and purposes of a national press, we therefore recommend its support to the colored people throughout North America.

13. Resolved, That the Convention recommend to the colored citizens of the several Free States, to assemble in Mass State Conventions annually, and petition the Legislatures thereof to repeal the Black Laws, or all laws militating against the interests of colored people.

14. Whereas, we firmly believe with the Fathers of '76, that "taxation and representation ought to go together;" therefore,

Resolved, That we are very much in doubt as to the propriety of our paying any tax upon which representation is based, until we are permitted to be represented.

15. Resolved, That, as a body, the professed Christian American Churches generally, by their support, defence, and participation in the damning sin of American Slavery, as well as cruel prejudice and proscription of the nominally free colored people, have forfeited every claim of confidence on our part, and therefore merit our severest reprobation.

16. Resolved, That Conventions of a similar character to this are well calculated to enhance the interests of suffering humanity, and the colored people generally, and that we recommend such assemblages to the favorable consideration of our people.

17. Resolved, That the next National Convention of Colored Freemen shall be held in Detroit, Michigan, or at Pittsburgh, Pa., some time in the year 1850.

18. Resolved, That among the many oppressive schemes against the colored people in the United States, we view the American Colonization Society as the most deceptive and hypocritical—"clothed with the livery of heaven to serve the devil in," with President Roberts, of Liberia, a colored man, for its leader.

19. Resolved, That we tender to the citizens of Cleveland our unfeigned thanks for the noble resolution passed by them in approval of the doings of this Convention.

20. Resolved, That the prejudice against color, so called, is vulgar, unnatural, and wicked in the sight of God, and wholly unknown in any country where slavery does not exist.

21. Resolved, That while we are engaged in the elevation of our people, we claim it to be our duty to inquire of our public lecturers and agents an explanation in reference to the disbursement of funds they may have collected from time to time for public purposes.

22.Whereas, we fully believe in the equality of the sexes, therefore,

Resolved, That we hereby invite females to hereafter to take part in our deliberations.

23. Whereas, a portion of those of our colored citizens called barbers, by refusing to treat colored men on the equality with the whites, do encourage prejudice among the whites of the several States; therefore,

Resolved, That we recommend to this class of men a change in their course of action relative to us; and if this change is not immediately made, we consider them base serviles, worthy only of the condemnation, censure, and defamation of all lovers of liberty, equality, and right.

Source: Report of the Proceedings of the Colored National Convention, Held at Cleveland, Ohio on Wednesday, September 6, 1848 (Rochester: Printed by John Dick, at the North Star Office, 1848).

17

John W. Lewis

A pastor in Providence, Rhode Island, John W. Lewis (1810–1861) cofounded the Second Freewill Baptist Church, widely considered one of the most militant black institutions in the city. In 1852, he prepared a reminiscence of the life of another of Second Freewill's founders, Charles Bowles, who had recently died. As an addendum, Lewis included an essay on race, which represents one of the few direct refutations by an antebellum black spokesperson of the claims of the emerging American School of racial science. This, pioneered by figures such as Louis Aggasiz, Samuel Morton, Josiah Nott, and George Gliddon, argued that blacks constituted an entirely distinct species of man, descended from entirely separate genesis. Following his contemporaries, Lewis conceded physical differences between the races, which he could not fully explain; he also claimed that such differences meant nothing in moral terms and that despite them blacks could be elevated. His historical environmentalism ascribed differences among the races to circumstantial, and hence transient, effects of environment. While effectively refuting many of the claims of the American School, Lewis's essay also may have conceded important terms of the debate. In addition to abandoning the universalistic claims of the American Revolution's Enlightenment roots, it tacitly endorsed contemporary Euro-American civilization as the standard by which societies (and races) should be measured.

"Essay on the Character and Condition of the African Race"

(1852)

"Human nature is human nature, the world over,
in the black man as well as the white."

CHAPTER I.

The sentiment uttered by the great Apostle Paul, in his admirable address to the Athenians, contained in Acts 17th; 26th, "That God hath made of one blood all nations of men to dwell on all the earth," is worthy the man and the christian. And a corresponding sentiment in the American Declaration of Independence, "That all men are created free and equal, and are endowed by their Creator with certain inalienable rights, among which are life, liberty, and the pursuits of happiness," is worthy the patriot and the statesman. But the most absurd idea of the present age, in the minds of many of the human race, is in the sentiment, that the standard to judge of a man's ability, and mental capacity to enjoy, and appreciate these blessings supported by self-evident truth, depends on his color or nationality; that one man has a right to throw aside his obligation to universal brotherhood, and proscribe a human being on account of his color, a cause over which he has no control.

It is insisted by American prejudice, that natural instinct in the human character leads one man to hate another of a different color, as a matter of physical necessity; that the intention of God in creating and diversifying the human race was to have set up between them a barrier, guarded by absolute hate, and supported by absolute will. This sentiment is incorporated into the theological creed of the American church, into the political system of American democracy, and into the civil jurisprudence of American law, and the social and domestic organization of American society; manifesting a spirit that well might shame the whole range of European Despotism, and aiming to drive the colored man from within the pale of human society. The spirit combines the priest and politician, with all the corruptness of political and ecclesiastical action of this American nation, in an attempt to unman the African race and doom them to a miserable degradation. Thank God, the privilege of man to enjoy "life, liberty, and the pursuit of happiness," is based on quite a different foundation, involving the great principles of infinite right, and demanding finite acquiescence to Divine benevolence.

If the wisdom of God has diversified the human race in complexion, habit, both national and local, his justice holds man responsible only for his moral conduct in the formation of his moral character, and on nothing more in his own existence has he control; and there cannot be any conceivable right under any circumstance in life, for one to prevent another from improving his moral, mental, or physical condition by the exercise of the faculties which God his Maker has given him. The existence of right is coeval with the Divine government, and right is right, God's no more, man's no less. God's right cannot abridge man's right, much less, man destroy his fellowman's. In the support and administration of the universal government, God has power to create and destroy; his power is unquestionable. But Infinite justice and Divine mercy stand between his power and my right, and he has no power to destroy my right and the privilege of my manhood, on account of my color, a cause in my existence for which he, and not myself, is wholly responsible.

Government grows out of the wants and necessities of our natures, not by arbitrary appointment, but as a matter of necessity. God proclaimed from Mount Sinai, in all the majesty and glory of his great name, the principles embodying the great organic code of his moral government, and which should be the corner stone of all human governments, whether a Theocracy, a Monarchy, or a Republic, and Christ re-proclaimed the same without taking away any of its obligation of man's part, or lessening the claims of the Divine government. In Matthew 7th:12th, Christ says, "Therefore all things that ye would that men do to you, do ye also to them, for this is the Law and the Prophets."

My natural rights is a gift of my Maker, growing but of my nature, and my relation to him. I have a right to read, write, work, in that way and department of labor that I like best, and use the avails of my labor in that way which is most satisfactory to my own mind; and go where I please. But in doing all this, I have no right to infringe on my neighbor's rights or withhold amenability to the Divine government. If then my fellow-men authorizing government to exercise arbitrary will over me it is a usurped and wicked dominion that is no law, not being founded in justice, and impartial justice demands the trampling such enactments under foot, as being opposed to God and humanity. For no power on earth, acting under legal authority, can trample down my right, without stepping over the boundaries of God's dominion. But the attempt to identify the Throne of God with the throne of iniquity, is one prominent feature of American depravity. And the attempt of civil government under a pretended sanction of the Divine authority, to legalize a system of wrong, to make it right, for the convenience of others in arbitrary will, tends to weaken the grand structure of christianity.

Infinite benevolence has always characterized all the efforts of God to benefit the human race, and could I believe that God, after creating me with the faculties as a man, and a heart to feel, and a soul to be benefitted by that religion whose author was sung in the rapture of the heavenly host, saying "Glory to God in the highest, on earth peace and good will to men;" and then stamp me with a colored skin as a black man, and by an act of arbitrary power despise his own work, and create in a white man, a principle in spirit to hate, abuse and injure me, to gratify his pride, and wicked ambition, it would destroy in my mind at once, all love and reverence to that God as a good being. I should be persuaded to believe, that the christian religion had become greatly corrupted by supreme selfishness and tradition, contrary to the spirit of God; or that God is an unjust, unmerciful, and inconsistent being; or that all things in the universe exist without a God, and are controlled by its own power, independent of Infinite will, and that the God and Devil of this world are combined in one, in the wicked, cruel disposition of men in their control of the governments of the world.—This I feel, and say as a colored man, and as a representative of the African race, and in defiance of a corrupt public opinions. I say it on the truth of eternal right. Human nature is human nature, the world over, in the black man as well as the white. And in human nature are the elements to form human character, in moral excellence, by the power and exercise of the intellectual and moral faculties in all the different races of men—the opinion of American despotism and American prejudice based on negro-hate, to the contrary notwithstanding.

Now all the base villainy that has attempted to snap the chain of human brotherhood, and involve the human family in hatred, is without the sanction of the God of Heaven. Like good Abraham, in true and fraternal fellowship with his Maker, we can say, "shall not the Judge of all the earth do right." Our religious sentiments teach our minds the great idea of right in the Infinite; hence whether we are thrown out of society, like the good John in banishment on the Isle of Patmos, or the multitude of Hindoos around the temple of Juggernaut, or the Indian in the western wild, bending to the Great Spirit, or the Native African, bowing to the serpent, or the many tribes of the earth in the darkness and superstition of heathen mythology, bowing to their uncouth idols, the divinity of the moral government of God, reaches the conscience, and dictates the sentiments of right, however much perverted human nature and the influence of sinful habits may lead them away from the true God.

Truth and justice are intuitive perceptions in the human soul, and even where there is no system of civil government, conscience often enforces these observances. But in coming into the United States, in the nineteenth century, a nation professing to acknowledge the Divine government, and talking of right in Congress, in the Legislature, Southern rights, and Northern rights, rights of Capitalist, or the Mechanic, the Manufacturer, and the Agriculturist, yes every body's rights are talked about, but nobody's rights are understood properly. A sort of judicial blindness obscures the moral perceptions of the great mass of the people of this nation, because of the supreme selfishness that leads man to infringe on his neighbor's rights to promote his own purposes; many of the people tread the holy courts of the Lord, and hear read and sung the following lines:—

> "Blessed Redeemer how Divine,
> How righteous is this rule of thine,
> Never to deal with others worse,
> Than we would have deal with us.

> This golden lesson short and plain,
> Gives not the mind or memory pain,
> And every conscience must approve,
> This universal law of love.

> 'Tis written in each mortal breast,
> Where all tenderest wishes rest."

Nothing can be more beautifully sublime than the language and sentiment of this poetical exhibition of the golden rule of the redeemer of the world. And happy would it be for the American nation if it were something more than a mere rhetorical flourish, or a splendid theory. This sentiment practically maintained, would abolish war; it would give a death blow to intemperance, and it would raze the citadel of despotism to the ground. It would proclaim this country the asylum, where love, the tenderest plant in Eden's garden, would fill every soul with a fragrance that would give joy to all the inhabitants of Zion. Honestly then every one should say, "One is our Master, even Christ, and all we are brethren. Enjoying one great plan of redemption, justification, and sanctification, through the spirit of the living God; and supporting the noble Apostolic declaration, "Neither Jew, nor Greek, Barbarian, Seythian, bond nor free, but all one in Christ Jesus." These sentiments are the cardinal virtues and excellences of bible christianity, designed to support the mighty structure of christian benevolence, and fraternity between man and man, of all the human race.

CHAPTER II.

Physical Condition of the African Race, as compared with the other Races of the Human Family.

It is extremely humiliating to America pride and arrogance, to be obliged to acknowledge the African race as a part of the human family, and in equality, in physical, intellectual and moral goodness, to be obliged by the obligation of universal brotherhood, to sustain fraternity with them as sentient beings. Many are in almost open rebellion with the Divine government of God. And the monopolizing proscription, a legitimate fruit of American despotism, will condemn the sentiment let it come from what source it may, if it dare advocate the equality of the human race, in the right to the enjoyment of life, liberty, and the pursuit of happiness. The honorable position of the Hon. Wm. H. Seward, of New York, in the Senate of the United States Congress, did not screen him from the aspersion of the enemies of freedom, when he dared utter the noble sentiment in that body, that "There is a Law above the Constitution of this Nation." It was condemned not only by the dominant political power of the nation, in its base subvserviency to Southern slavery. The popular, current religion, and the popular current literature of the whole country, aid in condemning Mr. Seward's sentiment, as dangerous to the interest of the nation, for the pulpit and presses, with unblushing effrontery to the Divine government, have raised the cry of treason, in concert with the voice of political demagogueism in the country. The Rev. D.D. Whedon, an esteemed Methodist minister, and a popular Professor in the Michigan University, has recently been made to feel the inquisitorial power of the popular, current religion, literature and politics of the country, by an expulsion from his place and standing with the Faculty of that College, for daring to preach the sentiments of the higher law from the pulpit.

It is insisted that there must have been more than one Head or Representative of the human races; that the 800,000,000 or 900,000,000 human beings on this globe, and speaking some 1,200 languages, and also diversified in color, from the blackest African to the whitest European, could not have obtained an existence from one Parental source. But all reasoning on this point is mere speculation, for whatever was the Parentage of the human race originally, the Deluge left Noah at the head of the human family, from whom the earth is now peopled. So that the oft-repeated declaration that the African race descended from Cain, absurd. It is said "the unnatural, and wicked conduct of Cain towards his brother Abel, brought down on him the displeasure of his God, and that he was marked by a black skin." But this is begging the question, and stating points without authority; for there is no proof that the original complexion of our first Parents was any nearer the European, than the African race, and if the mark of Cain was the color of the body, it is just as likely to be white as a black one.

And if an ugly, unnatural disposition is the result of that curse, is not the European on a level with the African? Has not jealousy, hatred and revenge, marked the conduct of the one as well as the other? Has not the pathway of human life of all nations been darkened by deeds of crime? Has not the soil of Europe, Asia and America, been stained by the blood of murdered brothers, as well as Africa? Has not human nature alike been vitiated by the original transgression of Adam? And, does not the Apostolic declaration of Peter before the household of Cornelius the Centurion, apply to man without regard to color, "Of a truth, I perceive that God is no respecter of persons, but in every nation, he that feareth him, and worketh righteousness is accepted with him."

And as in the bible declaration, man is made but a little lower than the Angels, in his condition as man, whatever be his color, him manhood bears him up in noble dignity above all the other animal creation, and viewed in his mechanical construction he is a mystery to himself. The frame of bones skillfully put together, to be willed into motion, is a master-piece of Infinite wisdom; this frame covered with muscles, forming a part of his existence, is supplied by a beautiful chemical process in himself, in operating the aliment carried into the stomach as the arrangement of the nerves throughout the whole system, as a sort of telegraphic communication to the soul; the blood vessels to convey the vital stream which contains animal life to all parts of the system; the heart, the great reservoir with its hydraulic principle to keep in perpetual motion the pulsation; all fitly and wisely arranged, and this whole system covered with a skin to guard it. Now in viewing this wonderful material construction of the human body, where is there any difference but simply in the covering of the body, and effect that classes and distinguishes the human race nationally; but which cannot add or detract from the perfection of their physical construction. This covering consists of three parts, viz: 1st, "The cuticle or scarf-skin; 2d, the reto mucorscum, and 3d, the cutis. The 2d lies between the 1st and 3d, and contains the color;'" so that it is not in the flesh, blood, bones, or the muscles, of which the human body is composed. Here is a phenomena, truly a philosophical wonder in the human existence. We see the effect, but the cause lies beyond the scope of finite minds. A great Infinite and Eternal God, has wisely arranged all this, and an attack on his Infinite prerogative, and the assault must in the end recoil on themselves, and will fix a guilt on their characters which must be answered to at the Judgement.

As the coloring is in the covering of the body, it cannot effect those laws peculiar to human beings, for the great principles of physical law, supported by Anatomy, Physiology, and Phrenology, are alike in all human beings, in natural or original character, irrespective of color. But national or local habits affecting the treatment of the body in its physical condition, will have a controlling influence in the development of the physical man. This united with the geographical locations, subjecting the body to different atmospheric temperatures, gives different character and appearance to the human system. Not that I would be understood as saying, in my opinion, that this is the whole and sole case of the difference in the complexion of the human race, without Infinite design for purposes fitly adapted to human convenience. But it is often argued farther, that "the African is wholly inferior to the European, as his color subjects him to a hot climate, where a natural imbecility incapacitates him to rank with intelligent beings." If this idea be carried to that extent, that the nature and condition of the colored man, compels him to a hot climate simply on account of color, I declare it false. I know by experience as a colored man, my physical habits having been formed in a cold and Northern climate, the ability to endure depends on an acclimated life, and if the physical habits of a white and colored man be formed alike in early life, in a tropical climate, they will be equally affected in a frigid climate, and so vice versa.

Another point is important to be well understood. All human bodies are subject alike to the same disease, and the color of the body does not require any variation in medical treatment, that is, in the same locality. I know that the principle of medical science is differently understood by different nations, in different stages of mental improvement, and diseases assume different character according to the different climates and modes of living, on all races alike, where the early habits are formed alike. In the American or European cities, where the population is made up of people of different nations, and forming quite a heterogeneous mass, in refined improvement, the manner of living becomes more complex in the human system, and a complex medical treatment is necessary. In the rural districts of the American or European civilized or enlightened countries, or in the rude and barbarous states of society in all parts of the world, a more simple of natural mode of living, gives to disease a more simple character. Hence where man is alike circumstanced irrespective of color, there are the same physical characteristics, and, in whatever state or condition of society they live, all have a system of medical science, and nature teaches all to go to earth's great laboratory either in the mineral or vegetable department, and find remedies for all disease of the body. And all the advantage the American or European has over the African or Indian, is, that civilization, and art, combined with native genius, has enabled them to systematize the theory and methodize the practice, in a more tangible manner; and yet they are not always more successful in their treatment.

Now I suppose some will object to the idea of equality of the races, on the ground that, "they are not equal in strength, in intelligence, and in talent." To convey the idea that the peasant is equal with the prince, the slave with the rich planter, or the weak and imbecile governments of some of the African, Asiatic, or European nations with the more power-ful nations of the earth, in moral or physical ability naturally, is absurd in the mind of modern despotism, because aristocracy cannot live without distinction? Well let us exam-ine this point a moment, and see if it cannot be shown by history, that individuals in different nations, at different periods of the world's history, in poverty, obscurity and apparently inferior talent, and looked down upon with scorn and indifference, by their more powerful neighbors, have not by dint of native talent and self-exertion risen to honor and distinction. And I ask, are the Europeans above others in this? I answer, No! What gave Russia the power over rude Circassian, to hold them as a part of that Empire in such base servility? It was art and civilization, giving the proud Russian intelligence over the Circassian, and nothing in the argument of superior natural ability; for when the Circass-ian in his turn became intelligent, he dared throw off Russian rule and assert his rights as a man. What gave England power over the poor China-man, to band their iron wills to British rule? It was the intelligence of England. So it is in the entire history of the human race, so that the superiority of one class over an inferior one, only the result of improved opportunity in becoming intelligent, in the progress of civilization.

Source: John W. Lewis, "Essay On the Character and Condition of the African Race," in John Lewis, *The Life, Labors, And Travels Of Elder Charles Bowles, Of The Free Will Baptist Denomina-tions, By Eld. John W. Lewis. Together With An Essay On The Character And Condition Of The African Race, By The Same. Also, An Essay On The Fugitive Law Of The U.S. Congress Of 1850, By Rev. Arthur Dearing* (Watertown, CT: Ingalls & Stowell's Steam Press, 1852).

18

Mary Ann Shadd

Although since 1816 small numbers of blacks had demonstrated a willingness to flee the prejudice of their native country, the suspicious motives of the American Colonization Society, which sponsored schemes to "return" blacks to Africa, had dissuaded most. Frustrated by little change after years of struggle, however, African-American leaders in the 1850s began once again to consider seriously alternatives to America. Some contemplated black-led efforts to return to Africa; others considered migration to Haiti or other places in the Caribbean. Still others considered moving to nascent black colonies in North America—in particular, what was then known as Canada West, or the portion of Canada north of the Great Lakes, extending from eastern Michigan to western New York. In addition to promising a relatively feasible site for relocation, Canada also offered a final refuge for those African Americans who had fled slavery. As America's stringent fugitive slave laws increasingly rendered the lives of fugitives perilous, the sanctuary offered by Britain's avowedly antislavery legal codes grew ever more valued. Black settlements in Canada West, which began in earnest in the 1830s, provided opportunities for black leaders to demonstrate the capacity of African Americans for embodying ideals of independence and respectability. This pamphlet, prepared by Mary Ann Shadd (1823–1893), a newspaper editor who had relocated from Delaware to Canada West, is representative of the literature prepared by African-American spokespersons to encourage Northern blacks to migrate.

Mary Ann Shadd was an interesting spokesperson for emigration. Her father, Abraham Shadd, had been a prominent member of black conventions during the 1830s; and he took part in committees which considered Canadian resettlement plans. Mary Ann Shadd was born in Delaware and moved with her family to West Chester, Pennsylvania, in the 1830s. Her father made sure she received a quality education. She soon became a teacher, opening a school in Wilmington, Delaware, in the early 1840s before moving on to educational institutions in Pennsylvania and New Jersey. She also displayed her talents as a writer. In 1849, she published her first pamphlet, "Hints to the Colored People" (which called on black leaders to set an even higher value on moral uplift and economic autonomy), and published her reform ideas in Frederick Douglass's *The North Star*. She then moved to Ontario, Canada (where about twenty thousand blacks had settled by the 1860s) and began editing the "Provincial Freeman."

Mary Ann Shadd returned to the United States after the Civil War (she was married by then to Isaac Cary) and taught in Washington, D.C. In her sixties, she completed a law degree during the 1880s, graduating as the only African American in her class. As her life and writing indicates, Shadd was one of the most determined and strong-willed activists of her day. She deserves wider recognition.

"A Plea For Emigration, or Notes of Canada West"

(1852)

"To set forth the advantage of a residence in a country, in which chattel slavery is not tolerated, and prejudice of color has no existence whatever . . ."

INTRODUCTORY REMARKS

THE increasing desire on the part of the colored people, to become thoroughly informed respecting the Canadas, and particularly that part of the province called Canada West— to learn of the climate, soil, and productions, and of the inducements offered generally to emigrants, and to them particularly, since that the passage of the odious Fugitive Slave Law has made a residence in the United States to many of them dangerous to the extreme,—this consideration, and the absence of condensed information accessible to all, is my excuse for offering this tract to the notice of the public. The people are in a strait,— on the one hand, a pro-slavery administration, with its entire controllable force, is bearing upon them with fatal effect: on the other, the Colonization Society, in the garb of *Christianity* and *Philanthropy*, is seconding the efforts of the first named power, by bringing into the lists a vast social and immoral influence, thus making more effective the agencies employed. Information is needed.—Tropical Africa, the land of promise of the colonizationists, teeming as she is with the breath of pestilence, a burning sun and fearful maladies, bids them welcome;—she feelingly invites to moral and physical death, under a voluntary escort of their most bitter enemies at home. Again, many look with dreadful forebodings to the probability of worse than inquisitorial inhumanity in the Southern States from the operation of the Fugitive Law. Certain that neither a home in Africa, nor in the Southern States, is desirable under present circumstances, inquiry is made respecting Canada. I have endeavored to furnish information to a certain extent, to that end, and believing that more reliance would be placed upon a statement of facts obtained in the country, from reliable sources and from observation, than upon a repetition of current statements made elsewhere, however honestly made, I determined to visit Canada, and to there collect such information as most persons desire. These pages contain the result of much inquiry— matter obtained both from individuals and from documents and papers of unquestionable character in the Province.

BRITISH AMERICA.

BRITISH AMERICA, it is well known, is a country equal in extent, at least, to the United States, extending on the north to the Arctic Ocean, from the Atlantic on the east, to the Pacific on the west, and the southern boundary of which is subject to the inequalities in latitude of the several Northern States and Territories belonging to the United States government. This vast country includes within its limits, some of the most beautiful lakes and rivers on the Western Continent. The climate, in the higher latitudes, is extremely severe, but for a considerable distance north of the settled districts, particularly in the western part, the climate is healthy and temperate: epidemics are not of such frequency as in the United States, owing to a more equable temperature, and local diseases are unknown. The province claiming especial attention, as presenting features most desirable in a residence, is Canada, divided into East and West; and of these Canada West is to be preferred . . .

• • •

SOIL,—TIMBER,—CLEARING LANDS.

The quality and different kinds of soil must form the second subject for consideration, because, in connection with climate, it enters largely into all our ideas of comfort and pecuniary independence; again, because so far as colored people are interested in the subject of emigration to any country, their welfare, in a pecuniary view, is promoted by attention to the quality of the soil. Lands out of the United States, on this continent, should have no local value, if the questions of personal freedom and political rights were left out of the subject, but as they are paramount, too much may not be said on this point. I mean to be understood, that a description of lands in Mexico would probably be as desirable as lands in Canada, if the idea were simply to get lands and settle thereof; but it is important to know if by this investigation we only agitate, and leave the public mind in an unsettled state, or if a permanent nationality is included in the prospect of becoming purchasers and settlers.

The question, does the soil of Canada offer inducements sufficient to determine prospective emigrants in its favor? may be answered by every one for himself, after having properly weighed the following item. Persons who have been engaged in agriculture the greater part of their lives,—practical and competent farmers, and judges of the capacity of different soils,—say, that the soil is unsurpassed by that of Kentucky and States farther south, and naturally superior to the adjoining northern States. It is not only indicated by the rich, dark and heavy appearance, and the depth of the soil, which is seldom reached by plows of the greatest capacity, but by the character of the products, and the unequalled growth and size of timber on uncleared lands. Wheat, the staple product of the country, averages sixty pounds to the bushel—often actually exceeding that; fifty-six is the standard weight in the United States; and leaving out Delaware, that is seldom reached. The forest consists of walnut, hickory, white and burr oak, burrwood, oak, pine, poplar—all of the largest size, and other inferior kinds of wood with which we are not familiar in our northern woods. There is a greater variety in them, and larger size, and knowing that the size of vegetables depends mainly upon the quantity of nutriment afforded by the soil, we are led in this instance to infer its superiority. Besides the well known wheat, oats, buckwheat, Indian corn, and other grains, are raised of good quality, and with profit, and more to the acre than is usually obtained in the States, except on the application of fertilizing materials—a mode not much practiced in Canada hitherto, the land not having been exhausted sufficiently to require such appliances to further its productiveness. The varieties of the soil, are a black loam, sandy loam, clay, and sand, but a black loam is the predominating kind . . .

• • •

PRICES OF LAND IN THE COUNTRY—CITY PROPERTY, &C.

The country in the vicinity of Toronto and to the eastward, being thickly settled, (farms being advertised "thirty miles on Yonge street,") the price of property is, of course, very much higher than in the western districts. City property varies according to location—two hundred dollars the foot, is the value of lots in good position in Toronto: in the suburbs very fine lots may be had at reasonable rates. Farms, at a few miles distant, range from thirty to fifty dollars the acre—fifty dollars being thought a fair price for the best quality of land without improvements; but in the western districts, farms may be bought for one thousand dollars, superior in every way, to farms near the city of Toronto, that are held at five thousand. Improved lands, near Chatham, London, Hamilton, and other towns near, may be bought at prices varying from ten up to one hundred: at a few miles distant, uncleared lands, belonging to the Government, may be had by paying one dollar sixty-two cents, two, and two fifty, according to locality—well timbered and watered, near culti-vated farms on the river and lake shore. Thousands of acres, of the very best land in the Province, are now in the market at the above prices, and either in the interior, or well situ-ated as to prospect from the lakes, and near excellent markets. The land is laid out in what are called concessions, these concessions, or blocks, being sub-divided into lots. There is, therefore, a uniformity of appearance throughout in the farms, and no contest about roads on individual property can result—the roads being designed to benefit equally contiguous property, and under jurisdiction of Government. One hundred acres is the smallest quan-tity to be had of Government, but individual holders sell in quantities to suit purchasers. Large quantities of land are held by individuals, though at a higher rate generally than that held by Government; and their titles are said to be often defective. In every respect, the preference should be for purchase of Government –land is cheaper, as well situated, and below a specified number of acres, may not be bought; a prohibition of advantage to many who would buy, as there is induced a spirit of enterprise and competition and a sense of responsibility. Too many are now *independently* dragging along miserably, on the few acres, ten, twenty, or such a matter, bought at the high rates of individual holders, in a country in which the prices must, for a long time, require more land in process of culture, to afford a comfortable support. There is every inducement to buy, near or in towns, as well as in the country, as land is cheap, business increasing, with the steady increase of population, lack of employment at fair prices, and no complexional or other qualification in existence.

LABOR—TRADES.

In Canada, as in other recently settled countries, there is much to do, and comparatively few for the work. The numerous towns and villages springing up, and the great demand for timber and agricultural products, make labor of every kind plenty; all trades that are practiced in the United States, are there patronized by whosoever carried on—no man's complexion affecting his business. If a colored man understands his business, he receives the public patronage the same as a white man. He is not obliged to work a little better, and at a lower rate—there is no degraded class to identify him with, therefore every man's work stands or falls according to merit, not as is his color. Builders, and other tradesmen, of different complexions, work together on the same building and in the same shop, with perfect harmony, and often the proprietor of an establishment is colored, and the major-ity or all of the men employed are white. Businesses that in other communities have ceased to remunerate, yield a large percentage to the money invested.

The mineral resources of the Canadas not being developed, to any extent, for fuel wood is generally used, and a profitable trade in that commodity is carried on; and besides lumber for buildings, the getting out of materials for staves, coopers' stuff, and various purposes, affords steady employment and at fair prices, for cash. This state of things must increase, and assume more importance in Canada markets, as the increasing population of the western United States burn and otherwise appropriate their timber. Railroads are in process of construction—steamboats now ply between Toronto and the several towns on the lakes; and in process of time, iron and other works will be in operation, it is said, all requiring their quota, and of course keeping up the demands. Boards for home and foreign markets, are successfully manufactured, and numerous mill-sites are fast being appropriated to saw and grist mills. In some sections, colored men are engaged in saw mills on their own account. At Dawn, a settlement on the Saydenham, (of which hereafter,) and at other points, this trade is prosecuted with profit to them. To enumerate the different occupations in which colored persons are engaged, even in detail, would but fatigue, and would not further the end in view, namely: To set forth the advantage of a residence in a country, in which chattel slavery is not tolerated, and prejudice of *color* has no existence whatever—the adaptation of that country, by climate, soil, and solid character, to their physical and political necessities; and that a country of a residence there over their present position at *home*. It will suffice, that colored men prosecute all the different trades; are store keepers, farmers, clerks, and laborers; and are not only unmolested, but sustained and encouraged in any business for which their qualifications and means fit them; and as the resources of the country develop, new fields of enterprise will be opened to them, and consequently new motives to honorable effort.

CHURCHES—SCHOOLS.

In the large towns and cities, as in similar communities in other Christian countries, the means for religious instruction are ample. There are costly churches in which all classes and complexions worship, and no "negro pew," or other seat for colored persons, especially. I was forcibly struck, when at Toronto, with the contrast the religious community there presented, to our own large body of American Christians. In the churches, originally built by the white Canadians, the presence of colored persons, promiscuously seated, elicited no comment whatever. They are members, and visitors, and as such have their pews according to their inclination, near the door, or remote, or central, as best suits them. The number of colored persons, attending the churches with whites, constitutes a minority, I think. They have their "own churches." That that is the feature in their policy, which is productive of mischief to the entire body, is evident enough; and the opinion of the best informed and most influential among them, in Toronto and the large towns, is decided and universal. I have heard men of many years residence, and who have, in a measure, been moulded by the better sentiment of society, express deep sorrow at the course of colored persons, in pertinaciously refusing overtures of religious fellowship from the whites; and in the face of all experience to the contrary, erecting Colored Methodist, and Baptist, and other Churches. This opinion obtains amongst many who, when in the United States, were connected with colored churches. Aside from their caste character, their influence on the colored people is fatal. The character of the exclusive church in Canada tends to perpetuate ignorance, both of their true position as British subjects, and of the Christian religion in its purity. It is impossible to observe thoughtfully the workings of that incipient Zion, (the Canadian African Church, of whatever denomination,) in its present imperfect state, without seriously regretting that it should have been thought necessary to call it into existence. In her bosom is nurtured the long-standing and rankling prejudices, and hatred against whites, without exception, that had their origin in American oppression, and that should have been left in the country in which they orig-inated— 'tis that species of animosity that is not bounded by geographical lines, nor suffers discrimination.

A goodly portion of the people in the western part of the Province, (for there are but few in the eastern,) are enjoying superior religious opportunities, but the majority greatly need active missionary effort: first, to teach them love to their neighbor; and, again, to give them an intelligent and correct understanding of the Sacred Scriptures. The missionary strength, at present, consists of but six preachers—active and efficient gentlemen, all of them, and self-sacrificing in the last degree; and several women engaged in teaching, under the same auspices. Much privation, suffering, opposition, and sorrow await the missionary in that field. If it were possible for him to foresee what is in store for him there, a mission to India, or the South Sea Islands, would be preferable; for, in that case, the sympathy of the entire community is enlisted, and his sojourn is made as pleasant as possible—the people to whom he is sent, are either as little children, simple and confid-ing, or out-right savages; and in that case, deadly enemies. In this less remote field—almost in speaking distance—neglect from friends, suspicion, abuse, misrepresen-tation, and a degrading surveillance, often of serious and abiding consequences, await him. Not directly from the fugitives—those designed primarily to be benefitted—may assaults be looked for, at first. They possess a desire for the light, and incline to cluster around the missionary invariably. There are those who pretend to have been enlightened, and to have at heart the common good, whose influence and operations, he will find designedly counteracting his conscientious efforts, the most effectively appealing to a common origin and kindred suffering secretly striking behind, and bringing his character as a missionary, and his operations, into discredit in the eyes of a sympathizing Christian community. This, and more, awaits those who may be called to the field; but the case is not a hopeless one. The native good sense of the fugitives, backed by proper schools, will eventually develop the real character of their operations and sacrifices. They and their families, of all others, should have the support of Christians.

The refugees express a strong desire for intellectual culture, and persons often begin their education at a time of life when many in other countries think they are too old. There are no separate schools: at Toronto and in many other places, as in the churches, the colored people avail themselves of existing schools; but in the western country, in some sections, there is a tendency to "exclusiveness." The colored people of that section peti-tioned, when the School Law was under revision, that they might have separate schools: there were counter petitions by those opposed, and to satisfy all parties, twelve freehold-ers among *them*, can, by following a prescribed form, demand a school for their children; but if other schools, under patronage of Government, exist, (as Catholic or Protestant,) they can demand admission into them, if they have not one. They are not compelled to have a colored school. . . .

As before said, the facilities for obtaining a liberal education, are ample in the large towns and cities. In Toronto, students of all complexions associate together, in the better class schools and colleges. The operations of missionaries being chiefly among colored people, they have established several schools in connection with their labors, yet they are open to children without exception. The colored common schools have more of a complexional character than the private, which, with no exception that I have heard of, are open to all. The Act of Parliament above referred to, was designed to afford the fullest and most equable facilities for instruction to all, and that particular clause was inserted with the view to satisfy them, though less objectionable to the body of them, than what they asked for.

The fugitives, in some instances, settled on Government land before it came into market, cleared away and improved it. Their friends established schools which were flourishing, when they were obliged to break up, and the people to disperse, because of inability to purchase and other persons buying. This cause has, in a measure, retarded the spread of general information amongst them.

Again, ten, twenty or more families are often settled near one another, or interspersed among the French, Dutch, Scotch, Irish and Indians, in the woodland districts: often, English, is not spoken. There may not be an English school, and all revel together in happy ignorance. Nothing but the sound of the axe, and their own crude ideas of independence, to inspire them, unless it be an Indian camp fire occasionally. This may be rather an uninviting state of affairs to those living in crowded cities, but it is true there are numerous grown up families, of white and colored, who do not know B. But as uninteresting as is the detail, in this particular aspect of these affairs, the signs are encouraging. If they went to labor honestly, in a region semi-barbarous, they have cut their way out, and are now able to make themselves heard in a demand for religious instructors of the right kind, and schools. Many efficient persons have devoted their time and talents to their instruction, but there has not been anything like an equal number to the work: neither are they often found to have materials to work with. Individuals in the United States often send books to those most needy, yet they are usually of such a character as to be utterly useless. I have often thought, if it is really a benevolent act to send old almanacs, old novels, and all manner of obsolete books to them, what good purpose was accomplished, or even what sort of vanity was gratified, by emptying the useless contents of old libraries on destitute fugitives? It would be infinitely better not to give, it seems, though probably persons sending them think differently. The case is aggravated from the fact of a real desire, on the part of the recipients, to learn, and their former want of opportunity. Probably the propensity to give is gratified, but why not give, when gifts are *needed*, of that which is useful? But the question, if it is answering any good purpose to give such things as books even, has not been satisfactorily answered in the affirmative, to persons who have seen the fugitives in their Canadian homes.

SETTLEMENTS—DAWN—ELGIN—INSTITUTION—FUGITIVE HOME.

Much has been said of the Canada colored settlements and fears have been expressed by many, that by encouraging exclusive settlements, the attempt to identify colored men with degraded men of like color in the States would result, and as a consequence, estrangement, suspicion, and distrust would be induced. Such would inevitably be the result, and will be, shall they determine to have entirely proscriptive settlements. Those in existence, so far as I have been able to get at facts, do not exclude whites from their vicinity; but that settlements may not be established of that character, is not so certain. Dawn, on the Suydenham river, Elgin, or King's Settlement, as it is called, situated about ten miles from Chatham, are settlements in which there are regulations in regard to morals, the purchase of lands, etc., bearing only on the colored people; but whites are not excluded because of dislike. When purchase was made of the lands, many white families were residents,—at least, locations were not selected in which none resided. At first, a few sold out, fearing that such neighbors might not be agreeable; others, and they the majority, concluded to remain, and the result attests their superior judgement. Instead of an increase of vice, prejudice, improvidence, laziness, or a lack of energy, that many feared would characterize them, the infrequency of violations of law among so many, is unprecedented; due attention to moral and intellectual culture has been given; the former prejudices on the part of the whites, has given place to a perfect reciprocity of religious and social intercommunication. Schools are patronized equally; the gospel is common, and hospitality is shared alike by all. The school for the settlers, at Elgin, is so far superior to the one established for white children, that the latter was discontinued, and, as before said, all send together, and visit in common the Presbyterian church, there established. So of Dawn; that settlement is exceedingly flourishing, and the moral influence it exerts is good, though, owing to some recent arrangements, regulations designed to further promote its importance are being made. Land has increased in value in those settlements. Property that was worth but little, from the superior culture given by colored persons over the method before practised, and the increasing desires for country homes, is held much higher. Another fact that is worth a passing notice, is, that a spirit of competition is active in their vicinity. Efforts are now put forth to produce more to the acre, and to have the land and tenements present a tidy appearance. That others than those designed to be benefited by the organization, should be, is not reasonable, else might persons, not members of a society justly claim equal benefits with members. If Irishmen should subscribe to certain regulations on purchasing land, no neighboring landholders could rightfully share with them in the result of that organization. But prejudice would not be the cause of exclusion. So it is of those two settlements; it cannot be said of them, that they are caste institutions, so long as they do not express hostility to the whites; but the question of their necessity in the premises may be raised, and often is, by the settlers in Canada as well as in the States. The "Institution" is a settlement under the direction of the A. M. E. Church; it contains, at present, two hundred acres, and is sold out in ten acre farms, at one dollar and fifty cents per acre, or one shilling less than cost. They have recently opened a school, and there is a log meeting house in an unfinished state, also a burying ground. There are about fifteen families settled on the land, most of whom have cleared away a few trees, but it is not in a very prosperous condition, owing, it is said, to bad management of agents—a result to be looked for when a want of knowledge characterise them. This "Institution" bids fair to be one nucleus around which caste settlements will cluster in Canada.

The Refugees' Home is the last of the settlements of which I may speak in this place. How many others are in contemplation I do not know, though I heard of at least two others. This Society is designed to appropriate fifty thousand acres of land for fugitives from slavery, *only*, but at present the agents have in possession two hundred acres, situated about eight miles from Windsor, in the western district. The plan is to sell farms of twenty-five acres, that is, to give five acres to actual settlers, with the privilege of buying the adjoining twenty acres, at the market value—one-third of the purchase money constitutes a fund for school and other purposes; and ten years are given to pay for the twenty acres, but no interest may accumulate. This society may now be considered in operation, as they have made a purchase, though, as yet, no one has settled thereon, and the results to be looked for from it, from the extent of the field of operations, will have an important bearing on the colored people who are now settled in Canada, or who may emigrate thither. The friends of the society, actuated by benevolent feelings towards victims of American oppression and the odious Fugitive Law, are sanguine as to the success of the measure, but not so universal is the opinion in its favor, even among those designed to be benefited; in fact, all the objections raised against previously existing settlements, hold good against these, with the additional ones of greater magnitude. It is well known that the Fugitive Bill makes insecure every northern colored man,—those *free* are alike at the risk of being sent south,—consequently, many persons, always free, will leave the United States, and settle in Canada, and other countries, who would have remained had not that law been enacted. In pro-slavery communities, or where colonization influence prevails, they would leave at a sacrifice; they arrive in Canada destitute, in consequence, but may not settle on the land of the Refugees' Home, from the accident of nominal freedom, when it is well known that even slaves south, from the disgrace attending manual labor when performed by whites, have opportunities, in a pecuniary way, that colored men have not in some sections north. Again, the policy of slaveholders has been to create a contempt for *free* people in the bosom of their slaves, and pretty effectually have they succeeded. Their journey to Canada for liberty has not rooted out that prejudice, quite, and reference to a man's birth, as free or slave, is generally made by colored persons, should he not be as prosperous as his better helped fugitive brethren. Thus, discord among members of the same family, is engen-dered; a breach made, that the exclusive use by fugitives of the society lands is not likely to mend. Again, the society, with its funds, is looked upon in the light of a powerful rival, standing in the way of poor *free* men, with its ready cash, for its lands will not all be govern-ment purchases; neither does it contemplate large blocks, exclusively, but, as in the first purchase, and wherever found, and in small parcels also. From the exclusive nature of the many settlements, (as fugitive homes,) when it shall be known for what use it is wanted, individual holders will not sell but for more than the real value, thus embarrassing poor men who would have bought on time, and as an able purchaser from government, the society must have a first choice. The objections in common with other settlements are: the individual supervision of resident agents, and the premium indirectly offered for good behavior. "We are free men," say they who advocate independent effort, "we, as other subjects are amenable to British laws; we wish to observe and appropriate to ourselves, *ourselves*, whatever of good there is in the society around us, and by our individual efforts, to attain to a respectable position, as do the many foreigners who land on the Canada shores, as poor in purse as we were; and we do not want agents to beg for us." The accom-panying are articles in the Constitution:

Article 2. The object of this society shall be to obtain permanent homes for the refugees in Canada, and to promote their moral, social, physical, intellectual, and political elevation.

Article 11. This society shall not deed lands to any but actual settlers, who are refugees from southern slavery, and who are the owners of no land.

Article 12. All lands purchased by this society, shall be divided into twenty-five acre lots, or as near as possible, and at least one-tenth of the purchase price of which shall be paid down by actual settlers before possession is given, and the balance to be paid in equal annual installments.

Article 13. One-third of all money paid in for land by settlers shall be used for educa-tional purposes, for the benefit of said settlers' children, and the other two-thirds for the purchase of more lands for the same object, while chattel slavery exists in the United States.

BY-LAWS.

No person shall receive more than five acres of land from the society, at less than cost.

Article 4. No person shall be allowed to remove any timber from said land until they have first made payment thereon.

These are the articles of most importance, and, as will be seen, they contemplate more than fifty thousand acres continual purchases, till slavery shall cease; and other terms, as will be seen by Art. 13 of Con., and Art. 4, By-Laws, than most fugitives just from slavery can comply with, (as destitute women with families, old men, and single women,) until after partial familiarity with their adopted country. This, say many colored Canadians, begins not to benefit until a man has proven his ability to act without aid, and is fit for political equality by his own industry, that money will get for him at any time.

POLITICAL RIGHTS—ELECTION LAW—OATH—CURRENCY.

There is no legal discrimination whatever effecting colored emigrants in Canada, nor from any cause whatever are their privileges sought to be abridged. On taking proper measure, the most ample redress can be obtained. The following "abstracts of acts," bearing equally on all, and observed fully by colored men qualified, will give an idea of the measures given them:*

"The qualifications of voters at municipal elections in townships, are freeholders and householders of the township or ward, entered on the roll for rateable real property, in their own right or that of their wives, as proprietors or tenants, and resident at the time in the township or ward."

"In towns, freeholders and householders for rateable real property in their own names or that of their wives, as proprietors or tenants to the amount of five pounds per annum or upwards, resident at the time in the ward. The property qualification of town voters may consist partly of freehold and partly of leasehold."

In villages it is three pounds and upwards, with freehold or leasehold; in cities, eight pounds.

The laws regulating elections, and relating to the electors, are not similar in the two Canadas; but colored persons are not affected by them more than others.

"No person shall be entitled to vote at country elections, who has not vested in him, by legal title, real property in said county of the clear yearly value of forty-four shillings and five pence and one farthing, currency. Title to be in fee simple or freehold under tenure of free and common soccage, or in *fief* in *rature*, or in *franc allen*, or derived from the Governor and Council of the late Province of Quebec, or Act of Parliament. Qualificatiori, to be effective, requires actual and uninterrupted possession on the part of the elector, or that he should have been in receipt of the rents and profits of said property for his own use and benefit at least six months before the date of the writ of election. But the title will be good without such anterior possession, if the property shall have come by inheritance, devise, marriage or contract of marriage, and also if the deed or patent from the Crown on which he holds to claim such estate in Upper Canada, have been registered three calendar months before the date of the writ of election. In Lower Canada, possession of the property under a written promise of sale registered, if not a notarial deed, for twelve months before the election, to be sufficient title to vote. In Upper Canada, a conveyance to wife after marriage must have been registered three calendar months, or husband have been in possession of property six months before election."

"Only British subjects of the full age of twenty-one are allowed to vote. Electors may remove objection by producing certificate, or by taking the oath."

These contain no proscriptive provisions, and there are none. Colored men comply with these provisions and vote in the administration of affairs. There is no difference made whatever; and even in the slight matter of taking the census it is impossible to get at the exact number of whites or colored, as they are not designated as such. There is, it is true, petty jealousy manifested at times by individuals, which is made use of by the designing; but impartiality and strict justice characterize proceedings at law, and the bearing of the laws. The oath, as prescribed by law, is as follow:

"I, A. B., do sincerely promise and swear, that I will bear faithful and true allegiance to Her Majesty Queen Victoria, as lawful Sovereign of the United Kingdom of Great Britain and Ireland, and of this Province of Canada, dependent on and belonging to the said United Kingdom, and that I will defend her to the uttermost of my power against all traitors, conspiracies, and attempts whatever which shall be made against Her Person, Crown and Dignity, and that I will do my utmost endeavor to disclose and make known to Her Majesty, Her Heirs and Successors all treasons and traitorous conspiracies and attempts which I shall know to be against her Her or any of them, and all this I do swear without any equivocation, mental evasion, or secret reservation, and renouncing all pardons and dispensations from persons whatever, to the contrary. So help me God."

"The Deputy Returning Officer may administer oath of allegiance to persons who, according to provisions of any Act of Parliament, shall become, on taking such oath, entitled to the privileges of British birth in the Province."

"Persons knowing themselves not to be qualified, voting at elections, incur penalty of 10 pounds; and on action brought, the burden of proof shall be on the defendant. Such votes null and void."

"The qualifications of Municipal Councillors are as follows:—Township Councillor must be a freeholder or householder of the township or ward, * * * as proprietor or tenant rated on the roll, in case of a freeholder for 100 pounds or upwards; householder for 200 pounds or upwards; Village Councillor, in case of a freeholder, for 10 pounds or upwards; a householder for 20 pounds and upwards: Town Councillor, in case of a freeholder 20 pounds per annum; if a householder to the amount of 40 pounds and upwards. The property qualification of Town Councillors may be partly freehold and partly leasehold."

A tenant voter in town or city must have occupied by actual residence, as a separate tenant, a dwelling house or houses for twelve months, of the yearly value of 11 pounds, 2 s. $1^1/_2$ d. currency, and have paid a year's rent, or that amount of money for the twelve months immediately preceding the date of election writ. A person holding only a shop or place of business, but not actually residing therein, is not entitled to vote. And a voter having changed his residence within the town during the year, does not affect his right to vote, but must vote in the ward in which he resides on the day . . .

• • •

THE THIRTY THOUSAND COLORED FREEMEN OF CANADA.

The colored subjects of her Majesty in the Canadas are, in the general, in good circumstance, that is, there are few cases of positive destitution to be found among those permanently settled. They are settled promiscuously in cities, towns, villages, and the farming districts, and no equal number of colored men in the States, north or south, can produce more freeholders. They are settled on, and own portions of the best farming lands in the province, and own much valuable property in the several cities, etc. There is, of course, a difference in the relative prosperity and deportment in different sections, but a respect for, and observance of the laws, is conceded to them by all; indeed, much indifference on the part of whites has given place to genuine sympathy, and the active abolitionists and liberal men of the country, look upon that element in their character as affording ground for hope of a bright future for them, and as evidence that their sympathy for the *free* man is not misplaced, as more than compensation for their own exertions for those yet in bonds. I have said, there is but little actual poverty among them. They are engaged in the different trades and other manual occupations. They have a paper conducted by the Rev. Henry Bibb, and other able men, white and colored, are laboring among them, and in view of the protection afforded, there is no good reason why they should not prosper. After the passage of the fugitive law, the sudden emigration of several thousand in a few months, destitute as they necessarily were, from having, in many instances, to leave behind them all they possessed, made not a little suffering for a brief period, (only among them,) and the report of *their* condition had an injurious bearing upon all the colored settlers. Clothing, provisions, and other articles were sent them, but often so disposed of, or appropriated, as not to benefit those for whom intended. Distrust of agents, indiscriminately, and altogether but little real good has followed from the charity. The sensible men among them, seeing the bad results from a general character for poverty and degradation, have not been slow to express their disapprobation in the social circle, in meetings, and through the public papers. The following extracts express fully the sentiments of nine-tenths of the colored men of Canada; they think they are fully able to live without begging. There are others (very ignorant people,) who think differently, as there will be in all communities, though they are in the minority. There are those, also, and they are a respectable minority, (in point of numbers,) who are in favor of distinctive churches and schools, and of being entirely to themselves; they will come in for especial notice, but first, let us hear the people of Buxton and other places:

"If facts would bear out the statements made, the fugitives would have little to choose between slavery on one side of the line, and starvation on the other; but we rejoice that he is not reduced to the alternative. The man who is willing to work need not suffer, and unless a man supports himself he will neither be independent nor respectable in any country." * * * "The cry that has been often been raised, that we could not support ourselves, is a foul slander, got up by our enemies, and circulated both on this and the other side of the line, to our prejudice. Having lived many years in Canada, we hesitate not to say that all who are able and willing to work, can make a good living." * * * It is time the truth should be known concerning the relief that has been sent to the "suffering fugitives in Canada," and to what extent it has been applied. The boxes of clothing and barrels of provisions which have been sent in , from time to time, by the praiseworthy, but misguided zeal of friends in the United States, has been employed to support the idle, who are too lazy to work, and who form but a small portion of the colored population in Canada. There are upwards of thirty thousand colored persons in Canada West, and not more than three thousand of them have ever received aid, and not more than half of them required it had they been willing to work. We do not think it right that twenty-seven thousand colored persons, who are supporting themselves by their own industry, should lie under the disgrace of being called public beggars, when they receive nothing, and don't want anything. * * * We wish the people of the United States to know that there is one portion of Canada West where the colored people are self-supporting, and they wish them to send neither petticoat nor pantaloons to the county of Kent. * * * The few cases of real want which arise from sickness or old age, can, with a trifling effort, be relieved here, without making it a pretext for a system of wholesale begging in the United States."

> EDWARD R. GRANTS,
> SAMUEL WICKHAM,   Committee.
> ROBERT HARRIS.

"As to the state of things in Toronto and in Hamilton, I can say, from actual observation, that extreme suffering is scarcely known among the black people, while some who are far from being as industrious and deserving as they ought to be, receive aid to which they would hardly seem entitled."— *S. R. Ward's Letter to the Voice of the Fugitive.*

Notwithstanding the prosperity and liberal sentiment of the majority, there is yet a great deal of ignorance, bigotry, prejudice, and idleness. There are those who are only interested in education so far as the establishment of separate schools, churches, &c., tend to make broad the line of separation they wish to make between them and the whites; and they are active to increase their numbers, and to perpetuate, in the minds of the newly arrived emigrant or refugee, prejudices, originating in slavery, and as strong and objectionable in their manifestations as those entertained by whites towards them. Every casual remark by whites is tortured into a decided and effective negro hate. The expressions of an individual are made to infer the existence of prejudice on the part of the whites, and partiality by the administrators of public affairs. The recently arrived fugitives, unacquainted with the true state of things, is "*completely convinced* by the noisy philippic against all the "white folks," and all colored ones who think differently from them, and he is thus prepared to aid demagogues in preventing the adoption of proper measures for the spread of education and general intelligence, to maintain an ascendency over the inferior minds around them, and to make the way of the missionary a path of thorns. Among that portion, generally, may those be found, who by their indolent habits, tend to give point to what of prejudice is lingering in the minds of the whites; and it is to be feared that they may take some misguided step now, the consequences of which will entail evil on the many who will hereafter settle in Canada. The only ground of hope is in the native good sense of those who are now making use of the same instrumentalities for improvement as are the whites around them.

THE FRENCH AND FOREIGN POPULATION.

The population of Canada consists of English, Scotch, French, Irish and Americans; and, including colored persons, numbers about 1,582,000. Of the whites, the French are in the majority, but the increasing emigration of Irish, Scotch, English and other Europeans, is fast bringing about an equality in point of numbers that will be felt in political circles. In Canada West the French are in the minority.

The disposition of the people generally towards colored emigrants, that is, so far as the opinions of the old settlers may be taken, and my own observation may be allowed, is as friendly as could be looked for under the circumstances. The Yankees, in the country and in the States adjoining, leave no opportunity unimproved to embitter their minds against them. The result is, in some sections, a contemptible sort of prejudice, which, among English, is powerless beyond the individual entertaining it—not even affecting *his circle*. This grows out of the constitution of English society, in which people are not obliged to think as others do. There is more independent thought and free expression than among Americans. The affinity between the Yankees and French is strong; said to grow out of similar intentions with respect to political affairs: and they express most hostility, but it is not of complexional character only, as that serves as a mark to identify men of a different policy. Leaving out Yankees—having but little practical experience of colored people— they, (the French,) are predisposed, from the influence alluded to, to deal roughly with them; but in the main benevolence and a sense of justice are elements in their character. They are not averse to truth. There is a prevailing hostility to chattel slavery, and an honest representation of the colored people: their aims and progressive character, backed by uniform good conduct on their part, would in a very short time destroy every vestige of prejudice in the Province.

"The public mind literally thirsts for the truth, and honest listeners, and anxious inquirers will travel many miles, crowd our country chapels, and remain for hours eagerly and patiently seeking the light. * * * * Let the ignorance now prevalent on the subject of slavery be met by fair and full discussion, and open and thorough investigation, and the apathy and prejudice now existing will soon disappear."—*S. R. Ward.*

Colored persons have been refused entertainment in taverns, (invariably of an inferior class,) and on some boats distinction is made; but in all cases, it is that kind of distinction that is made between poor foreigners and other passengers, on the cars and steamboats of the Northern States. There are the emigrant train and the forward deck in the United States. In Canada, colored persons, holding the same relation to the Canadians, are in some cases treated similarly. It is an easy matter to make out a case of prejudice in any country. We naturally look for it, and the conduct of many is calculated to cause unpleasant treatment, and to make it difficult for well-mannered persons to get comfortable accommodations. There is a medium between servility and presumption, that recommends itself to all persons of common sense, of whatever rank or complexion; and if colored people would avoid the two extremes, there would be but few cases of prejudices to complain of in Canada. In cases in which tavern keepers and other public characters persist in refusing to entertain them, they can, in common with the traveling public generally, get redress at law.

Persons emigrating to Canada, need not hope to find the general state of society as it is in the States. There is as in the old country, a strong class feeling—lines are as completely drawn between the different classes, and aristocracy in the Canadas is the same in its manifestations as aristocracy in England, Scotland and elsewhere. There is no approach to Southern chivalry, nor the sensitive democracy prevalent at the North; but there is an aristocracy of birth, not of skin, as with Americans. In the ordinary arrangements of society from wealthy and titled immigrants and visitors from the mother country, down through the intermediate circles to Yankees and Indians, it appears to have been settled by common consent that one class should not "see any trouble over another;" but the common ground on which all honest and respectable men meet, is that of innate hatred of American Slavery.

RECAPITULATION.

The conclusion arrived at in respect to Canada, by an impartial person, is, that no settled country in America offers stronger inducements to colored people. The climate is healthy, and they enjoy as good health as other settlers, or as the natives; the soil is of the first quality; the laws of the country give to them, at first, the same protection and privileges as to other persons not born subjects; and after compliance with Acts of Parliament affecting them, as taking oath, &c., they many enjoy full "privileges of British birth in the Province." The general tone of society is healthy; vice is discountenanced, and infractions of the law promptly punished; and, added to this, there is an increasing anti-slavery sentiment, and a progressive system of religion.

• • •

The question whether or not an extensive emigration by the free colored people of the United States would affect the institution of slavery, would then be answered. I have here taken the affirmative of that question, because that view of the case seems to me most clear. The free colored people have steadily discountenanced any rational scheme of emigration, in the hope that by remaining in the States, a powerful miracle for the overthrow of slavery would be wrought. What are the facts. More territory has been given up to slavery, the Fugitive Law has passed, and a concert of measures, seriously affecting their personal liberty, has been entered into by several of the Free states; so subtle, unseen and effective have been their movements, that, were it not that we remember there is a Great Britain, we would be overwhelmed, powerless, from the force of such successive shocks; and the end may not be yet, if we persist in remaining for targets, while they are strengthening themselves in the Northwest, and in the Gulf. There would be more of the right spirit, and infinitely more of real manliness, in a peaceful but decided demand for freedom to the slave from the Gulf of Mexico, than in a miserable scampering from state to state, in a vain endeavor to gather the crumbs of freedom that a pro-slavery besom may sweep away at any moment. May a selection for the best be made, now that there are countries between which and the United States a comparison may be instituted. A little folding of the hands, and there may be a retreat from the clutches of the slave power.

Source: Mary Ann Shadd, *A Plea for Emigration, or Notes of Canada West, in its Moral, Social, and Political Aspect: with Suggestions Respecting Mexico, West Indies, and Vancouver Island, for the Information of Colored Emigrants* (Detroit: Printed by George W. Pattison. 1852).

19.

Frederick Douglass, et al.

Written appeals to the citizens of the United States were staples of the proceedings produced and published by black national conventions. The most powerful of these appeared in the minutes of the 1853 national convention held in Rochester. Penned largely by Frederick Douglass (1818–1895), the work represents a master of rhetoric at the height of his game. Douglass's gift was not so much his originality as his ability to concisely and vibrantly express moral outrage—the outrage due a nation which lauded itself on its commitment to freedom while denying liberty to people of African descent. Marshaling potent moral claims and facts drawn from American history, the address exhibited a tension that characterized much of the antebellum black protest tradition—a forthright demand for redress through appeal to the nation's most cherished principles. This strategy challenged a hostile society to reform the racial order or expose itself to the charge of hypocrisy.

"Address to the People of the United States"

(1853)

" . . . we address you as American citizens asserting
their rights on their own native soil."

ADDRESS, OF THE COLORED NATIONAL CONVENTION
TO THE PEOPLE OF THE UNITED STATES.

FELLOW CITIZENS: Met in convention as delegates, representing the Free Colored people of the United States; charged with the responsibility of inquiring into the general condition of our people, and of devising measures which may, with the blessing of God, tend to our mutual improvement and elevation; conscious of entertaining no motives, ideas, or aspirations, but such as are in accordance with truth and justice, and are compatible with the highest good of our country and the world, with a cause as vital made worthy as that for which (nearly eighty years ago) your fathers and our fathers bravely contended, and in which they gloriously triumphed- we deem it proper, on this occasion, as one method of promoting the honorable ends for which we have met, and of discharging our duty to those in whose name we speak, to present the claims of our common cause to your candid, earnest, and favorable consideration.

As an apology for addressing you, fellow- citizens! we cannot announce the discovery of any new principle adapted to ameliorate the condition of mankind. The great truths of moral and political science, upon which we rely, and which we press upon your consideration, have been evolved and annunciated by you. We point to your principles, your wisdom, and to your great example as the full justification of our course this day. That ALL MEN ARE CREATED EQUAL: that "LIFE, LIBERTY, AND THE PURSUIT OF HAPPINESS" ARE THE RIGHT OF ALL; that "TAXATION AND REPRESENTATION" SHOULD GO TOGETHER; that GOVERNMENTS ARE TO PROTECT, NOT TO DESTROY, THE RIGHTS OF MANKIND; that THE CONSTITUTION OF THE UNITED STATES WAS FORMED TO ESTABLISH JUSTICE, PROMOTE THE GENERAL WELFARE, AND SECURE THE BLESSING OF LIBERTY TO ALL THE PEOPLE OF THIS COUNTRY; THAT RESISTANCE TO TYRANTS IS OBEDIENCE TO GOD — are American principles and maxims, and together they form and constitute the constructive elements of the American government. From this elevated platform, provided by the Republic for us, and for all the children of men, we address you. In doing so, we have our spirit properly discerned. On this point we would gladly free ourselves and our cause from all misconception. We shall affect no especial timidity, nor can we pretend to any great boldness. We know our poverty and weakness, and your wealth and greatness.

Yet we will not attempt to repress the spirit of liberty within us, or to conceal, in any wise, our sense of the justice and the dignity of our cause.

We are Americans, and as Americans, we would speak to Americans. We address you not as aliens nor as exiles, humbly asking to be permitted to dwell among you in peace; but we address you as American citizens asserting their rights on their own native soil. Neither do we address you as enemies, (although the recipients of innumerable wrong;) but in the spirit of patriotic good will. In assembling together as we have done, our object is not to excite pity for ourselves, but to command respect for our cause, and to obtain justice for our people. We are not malefactors imploring mercy; but we trust we are honest men, honestly appealing for righteous judgment, and ready to stand or fall by that judgment. We do not solicit unusual favor, but we will be content with roughhanded "fair play." We are neither lame or blind, that we should seek to throw off the responsibility of our own existence, or to cast ourselves upon public charity for support. We would not lay our burdens upon other men's shoulders; but we do ask, in the name of all that is just and magnanimous among men, to be freed from all the unnatural burdens and impediments with which American customs and American legislation have hindered our progress and improvement. We ask to be disencumbered of the load of popular reproach heaped upon us- for no better cause than that we wear the complexion given us by our God and our Creator.

We ask that in our native land, we shall not be treated as strangers, and worse than strangers.

We ask that, being friends of America, we should not be treated as enemies of America.

We ask that, speaking the same language and being of the same religion, worshipping the same God, owing our redemption to the same Savior, and learning our duties from the same Bible, we shall not be treated as barbarians.

We ask that the doors of the school-house, the work- shop, the church, the college, shall be thrown open as freely to our children as to the children of other members of the community.

We ask that the American government shall be so administered as that beneath the broad shield of the Constitution, the colored American seaman, shall be secure in his life, liberty and property, in every State in the Union.

We ask that as justice knows no rich, no poor no black, no white, but, like the government of God, renders alike to every man reward or punishment, according as his works shall be- the white and black man may stand upon an equal footing before the laws of the land.

We ask that (since the right of trial by jury is a safeguard to liberty, against the encroachments of power, only as it is a trial by impartial men, drawn indiscriminately from the country) colored men shall not, in every instance, be tried by white persons; and that colored men shall not be either by custom or enactment excluded from the jury-box.

We ask that (inasmuch as we are, in common with other American citizens, supporters of the State, subject to its laws, interested in its welfare, liable to be called upon to defend it in time of war, contributors to its wealth in time of peace) the complete and unrestricted right of suffrage, which is essential to the dignity even of the white man, be extended to the Free Colored man also.

Whereas the colored people of the United States have too long been retarded and impeded in the development and improvement of their natural faculties and powers, ever to become dangerous rivals to white men, in the honorable pursuits of life, liberty, and happiness; and whereas, the proud Anglo-Saxon can need no arbitrary protection from open and equal competition with any variety of the human family; and whereas, laws have been enacted limiting the aspirations of colored men, as against white men- we respectfully submit that such laws are flagrantly unjust to the man of color, and plainly discreditable to white men; and for these and other reasons, such laws ought to be repealed.

We especially urge that all laws and usages which preclude the enrollment of colored men in the militia, and prohibit their bearing arms in the navy, disallow their rising, agreeable to their merits and attainments- are unconstitutional- the constitution knowing no color- are anti-Democratic, since Democracy respects men as equals- are unmagnimonious, since such laws are made by the many, against the few, and by the strong against the weak.

We ask that all those cruel and oppressive laws, whether enacted at the South or the North, which aim at the expatriation of the free people of color, shall be stamped with national reprobation, denounced as contrary to the humanity of the American people, and as an outrage upon the Christianity and civilization of the nineteenth century.

We ask that the right of pre-emption, enjoyed by all white settlers upon the public lands, shall also be enjoyed by colored settlers; and that the word "white" be struck from the pre-emption act. We ask that no appropriations whatever, state or national, shall be granted to the colonization scheme; and we would have our right to leave or to remain in the United States placed above legislative interference.

We ask that the Fugitive Slave Law of 1850, that legislative monster of the modern times, by whose atrocious provisions the writ of "habeas corpus," the "right of trial by jury," have been virtually abolished, shall be repealed.

We ask, that the law of 1793 be so construed as to apply only to apprentices, and others really owing service or labor; and not to slaves, who can *owe* nothing. Finally, we ask that the slavery in the United States shall be immediately, unconditionally, and forever abolished.

To accomplish these just and reasonable ends, we solemnly pledge ourselves to God, to each other, to our country, and to the world, to use all and every means consistent with the just rights of our fellow men, and with the precepts of our Christianity.

We shall speak, write and publish, organize and combine to accomplish them.

We shall invoke the aid of the pulpit and the press to gain them.

We shall appeal to the church and to the government to gain them.

We shall vote, and expend our money to gain them.

We shall send eloquent men of our own condition to plead our cause before the people.

We shall invite the co-operation of good men in this country and throughout the world- and above all, we shall look to God, the Father and Creator of all men, for wisdom to direct us and strength to support us in the holy cause to which we this day solemnly pledge ourselves.

Such, fellow citizens, are our aims, ends, aspirations and determinations. We place them before you, with the earnest hope, that upon further investigation, they will meet your cordial and active approval.

And yet, again, we would free ourselves from the charge of unreasonableness and self-sufficiency.

In numbers we are few and feeble; but in the goodness of our cause, in the rectitude of our motives, and in the abundance of argument on our side, we are many and strong.

We count our friends in the heavens above, in the earth beneath, among good men and holy angels. The subtle and mysterious cords of human sympathy have connected us with the philanthropic hearts throughout the civilized world. The number in our own land who already recognize the justice of our cause, and are laboring to promote it, is great and increasing.

It is also a source of encouragement, that the genuine American, brave and independent himself, will respect bravery and independence in others. He spurns servility and mean-ness, whether they be manifested by nations or by individuals. We submit, therefore, that there is neither necessity for, nor disposition on our part to assume a tone of excessive humility. While we would be respectful, we must address you as men, as citizens, as broth-ers, as dwellers in a common country, equally interested with you for its welfare, its honor and for its prosperity.

To be still more explicit: we would, first of all, be understood to range ourselves no lower among our fellow-countrymen than is implied in the high appellation of "citizen."

Notwithstanding the impositions and deprivations which have fettered us- notwith-standing the disabilities and liabilities, pending and impending- notwithstanding the cunning, cruel, and scandalous efforts to blot out that right, we declare that we are, and of right we ought to be *American Citizens*. We claim this right, and we claim all the rights and privileges, and duties which, properly, attach to it.

It may, and it will, probably, be disputed that we are citizens. We may, and, probably, shall be denounced for this declaration, as making an inconsiderate, impertinent and absurd claim to citizenship; but a very little reflection will vindicate the position we have assumed, from so unfavorable a judgment. Justice is never inconsiderate; truth is never impertinent; right is never absurd. If the claim we set up be just, true and right, it will not be deemed improper or ridiculous in us so to declare it. Nor is it disrespectful to our fellow-citizens, who repudiate the aristocratic notions of the old world that we range ourselves with them in respect to all the rights and prerogatives belonging to American citizens. Indeed, we believe, when you have duly considered this subject, you will commend us for the mildness and modesty with which we have taken our ground.

By birth, we are American citizens; by the principles of the Declaration of Indepen-dence, we are American citizens; within the meaning of the United States Constitution, we are American citizens; by the facts of history, and the admissions of American statesmen, we are American citizens; by the hardships and trials endured; by the courage and fidelity displayed by our ancestors in defining the liberties and in achieving the independence of our land, we are American citizens. In proof of the justice of this primary claim, we might cite numerous authorities, facts and testimonies,- a few only must suffice.

In the Convention of New York, held for amending the Constitution of that State, in the year 1821, an interesting discussion took place, upon the proposition to prefix the word "*white*" to male citizens. Nathan Sandford, then late Chancellor of the State, said:

> Here there is but one estate- the people-and to me the only qualification seems to be their virtue and morality. If they may be safely trusted to vote for one class of rulers, why not for all? The principle of the scheme is, that those who bear the burdens of the State, shall choose those that rule it."

Dr. Robert Clark, in the same debate, said:

> "I am unwilling to retain the word 'white,' because it is repugnant to all the prin-ciples and notions of liberty, to which we have heretofore professed to adhere, and to our Declaration of 'Independence,' which is a concise and just expose of those principles." He said, "it had been appropriately observed by the Hon. gentleman from Westchester, (Mr. Jay,) that by retaining this word, you violate the Constitution of the States."

Chancellor Kent supported the motion of Mr. Jay to strike out the word "*white*."

"He did not come to this Convention," said he, "to disfranchise any portion of the community."

Peter A. Jay, on the same occasion, said, "It is insisted that this Convention, clothed with all the powers of the sovereign people of the State, have a right to construct the government in a manner they think most conducive to the general good. If, Sir, right and power be equivalent terms, then I am far from disputing the rights of this assembly. We have power, Sir, I acknowledge, as we may think expedient. We may place the whole government in the hands of a few and thus construct an aristocracy * * * * * * But, Sir, right and power are not convertible terms. No man, no body of men, however powerful, have a right to do wrong."

In the same Convention, Martin Van Buren said:

"There were two words which has come into common use with our revolutionary struggle- words which contained an abridgment of our political rights - words which, at that day, had a talismanic effect- which led our fathers from the bosom of their families to the tented field- which for seven long years of toil and suffering, had kept them to their arms, and which, finally conducted them to a glorious triumph. They were '*taxation and representation*.' Nor did they lose their influence with the close of the struggle. They were never heard in our halls of legislation without bringing to our recollection the consecrated feelings of those who won our liberties, or, reminding us of everything that was sacred in principle."

Ogden Edwards without, said, "he considered it no better than robbery to demand the contributions of colored people towards defraying the public expenses, and at the same time to disfranchise them."

But we must close our quotations from these debates. Much more could be cited, to show that colored men are not only citizens, but that they have a right to the exercise of the elective franchise in the State of New York. If the right of citizenship is established in the State of New York, it is in consequence of the same facts which exist at least in every free State of the union. We turn from the debates in the State of New York to the nation; and here we find testimony abundant and incontestible, that Free Colored people are esteemed as citizens, by the highest authorities in the United States.

The Constitution of the United States declares "that the citizens of each State shall be entitled to all the privileges and immunities of citizens in the "United States."

There is in this clause of the Constitution, nothing whatever, of that watchful malignity which has manifested itself lately in the insertion of the word "*white*," before the term "*citizen*." The word "*white*" was unknown to the framers of the Constitution of the United States in such connections- unknown to the signers of the Declaration of Independence- unknown to the brave men at *Bunker Hill, Ticonderoga and at Red Bank*. It is a modern word, brought into use by modern legislators, despised in revolutionary times. The question of our citizenship came up as a national question, and was settled during the pendency of the Missouri question, 1820.

It will be remembered that the State presented herself for admission into the Union, with a clause in her Constitution prohibiting the settlement of colored citizens within her borders.

Resistance was made to her admission into the Union, upon that very ground; and it was not until that State receded from her unconstitutional position, that President Monroe declared the admission of Missouri into the Union to be complete.

According to Nile's Register, August 18th, vol. 20, page 338–339, the refusal to admit Missouri into the Union was not withdrawn until the General Assembly of that State, in conformity to a fundamental condition imposed by Congress, had, by an act passed for that purpose, solemnly enacted and declared:

> "That this State [Missouri] has assented, and does assent, that the fourth clause of the 26th section of the third article of their Constitution should never be construed to authorize the passage of any law, and that no law shall be passed in conformity thereto, by which any citizen of either of the United States shall excluded from the enjoyment of any of the privileges and immunities to which such citizens are entitled, under the Constitution of the United States"

Upon this action by the State of Missouri, President Monroe proclaimed the admission of Missouri into the Union:

Here, fellow-citizens, we have a recognition of our citizenship by the highest authority of the United States; and here we might rest our claim to citizenship. But there have been services performed, hardships endured, courage displayed by our fathers, which modern American historians forget to record- a knowledge of which is essential to an intelligent judgment of the merits of our people. Thirty years ago, slavery was less powerful than it is now; American statesmen were more independent then, than now; and as a consequence, the black man's patriotism and bravery were more readily recognized. The age of slave-hunting had not then come on. In the memorable debate on the Missouri question, the meritorious deeds of our fathers obtained respectful mention. The Hon. Wm. Eustis, who had himself been a soldier of the revolution, and Governor of the State of Massachusetts, made a speech in the Congress of the United States, 12th December, and said:

> "The question to be determined is, whether the article in the Constitution of Missouri, requiring the legislature to provide by law, 'that free negroes and mulattoes shall not be admitted into that State,' is, or is not repugnant to that clause of the Constitution of the United States which declares 'that the citizens of each State shall be entitled to all the privileges and immunities of citizens in the several States?' This is the question. Those who contend that the article is not repugnant to the Constitution of the United States, take the position that free blacks and mulattoes are not citizens. *Now I invite the gentlemen who maintain this to go with me and examine this question to the root.* At the early part of the revolutionary war, there were found in the middle and northern States, many blacks and other people of color, capable of bearing arms, a part of them free, and a greater part of them slaves. The freeman entered our ranks with the whites. The time of those who were slaves were purchased by the State, and they were induced to enter the service in consequence of a law, by which, on condition of their serving in the ranks during the war, they were made freemen. In Rhode Island, where their numbers were more considerable, they were formed under the same considerations into a regiment, commanded by white officers; and it is required in justice to them, to add that they discharged their duty with zeal and fidelity. The gallant defence of Red Bank, in which the black regiment bore a part, is among the proofs of their valor."

> "Not only the rights but the character of those men do not seem to be understood; nor is it to me all that extraordinary that gentlemen from other States, in which the condition, character, the moral facilities, and the rights of men of color differ so widely, should entertain opinions so variant from ours. In Massachusetts,

Sir, there are among them who possess all the virtues which are deemed estimable in civil and social life. They have their public teachers of religion and morality- their schools and other institutions. On anniversaries which they consider interesting to them, they have their public processions, in all of which they conduct themselves with order and decorum. Now, we ask only, that in a disposition to accommodate others, their avowed rights and privileges be not taken from them. If their number be small, and they are feebly represented, we, to whom they are known, are proportionately bound to protect them. But their defence is not founded on their numbers; it rests on the immutable principles of justice. If there be only one family, or a solitary individual who has rights guaranteed to him by the Constitution, whatever may be his color or complexion, it is not in the power, nor can it be in the inclination of Congress to deprive him of them. And I trust, Sir, that the decision on this occassion will show that we will extend good faith even to the blacks." -*National Intelligencer*, Jan. 11, 1821:

The following is an extract from a speech of the Hon. Mr. Morrill, of New Hampshire, delivered in the United States Senate in the same month, and reported in the *National Intelligencer*, Jan 11th, 1821:

"Sir, you excluded, not only the citizens from their constitutional privileges and immunities, but also your soldiers of color, to whom you have given patents of land. You had a company of this description. They have fought your battles. They have defended your country. They have preserved your privileges; but have lost their own. What did you say to them on their enlistment? 'We will give you a monthly compensation, and, at the end of the war, 160 acres of good land, on which you may settle, and by cultivating the soil, spend your declining years in peace and in the enjoyment of those immunities for which you have fought and bled.' Now, Sir, you restrict them, and will not allow them to enjoy the fruit of their labor. Where is the public faith in this case? Did they suppose, with a patent in their hand, declaring their title to land in Missouri, with the seal of the nation, and the President's signature affixed thereto, it would be said unto them by any authority, you shall not possess the premises? This could never have been anticipated; and yet this must follow, if colored men are not citizens."

Mr. Strong, of New York, said, in the same great debate, "The federal constitution knows but two descriptions of freemen: these are citizens and aliens. Now Congress can naturalize only aliens- i.e. persons who owe allegiance to a foreign government. But a slave has no country, and owes no allegiance except to his master. How, then, is he an alien? If restored to his liberty, and made a freeman, what is his national character? It must be determined by the federal constitution and without reference to policy; for it respects liberty. Is it that of a citizen, or alien? But it has been shown that he is not an alien. May we not, therefore, conclude- nay, are we not bound to conclude that he is a citizen of the United States?"

Charles Pinckney, of South Carolina, speaking of the colored people, in Congress, and with reference to the same question, bore this testimony:

"They then were (during the Revolution) as they still are, as valuable a part of our population to the Union, as any other equal number of inhabitants. They were, in numerous instances, the pioneers; and in all the labors of your armies, to their hands were owing the erection of the greatest part of the fortifications raised for the protection of our country. Fort Moultrie gave, at an early period the experience and untired valor of our citizens immortality to American arms; 'and in the Northern State, numerous bodies of them were enrolled, and fought, side by side, with the whites, the battles of the Revolution."

General Jackson, in his celebrated proclamations to the free colored inhabitants of Louisiana, uses these expressions: "Your white-fellow citizens;" and again: "Our brave citizens are united, and all contention has ceased among them."

FIRST PROCLAMATION.
EXTRACTS.
Head Quarters, 7th Military Dis't.,
Mobile, Sept. 21st, 1814.

To the Free Colored Inhabitants of Louisiana:
Through a mistaken policy you have heretofore been deprived of a participation in the glorious struggle for national rights, in which your country is engaged.

This no longer shall exist.

As sons of freedom, you are now called on to defend our most inestimable blessings. As *Americans*, your country looks with confidence to her adopted children for a valorous support. As fathers, husbands, and brothers, you are summoned to rally round the standard of the Eagle, to defend all which is dear to existence.

Your country, although calling for your exertions, does not wish you to engage in her cause without remunerating you for the services rendered.

In the sincerity of a soldier, and in the language of truth, I address you.- To every noble-hearted free man of color, volunteering to serve during the present contest with Great Britain, and no longer, there will be paid the same bounty in money and land now received by the white soldiers of the United States, viz.: $124 in money, and 160 acres of land. The non-commissioned officers and privates will also be entitled to *the same* monthly pay and daily rations, and clothes, furnished to *any American soldier*.

The Major General commanding will select officers for your government from your white-fellow citizens. Your non-commissioned officers will be selected from yourselves. Due regard will be paid to the feelings of freemen and soldiers. As a distinct, independent battalion or regiment, pursuing the path of glory, you will, undivided, receive the applause and gratitude of *your* countrymen.

ANDREW JACKSON
Maj. Gen. Commanding.

– *Niles' Register, Dec. 3, 1814, Vol. 7, p.205.*

SECOND PROCLAMATION

To the Free People of Color:
Soldiers! when on the banks of the Mobile I called you to take up arms, inviting you to partake the perils and glory of your *white fellow*-citizens, I expected much from you; for I was not ignorant that you possessed qualities most formidable to an invading enemy. I

knew with what fortitude you could endure hunger and thirst, and all the fatigues of a campaign.

I knew well how you loved our native country, and that you, as well as ourselves, had to defend what *man* holds most dear- his parents, wife, children, and property. You have done more than I expected. In addition to the previous qualities I before knew you to possess, I found among you a noble enthusiasm which leads to the performance of great things.

Soldiers! the President of the United States shall hear how praiseworthy was your conduct in the hour of danger, and the representatives of the American people will give you the praise your exploits entitle you to. Your General anticipates them in applauding your noble ardor.

> The enemy approaches- his vessels cover our lakes- our brave citizens are united, and all contention has ceased among them. Their only dispute is, who shall win the prize of valor, or who the most glory, its noblest reward.-
> By order,   THOMAS BUTLER, Aid-de-Camp.

Such, fellow-citizens, is but a sample of a mass of testimony, upon which we found our claim to be American citizens. There is, we think, no flaw in the evidence. The case is made out. We and you stand upon the same broad national basis. Whether at home or abroad, we and you owe equal allegiance to the same government- have a right to look for protection on the same ground. We have been born and reared on the same soil; we have been animated by, and have displayed the same patriotic impulses; we have acknowledged and performed the same duty; we have fought and bled in the same battles; we have gained and gloried in the same victories; and we are equally entitled to the blessings resulting therefrom.

In view of this array of evidence of services bravely rendered, how base and monstrous would be the ingratitude, should the republic disown us and drive us into exile!- how faithless and selfish, should the nation persist in degrading us! But we will not remind you of obligations- we will not appeal to your generous feelings- a naked statement of the case is our best appeal. Having, now, upon the testimony of your own great and venerated names completely vindicated our right to be regarded and treated as American citizens, we hope you will now permit us to address you in the plainness of speech becoming the dignity of American citizens.

Fellow-citizens, we have had, and still have, great wrongs of which to complain. A heavy and cruel hand has been laid upon us.

As a people, we feel ourselves to be not only deeply injured, but grossly misunderstood. Our white fellow-countrymen do not know us. They are strangers to our character, ignorant of our capacity, oblivious of our history and progress, and are misinformed as to the principles and ideas that control and guide us as a people. The great mass of American citizens estimate us as being a characterless and purposeless people; and hence we hold up our heads, if at all, against the withering influence of a nation's scorn and contempt.

It will not be suprising that we are so misunderstood and misused when the motives for misrepresenting us and for degrading us are duly considered. Indeed, it will seem strange, upon such consideration, (and in view of the ten thousand channels through which malign feelings find utterance and influence,) that we have not even fallen lower in public estimation than we, have done. For, with the single exception of the Jews, under the whole heavens, there is not to be found a people pursued with a more relentless prejudice and persecution, than are the Free Colored people of the United States.

Without pretending to have exerted ourselves as we ought, in view of an intelligent understanding of our interest, to avert from us the unfavorable opinions and unfriendly action of the American people, we feel that the imputations cast upon us, for our want of intelligence, morality and exalted character, may be mainly accounted for by the injustice we have received at your hands. What stone has been left unturned to degrade us? What hand has refused to fan the flame of popular prejudice against us? What American artist has not caricatured us? What wit has not laughed at us in our wretchedness? What song-ster has not made merry over our depressed spirits? What press has not ridiculed and contemned us? What pulpit has withheld from our devoted heads its angry lightning, or its sanctimonious hate? Few, few, very few; and that we have borne up with it all- that we have tried to wise, though denounced by all to be fools- that we have tried to be upright, when all around us have esteemed us as knaves- that we have striven to be gentlemen, although all around us have been teaching us its impossibility- that we have remained here, when all our neighbors have advised us to leave, proves that we possess qualities of head and heart, such as cannot but be commended by impartial men. It is believed that no other nation on the globe could have made more progress in the midst of such an univer-sal and stringent disparagement. It would humble the proudest, crush the energies of the strongest, and retard the progress of the swiftest. In view of our circumstances, we can, without boasting, thank God, and take courage, having placed ourselves where we may fairly challenge comparison with more highly favored men.

Among the colored people, we can point, with pride and hope, to men of education and refinement, who have become such, despite of the most unfavorable influences; we can point to mechanics, farmers, merchants, teachers, ministers, doctors, lawyers, editors, and authors, against whose progress the concentrated energies of American prejudice have proved quite unavailing.- Now, what is the motive for ignoring and discouraging our improvement in this country? The answer is ready. The intelligent and upright free man of color is an unanswerable argument in favor of liberty, and a killing condemnation of American slavery. It is easily seen that, in proportion to the progress of the free man of color, in knowledge, temperance, industry, and rightousness, in just that proportion will he endanger the stability of slavery; hence, all the powers of slavery are exerted to prevent the elevation of the free people of color.

The force of fifteen hundred million dollars is arrayed against us; hence, the *press*, the pulpit, and the platform, against all the natural promptings of uncontaminated manhood, point their deadly missiles of ridicule, scorn and contempt at us; and bid us, on pain of being pierced through and through, to remain in our degradation.

Let the same amount of money be employed against the interest of any other class of persons, however favored by nature they may be, the result could scarcely be different from that seen in our own case. Such a people would be regarded with aversion; the money-ruled multitude would heap contumely upon them, and money-ruled institutions would prescribe them. Besides this money consideration, fellow-citizens, an explanation of the erroneous opinions prevalent concerning us is furnished in the fact, less cred-itable to human nature, that men are apt to hate most those whom they have injured most.- Having despised us, it is not strange that Americans should seek to render us despicable; having enslaved us, it is natural that they should strive to prove us unfit for freedom; having denounced us as indolent, it is not strange that they should cripple our enterprise; having assumed our inferiority, it would be extraordinary if they sought to surround us with circumstances which would serve to make us direct contradictions to their assumption.

In conclusion, fellow-citizens, while conscious of the immense disadvantages which beset our pathway and fully appreciating our own weakness, we are encouraged to persevere in efforts adapted to our improvement, by a firm reliance upon God, and a settled conviction, as immovable as the everlasting hills, that all the truths in the whole universe of God are allied to our cause.

FREDERICK DOUGLASS,
J.M. WHITFIELD,
H.O. WAGONER,
REV. A.N. FREEMAN,
GEORGE B. VASHON.

Source: Proceedings of the Colored National Convention Held in Rochester, July 6th, 7th, and 8th 1853 (Rochester: Printed at the Office of Frederick Douglass' Paper, 1853).

20

Martin Delany

Martin Delany (1820–1876) has been described by several scholars as the foremost ante-bellum black nationalist. Born into a free black family in Charleston, West Virginia, Delany moved to western Pennsylvania. There, under the tutelage of Lewis Woodson, a prominent member of Pittsburgh's free African-American community, he learned the newspaper business, eventually becoming Frederick Douglass's coeditor for a time on the journal *The North Star*. He also attended medical school at Harvard University, where his attendance caused a furor among white students and likely shaped his increasingly pessimistic view of race relations. Delany's strand of black nationalism grew out of such frustrations and is exemplified in the selection below, an address prepared for a convention held in 1854 to espouse black emigration from the nation. It emphasized the need for black people to protect themselves from prejudice through the exercise of political power. Since such political power could be achieved only by becoming numerically dominant, this meant, in effect, migration to a new land where blacks would not need to compete against a white majority. Delany's emigrationism shifted black thinking toward a fundamentally antagonistic view of race relations in which exercises of raw power superceded efforts at moral suasion. It tacitly rejected the paternalism of white allies, whose strict focus on abolitionism too often neglected the interests of blacks once freed.

"Political Destiny of the Colored Race on the American Continent"

(1854)

"We propose for this disease a remedy.
That remedy is Emigration."

To the colored inhabitants of the United States.

FELLOW-COUNTRYMEN!—The duty assigned to us is an important one, comprehending all that pertains to our destiny and that of our posterity—present and prospectively. And while it must be admitted, that the subject is one of the greatest magnitude, requiring all that talents, prudence and wisdom might adduce, and while it would be folly to pretend to give you the combined result of these three agencies, we shall satisfy ourselves with doing our duty to the best of our ability, and that in the plainest, most simple and comprehensive manner.

Our object, then, shall be to place before you our true position in this country—the United States,Ñthe improbability of realizing our desires, and the sure, practicable and infallible remedy for the evils we now endure.

We have not addressed you as *citizens*—a term desired and ever cherished by us—because such you have never been. We have not addressed you as *freemen*,Ñbecause such privileges have never been enjoyed by any colored man in the United States. Why then should we flatter your credulity, by inducing you to believe that which neither has now, nor never before had an existence. Our oppressors are ever gratified at our manifest satisfaction, especially when that satisfaction is founded upon false premises; an assumption on our part, of the enjoyment of rights and privileges which never have been conceded, and which, according to the present system of the United States policy, we never can enjoy.

The *political policy* of this country was solely borrowed from, and shaped and modeled after, that of Rome. This was strikingly the case in the establishment of immunities, and the application of terms in their Civil and Legal regulations.

The term Citizen—politically considered—is derived from the Roman definition—which was never applied in any other sense—*Cives Ingenui*; which meant, one exempt from restraint of any kind. (*Cives*, a citizen; one who might enjoy the highest honors in his own free town—the town in which he lived—and in the country or commonwealth; and *Ingenui, freeborn*—of GOOD EXTRACTION.) All who were deprived of citizenship—that is, the right of enjoying positions of honor and trust—were termed *Hostes* and *Peregrini*; which are public and private *enemies*, and foreigners, or *aliens* to the country. (*Hostis*, a public—and sometimes—private enemy; and *Peregrinus*, an *alien, stranger*, or *foreigner*.)

The Romans, from a national pride, to distinguish their inhabitants from those of other countries, termed them all "citizens," but consequently, were under the necessity of specifying four classes of citizens: none but the *Cives Ingenui* being unrestricted in their privileges. There was one class, called the *Jus Quiritium*, or the wailing or *supplicating* citizens—that is, one who was *continually moaning, complaining, or crying for aid or succor*. This class might also include within themselves, the *jus suffragii*, who had the privilege of *voting*, but no other privilege. They could vote for one of their superiors—the *Cives Ingenui*—but not for themselves.

Such, then, is the condition, precisely, of the black and colored inhabitants of the United States; in some of the States they answering to the latter class, having the privilege of *voting*, to elevate their superiors to positions to which they need never dare aspire, or even hope to attain.

There has, of late years, been a false impression obtained, that the privilege of *voting* constitutes, or necessarily embodies, the *rights of citizenship*. A more radical error never obtained favor among an oppressed people. Suffrage is an ambiguous term, which admits of several definitions. But according to strict political construction, means simply "a vote, voice, approbation." Here, then, you have the whole import of the term suffrage. To have the "right of suffrage," as we rather proudly term it, is simply to have the *privilege*—there is no *right* about it—of giving our *approbation* to that which our *rulers may do*, without the privilege, on our part, of doing the same thing. Where such privileges are granted—privileges which are now exercised in but few of the States by colored men—we have but the privilege granted of saying, in common with others, who shall, for the time being, exercise *rights*, which in him, are conceded to be *inherent* and *inviolate*: Like the indented apprentice, who is summoned to give his approbation to an act which would be fully binding without his concurrence. Where there is no *acknowledged sovereignty*, there can be no binding power; hence, the suffrage of the black man, independently of the white, would be in this country unavailable.

Much might be adduced on this point to prove the insignificance of the black man, politically considered in this country, but we deem it wholly unnecessary at present, and consequently proceed at once to consider another feature of this important subject.

Let it then be understood, as a great principle of political economy, that no people can be free who themselves do not constitute an essential part of the ruling element of the country in which they live. Whether this element be founded upon a true or false, a just or an unjust basis; this position in community is necessary for personal safety. The liberty of no man is secure, who controls not his own political destiny. What is true of an individual, is true of a family; and that which is true of a family, is also true concerning a whole people. To suppose otherwise, is that delusion which at once induces its victim, through a period of long suffering, patiently to submit to every species of wrong; trusting against probability, and hoping against all reasonable grounds of expectation, for the granting of privileges and enjoyment of rights, which will never be attained. This delusion reveals the true secret of the power which holds in peaceable subjection, all the oppressed in every part of the world.

A people, to be free, must necessarily be *their own rulers*: that is, *each individual* must, in himself, embody the *essential ingredient*—so to speak—of the *sovereign principle* which composes the *true basis* of his liberty. This principle, when not exercised by himself, may, at his pleasure, be delegated to another—his true representative.

Said a great French writer: "A free agent, in a free government, should be his own governor;" that is, he must possess within himself the *acknowledged right to govern*: this constitutes him a *governor*, though he may delegate to another the power to govern himself.

No one, then, can delegate to another a power he never possessed; that is, he cannot *give an agency* in that which he never had a right. Consequently, the colored man in the United States, being deprived of the right of inherent sovereignty, cannot *confer* a suffrage, because he possesses none to confer. Therefore, where there is no suffrage, there can neither be *freedom* nor *safety* for the disfranchised. And it is a futile hope to suppose that the agent of another's concerns, will take a proper interest in the affairs of those to whom he is under no obligations. Having no favors to ask or expect, he therefore has none to lose.

In other periods and parts of the world—as in Europe and Asia—the people being of one common, direct origin of race, though established on the presumption of difference by birth, or what was termed *blood*, yet the distinction between the superior classes and common people, could only be marked by the difference in the dress and education of the two classes. To effect this, the interposition of government was necessary; consequently, the costume and education of the people became a subject of legal restriction, guarding carefully against the privileges of the common people.

In Rome, the Patrician and Plebian were orders in the ranks of her people—all of whom were termed citizens (*cives*)—recognized by the laws of the country; their dress and education being determined by law, the better to fix the distinction. In different parts of Europe, at the present day, if not the same, the distinction among the people is similar, only on a modified—and in some kingdoms—probably more tolerant or deceptive policy.

In the United States, our degradation being once—as it has in a hundred instances been done—legally determined, our color is sufficient, independently of costume, education, or other distinguishing marks, to keep up that distinction.

In Europe, when an inferior is elevated to the rank of equality with the superior class, the law first comes to his aid, which, in its decrees, entirely destroys his identity as an inferior, leaving no trace of his former condition visible.

In the United States, among the whites, their color is made, by law and custom, the mark of distinction and superiority; while the color of the blacks is a badge of degradation, acknowledged by statute, organic law, and the common consent of the people.

With this view of the case—which we hold to be correct—to elevate to equality the degraded subject of law and custom, it can only be done, as in Europe, by an entire destruction of the identity of the former condition of the applicant. Even were this desirable—which we by no means admit—with the deep seated prejudices engendered by oppression, with which we have to contend, ages incalculable might reasonably be expected to roll around, before this could honorably be accomplished; otherwise, we should encourage and at once commence an indiscriminate concubinage and immoral commerce, of our mothers, sisters, wives and daughters, revolting to think of, and a physical curse to humanity.

If this state of things be to succeed, then, as in Egypt, under the dread of the inscrutable approach of the destroying angel, to appease the hatred of our oppressors, as a license to the passions of every white, let the lintel of each door of every black man, be stained with the blood of virgin purity and unsullied matron fidelity. Let it be written along the cornice in capitals, "The *will* of the white man is the rule of my household." Remove all the protection to our chambers and nurseries, that the places once sacred, may henceforth become the unrestrained resort of the vagrant and rabble, always provided that licensed commissioner of lust shall wear the indisputable impress of *white* skin.

But we have fully discovered and comprehended the great political disease with which we are affected, the cause of its origin and continuance; and what is now left for us to do, is to discover and apply a sovereign remedy—a healing balm to a sorely diseased body—a wrecked but not entirely shattered system. We propose for this disease a remedy. That remedy is Emigration. This Emigration should be well advised, and like remedies applied to remove the disease from the physical system of man, skillfully and carefully applied, within the proper time, directed to operate on that part of the system whose greatest tendency shall be, to benefit the whole.

Several geographical localities have been named, among which rank the Canadas. These we do not object to as places of temporary relief, especially to the fleeing fugitive—which, like a paliative, soothes for the time being the misery—but cannot commend them as permanent places upon which to fix our destiny, and that of our children, who shall come after us. But in this connexion, we would most earnestly recommend to the colored people of the United States generally, to secure by purchase all of the land they possibly can, while selling at low rates, under the British people and government. As that time may come, when, like the lands in the United States territories generally, if not as in Oregon and some other territories and States, they may be prevented entirely from settling or purchasing them; the preference being given to the white applicant.

And here, we would not deceive you by disguising the facts, that according to political tendency, the Canadas—as all British America—at no very distant day, are destined to come into the United States.

And were this not the case, the odds are against us, because the ruling element there, as in the United States, is, and ever must be, white—the population now standing, in all British America, two and a half millions of whites, to but forty thousand of the black race; or sixty-one and a fraction, whites, to one black!—the difference being eleven times greater than in the United States—so that colored people might never hope for anything more than to exist politically by mere suffrance—occupying a secondary position to the whites of the Canadas. The Yankees from this side of the lakes, are fast settling in the Canadas, infusing, with industrious success, all the malignity and negro-hate, inseparable from their very being, as Christian Democrats and American advocates of equality.

Then, to be successful, our attention must be turned in a direction towards those places where the black and colored man comprise, by population, and constitute by necessity of members, the *ruling element* of the body politic. And where, when occasion shall require it, the issue can be made and maintained on this basis. Where our political enclosure and national edifice can be reared, established, walled, and proudly defended on this great elementary principle of original identity. Upon this solid foundation rests the fabric of every substantial political structure in the world, which cannot exist without it; and so soon as a people or nation lose their original identity, just so soon must that nation or people become extinct.—Powerful though they may have been, they must fall. Because the nucleus which heretofore held them together, becoming extinct, there being no longer a centre of attraction, or basis for a union of the parts, a dissolution must as naturally ensue, as the result of the nutrality of the basis of adhesion among the particles of matter.

This is the secret of the eventful downfall of Egypt, Carthage, Rome, and the former Grecian States, once so powerful—a loss of original identity; and with it, a loss of interest in maintaining their fundamental principles of nationality.

This, also, is the great secret of the present strength of Great Britain, Russia, the United States, and Turkey; and the endurance of the French nation, whatever its strength and power, is attributable only to their identity as Frenchmen.

And doubtless the downfall of Hungary, brave and noble as may be her people, is mainly to be attributed to the want of identity of origin, and consequently, a union of interests and purpose. This fact it might not have been expected would be admitted by the great Magyar, in his thrilling pleas for the restoration of Hungary, when asking aid, both national and individual, to enable him to throw off the ponderous weight placed upon their shoulders by the House of Hapsburg.

Hungary consisted of three distinct "races"—as they called themselves—of people, all priding in and claiming rights based on their originality—the Magyars, Celts, and Sclaves. On the encroachment of Austria, each one of these races—declaring for nationality—rose up against the House of Hapsburg, claiming the right of self-government, premised on their origin. Between the three a compromise was effected—the Magyars, being the majority, claimed the precedence. They made an effort, but for the want of a unity of interests—and identity of origin, the noble Hungarians failed.—All know the result.

Nor is this the only important consideration. Were we content to remain as we are, sparsely interspersed among our white fellow-countrymen, we never might be expected to equal them in any honorable or respectable competition for a livelihood. For the reason that, according to the customs and policy of the country, we for ages would be kept in a secondary position, every situation of respectability, honor, profit or trust, either as mechanics, clerks, teachers, jurors, councilmen, or legislators, being filled by white men, consequently, our energies must become paralysed or enervated for the want of proper encouragement.

This example upon our children, and the colored people generally, is pernicious and degrading in the extreme. And how could it otherwise be, when they see every place of respectability filled and occupied by the whites, they pandering to their vanity, and existing among them merely as a thing of conveniency.

Our friends in this and other countries, anxious for our elevation, have for years been erroneously urging us to lose our identity as a distinct race, declaring that we were the same as other people; while at the very same time their own representative was traversing the world and propagating the doctrine in favor of *a universal Anglo-Saxon predominence*. The "Universal Brotherhood," so ably and eloquently advocated by that Polyglot Christian Apostle of this doctrine, had established as its basis, a universal acknowledgment of the Anglo-Saxon rule.

The truth is, we are not identical with the Anglo-Saxon or any other race of the Caucasian or pure white type of the human family, and the sooner we know and acknowledge this truth, the better for ourselves and posterity.

The English, French, Irish, German, Italian, Turk, Persian, Greek, Jew, and all other races, have their native or inherent peculiarities, and why not our race? We are not willing, therefore, at all times and under all circumstances to be moulded into various shapes of eccentricity, to suit the caprices and conveniences of every kind of people. We are not more suitable to everybody than everybody is suitable to us; therefore, no more like other people than others are like us.

We have then inherent traits, attributes—so to speak—and native characteristics, peculiar to our race—whether pure or mixed blood—and all that is required of us is to cultivate these and develop them in their purity, to make them desirable and emulated by the rest of the world.

That the colored races have the highest traits of civilization, will not be disputed. They are civil, peaceable and religious to a fault. In mathematics, sculpture and architecture, as arts and sciences, commerce and internal improvements as enterprises, the white race may probably excel; but in languages, oratory, poetry, music and painting as arts and sciences, and in ethics, metaphysics, theology and legal jurisprudence; in plain language—in the true principles of morals, correctness of thought, religion, and law or civil government, there is not doubt but the black race will yet instruct the world.

It would be duplicity longer to disguise the fact, that the great issue, sooner or later, upon which must be disputed the world's destiny, will be a question of black and white; and every individual will be called upon for his identity with one or the other. The blacks and colored races are four-sixths of all the population of the world; and these people are fast tending to a common cause with each other. The white races are but one-third of the population of the globe—or one of them to two of us—and it cannot much longer continue, that two-thirds will passively submit to the universal domination of this one-third. And it is notorious that the only progress made in territorial domain, in the last three centuries, by the whites, has been a usurpation and encroachment on the rights and native soil of some of the colored races.

The East Indies, Java, Sumatra, the Azores, Madeira, Canary, and Capo Verde Islands; Socotra, Guardifui and the Isle of France; Algiers, Tunis, Tripoli, Barca and Egypt in the North, Sierra Leone in the West, and Cape Colony in the South of Africa; besides many other Islands and possessions not herein named. Australia, the Ladrone Islands, together with many others of Oceania; the seizure and appropriation of a great portion of the Western Continent, with all its Islands, were so many encroachments of the whites upon the rights of the colored races. Nor are they yet content, but, intoxicated with the success of their career, the Sandwich Islands are now marked out as the next booty to be seized, in the ravages of their exterminating crusade.

We regret the necessity of stating the fact—but duty compels us to the task—that for more than two thousands years, the determined aim of the whites has been to crush the colored races wherever found. With a determined will, they have sought and pursued them in every quarter of the globe. The Anglo-Saxon has taken the lead in this work of universal subjugation. But the Anglo-American stands pre-eminent for deeds of injustice and acts of oppression, unparalleled perhaps in the annals of modern history.

We admit the existence of great and good people in America, England, France, and the rest of Europe, who desire a unity of interests among the whole human family, of whatever origin or race.

But it is neither the moralist, Christian, nor philanthropist whom we now have to meet and combat, but the politician—the civil engineer and skillful economist, who direct and control the machinery which moves forward with mighty impulse, the nations and powers of the earth. We must, therefore, if possible, meet them on vantage ground, or, at least, with adequate means for the conflict.

Should we encounter an enemy with artillery, a prayer will not stay the cannon shot; neither will the kind words nor smiles of philanthropy shield his spear from piercing us through the heart. We must meet mankind, then, as they meet us—prepared for the worst, though we may hope for the best. Our submission does not gain for us an increase of friends nor respectability—as the white race will only respect those who oppose their usurpation, and acknowledge as equals those who will not submit to their rule. This may be no new discovery in political economy, but it certainly is a subject worthy the consideration of the black race.

After a due consideration of these facts, as herein recounted, shall we stand still and continue inactive—the passive observers of the great events of the times and age in which we live; submitting indifferently to the usurpation, by the white race, of every right belonging to the blacks? Shall the last vestige of an opportunity, outside of the continent of Africa, for the national development of our race, be permitted, in consequence of our slothfulness, to elude our grasp and fall into the possession of the whites? This, may Heaven forbid. May the sturdy, intelligent Africo-American sons of the Western Continent forbid.

Longer to remain inactive, it should be borne in mind, may be to give an opportunity to despoil us of every right and possession sacred to our existence, with which God has endowed us as a heritage on the earth. For let it not be forgotten, that the white race—who numbers but *one* of them to *two* of us—originally located in Europe, besides possessing all of that continent, have now got hold of a large portion of Asia, Africa, all North America, a portion of South America, and all of the great Islands of both Hemispheres, except Paupau, or New Guinea, inhabited by negroes and Malays, in Oceanica; the Japanese Islands, peopled and ruled by the Japanese; Madagascar, peopled by negroes, near the coast of Africa; and the Island of Haiti, in the West Indies, peopled by as brave and noble descendants of Africa, as they who laid the foundation of Thebes, or constructed the ever-lasting pyramids and catacombs of Egypt.—A people who have freed themselves by the might of their own will, the force of their own power, the unfailing strength of their own right arms, and their unflinching determination to be free.

Let us, then, not survive the disgrace and ordeal of Almighty displeasure, of two to one, witnessing the universal possession and control by the whites, of every habitable portion of the earth. For such must inevitably be the case, and that, too, at no distant day, if black men do not take advantage of the opportunity, by grasping hold of those places where chance is in their favor, and establishing the rights and power of the colored race.

We must make an issue, create an event, and establish for ourselves a position. This is essentially necessary for our effective elevation as a people, in shaping our national development, directing our destiny, and redeeming ourselves as a race.

If we but determine it shall be so, it *will* be so; and there is nothing under the sun can prevent it. We shall then be but in pursuit of our legitimate claims to inherent rights, bequeathed to us by the will of Heaven—the endowment of God, our common parent. A distinguished economist has truly said, "God has implanted in man an infinite progression in the career of improvement. A soul capacitated for improvement ought not to be bounded by a tyrant's landmarks." This sentiment is just and true, the application of which to our case, is adapted with singular fitness.

Having glanced hastily at our present political position in the world generally, and the United States in particular—the fundamental disadvantages under which we exist, and the improbability of ever attaining citizenship and equality of rights in this country—we call your attention next, to the places of destination to which we shall direct Emigration.

The West Indies, Central and South America, are the countries of our choice, the advantages of which shall be made apparent to your entire satisfaction.

Though we have designated them as countries, they are in fact but one country—relatively considered—a part of this, the Western Continent. . .

. . .

There is but one question presents itself for our serious consideration, upon which we must give a decisive reply—Will we transmit, as an inheritance to our children, the blessings of unrestricted civil liberty, or shall we entail upon them, as our only political legacy, the degradation and oppression left us by our fathers?

Shall we be persuaded that we can live and prosper nowhere but under the authority and power of our North American white oppressors; that this (the United States,) is the country most—if not the only one—favorable to our improvement and progress? Are we willing to admit that we are incapable of self-government, establishing for ourselves such political privileges, and making such internal improvements as we delight to enjoy, after American white men have made them for themselves?

No! Neither is it true that the United States is the country best adapted to *our* improvement. But that country is the best in which our manhood—morally, mentally, and physically—can be *best developed*—in which we have an untrammeled right to the enjoyment of civil and religious liberty; and the West Indies, Central and South America, present now such advantages, superiorly preferable to all other countries.

That the continent of America was designed by Providence as a reserved asylum for the various oppressed people of the earth, of all races, to us seems very apparent.

From the earliest period after the discovery, various nations sent a representative here, either as adventurers and speculators, or employed laborers, seamen, or soldiers, hired to work for their employers. And among the earliest and most numerous class who found their way to the new world, were those of the African race. And it has been ascertained to our minds beyond a doubt, that when the Continent was discovered, there were found in the West Indies and Central America, tribes of the black race, fine looking people, having the usual characteristics of color and hair, identifying them as being originally of the African race; no doubt, being a remnant of the Africans who with the Carthagenian expedition, were adventitiously cast upon this continent, in their memorable adventure to the "Great Island," after sailing many miles distant to the West of the "Pillars of Hercules"—the present Straits of Gibraltar.

We would not be thought to be superstitious, when we say, that in all this we can "see the finger of God." Is it not worthy of a notice here, that while the ingress of foreign whites to this continent has been voluntary and constant, and that of the blacks involuntary and but occasional, yet the whites in the southern part have *decreased* in numbers, *degenerated* in character, and become mentally and physically *enervated* and imbecile; while the blacks and colored people have studiously *increased* in numbers, *regenerated* in character, and have grown mentally and physically vigorous and active, developing every function of their manhood, and are now, in their elementary character, decidedly superior to the white race? So then the white race could never successfully occupy the southern portion of the continent; they must of necessity, every generation, be repeopled from another quarter of the globe. The fatal error committed by the Spaniards, under Pizarro, was the attempt to exterminate the Incas and Peruvians, and fill their places by European whites. The Peruvian Indians, a hale, hardy, vigorous, intellectual race of people, were succeeded by those who soon became idle, vicious, degenerated and imbecile. But Peru, like all the other South American States, is regaining her former potency, just in proportion as the European race decreases among them. All the labor of the country is performed by the aboriginal natives and the blacks; the few Europeans there, being the merest excrescences on the body politic—consuming drones in the social hive.

Had we no other claims than those set forth in a foregoing part of this Address, they are sufficient to induce every black and colored person to remain on this continent, unshaken and unmoved.

But the West Indians, Central and South Americans, are a noble race of people; generous, sociable and tractable—just the people with whom we desire to unite, who are susceptible of progress, improvement and reform of every kind. They now desire all the improvements of North America, but being justly jealous of their rights, they have no confidence in the whites of the United States, and consequently peremptorily refuse to permit an indiscriminate settlement among them of this class of people; but placing every confidence in the black and colored people of North America.

The example of the unjust invasion and forcible seizure of a large portion of the territory of Mexico, is still fresh in their memory; and the oppressive disfranchisement of a large number of native Mexicans, by the Americans—because of the color and race of the natives—will continue to rankle in the bosom of the people of those countries, and prove a sufficient barrier henceforth against the inroads of North American whites among them.

Upon the American continent, then, we are determined to remain despite every opposition that may be urged against us.

You will doubtless be asked—and that, too, with an air of seriousness—why, if desirable to remain on this continent, not be content to remain *in* the United States. The objections to this—and potent reasons, too, in our estimation—have already been clearly shown.

But notwithstanding all this, were there still any rational, nay, even the most futile grounds for hope, we still might be stupid enough to be content to remain, and yet through another period of unexampled patience and suffering, continue meekly to drag the galling yoke and clank the chain of servility and degradation. But whether or not in this, God is to be thanked and Heaven blessed, we are not permitted, despite our willingness and stupidity, to indulge even the most distant glimmer of a hope of attaining to the level of a well protected slave.

For years, we have been studiously and jealously observing the course of political events and policy, on the part of this country, both in a national and individual State capacity, as pursued toward the colored people. And he who, in the midst of them, can live with observation, is either excusably ignorant, or reprehensibly deceptions and untrustworthy.

We deem it entirely unnecessary to tax you with anything like the history of even one chapter of the unequalled infamies perpetrated on the part of the various States, and national decrees, by legislation, against us. But we shall call your particular attention to the more recent acts of the United States; because whatever privileges we may enjoy in any individual State, will avail nothing, when not recognized as such by the United States.

When the condition of the inhabitants of any country is fixed by legal grades of distinction, this condition can never be changed except by express legislation. And it is the height of folly to expect such express legislation, except by the inevitable force of some irresistible internal political pressure. The force necessary to this imperative demand on our part, we never can obtain, because of our numerical feebleness.

Were the interests of the common people identical with ours, we, in this, might succeed, because we, as a class, would then be numerically the superior. But this is not a question of the rich against the poor, nor the common people against the higher classes; but a question of white against black—every white person, by legal right, being held superior to a black or colored person.

In Russia, the common people might obtain an equality with the aristocracy; because, of the sixty-five millions of her population, forty-five millions are serfs or peasants—leaving but twenty millions of the higher classes, royalty, nobility and all included.

The rights of no oppressed people have ever yet been obtained by a voluntary act of justice on the part of the oppressors. Christians, philanthropists, and moralists, may preach, argue and philosophise as they may to the contrary; facts are against them. Voluntary acts, it is true, which are in themselves just, may sometimes take place on the part of the oppressor; but these are always actuated by the force of some outward circumstances of self-interest, equal to a compulsion.

The boasted liberties of the American people were established by a Constitution, borrowed from and modeled after the British *magna charta*. And this great charter of British liberty, so much boasted of and vaunted as a model bill of rights, was obtained only by force and extortion.

The Barons, an order of noblemen, under the reign of King John, becoming dissatisfied at the terms submitted to by their sovereign, which necessarily brought degradation upon themselves—terms prescribed by the insolent Pope Innocent III, the haughty sovereign Pontiff of Rome; summoned his majesty to meet them on the plains of the memorable meadow of Runnimede, where presenting to him their own Bill of Rights—a bill dictated by themselves, and drawn up by their own hands—at the unsheathed points of a thousand glittering swords, they commanded him, against his will, to sign the extraordinary document. There was no alternative; he must either do or die. With a puerile timidity, he leaned forward his rather commanding but imbecile person, and with a trembling hand and single dash of the pen, the name KING JOHN stood forth in bold relief, sending more terror throughout the world, that the mystic handwriting of Heaven throughout the dominions of Nebuchadnezzar, blazing on the walls of Babylon. A consternation, not because of the *name* of the King, but because of the rights of *others*, which that name acknowledged.

The King, however, soon became dissatisfied, and determined on a revocation of the act—an act done entirely contrary to his will—at the head of a formidable army, spread fire and sword throughout the kingdom.

But the Barons, though compelled to leave their castles—their houses and homes—and fly for their lives, could not be induced to undo that which they had so nobly done; the achievement of their rights and privileges. Hence, the act has stood throughout all succeeding time, because never annulled by those who *willed* it.

It will be seen that the first great modern Bill of Rights was obtained only by a force of arms: a resistence of the people against the injustice and intolerance of their rulers. We say the people—because that which the Barons demanded for themselves, was afterwards extended to the common people. Their only hope was based on *their superiority of numbers*.

But can we in this country hope for as much? Certainly not.—Our case is a hopeless one. There was but one John, with his few sprigs of adhering royalty; and but *one* heart at which the threatening points of their swords were directed by a thousand Barons; while in our case, there is but a handful of the oppressed, without a sword to point, and *twenty millions* of Johns or Jonathans—as you please—with as many hearts, tenfold more relentless than that of Prince John Lackland, and as deceptious and hypocritical as the Italian heart of Innocent III.

Where, then, is our hope of success in this country? Upon what is it based? Upon what principle of political policy and sagacious discernment, do our political leaders and acknowledged great men—colored men we mean—justify themselves by telling us, and insisting that we shall believe them, and submit to what they say—to be patient, remain where we are; that there is a "bright prospect and glorious future" before us in this country! May Heaven open our eyes from the Bartemian obscurity.

But we call your attention to another point of our political degradation. The acts of State and general governments.

In a few of the States, as in New York, the colored inhabitants have a partial privilege of voting a white man into office. This privilege is based on a property qualification of two hundred and fifty dollars worth of real estate. In others, as in Ohio, in the absence of organic provision, the privilege is granted by judicial decision, based on a ratio of blood, of an admixture of more than one-half white; while in many of the States, there is no privilege allowed, either partial or unrestricted.

The policy of the above named States will be seen and detected at a glance, which while seeming to extend immunities, is intended especially for the object of degradation.

In the State of New York, for instance, there is a constitutional distinction created among colored men—almost necessarily compelling one part to feel superior to the other; while among the whites no such distinction dare be known. Also, in Ohio, there is a legal distinction set up by an upstart judiciary, creating among the colored people, a privileged class by birth! All this must necessarily sever the cords of union among us, creating an almost insurmountable prejudices of the most stupid and fatal kind, paralysing the last bracing nerve which promised to give us strength.

It is upon this same principle, and for the same object, that the General Government has long been endeavoring, and is at present knowingly designing to effect a recognition of the independence of the Dominican Republic, while disparagingly refusing to recognize the independence of the Haitien nation—a people four-fold greater in numbers, wealth and power. The Haitiens, it is pretended, are refused because they are *Negroes*; while the Dominicans, as is well known to all who are familiar with the geography, history, and political relations of that people, are identical—except in language, they speaking the Spanish tongue—with those of the Haitiens; being composed of negroes and a mixed race. The government may shield itself by the plea that it is not familiar with the origin of those people. To this we have but to reply, that if the government is thus ignorant of the relations of its near neighbors, it is the heighth of presumption, and no small degree of assurance, for it to set up itself as capable of prescribing terms to the one, or conditions to the other.

Should they accomplish their object, they then will have succeeded in forever establishing a barrier of impassable separation, by the creation of a political distinction between those people, of superiority and inferiority of origin or national existence. Here, then, is another strategem of this most determined and untiring enemy of our race—the government of the United States.

We come now to the crowning act of infamy on the part of the General Government towards the colored inhabitants of the United States—an act so vile in its nature, that rebellion against its demands should be promptly made, in every attempt to enforce its infernal provisions.

In the history of national existence, there is not to be found a parallel to the tantalising and aggravating despotism of the provisions of Millard Fillmore's Fugitive Slave Bill, passed by the thirty-third Congress of the United States, with the approbation of a majority of the American people, in the year of the Gospel of Jesus Christ, eighteen hundred and fifty.

This bill had but one object in its provisions, which was fully accomplished in its passage; that is, the reduction of every colored person in the United States—save those who carry free papers of emancipation, or bills of sale from former claimants or owners—to a state of relative *slavery*; placing each and every one of us at the *disposal of any and every white* who might choose to *claim* us, and the caprice of any and every upstart knave bearing the title of "Commissioner."

Did any of you, fellow-countrymen, reside in a country the provisions of whose laws were such that any person of a certain class, who whenever he, she or they pleased might come forward, lay a claim to, make oath before (it might be,) some stupid and heartless person, authorized in such cases, and take, at their option, your horse, cow, sheep, house and lot, or any other property, bought and paid for by your own earnings—the result of your personal toil and labor—would you be willing, or could you be induced, by any reasoning, however great the source from which it came, to remain in that country? We pause, fellow-countrymen, for a reply.

If there be not one yea, of how much more importance, then, is your *own personal safety*, than that of property? Of how much more concern is the safety of a wife or husband, than that of a cow or horse; a child, than a sheep; the destiny of your family, to that of a house and lot?

And yet this is precisely our condition. Any one of us, at any moment, is liable to be *claimed*, *seized* and *taken* into custody by the white as his or her property—to be *enslaved for life*—and there is no remedy, because it is the *law of the land*! And we dare predict, and take this favorable opportunity to forewarn you, fellow-countrymen, that the time is not far distant, when there will be carried on by the white men of this nation, an extensive commerce in the persons of what now compose the free colored people of the North. We forewarn you, that the general enslavement of the whole of this class of people, is now being contemplated by the whites.

At present, we are liable to enslavement at any moment, provided we are taken *away* from our homes. But we dare venture further to forewarn you, that the scheme is in mature contemplation and has even been mooted in high places, of harmonizing the two discordant political divisions in the country, by again reducing the free to slave States.

The completion of this atrocious scheme, only become necessary for each and every one of us to find an owner and master at our own doors. Let the general government but pass such a law, and the States will comply as an act of harmony. Let the South but *demand* it, and the North will comply as a *duty* of compromise.

If Pennsylvania, New York and Massachusetts can be found arming their sons as watchdogs for southern slave hunters; if the United States may, with impunity, garrison with troops the Court House of the freest city in America; blockade the streets; station armed ruffians of dragoons, and spike artillery in hostile awe of the people; if free, white, highborn and bred gentlemen of Boston and New York, are smitten down to the earth, refused an entrance on professional business, into the Court Houses, until inspected by a slave hunter and his counsel; all to put down the liberty of the black man; then, indeed, is there no hope for us in this country!...

That, then, which is left for us to do, is to *secure* our liberty; a position which shall fully *warrant* us *against* the *liability* of such monstrous political crusade and riotous invasions of our rights.—Nothing less than a national indemnity, indelibly fixed by virtue of our own sovereign potency, will satisfy us as a redress of grievances for the unparalleled wrongs, undisguised impositions, and unmitigated oppression, which we have suffered at the hands of this American people.

And what wise politician would otherwise conclude and determine? None we dare say. And a people who are incapable of this discernment and precaution, are incapable of self-government, and incompetent to direct their own political destiny. For our own part, we spurn to treat for liberty on any other terms or conditions.

It may not be inapplicable, in this particular place, to quote from high authority, language which has fallen under our notice, since this report has been under consideration. The quotation is worth nothing, except to show that the position assumed by us, is a natural one, which constitutes the essential basis of self-protection.

Said Earl Aberdeen recently in the British House of Lords, when referring to the great question which is now agitating Europe:ÑÒOne thing alone is certain, that the only way to obtain a sure and honorable peace, is to *acquire a position* which may *command* it; and to gain such a position *every nerve and sinew* of the empire should be strained. The pickpocket who robs us is not to be let off because he offers to restore our purse;" and his Grace might have justly added, "should never thereafter be entrusted or confided in."

The plea doubtless will be, as it already frequently has been raised, that to remove from the United States, our slave brethren would be left without a hope. They already find their way in large companies to the Canadas, and they have only to be made sensible that there is as much freedom for them South, as there is North; as much protection in Mexico as in Canada; and the fugitive slave will find it a much pleasanter journey and more easy of access, to wend his way from Louisiana and Arkansas to Mexico, than the thousands of miles through the slave-holders of the South and slave-catchers of the North, to Canada.

Once into Mexico, and his farther exit to Central and South America and the West Indies, would be certain. There would be no obstructions whatever. No miserable, half-starved, servile Northern slave-catchers by the way, waiting cap in hand, ready and willing to do the bidding of their contemptible southern masters.

No prisons, nor Court Houses, as slave-pens and garrisons, to secure the fugitive and rendezvous the mercenary gangs, who are bought as military on such occasions. No perjured Marshals, bribed Commissioners, nor hireling counsel, who, spaniel-like, crouch at the feet of Southern slave-holders, and cringingly tremble at the crack of their whip. No, not as may be encountered throughout his northern flight, there are none of these to be found or met with in his travels from the Bravo del Norte to the dashing Oronoco—from the borders of Texas to the boundaries of Peru.

Should anything occur to prevent a successful emigration to the South—Central, South America and the West Indies—we have no hesitancy, rather than remain in the United States, the merest subordinates and serviles of the whites, should the Canadas still continue separate in their political relations from this country, to recommend to the great body of our people, to remove to Canada West, where being politically equal to the whites, physically united with each other by a concentration of strength; when worse comes to worse, we may be found, not as a scattered, weak and impotent people, as we now are separated from each other throughout the Union, but a united and powerful body of freemen, mighty in politics, and terrible in any conflict which might ensue, in the event of an attempt at the disturbance of our political relations, domestic repose, and peaceful firesides.

Now, fellow-countrymen, we have done. Into your ears have we recounted your own sorrows; before your own eyes have we exhibited your wrongs; in your own hands have we committed your own cause. If there should prove a failure to remedy this dreadful evil, to assuage this terrible curse which has come upon us; the fault will be yours and not ours; since we have offered you a healing balm for every sorely aggravated wound.

Source: "Political Destiny of the Colored Race, on the American Continent," *Proceedings of the National Emigration Convention of Colored People, held at Cleveland, Ohio, August 24, 1854* (Pittsburgh, Pa.: A. A. Anderson, Printer, 1854).

21.

William Wells Brown

In 1791, in the midst of the French Revolution, hundreds of thousands of enslaved Africans on the Caribbean island of St. Dominique rose up against their French colonial masters. During the revolution that followed, white colonists, free people of color, and enslaved blacks vied for control of the richest European colony in the New World. An alliance of free people of color and formerly enslaved blacks eventually defeated white colonials and—to the horror of whites everywhere—the best of Europe's armies. In 1804 they declared the Republic of Haiti, the first independent black republic in the modern world. The success of African-descended people against white armies in the revolution captured the imaginations of many black activists in the United States, including that of William Wells Brown (1815–1884). Brown, a former slave and conductor on the Underground Railroad, composed this lecture in 1854 as sectional tensions in the United States mounted alongside blacks' frustrations with the pace of change. Brown's lecture offers a lucid account of the immeasurably complex events of the revolution, marred only by a focus on events from the "top down" (the initial uprising by the Vodun priest Boukman is never mentioned, for example). It helps illustrate the ways color and caste played roles in Caribbean slave societies quite different from the ones they played in the United States: as Brown notes, the slaves initially harbored as much antipathy toward their free, light-complected brethren as toward their white overlords. More importantly, the lecture typifies arguments made frequently by white and black abolitionists, who raised the fearful specter of bloody slave revolt as the inevitable consequence of a dehumanizing system of bound labor. By invoking the Enlightenment spirit of the Age of Democratic Revolution that America's founding fathers had used to justify their bloody revolt against England, such arguments added considerable legitimacy to violent resistance.

"The History of the Haitian Revolution"

(1855)

" . . . the advantage of numbers and physical strength was on the side of the oppressed. Right is the most dangerous of weapons,—woe to him who leaves it to his enemies!"

LADIES AND GENTLEMEN:

THE Island of St. Domingo is situated at the entrance to the Gulf of Mexico, in one of the four Antilles, and holds the second rank after Cuba, from which it is distant only about twenty leagues. When the island was discovered by Columbus, in 1492, it was thought to have had a population of a million of people of the Caribbean race; a people of a dark brown complexion, short and small in stature, and exceedingly simple in their domestic habits, and who were but little removed from barbarism. The Caribbeans were under the dominion of four or five petty kings or chiefs, to whom they were very obedient. They acknowledged a Supreme Power, the Author of all things, and entertained a dim idea of a future state, involving rewards and punishments correspondent to their low moral condition and gross conceptions. As might have been anticipated, the natives were much alarmed at the arrival of the Spaniards, and withdrew into the interior. However, by the superior judgment of Columbus, they were gradually won back, and rendered the illustrious strangers all the assistance they could. After the return of Columbus to Spain, Dovadillo, his successor, began a system of unmitigated oppression towards the Caribbeans, and eventually reduced the whole of the inhabitants to slavery; and thus commenced that hateful sin in the New World. As fresh adventurers arrived in the island, the Spanish power became more consolidated and more oppressive. The natives were made to toil in the gold mines without compensation, and in many instances without any regard whatever to the preservation of human life; so much so, that in 1507 the number of natives had, by hunger, toil, and the sword, been reduced from a million to sixty thousand. Thus, in the short space of *fifteen years*, more than *nine hundred thousand* persons perished under the iron hand of slavery in the island of St. Domingo.

The most important town built by the Spaniards was Santo Domingo, situated on the south side of the island. The island was too valuable not to attract other adventurers, and, in a short period after its discovery, the French planted a colony on the north-west side of the island, which in a few years surpassed the Spanish portion in the elements of social well-being, and in commerce and agriculture.

St. Domingo suffered much from the loss of its original inhabitants; and the want of laborers to till the soil and to work in the mines first suggested the idea of importing slaves from the coast of Africa. The slave-trade was soon commenced and carried on with great rapidity. Before the Africans were shipped, the name of the owner and the plantation on which they were to toil was stamped on their shoulders with a burning-iron. For a number of years St. Domingo opened its markets annually to more than 20,000 newly-imported slaves. With the advance of commerce and agriculture, opulence spread in all parts of the island, and poured untold treasures into France and Spain. In a similar proportion the population increased, so that, at the beginning of the French Revolution, in 1789, there were 900,000 souls on the island. Of these, 700,000 were Africans, 60,000 men of mixed blood, and the remainder were whites and Caribbeans.

As in all countries where involuntary slavery exists, morality was at a low stand. Owing to the amalgamation of whites and blacks, there arose a class known as mulattoes and quadroons. This class, though allied to the whites by the tenderest ties of nature, were their most bitter enemies. Although emancipated by law from the dominion of individuals, the mulattoes had no rights; shut out from society by their color, deprived of religious and political privileges, they felt their degradation even more keenly than the bond slaves. The mulatto son was not allowed to dine at his father's table, kneel with him in his devotions, bear his name, inherit his property, nor even to lie in his father's graveyard. Laboring as they were under the sense of their personal social wrongs, the mulattoes tolerated, if they did not encourage, low and vindictive passions. They were haughty and disdainful to the blacks, whom they scorned, and jealous and turbulent to the whites, whom they hated and feared.

Many of the mulattoes having received their education in Paris, where prejudice against color was unknown, experienced great dissatisfaction at their proscription on their return to St. Domingo. White enough to make them hopeful and aspiring, many of them possessed wealth enough to make them influential. Aware by their education of the principles of freedom that were being advocated in Europe and the United State, they were also ever on the watch to seize opportunities to better their social and political condition. In the French part of the island alone, 20,000 whites lived in the midst of 30,000 free mulattoes and 500,000 slaves. Thus the advantage of numbers and physical strength was on the side of the oppressed. Right is the most dangerous of weapons,—woe to him who leaves it to his enemies!

In England, Wilberforce, Sharpe, and Clarkson were using their great talents to abolish the African slave-trade, and to emancipate the slaves in the English colonies. The principles which they advocated were taken up by the friends of the blacks in Paris, and a society was formed, with Gregoire, Raynal, Barnave, Brissot, Condorcet, and Lafayette at its head. The English philanthropists issued their publications in London; they found their way to Paris, and thence to St. Domingo. These made the blacks aware of their rights, as well as of their strength. The island had already assumed the name of *Hayti*. The French nation, after suffering for centuries under the misrule of its profligate princes, arose *en masse* to throw off their yoke, and the news of the oath of the Tennis Court and the taking of the Bastile was received with the wildest enthusiasm by the mulattoes in Hayti. The announcement of these events was hailed with delight by both the white planters and the mulattoes; the former, because they thought that they saw in the dim distance the independence of the colony; the latter, because they viewed it as a movement that would secure to them equal rights with the whites. And even the slaves regarded it as a precursor to their own emancipation.

However, the general excitement which the revolution in Paris created amongst the mulattoes soon satisfied the planters that they could not retain their power without the aid of France. The mulattoes immediately dispatched a deputation to Paris, to urge upon the Constituent Assembly their claims to equal rights with the whites. The whites sent a deputation to oppose the mulattoes. Both parties were well received at Paris, but the men of color were objects of special favor. Oge, one of the mulatto deputies, became known to Brissot, Barnave, Raynal, and Gregoire, and was allowed to appear in the Assembly, where he laid the wrongs of his race before that august body. In urging his claims, he said, if equality was withheld from the mulattoes, they would appeal to force. This was ably seconded in an eloquent speech by the noble-hearted and philanthropic Barnave, who exclaimed at the top of his voice, so as to be heard at the remotest part of the Assembly, *"Perish the colonies, rather than a principle!"* Noble language this! Would that the fathers of the American Revolution had been as consistent! The Assembly passed a decree giving the mulattoes equal rights with the whites, and Oge was made bearer of the news to his brethren. As might have been expected, this news created a great sensation amongst the planters in Hayti, who, as soon as the intelligence reached them, resolved that the decree should not be carried into effect. A portion of the mulattoes determined that the decree should be enforced, and assembled in arms, with Oge as their leader. This chief addressed the following letter to the Colonial Assembly:

"SIRS: A prejudice, for a long time upheld, is at last about to fall. Charged with a commission honorable to myself, I call upon you to proclaim throughout the colony the decree of the National Assembly, of the 28th of March, which gives, without distinction, to every *free* citizen the right of being admitted to all duties and functions whatever. My pretensions are just, and I do hope you will regard them. *I shall not have recourse to any raising of the slave gangs*. It is unnecessary, and would be unworthy of me. I wish you to appreciate duly the purity of my intentions. When I solicited of the National Assembly the decree I obtained in favor of our American colonists, known under the hitherto injurious distinction of the mixed race, *I never comprehended in my claims the negroes in a state of slavery*. You, and our adversaries, have mixed this with my proceedings, to destroy my estimation in the minds of all well-disposed people; but I have demanded only concessions for a class of *free men*, who have endured the yoke of your oppression for two centuries. We have *no wish* but for the execution of the decree of the 28th March. We insist on its promulgation; and we cease not to repeat to our friends, that our adversaries are not merely unjust to us, but to them-selves, for they do not seem to know *that their interests are with ours*. Before employing the means at my command, I will see what good temper will do; but if, contrary to my object, you refuse what is asked, I will not answer for those disorders which may arise from merited revenge."

The shout of battle was the only answer returned to this letter. The free blacks were defeated, and their brave leader, being taken prisoner, was, with a barbarity equalled only by its folly, broken alive on the wheel.

The revolt was suppressed for the moment, but the blood of Oge and his companions bubbled silently in the hearts of the negro race; they swore to avenge them. The mulat-toes, many of whom held slaves themselves, and, therefore, were opposed to their liberation, now saw that nothing short of a general emancipation of the slaves would secure for them their rights, and they began to make common cause with them, with the hope of extorting from the planters an acknowledgment of their equality. The habits of the mulat-toes, their intelligence, energy, and boldness, naturally pointed them out as the leaders of the slaves. They fraternized with them; they became popular from the very tinge of their skin, for which they had recently blushed when in company with the whites. The mulat-toes secretly fomented the germs of insurrection at the nightly meetings of the slaves. They also kept up a clandestine correspondence with the friends of the blacks at Paris. The planters trembled, and terror urged them to violence. The blood of Oge and his accomplices had sown everywhere despair and conspiracy.

The news of the insurrection and the death of Oge reached even the halls of the National Assembly in Paris, and gave rise to various opinions. Some sided with the blacks, others with the planters. Gregoire ably defended the course which the colored men had pursued; and said, "If liberty be right in France, it is right in Hayti; if our cause be a good one, so is the cause of the oppressed in St. Domingo." He well knew that the crime for which Oge and his friends had suffered in Hayti, had constituted the glory of Mirabeau and Lafayette at Paris.

While the National Assembly at Paris was discussing the merits of the outbreak in the colony, the Colonial Assembly, which was in session at St. Marc, took the title of General Assembly, and declared that they would never share their rights with the mulattoes. Moreover, the Colonial Assembly threw off their allegiance to the mother country, and declared themselves the sole legitimate representatives of St. Domingo, and dismissed the governor-general, whose power emanated from France alone. When this news reached Paris, the National Assembly held in Hayti, and sent out troops to enforce their decrees. This intelligence was received with joy by the mulattoes, for they now saw that the authorities in the mother country, and the planters, were at war with each other, and that they would profit by the quarrel.

The planters repelled with force the troops sent out by France; denying its perogatives, and refusing the civic oath. In the midst of these thickening troubles, the planters who resided in France were invited to return, and to assist in vindicating the civil independence of the island. Then was it that the mulattoes earnestly appealed to the slaves, and the result was appalling. The slaves awoke as from an ominous dream, and demanded their rights with sword in hand. Gaining immediate success, and finding that their liberty would not be granted by the planters, they rapidly increased in numbers; and, in less than a week from its commencement, the storm had swept over the whole plain of the north, from east to west, and from the mountains to the sea. The splendid villas and rich factories yielded to the fury of the devouring flames; so that the mountains, covered with smoke and burning cinders borne upwards by the wind, looked like volcanoes; and the atmosphere, as if on fire, resembled a furnace.

Such were the outraged feelings of a people whose ancestors had been ruthlessly torn from their native land, and sold in the shambles of St. Domingo. During these excesses, a new General Assembly, composed entirely of planters and their immediate friends, opened its sessions, under the title of the "New Colonial Assembly;" and its first step was an act of rebellion. Refusing to apply to France for aid, and having taken measures of defence, it sought protection from England. But without waiting to hear from the English government, the Colonial Assembly laid aside their own uniform, put on the round English hat, and substituted the black cockade for the French national flag. The men of color placed themselves under the standard of royalty; they gave themselves the name of the "King's Own," and their chief assumed the title of "High Admiral of the French Army." By this movement the blacks became the government troops, and the planters the insurgents. Although the men of color were now the acknowledged soldiers of France, as yet they had no leaders of any note, and were scarcely more than an armed banditti. Jean Francois, an emancipated mulatto, intellectual, but possessing little courage, was its chief. Without either regular arms or uniform, the blacks attired themselves in the spoils taken in their engagements, and were mounted on old, broken-down horses and mules. The infantry, many of them, made a still more ridiculous appearance. The commanding chief was decorated with ribbons, orders, and medals which had been worn in former days by the whites, and announced himself as "a Chevalier of the Order of St. Louis, and Great Grand High-Admiral and Generalissimo of the French Army."

Like white men, the blacks no sooner met with success than they disagreed amongst themselves, and Bissou, an inferior general, drew off his forces, and assumed the title of "Viceroy of the Conquered Territories."

For the purpose of striking terror into the minds of the blacks, and to convince them that they should never have their freedom, the French planters were murdering them on every hand by the thousands. In a single day, at the Cape, more than five hundred faithful servants, who had not taken up arms against their masters, but who refused to fight for them, were put to death. This example set by the whites taught the men of color that the struggle was for liberty or death. Crime was repaid with crime, and vengeance followed vengeance. The educated, refined, and civilized whites degraded themselves even more than the barbarous and ignorant slaves.

While matters were thus transpiring in Hayti, the people in France were scarcely less agitated with dissensions at home. Louis XVI, in his attempt to escape from his own dominions, had been arrested and taken back to his capital, there to be insulted and humiliated by his subjects. Although the mother country had enough to do at home, she resolved to send three commissioners to St. Domingo, on a mission of peace. On their arrival in the island, these men did but little more than fan the flame which had already been kindled.

The struggle in St. Domingo was watched with intense interest by the friends of the blacks, both in Paris and in London, and all appeared to look with hope to the rising up of a black chief, who should prove himself adequate to the emergency. Nor did they look in vain. In the midst of the disorders that threatened on all sides, the negro chief made his appearance in the form of an old slave named Toussaint. This man was the grandson of the king of Arradas, one of the most wealthy, powerful, and influential monarchs on the west coast of Africa. Toussaint was a man of prepossessing appearance, of middle stature, and possessed an iron frame. His dignified, calm, and unaffected features, and broad and well-developed forehead, would cause him to be selected, in any company of men, as one who was born for a leader. By his energy and perseverance he had learned to read and write, and had carefully studied the works of Raynal, and a few others who had written in behalf of human freedom. This class of literature, no doubt, had great influence over the mind of Toussaint, and did much to give him the power that he afterwards exercised in the island. His private virtues were many, and he had a deep and pervading sense of religion, and, in the camp, carried it even as far as Oliver Cromwell. It might be said that an inward and prophetic genius revealed to him the omnipotence of a firm and unwearied adherence to a principle. He was not only loved by fellow-slaves, but the planters held him in high consideration.

When called into the camp, Toussaint was fifty years of age. One of his great characteristics was his humanity. Before taking any part in the revolution, he aided his master's family to escape from the impending danger. After seeing his master's household beyond the reach of the revolutionary movement, he entered the army as an inferior officer; but was soon made aide-de-camp to General Bissou. Disorder and bloodshed reigned triumphant throughout the island, and every day brought fresh intelligence of depredations committed by whites, mulattoes, and blacks. Such was the condition of affairs when a decree was passed by the Colonial Assembly, giving equal rights to the mulattoes, and asking their aid in restoring order, and reducing the slaves again to their chains. Overcome by this decree, and having gained all they wished, the mulattoes joined the planters in a murderous crusade against the blacks, who were the slaves. The union of the whites and mulattoes made an army too strong and powerful for the slaves, and the latter were defeated in several pitched battles. But the blacks were fighting for personal liberty, and therefore were not to be easily conquered. The never-to-be-forgiven course of the mulattoes in fraternizing with the whites to prevent the slaves getting their liberty, created an ill feeling between these two proscribed classes, which a half a century has not been able to efface.

While the people of St. Domingo were thus pitted against each other, the revolution in France was making sad havoc. Robespierre and Danton ruled in Paris; the Swiss Guard had been massacred; the royalists and nobility had fled, and the guillotine had once more fallen; and the head of Louis XVI had rolled into the basket. At the news of the king's death, the slaves in Hayti gave up all hope and thought of peace and freedom under the French, renounced the revolutionary movements in Paris, and passed over into the service of the king of Spain. Toussaint was appointed brigadier-general in the Spanish army, and soon appeared in the field as a most powerful and determined foe to the French planters.

While the blacks were becoming formidable under the protection of Spain, the mulattoes were gaining strength and influence under the French. Affairs had scarcely assumed this shape in Hayti, when General Galbeaud was sent out from France to take command of the army in St. Domingo. The commissioners in the island refused to give up their authority, and a civil war commenced between the new general and the commissioners. The Haytian national guard and volunteers joined the general, while the troops of the line and the mulattoes took sides with the commissioners. A fierce and sanguinary struggle followed, in which both parties showed that they thought they were in the right, and which was attended with the most fatal results. The commissioners, seeing a defeat at hand, let loose fifteen hundred slaves, and a large number of outlaws, who were confined in the prisons, and declared them free if they would fight in their behalf. Slaves, who had been many months in the mountains, where they had been committing the most unlawful depredations, were also invited by the commissioners to join their standard. The two armies met; a battle was fought in the streets, and many thousands were slain on both sides; the French general, however, was defeated, and, in company with several hundreds of refugees, set sail for France. During the conflict the city was set on fire, and on every side presented shocking evidence of slaughter, conflagration, and pillage. The strifes of political and religious partisanship, which had raged in the clubs and streets of Paris, and had caused the guillotine to send its two hundred souls every day for many weeks, unprepared, to eternity, were transplanted to St. Domingo, where they raged with all the heat of a tropical clime, and the animosities of a civil war. Truly did the flames of the French Revolution at Paris, and the ignorance and self-will of the planters, set the island of St. Domingo on fire. The commissioners with their retinue retired from the burning city into the neighboring highlands, where a camp was formed to protect the ruined town from the opposing party. Having no confidence in the planters, and fearing a reaction, the commissioners proclaimed a general emancipation to the slave population, and invited the blacks who had joined the Spaniards to return. Toussaint and his followers accepted the invitation, returned, and were enroled in the army under the commissioners. Fresh troops arrived from France, who were no sooner in the island than they separated—some siding with the planters, and others with the commissioners; and never, perhaps, did any conflict present more heterogeneous combinations than this civil commotion. The white republicans of the mother country were arrayed against the white republicans of Hayti, whom they had been sent out to assist; the blacks and mulattoes were at war with each other; old and young of both sexes, and of all colors, were put to the sword, while the fury of the flames swept from plantation to plantation and from town to town. On one day four flags, representing as many political influences, were hoisted in sight of each other. Each had a cockade, denoting the opinions entertained by its members. Here were whites who wore the black cockade; there were other whites who wore the white cockade. The main body of mulattoes wore the red cockade; while a company made up of all shades of complexions wore the tri-colored cockade.

These parties were a lamentable illustration of the rival opinions that pervaded the minds of the masses; and miserably was poor, unfortunate St. Domingo torn asunder by Spaniards, French, English, and Africans,—by enemies and friends of emancipation.

During these sad commotions, Toussaint, by his superior knowledge of the character of his race, his generosity, humanity, and courage, had won his way up to the highest position in the French army. Becoming aware that they were equal to the emergency, and wearied with internal commotion, the commissioners offered Toussaint the entire command of the army; and Lavaux, the governor, nominated the negro chief as second in the government in the island. Lavaux being soon after recalled to France, Toussaint was declared Governor-General of St. Domingo; and, by his genius and surpassing activity, he levied fresh forces, raised the reputation of the army, and drove the English troops out of the island.

The power of the French had now ceased, the English had been driven from the island, Spanish rule was at an end, and yet the war was carried on as fiercely as ever. But it was a war of color, and not condition. During the revolution a chief had appeared in the south, who, by his bravery and intellectual gifts, was second only to Toussaint. This was Rigaud, the son of a wealthy planter by a woman of mixed blood. Nature had been profligate in bestowing her gifts upon Rigaud. He was tall and slim, with features beautifully defined; and having been educated in Paris, in the finest military school in the world, and where he had been introduced into good society, his manners were polished and his language elegant. On his return to Hayti, Rigaud joined the militia in Les Cayes, his native town. In religion he was the very opposite of Toussaint. An admirer of Voltaire and Rousseau, he had made their works his study. A long residence in Paris had enabled him to become acquainted with many of the followers of these two distinguished philosophers. He had seen two hundred thousand persons following the bones of Voltaire, when removed to the Pantheon; and, in his admiration for the great writer, had confounded liberty with infidelity. In Asia he would have founded and governed an empire; in Hayti he was scarcely more that an outlawed chief; but he had in his soul the elements of a great man. Rigaud was the first man amongst the mulattoes; Toussaint was first with the blacks. After the whites had abandoned the government, these two powerful chiefs made war upon each other. Toussaint ruled in the west, and Rigaud in the south. . . .

The army for the expedition to St. Domingo was fitted out, and no pains or expense spared to make it an imposing one. Fifty-six ships of war, with twenty-five thousand men, left France for Hayti. It was, indeed, the most valiant fleet that had ever sailed from the French dominions. The Alps, the Nile, the Rhine, and all Italy, had resounded with the exploits of the men who were now leaving their country for the purpose of placing the chains again on the limbs of the heroic people of St. Domingo. There were men in that army that had followed Bonaparte from the siege of Toulon to the battle under the shades of the pyramids of Egypt,—men who had grown gray in the camp. Among them were several distinguished men of color. There was Rigaud, the educated, refined, and accomplished gentlemen, whose language was of the drawing-room, and who was as brave as he was handsome, and whose valor had disputed the laurel with Touissant. There, too, was Petion, a man destined to make an impression that should be recorded in the history of his native island. And last, though not the least, there was Boyer, who was to wait his turn to be placed in the presidential chair. These three were mulattoes, were haters of the blacks, and consequently had become the dupes and tools of Bonaparte, and were now on their way to assist in reducing the land of their birth to slavery. . . .

News of the intended invasion reached St. Domingo some days before the squadron had sailed from Brest; and therefore the blacks had time to prepare to meet their enemies. Touissant had concentrated his forces at such points as he expected would be first attacked. Christophe, who stood next to Touissant in command, had Cape City in his charge. This chief was born a slave in the island of New Grenada, was emancipated, and went to Hayti, where he became the keeper of an inn. He subsequently dealt in cattle, at which business he made a small fortune. Being six feet three inches in height, Christophe made an imposing appearance on horseback, when dressed in his uniform of a general. He had a majestic carriage, and an eye full of fire; and a braver man never lived. Next to Christophe was Dessalines. The furrows and incisions on the face, neck, and arms of this man pointed out the coast of Africa as his birthplace. He was a bold, turbulent, and ferocious spirit, whose barbarous eloquence lay in expressive signs rather than in words. Hunger, thirst, fatigue, and loss of sleep, he seemed made to endure, as if by peculiarity of constitution. He had a fierce and sanguinary look, beneath which was concealed an impenetrable dissimulation. Like Leclerc, Dessalines was of small, neat figure. Port-au-Prince was under the command of this chief, and it could not have been left in better hands. . . .

With no navy, and by little means of defence, the Haytians determined to destroy their towns rather than they should fall into the hands of the enemy. Late in the evening the French ships were seen to change their position, and Christophe, satisfied that they were about to effect a landing, set fire to his own mansion, which was the signal for the burning of the town. The French general wept as he beheld the ocean of flames rising from the tops of the houses in the finest city in St. Domingo. Another part of the fleet landed at Samana, where Toussaint happened to be himself. On seeing the ships, the great general said, "Here come the enslavers of our race. All France is coming to Hayti, to try to put the chains again on our limbs; but not France, with all her troops of the Rhine, the Alps, the Nile, the Tiber, nor all Europe to help her, can extinguish the soul of Africa. That soul, when once the soul of a man, and no longer that of a slave, can overthrow the Pyramids and the Alps themselves, sooner than again be crushed down into slavery." . . .

After the abandonment of the Cape, Christophe joined Toussaint, and the two generals raised fire and flames everywhere. Although the French had all the strongholds in the island, they found that they were not masters of Hayti. Like Nat Turner, the Spartacus of the Southampton revolt, who fled with his brave band to the Virginia swamps, Toussaint and his generals took to the mountains. Leclerc now resorted to the most ungenerous and dishonest means that could be devised to induce the brave Toussaint to surrender the island to him. Isaac and Placide, sons of Toussaint, who had been at school in Paris, were given commissions as French officers, by Bonaparte, and sent out with Leclerc. These sons were sent by Leclerc to Toussaint to persuade and to work upon the feelings of their father, and cause him to betray his trust, and the liberty of St. Domingo. But the heroic old chief, though born a slave, and without the refinements that adorned the most polished and educated Leclerc, rose from the position of the slave to that of a patriot. Toussaint received his sons, embraced them, and told them that they were at liberty to return to the French army if they wished, but that he would not yield the island.

Again Leclerc addressed Toussaint, telling him that he had a force sufficient to crush him if he did not surrender. Like Leonidas, when Xerxes sent him word that his "forest of arrows would darken the sun-light," "So much the better, we shall then fight in the shade," was the reply of the former. "I have a sword, and will not sheathe it," said Toussaint to Leclerc's messenger. The black general then issued a proclamation to the people of Hayti, in which he said, "You are going to fight against enemies who have neither faith, law nor religion; they promise you liberty—they intend your servitude. Why have so many ships traversed the ocean, if not to throw you again in chains? During the last ten years what have you not endured for liberty? The French do not come here to fight for their country, or for liberty, but for slavery. Let us resolve that these troops shall never leave our shores. Fortune seems to have delivered them as victims into our hands. Those whom our swords spare will be struck dead by an avenging climate; their bones will be scattered among these mountains and rocks, and tossed about by the waves of our sea. Never more will they behold their native land; never more will they be received by their mothers, their wives and their sisters; but liberty will reign over their tomb."

"To arms! To arms!" was the cry all over the island, until every one who could use even the lightest instrument of death, was under arms. General Maurepas, a brave black, defeated the French general at St. Marc, and forced him to put to sea with two ships of war. Dessalines, Belair and Lemartiniere, defeated the French general at Verettes; in no place was the slaughter so terrible as there. At the mere nod of Dessalines, men who had been slaves, and who dreaded the new servitude with which they were threatened, massacred seven hundred of the whites that Dessalines had amongst his prisoners. The child died in the arms of its sick and terrified mother; the father was unable to save the daughter; the daughter unable to save the father. Mulattoes took the lives of their white fathers, to whom they had been slaves, or who, allowing them to go free, had disowned them; thus revenging themselves for the mixture of their blood. So frightful was this slaughter, that the banks of the Artibonite were strewed with dead bodies, and the waters dyed with the blood of the slain. Not a grave was dug, for Dessalines had prohibited interment, in order that the eyes of the French might see his vengeance in even in the repulsive remains of carnage. He had a mother put to death for having buried her son.

Let the slave-holders in our Southern States tremble when they shall call to mind these events. While Dessalines was carrying fire and sword amongst the planters where he had command, Toussaint and Christophe were cutting the French to pieces at Crete-a-Pierrat, where they had to meet the bravery and experience of Rigaud and Petion, who fought nobly, but in a bad cause. Rochambeau was doing the work of death amongst the blacks. He caused wives to be murdered before the eyes of their husbands, and children to be thrown into burning pits in presence of their agonizing mothers. But Leclerc saw that this was slaughter without any prospect of reducing the blacks to their former condition as slaves, and he determined to resort to a stratagem, in which he succeeded too well.

A correspondence was opened with Toussaint, in which the captain-general promised to acknowledge the liberty of the blacks, and the equality of all, if he would yield. In the mean time, Dessalines and Christophe had joined the French, under the solemn promise that liberty should be guaranteed to the colored race throughout the island. Overcome by the persuasions of his other generals, and the blacks who surrounded him, and who were sick and tired of the shedding of blood, Toussaint gave in his adhesion to the French authorities. This was the great error of his life. But even in this Christophe and Dessalines cannot escape blame. As inferior officers, they should not have listened to Leclerc's terms without the consent of Toussaint. Suffice it to say, that both of these generals regretted that act in after life.

The loss that the French army had sustained during the war was great. Fifteen thousand of their best troops, and some of their bravest generals, had fallen before the arms of these negroes, whom they despised. Soon after Toussaint gave in his adhesion, the yellow fever broke out in the French army, and carried nearly all of the remaining men off, —Debelle, who had rare virtues, and who was beloved by many of the blacks; Dugua, an old man, whose warlike exploits on the banks of the Nile had placed him high in the list of fame; Hardy, a man second only to Bonaparte, in the wars of the East; more than seven hundred medical men, besides twenty-two thousand sailors and soldiers. Among these were fifteen hundred officers. It was at this time that Toussaint might have renewed the war with great success. But he was a man of his word, and would not take advantage of the sad condition of the French army.

The forcible capture of Toussaint, which took place about this time, is too well known to be recapitulated here. The great chief of St. Domingo had scarcely been conveyed on board the ship Creole, and she out of the harbor, ere Rigaud, the mulatto general who had accompanied Leclerc to Hayti, was also seized and sent to France. After being imprisoned a short time in the Temple, Toussaint was conveyed to the Castle of Joux, and placed in one of its cold, damp cells. It was a strange coincidence, that Toussaint and Rigaud, who had hated each other in their native land, were incarcerated in the same prison in France. But, even in this dismal place, these chiefs were too illustrious to be permitted to see and converse with each other. The arrest of Toussaint caused suspicion and alarm amongst the blacks; and that of Rigaud told the mulattoes that they could put no confidence in the promises of the captain-general.

The disarming of the blacks, with the exception of those under Christophe and Dessalines, now took place. Belair, in the mountain of St. Marc, and Sans-Souci, two veteran chiefs, who had followed Toussaint in nearly all his battles, were arrested and put to death. But the death of General Maurepas, the heroic black chief, who had defeated a portion of the French when they numbered two to his one, caused a general rising of the blacks. This general, who commanded a battalion of blacks attached to the French army, was invited by Leclerc to go to the Cape to take the command of that post. No sooner had he arrived than he and his soldiers were disarmed and put on board a vessel lying in the bay. Maurepas was bound to the mast of the ship and tortured in the presence of his wife and children. They were then, one after another, thrown into the sea; the father being the last put to death, so that he should witness the drowning of his wife, children, and officers, to increase his grief. Thus died the frank, brave, and generous Maurepas, who loved liberty for the sake of his race. The murder of Maurepas and his companions had scarce been told to the blacks, before the news reached them that Rochambeau had put five hundred blacks to death. These brutal murders by the French filled the blacks with terror.

Hearing of the death of his old friend and camp-mate, Dessalines, with all under his command, joined the insurgents, and started for the Cape, for the purpose of meeting Rochambeau, and avenging the death of the blacks. In his impetuous and terrible march, he surrounded and made prisoners a body of Frenchmen, and, with branches of trees, that ferocious chief raised, under the eyes of Rochambeau, five hundred gibbets, on which he hanged as many prisoners.

Twenty thousand fresh troops arrived from France; but they were not destined to see Leclerc, for the yellow fever had taken him off. In the mountains were many barbarous and wild blacks, who had escaped from slavery soon after being brought from the coast of Africa. One of these bands of savages were commanded by Lamour de Rance, an adroit, stern, savage man, half naked, with epaulets tied to his bare shoulders for his only token of authority.

At home, in the mountains, he passed from one to another with something of the ease of the birds in his own sunny land. Toussaint, Christophe, and Dessalines, had each in their turn pursued him, but in vain. His mode of fighting was in keeping with his dress.

Another gang of these savages was commanded by a woman named Vida. She was a native of Africa, and, like Lamour, had been ruthlessly torn from her native land. Her face was all marked with incisions, and large pieces had been cut out of her ears. Vida kept a horse, which she had caught with her own hands, and had broken to the bit. When on horseback, she rode like a man. On arriving at places too steep to ascend, she would dismount, and her horse would at once follow her. This woman, with her followers, met and defeated a batallion of the French, who had been sent into the mountains. Lamour and Vida united, and they were complete masters of the wilds of St. Domingo;—and, even to the present day, their names are used to frighten children into obedience. These two savages came forth from their mountain homes, and made war on the whites wherever they found them.

The desertion from the French army by Dessalines was soon after followed by Christophe, who carried over to the blacks a large and well disciplined force. Clervaux and Petion, the mulatto generals who succeeded Rigaud in the south, also joined the blacks, and these four chiefs caused dismay in all parts of the island where they appeared. Leclerc was now dead, and Rochambeau, who succeeded him in the government of St. Domingo, began to resort to the most atrocious means to subdue the blacks. He sent a ship of war to Cuba for blood-hounds; and, on their arrival, cannons were fired, and demonstrations of joy were shown in various ways. Even the women, wives of the planters, went to the sea-side, met the animals, put garlands about their necks, and some kissed and caressed the dogs. Such was the degradation of human nature. While white women were cheering on the French, who had imported blood-hounds as their auxiliaries, the black women were using all of their powers of persuasion to rouse the blacks to the combat. Many of these women walked from camp to camp, and from battalion to battalion, exhibiting their naked bodies, showing their lacerated and scourged persons;—these were the marks of slavery, made many years before, but now used for the cause of human freedom.

Christophe, who had taken command of the insurgents, now gave unmistakable proof that he was a great general, and scarcely second to Toussaint. Twenty thousand fresh troops arrived from France to the aid of Rochambeau; yet the blacks were victorious wherever they fought. The French blindly thought that cruelty to the blacks would induce their submission, and to this end they bent all their energies. An amphitheater was erected, and two hundred dogs, sharpened by extreme hunger, put there, and black prisoners thrown in. The raging animals disputed with each other for the limbs of their victims, until the ground was dyed with human blood. Three hundred brave blacks were put to death in this horrible manner. The blacks, having spread their forces in every quarter of the island, were fast retaking the forts and towns. Christophe commanded in the north, Dessalines in the west, and Terrou in the south.

Rochambeau, surrounded on all sides, drew his army together for defence, rather than aggression. But even in this he foresaw a failure. Exulting in their triumph, the blacks commenced hostilities on the sea. In light boats, with the aid of the wind and tide and of oars, they went up and down the rivers, passed from the mountains, spreading terror wherever they appeared. At last Rochambeau was besieged by the blacks on land, and the English on sea, and never was a general in a more deplorable condition. Horses had been used for food; and even the very dogs that had been brought from Cuba to hunt down the blacks were used as food by the proud and oppressive French. The French general now sued for peace, and promised that he would immediately leave the island; it was accepted by the blacks, and Rochambeau prepared to return to France. The French embarked in their vessels of war, and the standard of the blacks once more waved over Cape City, the capital of St. Domingo. As the French sailed from the island, they saw the tops of the mountains lighted up;—it was not a blaze kindled for war, but for freedom. Every heart beat for liberty, and every voice shouted for joy. From the ocean to the mountains, and from town to town, the cry was Freedom! Freedom! And the women formed themselves into bands, and went from house to house, serenading those who had been most conspicuous in expelling their invaders. Thus ended Napoleon's expedition to Hayti. In less than two years, the French lost more than fifty thousand persons, and the blacks less than fifteen thousand. . . .

Who knows but that a Toussaint, a Christophe, a Rigaud, a Clervaux, and a Dessaline, may some day appear in the Southern States of this Union? That they are there, no one will doubt. That their souls are thirsting for liberty, all will admit. The spirit that caused the blacks to take up arms, and to shed their blood in the American revolutionary war, is still amongst the slaves of the south; and, if we are not mistaken, the day is not far distant when the revolution of St. Domingo will be reenacted in South Carolina and Louisiana. The Haytian revolution was not unlike that which liberated the slaves of Sparta. . . .

What the Helots were to Sparta at the time of the earthquake, the blacks were to St. Domingo at the time of the French revolution. And the American slaves are only waiting for the opportunity of wiping out their wrongs in the blood of their oppressors. No revolution ever turned up greater heroes that that of St. Domingo. But no historian has yet done them justice. If the blacks were guilty of shedding blood profusely, they only followed the example set them by the more refined and educated whites.

After the French had been driven from the island, Dessalines soon set his companions at naught, and caused himself to be elected governor; and a few months after, he threw aside the disguise, and proclaimed himself emperor. That he was a cruel man, no one will deny. It was this hatred to the whites, and his indomitable courage, that place him in favor with the people. The act of Cortes, in destroying his ships, after arriving in Mexico, was not more heroic or courageous than that of Dessalines, when, fearing that his soldiers would surrender the fort at Crete-a-Pierrat, he seized a torch, held it to the door of the magazine, and threatened to blow up the fort, and himself with it, if they did not defend it. What is most strange in the history of this man is, that he was a savage, a slave, a soldier, a general, and died, when an emperor, under the dagger of a Brutus. . . .

We cannot close without once more reviewing the character of Toussaint. Of all the great men of St. Domingo, the first place must be given to him. He laid the foundation for the emancipation of his race and the independence of the island. He fought her battles, and at last died in a cold prison for her sake and his fidelity to the cause of freedom. As an officer in battle he had no superior in Hayti. He defeated the French in several pitched battles, drove the English from the island, and refused a crown when it was offered to him. When his friends advised him to be on his guard against the treachery of Leclerc, he replied, "For one to expose one's life for one's country when in danger is a sacred duty; but to arouse one's country in order to save one's life is inglorious." From ignorance he became educated by his own exertions. From a slave he rose to be a soldier, a general, and a governor, and might have been a king. He possessed a rare genius, which showed itself in the private circle, in the council-chamber, and on the field of battle. His very name became a tower of strength to his friends and a terror to his foes.

The history of Toussaint, placed by the side of that of Napoleon, presents many striking parallels. Both born in a humble position, they raised themselves to the height of power by the force of their character. Both gained renown in legislation and government, as well as in war. Both fell the moment they had attained supreme authority. Both finished their career on a barren rock.

The parallels, however, have their contrast. Toussaint fought for liberty; Napoleon fought for himself. Toussaint gained fame by leading an oppressed and injured race to the successful vindication of their rights; Napoleon made himself a name and acquired a sceptre by supplanting liberty and destroying nationalities, in order to substitute his own illegitimate despotism. Napoleon transferred Toussaint from the warm and sunny climate of the West Indies to the cold climate of the north of France; the English transferred Napoleon from the cold climate of France to the warm climate of St. Helena.

This was indeed retribution; for the man of the cold regions died in the tropics, to atone for his crime in having caused the man of the tropics to end his days in the cold regions. While Toussaint's memory will be revered by all lovers of freedom, Napoleon's will be detested.

And, lastly, Toussaint's career as a Christian, a statesman, and a general, will lose nothing by a comparison with that of Washington. Each was the leader of an oppressed and outraged people, each had a powerful enemy to contend with, and each succeeded in founding a government in the New World. Toussaint's government made liberty its watchword, incorporated it in its constitution, abolished the slave-trade, and made freedom universal amongst the people. Toussaint liberated his countrymen; Washington enslaved a portion of his, and aided in giving strength and vitality to an institution that will one day rend asunder the UNION that he helped to form. Already the slave in his chains, in the rice swamps of Carolina and the cotton fields of Mississippi, burns for revenge.

In contemplating the fact that the slave would rise and vindicate his right to freedom by physical force, Jefferson said:—

"Indeed, I tremble for my country when I reflect that God is just, that his justice cannot sleep forever; that, considering numbers, nature, and natural means only, a revolution of the wheel of fortune, and exchange of situation, is among possible events; that it may become probable by supernatural interference! The Almighty has no attribute which can take side with us in such a contest.

"What an incomprehensible machine is man! who can endure toil, famine, stripes, imprisonment, and death itself, in vindication of his own liberty, and the next moment be deaf to all those motives whose power supported him through his trial, and inflict on his fellow-men a bondage, one hour of which is fraught with more misery than ages of that which he rose in rebellion to oppose."

And, should such a contest take place, the God of Justice will be on the side of the oppressed blacks. The exasperated genius of Africa would rise from the depths of the ocean, and show its threatening form; and war against the tyrants would be the rallying cry. The indignation of the slaves of the south would kindle a fire so hot that it would melt their chains, drop by drop, until not a single link would remain; and the revolution that was commenced in 1776 would then be finished, and the glorious sentiments of the Declaration of Independence, "That all men are created equal, and endowed by their Creator with certain inalienable rights, among which are life, liberty, and the pursuit of happiness," would be realized, and our government would no longer be the scorn and contempt of the friends of freedom in other lands, but would really be the LAND OF THE FREE AND HOME OF THE BRAVE.

Source: William Wells Brown, *St. Domingo: Its Revolutions and its Patriots. A Lecture, Delivered Before the Metropolitical Athenæum, London, May 16, and at St. Thomas' Church, Philadelphia, December 20, 1854* (Boston: Bela March, 1855).

22

Mary Still

A member of a Philadelphia family with deep roots in the black freedom struggle, Mary Still (1808–1889) served as an educator and later a missionary in the Reconstruction South with the African Methodist Episcopal (AME) church. These dual roles are evident in this pamphlet, the first and larger part of which served as an introduction by unknown members of the church. Still's portion, which follows, advocates an idealized feminine role of nurturing domestic virtues and literary accomplishments—an idea becoming increasingly common in the antebellum North. Still included particular racial resonances as well. In the same way that black spokesmen illuminated the role of African-American men in a progressive American history, Still highlights the role of women in the history of black community building and black antislavery activity, often in the face of male opposition. Much of her pamphlet is a brief in support of the fledgling denomination newspaper *The Christian Recorder*, begun in 1854 and suspended in 1856 for lack of funds. As the journal of the largest national institution under black control, she argues, the newspaper would help unite free blacks in promoting education and culture in the AME ranks. In championing the role of the black press in combating the debilitating effects of racism, she hopes such an organ would give expression to the best voices of black America for the inspiration and education of African-American readers. In appealing to the women of the church, she claims for African-American women the primary role of educators of black youth, urging women to organize fundraising fairs and other activities to generate support for a revitalized national African-American newspaper. *The Christian Recorder* did not resume publication until 1861.

"An Appeal to the Females
of the African Methodist Episcopal Church"

(1857)

"Shall it ever be said by human lips again, that the Christian Recorder, the organ of the A.M.E. Church has been suspended for want of support? Heaven forbid it."

AN APPEAL:

BY this appeal we wish to call the serious attention of the female part of the Church, to consider an important subject that is about to be laid before them. We again come before the public in behalf of thousands that now are, and thousands yet unborn; moved by a Divine impulse, and led on by hope, we make one more effort to resuscitate again our Organ that now lays buried beneath its pecuniary difficulties; and which is so essentially necessary for our progress as an organized body. We hail the present as a glorious epoch in the history of our Church. One which animates every pulsation of my heart, and swells every fibre of my soul, and will inevitably speak volumes in behalf of this connection. Some forty years have rolled rapidly away since the fathers declared Independence in this connection. Since that time the scene has been one of care, opposition, and extream perplexity. Many noble and pious hearted sons have ministered at her altars, and many, very many have been begotten in the Gospel, from dead works to a lively hope in Christ. And many have found their way through this state of things to a land of blessedness and calm repose. We have stood by them when in Jorden, and have heard them say in language emphatical, that the waves would not overflow them, though they are deeper than the grave. Yet much remains to be done at this present crisis. The peculiar circumstances with which our people are surrounded, makes their condition one of deep sympathy. Slavery, oppression, insult and wrong which in their effects are as strong as death and as cruel as the grave, they have stung our noblest and best men to their vitals; and in a measure drownded the sensibilities of our whole race. The people who compose the connection were reared in all of the different parts of the United States, and most of them without common school advantage, and many of them in places where learning to the colored man is considered a crime, and is punished with stripes, extermination, or exile. Is it any wonder then that our progress is so tardy, and our literary platform is so weakly constructed? Is it any wonder then that we issue papers one half of the year, and suspend them the next? Is it strange that resolution after resolution pass our Ecclesiastical Bodies, and then fall to the leward? Is it strange that there are so many breaches of trust, and so many woful mistakes when we have had to feel our way through a cloud as dark as that of Egypt and as destroying in its effect? But thus sayeth the Lord, "in the place were I record My Name, there do I delight to meet my people." Then why should we dispond in the way? or why should we distrust his goodness, Allen, Webster, Tapsico, Cox and Corr, with an innumerable host of other worthies, labored faithfully and successfully in the field; but they had to meet the fate common to all men, to taste of death and to see corruption. The sisters too, stood collateral with the fathers in that religious campaign, though their weapons were not carnal but mighty through faith to the pulling down of the strong holds of the enemy in time of hot persecution, sore conflict and extream want and disunion, they were faithful in giving their aid to the cause and thus leveling the high way and lighting up the gloomy desert. Ever ready with a scanty pittance, earned by hard toil, to respond to the claims of the Church. When were as castouts and spurned from the large churches, driven from their knees, pointed at by the proud, neglected by the careless, without a place of worship. Allen, faithful to the heavenly calling, came forward and laid the foundation of this connection. The women, like the women at the Sepulchre, were early to aid in laying the foundation of the temple, and in helping to carry up the noble structure, and in the name of their God, set up their banner but most of our aged mothers are gone from this to a better state of things. Yet some linger still on their staves watching with intense interest the ark as it moves over the tempestuous waves of opposition and ignorance. Still guided by her polar star, that now and then reflects light and brilliancy in her pathway. But the labors of these women stopped not here, for they knew well that they were subject to affliction and death. For the purpose of mutual aid, they banded themselves together in society capacity, that they might be the better able to administer to each others necessities in time of distress, and thus alleviate each others sufferings, and to soften their own pillows. So we find the females in the early history of the Church, abounded in good works, and in acts of true benevolence. "Instant in season and out of season," in visiting the sick and the distressed, and in administering both spiritual and temporal blessings to those who stood in need. The advantages that we enjoy are far superior, for the light of science and learning have in a great measure illuminated our understanding, and our path is strewed with roses when compared with the dark thorny maze our mothers walked in, "for many have run to and fro, and knowledge have increased," Is it not our duty then to take some more efficient means to carry on this great enterprise that now lays before us?—Surely a great moral duty devolves upon us. Before us is opening a field already white for harvest, and is every day extending in weadth and in length, and one in which offers ample reward to labor, in this possition females can do much to repel the cloud that lowers over the minds of our people, which blinds their sensibilities and threatens mental death. By a wise and judicious extention, they may be very efficient in extending the borders of the Church, and in strengthening her stakes.

We are sometimes told that females should have nothing to do with the business of the Church. But they have yet to learn that when female labor is withdrawen the Church must cease to exist. Upon our doings greatly depends the future prosperity of the young. By our decission in all important matters, will they direct their future course. As it is women, who gives impress to society; and her who teaches the young mind how to shoot, and how to articulate its earliest thoughts. How important then that we should deside wisely and judiciously upon a subject that involves the interest of so many intiligent beings. There are many temples of learning established in different sections of the country, where children and youth may be prepared to fill respectable situations in life. But they need the encouragement of their seniors. Therefore, let us encourage learning in all of its useful branches, we should be careful to aid religious and benevolent institutions with christian fidelity.—We should be careful also to have our conduct modest and our conversation chaste, that our fruit may be unto holiness and that our end may be unto everlasting life. We should ever keep in mind that the scrutinizing eye of the world which is no friend to our progress is upon us, and the claimes of the Church call for our help; and angels are waiting our decission. "Therefore, seeing that we are surrounded with so great a cloud of witnesses, we should take the more earnest heed to our way," so they that run may read in our lives lessons of usefulness and true benevolence. The present is a crisis of great interest to the people of color in the United States; and we fear greatly, but too little considered or understood by the majority of us. Who that reads the daily news, or watches the daily course of things, but sees that the subject relating to our present and future possition in convulsing the whole country, from Main to Florida, and from the Atlantic on the East, to the shore of the great Pacific on the West. Upon our doings may depend the weak or woe of millions now in slavery, dark and doleful vault, our eyes weep and our hearts is made sad with every days report that comes wafted to us on the Western breeze, of many that are sacrificed on the altar of slavery. The wails and groans of those of our brethren who are burned at the stake, whipped to death, hanged upon the gallows, shock our sensibilities and fill us with wild indignation. We say again, that we hail the present as a glorious epoch in our history; when females are about to step upon that glorious platform of moral enterprize, and in that elevated possition and with a concentrated effort bring their influence to bear against the powers of mental darkness, the time now is, when their labor is most needed; and hence it will be most appreciated by a wise and judicious course, we may move the difficulties that tower like mountains before our Publication Committee, and thus throw a hallo around the head of our Editor. In modern as well as in ancient times, have women been a means either primary or secondary to the advancement of great moral enterprizes. In war the sound of musketry have ceased at her entreaties, and the most stern difficulties have crumbled at her touch. Cities have been raised to the earth at her bidding, and in reversion raised again to eminence and fame at her command, woman was given in the very onset of human existance as a helpmate to man in his Edin; being equal in structure, pure in virtue, clear in power of perseption, she stands collateral with her Lord; and when he is bowed with the wait of busy life, care-worn, tempest tost and in dispair, from woman he catches the first beam of light as it reflected from the countenance of a well cultivated understanding. The moral or degraded condition of society depends solely upon the influence of woman, if she be virtuous, pious and industrious, her feet abiding in her own house, ruleing her family well. Such a woman is like a tree planted by the river side, whose leaves are ever-green; she extends in her neighborhood a healthy influence, and all men calleth her blessed. But if unhappily she should be the reverse, loud, clamourous, her feet wandering from the path of virtue, neglecting to rule her family, then indeed is the demoralizing effect of a bad influence felt in all the avenues of her life. By this short address we hope to awake the latent faculties of the female part of our beloved Church to a consideration of a great moral duty; we wish to stimulate them to an immediate action in the literary department of the A. M. E. Church. It is the desire of the General Conference, as soon as the means can be raised to re-issue the Organ of the Church, and to do that, we must bring her piety, intelligence and monies, too, to bear against ignorance, superstition and poverty. Several attempts have been made to sustain a circulating newspaper, have in every case proved unsuccessful; the great difficulty arises mainly from the want of a stronger literary force. We are sorry to say there are many among us who are not able to read a common newspaper; therefore, they do nothing for the publication purposes. There are many who do read, but not sufficient enough to make reading interesting for them, hence the burden devolves on a few;

Some are silly enough to offer this as a reason why another effort should be made. But any intelligent mind can see at a glance that such objections are weak, unfounded and arises from a lack of enterprize and for the want of a concert of action. No organized body can exist with any credit to itself, or with any real benefit to its patrons without an Organ. The great amount of intelligence that will be derived from its circulation, is incalculable at present, we can only imagine of some of the good effects it would have from the influence it has had in time past; it will open avenues to religious and moral discussions for those who are seeking self-improvement. Its columns also will be open to the development of the minds of our youth, who as a natural consequence would feel more freedom to write for their own paper than any other. The human mind is a faculty capable of high attainment, being comprehensive in its character, it is able to grasp the most stern difficulties and by the power of perception, enter the most secret mistries. And the body that needs nutriment to give life, health and activity to the limbs and muscles, even so much the mind have nutriment by careful study and diligent perserverance in the various branches of science and literature. A Periodical is in the highest sence essential to our moral and intellectual improvement, and will serve as a connecting link to our Church organization, and will greatly facilitate the march of improvement that is going on so rapidly among us, other religious Societies expect much from the A. M. E. Church, from the fact that they were the first who put forth an effort to elevate and christinize their outcast brothers and sisters by encircling them within the enclosure of the Church, and by faithfully administering and constantly instructing and encouraging them in the way to respectablility and to Heaven. Their Temple at that time was a blacksmith's shop, mean, low, and humble, with no guilded pulpit, nor gaudy furniture, with no learned Oritors to expound the word of life to their hearers, so in truth it many be said, that the Gospel to them was not in wisdom of words, nor in excellency of speech, but in power. Thither the people resorted for instruction and to mingle their kindred voices in prayer and praise to the God they adored. We have unfrequently heard it said that Bethel Church is opposed to human learning, and to general intelligence, this in some degree may be true as it regards a portion of the Lay Members. But to charge the head of the Church with such indifferance, is highly culpable and unjust. The first Bishop who presided over them set a worthy example by educating his own children, which was attended with great expence, as private teachers had to be imployed as there were no colored schools established at that period, he also held out strong inducements to show those whom he presided over, the great utility of educating the children and youth, by carefully admonishing and instructing them in their parental duties, which he termed an imperative duty. But the General and Annual Conferences, have laid out a course of studies to be pursued by young men who are preparing for the Ministery; and resolutions, past making it a duty incumbent upon them, we have great reason to rejoice for what has been done, and also for what now is doing for the elevation of our hapless race; and do graciously hope for what is to come.

The minutes of the Quadreniel Conference, show that in the Ministerial rank, is blended some of the noblest talent and best cultivated minds to be found among the colored people. The Editor and General Book Steward's Report passed an honorable examination by a wise and judicious Committee, from the same, we learn that the business of the concern is in a more prosperous condition than has been for twelve years before; those things are truly encouraging and should stimulate us to immediate action in this great struggle, cold indeed, is the heart who does not feel the interest of the Church to be her interest; on the welfare of souls to linger about her soul. We would that our Church should stand as a star of the first magnitude among the churches; and that her light may be reflected from the center to the Isles of the sea, that thousands who now sit in darkness may see rays of living light eminating from her altar, and with holy zeal rush to her gates for instruction.

Now, may the God of all Grace, and the Father of our Lord Jesus Christ, so inspire our hearts with zeal from on high, to a patient labor, and to a diligent perserverance to act in the vineyard of the Lord, that our Church may be benefited and to His grace promoted. We hope that this short appeal will be received in good faith by our friends in this A. M. E. Church as coming from one who desires your present and future prosperity, and hope by your faithful adherance to all that good, that you will attain unto that, rest that remains for the people of God.

> Be not discouraged or dismayed,
> Because of the gibes of men,
> Tho' high and towering is the mount,
> But upward we'll assend.

NECESSITY AND MEANS FOR THE DIFFUSION OF KNOWLEDGE

BEING deeply impressed with the utility of a Periodical, devoted to Religion, Morality, Science, and Literature, for the dissemination of useful knowledge among a downtrodden and an oppressed race and for promoting a more general interest in our ranks, the ecclesiastical power in the A. M. E. Church, have provided for publishing an organ devoted to those principles made sacred by the God of nature. This organ comes to us by the name of the Christian Recorder. They saw with sorrow and deep regret the moral and mental condition of thousands who mingle in our societies, and urged on by the influence of that holy religion and Christian obligation which binds man to his fellow man, and points him to deeds of charity, and to labors of love. The impulse that moved them to action, was doubtless of divine origin, having a desire to light up the literary path for thousands yet unborn: and to raise a monument in honor of our sainted fathers who have long since fallen asleep, and while their bodies lie mingled with their mother dust, their happy spirits are watching and guiding our little bark over the waves of opposition, and the storm of difficulties to higher and nobler deeds on earth.

The importance of such an act is unquestionable, as it is a given point and well understood by all intelligent nations, that knowledge is power. To no people under heaven is this proverb more applicable than to ourselves. In accordance with certain resolutions put in their own assembly, they have, after grappling with the tide of opposition, and a cloud of mental darkness, and a host of pecuniary difficulties to some extent succeeded in this noble and praiseworthy enterprize. The oaks, the cedars, the pines and maples have been like Sampson's fetters made to bend to their wishes, and its name given to the public, and its banner hoisted to the breezes of heaven. This being done some of us may think all is done. We seem to forget, or know nothing about the expenses and embarrassments which such a publication may lead to, or the amount of material calls for. The great difficulty among us arises mainly from the want of a stronger literary force. There are many who do not read at all, therefore, they do not trouble themselves about books or papers. Many who do read care but nothing about mental culture; a third class, who are not able to pay for their reading, hence the burden dissolves on a few. Nevertheless it is a valuable and interesting little sheet, and promises much in the way of bringing out those latent faculties which lie imbeded in broken fragments of a once powerful honored nation. More especially is it interesting to us on account of its having origin among our own people, and is under the supervision of our Church organization. It will also wield a powerful influence in the removal of these unholy prejudices and disunions that hang over us like the pall of death, and does more to impede the march of improvement than the "pestilence that walks at midnight, or the disease that wastes at noonday." It will also facilitate an acquaintance with each other, and open avenues to religious and moral discussions, and enables us to read from its pages sentiments of high and noble origin. It will in some measure unite again the national chain which has long been broken by slavery, prejudice, and oppression, and bind us together in love and respect for each other's welfare. Its pages have been embellished with some of the richest specimens of literary talent we have in our ranks. Such we view with delight as stars of no small magnitude in our literary circle, reflecting light and refinement to those whose opportunities, have been less favorable to improvement. There appears to be a unity of feeling on the subject with the more mature minds, and a general prayer for its welfare. Some have hailed it with loud acclamations of praise, and others bid it welcome, while a third bids it go forth as on angels wings. But neither flattery nor raises alone will prove a sufficient means to carry out the aim and object of this paper. The time now is, when faith and works must unite. How many of the votaries of the Recorder are willing to step in front of the cause, leaving the masses behind and plant themselves in its defence to aid and support it through all its pecuniary embarrassments, and the various changes which it may be obliged to make. This is the third attempt that has been made through the medium of the A. M. E. Church connection, to establish an organ. But in each preceding case have failed for the want of support. But friends of education, shall this failure ever take place again? shall it ever be said of this connection, which boasts of its number, and hundreds of branches—its extension two thousands of miles to the far west—through the six eastern States into the Canadas, and through all the middle and most of the Southern States down into Louisiana, and even into California. Shall it ever be said by human lips again, that the Christian Recorder, the organ of the A. M. E. Church has been suspended for want of support? Heaven forbid it.

Oh, may he who is the foundation of all knowledge, and the Author of all good, so inspire our hearts with zeal from on high to a diligent perserverance to labor in the cause of moral and mental improvement of our race, to the establishing our press on the hill of science and literature that thousands may yet see the rays of living light emanating from its influence and words of everlasting truth to those who sit in darkness. In order to facilitate the desire of our paper, and to make the wish less irksome for our official brethren, and to throw around it a more substantial bulwark to enable it to stem from the rolling current and to settle its basis on a more sure foundation, we suggest to our friends the idea of a Fair known as the district or state Fair. We have known some benevolent Institutions who realize thousands of dollars annually in this way, and by these means publish hundreds of volumes in each year, and give respect and dignity to their committee. If they can raise thousands, surely we can hundreds. We know of nothing, at present, that will meet the condition of the people better than the idea above mentioned. Because our country and city friends can all participate in this, our sister cities also would have an equal chance for helping in carrying on the enterprize. We can but hope that our friends will consider the utility of the case, and pray that it will meet with the attention which it so highly merits.

In behalf of the thousands that now are and thousands yet unborn.

DAUGHTERS OF BETHEL
    Awake ye daughters of Bethel,
        No longer in idleness repose,
    Gird on the armor of holy resolution,
        And go forth to meet your foes.

    Why sleep ye daughters of Jerusalem,
        The promise to you is given,
    Through patience, hope and perserverance,
        We'll gain the port of Heaven.

    Go forth with holy zeal,
        With lamp and pitcher in your hand,
    War with ignorance and superstition,
        Until you gain the desired end.

    Go forth with courage bold,
        Nor fear the opponents power,
    The star that shone o'er Judea's plain,
        Will guide you in that hour.

    Your path through deserts, dark and dreary,
        And clouds beset the way,
    Yet by faith and perserverance,
        We'll hail an opening day.

    Be not discouraged or dismayed,
        In truth and righteousness the promise stands,
    Princes shall come out of Egypt,
        And Ethiopia shall stretch forth her hand.

    Some tell us we would better tarry,
        There's danger in the way,
    But to the stronger we will rally,
        To hail a rising day.

Source: Mary Still, *An Appeal to the Females of the African Methodist Episcopal Church* (Philadelphia: Peter Mckenna and Son, 1857).

23

J. Theodore Holly

James Theodore Holly (1829–1911), black nationalist, emigration activist, missionary, and Protestant Episcopal Bishop of Haiti, was born to free black parents in Washington, D.C. Resettled in Brooklyn, New York, Holly in 1848 worked as a clerk for abolitionist Lewis Tappen. In 1851, he settled in Windsor, Ontario, to coedit with Henry Bibb the newspaper *Voice of the Fugitive*. He joined the Protestant Episcopal church, was ordained a priest in 1856, and that year relocated to New Haven, where he headed St. Luke's Church until 1861.

Holly's years with the Canadian fugitive slave communities convinced him that emigration was the only solution for the development of African-American potential. He was active in the National Emigration Conventions of 1854 and 1856. Like many African Americans, Holly was drawn to Haiti, the only nation created by revolutionary black slaves. He hoped to convince the Protestant Episcopal church to support a mission in Haiti under his charge. He worked with Haitian recruiting agent James Redpath and others to promote a settlement of African Americans in Haiti and, in 1861, left for Haiti with 110 settlers from his New Haven flock. Though disease and poor planning decimated his group, Holly persisted in promoting emigration to Haiti and finally won church support for his mission. Except for a few visits to the United States, Holly remained active as a priest and missionary in Haiti until his death in 1911.

Holly's pamphlet printing of his lecture in 1857 is one of the only productions of the Afric-American Printing Company, established by the National Emigration Convention "for the publication of Negro literature." His celebration of black accomplishment in Haiti defied conventional white American opinion by holding up the black revolution and the nation it founded as deserving of African-American admiration, emulation, and support.

"A Vindication of the Capacity of the Negro for Self-Governement and Civilized Progress"

(1857)

". . . who, after this convincing proof to the contrary, shall dare to say that the negro race is not capable of self-government?"

DEDICATION

To REV. WILLIAM C. MUNROE
RECTOR OF ST. MATTHEW'S CURCH, DETROIT MICHIGAN

REV. AND DEAR SIR :-Permit me the honor of inscribing this work to you. It is a lecture that I prepared and delivered before a Literary Society of Colored Young Men, in the City of New Haven, CT. after my return from Hayti, in the autumn of 1855 ; and subsequently repeated in Ohio, Michigan, and Canada West, during the summer of 1856.

I have permitted it to be published at the request of the Afric-American Printing Company, an association for the publication of negro literature. organized in connection with the Board of Publication, which forms an constituent part of the National Emigration Convention, over which you so ably presided, at its sessions, held in Cleveland, Ohio, in the years 1854–6.

LECTURE

The task that I propose to myself in the present lecture, is an earnest attempt to defend the inherent capabilities of the negro race, for self-government and civilized progress. For this purpose, I will examine the events of Haytian History, from the commencement of their revolution to the present period.

REASONS FOR ASSUMING SUCH A TASK.

Notwithstanding the remarkable progress of philanthropic ideas and humanitarian feelings, during the last half century . . . the great mass of the Caucasian race still deem the negro as entirely destitute of those qualities, on which they selfishly predicate their own superiority.

And we may add to this overwhelming class a large quota also of that small portion of the white race, who profess to believe the truths, "That God is no respector of persons", because too many of those pseudo-humanitarians have lurking in their hearts, a secret infidelity in regard to the black man, which is ever ready to manifest its concealed sting, when the full and unequivocal recognition of the negro, in all respects, is pressed home upon their hearts.

Hence, between this downright prejudice against this long abused race, which is flauntingly maintained by myriads of their oppressors on the one hand; and this woeful distrust of his natural equality, among, those who claim to be his friends, on the other; no earnest and fearless efforts are put forth to vindicate their character, by even the few who may really acknowledge this equality of the races.

I wish, by the undoubted facts of history, to cast back the vile aspersions and foul calumnies that have been heaped upon my race for the last four centuries, by our unprincipled oppressors.

But this is not all. I wish to do all in my power to inflame the latent embers of self-respect, that the cruelty and injustice of our oppressors, have nearly extinguished in our bosoms, during the midnight chill of centuries, that we have clanked the galling chains of slavery.

THE REVOLUTIONARY HISTORY OF HAYTI.
THE BASIS OF THIS ARGUMENT.

This revolution is one of the noblest, grandest, and most justifiable outbursts against tyrannical oppression that is recorded on the pages of the world's history.

A race of almost dehumanized men made so by an oppressive slavery of three centuries arose from their slumber of ages, and redressed their own unparalled wrongs with a terrible hand in the name of God and humanity.

The Haytian Revolution is also the grandest political event of this or any other age. In weighty causes, and wondrous and momentous features, it surpasses the American revolution, in an incomparable degree. The revolution of this country was only the revolt of a people already comparatively free, independent, and highly enlightened. But the Haytian revolution was a revolt of an uneducated and menial class of slaves, against their tyrannical oppressors.

These oppressors, against whom the negro insurgents of Hayti had to contend, were not only the government of a far distant mother country, as in the case of the American revolution; but unlike and more fearful than this revolt, the colonial government of Hayti was also thrown in the balance against the negro revolters. The American revolters had their colonial government in their own hands, as well as their individual liberty at the commencement of the revolution. The black insurgents of Hayti had yet to grasp both their personal liberty and the control of their colonial government, by the might of their own right hands, when their heroic struggle began.

The obstacles to surmount, and the difficulties to contend against, in the American revolution, when compared to those of the Haytian, were, (to use a homely but classic phrase,) but a "tempest in a teapot," compared to the dark and lurid thunder storm of the dissolving heavens.

Never before, in all the annals of the world's history, did a nation of abject and chattel slaves arise in the terrific might of their resuscitated manhood, and regenerate, redeem, and disenthrall themselves; by taking their station at one gigantic bound, as an independent nation, among the sovereignties of the world.

It is, therefore, the unparalleled incidents that led to this wonderful event, that I now intend to review rapidly, in order to demonstrate progress, to the fullest extent and in the highest sense of these terms.

Preliminary Incidents of the Revolution

I shall proceed to develop the first evidence of the competency of the Negro race for self-government, amid the historical incidents that preceded their terrible and bloody revolution; and in the events of that heroic struggle itself.

When the cosmopolitan ideas of "Liberty, Fraternity, and Equality," which swayed the mighty minds of France, toward the close of the 18th century, reached the colony of St. Domingo, through the Massaic club, composed of wealthy colonial planters, organized in the French capital; all classes in that island, except the black slave and the free colored man, were instantly wrought up to the greatest effervescence, and swayed with the deepest emotions, by the startling doctrines of the equal political rights of all men, which were then so boldly enunciated in the face of the tyrannical despotisms and the immemorial assumptions of the feudal aristocracies of the old world.

The colonial dignitaries, the military officers, and other agents of the government of France, then resident in St. Domingo, the rich planters and the poor whites, (these latter called in the parlance of that colony "*Les petits blancs,*") were all from first to last, swayed with the intensest and the most indescribable feelings, at the promulgation of these bold and radical theories.

All were in a perfect fever to realize and enjoy the priceless boon of policitcal and social privileges that these revolutionary ideas held out before them. And in their impatience to grasp these precious prerogatives, they momentarily forgot their colonial dependence on France, and spontaneously came together in general assembly, at a small town of St. Domingo, called St. Marc: and proceeded to deliberate seriously about taking upon themselves all the attributes of national sovereignty and independence.

And when they had deliberately matured plans to suit themselves, they did not hesitate to send representatives to propose them to the national government of France, for its acknowledgment and acquiescence in their desires.

Such was the radical consequence to which the various classes of white colonists in St. Domingo seized upon, and carried the cosmopolitan theories of French philosophers and political agitators of the last century.

But from all this excitement and enthusiasm, I have already excepted the black and colored inhabitants of that island.

The white colonists of St. Domingo, like our *liberty loving* and *democratic* fellow citizens of the United States, never meant to include this despised race, in their glowing dreams of "Liberty, Equality, and Fraternity."

Like our model Republicans, the looked upon this hated race of beings, as placed so far down the scale of humanity, that when the "Rights of man" were spoken of, they did not imagine that the most distant reference was thereby made to the Negro; or any one through whose veins his tainted blood sent its crimsoned tide.

And so blind were they to the fact that the "Rights of Man" could be so construed as to recognise the humanity of that oppressed race; that when the National assembly of France, swayed by the just representations of the "Friends of the Blacks" was led to extend equal political rights to the free men of color in St. Domingo, at the same time that this National body ratified the doings of the General Colonial assembly of St. Marc: these same colonists who had been so loud in their hurrahs for the Rights of Man, now ceased their clamors for liberty in the face of this just national decree, and sullenly resolved " To die rather than share equal political rights with a bastard race." Such was the insulting term that this colonial assembly then applied to the free men of color, in whose veins coursed the blood of the proud planter, commingled with that of the lowly Negress.

THE SELF-POSSESSION OF THE BLACKS;
AN EVIDENCE OF THEIR CAPACITY FOR SELF-GOVERMENT.

The exceptional part which the blacks played in the moving drama that was then being enacted in St. Domingo, by their stern self-possession amid the furious excitement of the whites, is one of the strongest proofs that can be adduced to substantiate the capabilities of the negro race for self-government.

He remained heedless of the effervescence of liberty that bubbled over in the bosom of the white man; and continued at his sullen labors, biding his time for deliverance. And in this judicious reserve on the part of the blacks, we have one of the strongest traits of self-government.

When we look upon this characteristic of cool, self-possession, we cannot but regard it as almost a miracle under the circumstances. We cannot see whet magic power could keep such a warm blooded race of men in such an ice bound spell of cold indifference, when every other class of men in that colony was flush with the excitement of *liberty.*

And let no one dare to rob them of this glorious trait of character, either by alledging that they remained thus indifferent, because they were too ignorant to appreciate the blessings of liberty; or by saying, that if they understood the import of these clamors for the Right of Man," they were thus quiet, because they were too cowardly to strike for their disenthralment.

The change that they were thus ignorant of the priceless boon of freedom, is refuted by the antecedent history of the servile insurrections, which never ceased to rack that island from 1522 down to the era of negro independence.

And the desperate resolution to be free, that the Maroon negroes of the island maintained for 85 years, by their valorous struggles, in their wild mountain fastnesses, against the concentrated and combined operations of the French and Spanish authorities then in that colony; and which finally compelled these authorities to conclude a treaty with the intrepid Maroon chief, Santiago, and thereby acknowledging their freedom forever.

Hence nothing shall rob of the immaculate glory of exhibiting a stern self-possession, in that feverish hour of excitement, when every body around them were crying out Liberty. And in this judicious self-control at this critical juncture, when their destiny hung on the decision of the hour, we have a brilliant illustration of the capacity of the race for self-government.

SIMILAR EVIDENCE ON THE PART OF THE FREE MEN OF COLOR

But additional and still stronger evidence of this fact crowd upon us, when we see that the free men of color remained entirely passive during the first stage of this revolutionary effervescence. This class of men as a general thing, was educated and wealthy; and they were burthened with duties by the State, without being invested with corresponding political privileges.

They had greater cause to agitate than the whites, because they suffered under heavier burdens than that class. Nevertheless, in the first great outbreak of the water-floods of liberty tempting as the occasion was, and difficult as restraint must have been; yet the free men of color also possessed their souls in patience, and awaited a more propitious opportunity. Certainly no one will attempt to stigmatise the calm judgement of these men in this awful crisis of suspense, as the result of ignorance of the blessings of freedom, when it is known that many or this class were educated in the seminaries of France, under her most brilliant professors; and that they were also patrons of that prodigy of literature, the Encyclopedia of France.

Neither can they stigmatize this class of men as cowards, as it is also known that they were the voluntary Compeers of the Revolutionary heroes of the United States; and who, under the banners of France, mingled their sable blood with the Saxon and the French in the heroic battle of Savannah.

Then this calm indifference of the men of color in this crisis, notwithstanding the blood of three excitable races mingled in their veins with that of the African, viz: that of the French, the Spanish, and the Indian; and notwithstanding, they had glorious recollections of their services in the cause of American Independence, inciting them on – this calm indifference, on their part, I say, notwithstanding these exciting causes, is another grand and striking illustration of the conservative characteristics of the negro race, that demonstrate their capacity for self-government.

THE OPPORTUNE MOVEMENT OF THE FREE COLORED MEN

The tumultuous events of this excitement among the white colonists rolled onward, and brought the auspicious hour of negro destiny in that island nearer and nearer, when Providence designed that he should play his part in the great drama of freedom that was then being enacted. Of course the propitious moment for the free men of color to begin to move would present itself prior to that for the movement of the negro slaves.

The opportunity for the men of color presented itself when the general colonial assembly of St Mare's (already referred to) sent deputies to France, to present the result of its deliberations to the National Assembly; and to ask that august body to confer on the colony the right of self-government.

At this time, therefore, when the affairs of the colony were about to undergo examination in the supreme legislature of the mother country, the free men of color seized upon the occasion to send deputies to France also, men of their own caste, represent their grievances and make their wishes known to the National Assembly. This discreet discernment of such an opportune moment to make such a movement divested of every other consideration, shows a people who understand themselves, what they want, and how to seek it.

But when we proceed to consider the most approved manner in which the representations were made to the National Assembly, by the colored delegates in behalf of their case, in the colony of St. Domingo, and the influences they brought to bear upon that body, as exhibited hereafter: we shall perceive thereby that they showed such intimate acquaintance with the secret springs of governmental machinery, as demonstrated at once their capacity to govern themselves.

This deputation first drew up a statement in behalf of their caste in the colony, of such a stirring nature as would be certain to command the national sympathy in their cause, when presented to the National Assembly. But previously to presenting it to that assembly, they took the wise precaution to wait upon the honorable president of that august body, in order to enlist and commit him in their favor, as the first stepping stone to secure the success of their object before the Supreme Legislature.

They prevailed in their mission to the President of the Assembly; and succeeded in obtaining this very emphatic assurance from him: "No part of the nation shall vainly reclaim their rights before the assembly of the representatives of the French people."

Having accomplished this important step, the colored deputies next began to operate though the Abolition Society of Paris, called "Les Amis Des Noirs," upon such of the members of the assembly as were affiliated with this society, and thus already indirectly pledged to favor such a project as theirs, asking simple justice for their race. They were again successful, and Charles De Lameth, one of the zealous patrons of that society, and an active member of the National Assembly, was enraged to argue their cause before the Supreme Legislature of the nation, although strange to say, he was himself a colonial slaveholder at that time.

And at the appointed moment in the National Assembly, this remarkable man felt prompted to utter these astounding words in behalf of this oppressed and disfranchised class of the colony: "I am one of the greatest proprietors of St. Domingo; yet I declare to you, that sooner than lose sight of principles so sacred to justice and humanity, I would prefer to lose all that I possess. I declare myself in favor of admitting the men with color to the rights of citizenship; and in favor of the freedom of the blacks"

Now let us for a moment stop and reflect on the measures resorted to by colored deputies of St. Domingo, in Paris, who, by their wise stratagems, had brought their cause step by step to such an eventful and auspicious crisis as this.

Could there have been surer measures concocted for the success of their plans, than thus committing the president of the assembly to their cause in the first place; and afterwards pressing a liberty-loving slaveholder into their service, to thunder their measures through the National Assembly, by such a bold declaration?

Who among the old fogies of Tammany Hall could have surpassed these tactics of those much abused men of color, who thus swayed the secret springs of the National Assembly of France? And who, after this convincing proof to the contrary, shall dare to say that the negro race is not capable of self-government?

In order to make the very best impression on the popular heart of the nation, their petition demanding simple justice to their caste was accompanied with a statement very carefully drawn up.

In this statement they showed that their caste in the colony of St. Domingo possessed one-third of the real estate, and one-fourth of the personal effects of the island. They also set forth the advantages of their position in the political and social affairs of St. Domingo, as a balance of power in the hand of the imperial government of France, against the high pretensions of the haughty planters on the one hand, and the seditious spirit of the poor whites on the other. And, as an additional consideration, by way of capping the climax, they offered in the name, and in behalf of the free men of color in the colony, six millions of francs as a loyal contribution to the wants and financial exigencies of the National Treasury, to be employed in liquidating the debt of their common country.

They succeeded as a matter of course, in accomplishing their purpose; and the National Assembly of France promulgated a decree on the 8th of March, 1790, securing equal political rights to the men of color.

THE CRISIS PRODUCED IN THE COLONY BY THIS DECREE
THE MEN OF COLOR ON THE SIDE OF LEBERTY, LAW AND ORDER.

It was when this decree was made known in the colony of St. Domingo, that the General Assembly of the colony, then sitting at St. Maro's, expressed the malignant sentiments of the white colonists, in a resolution that I have already quoted, viz: they resolved that they would " Rather die, than share equal political rights with a bastard race."

Vincent Oje, a man of color, and one of the delegates to Paris, in behalf of this case, anticipated a venomous feeling of this kind against his race, on the part of the white colonists, when these decrees should be made known to them. He however, resolved to do whatever was within his power, to allay this rancorous feeling. He did not therefore hasten home to the colony immediately after the decree was promulgated. He delayed, in order to allow time for their momentary excitement as expressed in the resolution above, to cool off, by a more calm reflection on their sober second thought. He also tarried in France, to secure a higher political end, by which he would be personally prepared to return to St. Domingo, to make the most favorable impression in behalf of his race, and the objects of that decree, on the minds of the white colonists.

To this end he succeeds in getting the appointment of Commissioner of France, from the French government, to superintend the execution of the decree of the 8th of March, 1790, in the island of St. Domingo.

Certainly, he might hope, that being invested with the sacred dignity of France, his person, his race, (thus honored through him by that imperial government,) and the National defence itself, with which he was charged, would now be respected.

But not content with accumulating the national honors of republic; fearing lest the pro-Slavery colonists would disregard these high prerogatives, by looking upon them as having been obtained through the *fanatical* "Friends of the Blacks" at Paris, by those partisans exerting an undue influence on the National Government: he further proceeds to gather additional honors, by ingratiating himself into the favor of a potentate of Holland—the Prince of Limbourg; form whom he received the rank of Lieutenant Colonel, and the order of the Lion. Thus he wished to demonstrate to the infatuated colonists, who regarded his race as beneath their consideration, that he could not only obtain titles and reputation in France, by means of ardent friend, but that over and above these, and beyond the boundaries of France, he could also command an European celebrity.

This was indeed a splendid course of conduct on his part; and by thus gathering around him and centering within himself these commanding prestiges of respect, he demonstrated his thorough knowledge of one of the most important secrets in the art of governing; and so far made another noble vindication of the capacity of the negro race for self-government.

But as we proceed to consider the manner that he afterwards undertook to prosecute his high National Commission in promulgating in St. Domingo, the decree of the 8th of March, 1790, we shall see additional evidence of the same master skill crowd upon us.

He had now delayed his return from Europe in order to allow time for allaying of hasty excitement, and for the purpose of making the most favorable advent to the island.

He comes a commissioned envoy of the French nation, and an honored chevalier of Europe. Nevertheless, with that prudent foresight which anticipates all possible emergencies, he landed in St. Domingo in a cautious and unostentatious manner, so as not to provoke any forcible demonstration against him. Having landed, he gathered around him a suite of 200 men for his personal escort, which his station justified him in having as his cortage; and which might also serve the very convenient purpose of a body guard to defend him against any attempt at a cowardly assassination from any lawless or ruthless desperadoes of oppression in the colony.

At the head of this body of men, he at once proceeded to place himself in communication with the Colonial Assembly, then in session; to inform it officially of his commission and the national decree which he bore; and to require that assembly, as the legislative authority of the island, to enforce its observance, by enacting an ordinance in accordance with the same.

In this communication of Oje, being aware of their pro-slavery prejudices, he endeavored to conciliate them by a peace offering. That peace offering was the sanctioning of Negro Slavery; for he stated to the assembly that the decree did not refer to the blacks in servitude; neither did the men of color, said he, desire to acknowledge their equality.

This specific assurance on the part of Oje, although it does not speak much for his high sense of justice, when abstractly considered; yet it shows as much wisdom and tact in the science of government, as is evinced by the sapient or sap headed legislators of this country, who make similar compromises as a peace offering to the prejudice and injustice of the oligarchic despots of this nation.

Oje, however, failed to make the desired impression on the infatuated colonists, either by his National and European dignities, or by his peace offering of 500,000 of his blacker brethren.

He was captured; and after a mock trial, illustrative of pro-slavery justice; something similar, for instance, to our Fugitive Slave Law trials in Boston, Philadelphia, and Cincinnati-(though more merciful in its penalty than these)- this mock court of St. Domingo condemned Vincent Oje and his bravo lieutenant, Jean Chevanne, with their surviving compatriots, to be broken alive on the wheel.

We forget the error of the head committed by this right hearted, noble, and generous man, towards his more unfortunate brethren, in order to weep over his ignoble and unworthy fate, received at the hands of those monsters of cruelty in St. Domingo.

This untimely death of the great leader of the men of color, served only to develop how plentifully the race was supplied with sagacious characters, capable of performing daring deeds-it served to show how well the race was supplied with the material out of which great leaders are made, at any moment, and for any exigency.

Now came the hour for the patient, delving black slave to begin to move. He has manfully bided his time, whilst the white colonists were rampant in pursuit of high political prerogatives; and he has remained quiet, whilst his brother- the freed man of color, has carried his cause demanding equal political rights, triumphantly through the National Assembly of France.

But most intolerable of all, he has been perfectly still, whilst his more fortunate brethren have offered even to strike hands with the vile oppressor in keeping the iron yoke on his neck.

Nevertheless, he has lived to see both of these classes foiled by the over-ruling hand of Providence, from interpreting the words "Liberty, Equality, and Fraternity," to suit their own selfish and narrow notions. He finds these two parties now at open hostilities with one another. He sees, on one hand, the despicable colonists inviting foreign aid into the island, to resist the execution of the National decree and to prop up their unhallowed cause by the dread alternative of treason and rebellion, whilst on the other hand, he beholds the men of color fighting on the side of the nation, law, and order, against the white colonists. Amid this general commotion his pulsations grow quick, and he feels that the hour of destiny is coming for even him to strike.

Yet he still possesses his soul in patience until the destined moment. At last he hears that France now vacillates in carrying out the tardy measure of justice that her National Legislature had enacted. The mother country, that had so nobly commenced the work of justice, by the national decree, enfranchising the free men of color, now begins to recede from the high position she had assumed, in order to favor the frenzied prejudice of the infatuated colonists.

The toiling black slave at last hears that the National Government of France vacillates in her judgment, quails before the storm of pro-slavery invectives, hurled by the insensate bigots of St. Domingo against the men of color, and finally she recedes from her high position by the National Assembly repealing the decree of the 8th of March, 1790. Thus the slaves dawning ray of hope and liberty is extinguished, and there is nothing ahead but the impenetrable gloom of eternal slavery.

This, then, is the ominous moment reserved for the chained bondmen to strike; and he rises now from his slumber of degredation in the terrific power of brute force. Bouckman, (called by a Haytian historian the Spartacus of his race) was raised up as the leader of the insurgents, who directed their fury in the desperate struggle for liberty and revenge, until the work of devastation and death was spread throughout the island to a most frightful extent.

But when this first hero of the slaves was captured and executed by their oppressors, like Oje, the first hero of the free men of color, the capacity of the race to furnish leaders equal to any emergency, was again demonstrated.

A triumvirate of negro and mulatto chieftains now succeeded these two martyred heros.

Jean Francois, Biassou, and Jeannot, now appeared upon the stage of action, and directed the arms of the exasperated insurgents against a faithless nation, the cruel colonists and their English allies.

In order to contend against such overwhelming odds effectually, and for the purpose of obtaining the necessary supply of arms and ammunition, the insurgents went over, for a time, to the service of Spain. This government had always regarded the French as usurpers in the island; and the Spaniards were therefore glad of any prospect of expelling the French colonists entirely from St. Domingo. Hence they gladly accepted the proffered service of the blacks as a means to effect this end.

We may conclude that Spain was willing to use the blacks to subserve her end, and afterwards would doubtless have endeavored to reduce them to a state of slavery again.

Nevertheless the black slaves and free men of color went over to the cause of Spain, and used her to subserve their purpose in driving France not only to re-enact her previous decree in relation to the men of color; but also to proclaim the immediate emancipation of the blacks, and to invest them with equal political rights.

When this glorious result was thus triumphantly effected, they left the service of Spain and returned to the cause of France again.

During the struggles that took place while the insurgents were in the cause of Spain, the three leaders who headed them when they united with the Spaniards, were replaced by Toussaint and Rigaud -one a black, and the other a mulatto, when they returned to the service of France.

These two leaders, at the head of their respective castes in the service of France, fighting on the side of liberty, law, and order, compelled the turbulent and treasonable colonists to respect these last national decrees; drove their English allies from the colony, and extinguished the Spanish dominion therein, and thus reduced the whole island to the subjection of France.

When we duly consider this shrewd movement of the blacks in thus pressing, Spain in their service at that critical moment we have presented another convincing proof of the capacity of the negro to adopt suitable means to accomplish great ends; and it therefore demonstrates in the most powerful manner, his ability for self-government.

THE AUSPICIOUS DAWN OF NEGRO RULE.

Toussaint, by his acute genius and daring prowess, made himself the most efficient instrument in accomplishing these important results, contemplated by the three French Commissioners, who brought the last decrees of the National Assembly of France, proclaiming liberty throughout the island to all the inhabitants thereof; and thus, like another Washington, proved himself the regenerator and savior of his country.

On this account, therefore, he was solemnly invested with the executive authority of the colony; and their labors having been thus brought to such a satisfactory and auspicious result, two of the Commissioners returned home to France.

No man was more competent to sway the civil destinies of these enfranchised bondmen than he. And no one else could hold that responsible position of an official mediator between them and the government of France, with so great a surety and pledge of their continued freedom, as Toussaint L'Ouverture. And there was no other man that these rightfully jealous freemen would have permitted to carry out such stringent measures in the island, so nearly verging to serfdom, which were so necessary at that time in order to restore industry, but one of their own caste whose unreserved devotion to the cause of their freedom, placed him beyond the suspicion of any treacherous design to re-enslave them.

Thus had the genius of Toussaint developed itself to meet an emergency that no other man in the world was so peculiarly prepared to fulfil; and thereby he has added another inextinguishable proof of the capacity of the negro for self-government.

But if the combination of causes, which thus pointed him out as the only man that could safely undertake the fulfillment of the gubernatorial duties, are such manifest proofs of negro capacity; then the manner in which we shall see that he afterwards discharged the duties of that official station, goes still further to magnify the self-evident fact of negro capability.

He established commercial relations between that island and foreign nations; and he is said to be the first statesman of modern times, who promulgated the doctrine of free trade and reduced it to practice. He also desired to secure a constitutional government to St. Domingo, and for this purpose he assembled around him a select council of the most eminent men in the colony, who drew up a form of constitution under his supervision and approval, and which he transmitted, with a commendatory letter to Napoleon Bonaparte, then First Consul of France, in order to obtain the sanction of the imperial government.

But that great bad man did not even acknowledge its receipt to Toussaint; but in his mad ambition he silently meditated when he should safely dislodge the negro chief from his responsible position, as the necessary prelude to the re-enslavement of his sable brethren, whose freedom was secure against his nefarious designs, so long as Toussaint stood at the helm of affairs in the colony.

But decidedly the crowning act of Toussaint L'Ouverture's statesmanship, was the enactment of the Rural Code, by the operation of which, he was successful in restoring industrial prosperity to the island, which had been sadly ruined by the late events of sanguinary warfare. He effectually solved the problem of immediate emancipation and unimpaired industry, by having the emancipated slaves produce thereafter, as much of the usual staple productions of the country, as was produced under the horrible regime of slavery; nevertheless, the lash was entirely abolished, and a system of wages adopted, instead of the uncompensated toil of the lacerated and delving bondman.

In fact, the island reached the highest degree of prosperity that it ever attained, under the negro governorship of Toussaint.

The rural code, by which so much was accomplished, instead of being the horrible nightmare of despotism-worse than slavery, that some of the pro-slavery calumniators of negro freedom and rule would have us believe; was, in fact, nothing more than a prudent government regulation of labor-a regulation which made labor the first necessity of a people in a state of freedom.

This Haytian Code compelled every vagabond or loafer about the towns and cities, who had no visible means of an honest livelihood, to find an employer and work to do in the rural districts. And if no private employer could be found, then the government employed such on its rural estates, until they had found a private employer. The hours and days of labor were prescribed by this code, and the terms of agreement and compensation between employer and employed were also determined by its provisions. Thus, there could be no private imposition on the laborers; and, as a further security against such a spirit, the government maintained rural magistrates and a rural police, whose duty it was to see to the faithful execution of the law on both sides.

By the arrangement of this excellent and celebrated code, every body in the commonwealth was sure of work and compensation for the same, either from private employers or from the government.

And Toussaint showed that he had not mistaken his position by proving himself equal to that trying emergency when that demigod of the historian Abbott, Napoleon Bonaparte, first Consul of France, conceived the infernal design of re-enslaving the heroic blacks of St. Domingo; and who for the execution of this nefarious purpose sent the flower of the French Army, and a naval fleet of fifty-six vessels under command of General Leclerc, the husband of Pauline, the voluptuous and abandoned sister of Napoleon.

When this formidable expedition arrived on the coast of St, Domingo, the Commander found Toussaint and his heroic compeers ready to defend their God given liberty against even the terrors of the godless First Consul of France. Wheresoever these minions of slavery and despotism made their sacrilegious advances, devastation and death reigned under the exasperated genius of Toussaint.

He made that bold resolution and unalterable determination, which, in ancient times, would have entitled him to be deified among the gods; that resolution was to reduce the fair eden-like Isle of Hispaniola to a desolate waste like Sahara; and suffer every black to be immolated in a manly defense of his liberty, rather than the infernal and accursed system of negro slavery should again be established on that soil. He considered it far better, that his sable countrymen should be DEAD FREEMEN than LIVING SLAVES.

The French veterans grew pale at the terrible manner that the blacks set to work to execute this resolution. Leclerc found it impossible to execute his design by force; and he was only able to win the reconciliation of the exasperated blacks to the government of France, by abandoning his hostilities and pledging himself to respect their freedom thereafter. It was then that the brave Negro Generals of Toussaint went over in the service of Leclerc; and it was then, that the Negro Chieftain himself, resigned his post to the Governor General appointed by Napoleon, and went into the shades of domestic retirement, at his home in Ennery.

I know it may be said that, after all Toussaint was found wanting in the necessary qualities to meet, and triumph in, the last emergency, when he was finally beguiled, and sent to perish in the dungeons of France, a victim of the perfidious machinations of the heartless Napoleon.

On this point I will frankly own that Toussaint was deficient in those qualities by which his antagonist finally succeeded in getting him in his power.

So long as manly skill and shrewdness-so long as bold and open tactics and honorable stratagems were resorted to, the black had proved himself, in every respect, the equal of the white man. But the negro's heart had not yet descended to that infamous depth of subtle depravity, that could justify him in solemnly and publicly taking an oath, with the concealed, Jesuitical purpose, of thereby gaining an opportunity to deliberately violate the same. He had no conception therefore, that the white man from whom he had learned all that he knew of true-religion I repeat it-he had no conception that the white man, bad as he was, slaveholder as he was-that even he was really so debased, vile, and depraved, as to be capable of such a double-dyed act of villainy, as breaking an oath solemnly sealed by invoking the name of the Eternal God of Ages.

Hence, when the Captain General, Leclerc, said to Toussaint, in presence of the French and Black Generals, uplifting his hand and jeweled sword to heaven: " I swear before the face of the Supreme Being, to respect the liberty of the people of St. Domingo," Toussaint believed in the sincerity of this solemn oath of the white man. He threw down his arms, and went to end the remainder of his days in the bosom of his family. This was, indeed, a sad mistake for him, to place so much confidence in the word of the white man. As the result of this first error, he easily fell into another equally treacherous. He was invited by General Brunet, another minion of Napoleon, in St. Domingo, to partake of the social hospitalities of his home; but, Toussaint, instead of finding the domestic civilities that he expected, was bound in chains, sent on board the Hero, a vessel already held in readiness for the consummation of the vile deed, in which he was carried a prisoner to France.

A BLOODY INTERLUDE FINALLY ESTABLISHES NEGRO SOVEREIGNTY

But if the godlike Toussaint had thus proved himself deficient in those mean and unhallowed qualities that proved his sad overthrow, nevertheless, the race again proved itself equal to the emergency, by producing other leaders to fill up the gap now left open.

The negro generals, who had gone over to the service of France, on the solemn assurances and protestations of Leclerc, soon learned to imitate this new lesson of treachery, and accordingly deserted his cause, and took up arms against France again.

And, if afterwards, the heroic but sanguinary black chief, Dessalines, who had previously massacred 500 innocent whites (if any of these treacherous colonists can be called innocent) at Mirebalais ; 700 more at Verettes, and several hundred others at La Riviere- I say again, if we now see him resume his work of slaughter and death, and hang 500 French prisoners on gibbets erected in sight of the very camp of General Rochambeau, we may see in this the bitter fruit of the treachery of the whites, in this dreadful reaction of the blacks.*

<* General Leclerc had now fallen a victim to the ravages of Yellow Fever, and Rochambeau had succeeded to the supreme command of the invading forces.>

Thus, if shocking depravity in perfidiousness and covenant breaking, is needed as another evidence of the negro's equality with the white man, in order to prove his ability to govern himself, then the implacable black chief, Dessalines, furnishes us with that proof.

Having now arrived at the epoch when the banners of negro independence waved triumphantly over the Queen of the Antilles; if we look back at the trials and tribulations through which they came up to this point of National regeneration, we have presented to us, in the hardy endurance and perseverance manifested by them, in the steady pursuit of Liberty and Independence, the overwhelming evidence of their ability to govern themselves. For fourteen long and soul-trying years-twice the period of the revolutionary struggle of this country-they battled manfully for freedom. It was on the 8th of March, 1790, as we have seen, that the immortal man of color, Vincent Oje, obtained a decree from the National Assembly guaranteeing equal political privileges to the free men of color in the island. And, after a continued sanguinary struggle dating from that time, the never-to-be-forgotten self-emancipated black slave, Jean Jacque Dessalines, on the 1st of January, 1804, proclaimed negro freedom and independence throughout the island of St. Domingo.

That freedom and independence are written in the world's history in the ineffaceable characters of blood; and it's crimson letters will ever testify of the determination and of the ability of the negro to be free, throughout the everlasting succession of ages.

EVIDENCES OF SELF-GOVERNMENT SINCE 1804

I will now proceed to give a hasty synopsis of the evidences that the Haytians have continued to manifest since their independence in demonstration of the Negros' ability to govern themselves.

Dessalines the Liberator of his country was chosen as a matter of course the first Ruler of Hayti. During his administration, the efficient organization of an army of 60,000 men to defend the country against invaders-the erection of immense fortifications, and the effort to unite and consolidate the Spanish part of the Island in one government with the French portion over which he presided, showed that he understood the precautionary measures necessary to preserve the freedom and independence of his country.

In the succeeding administrations of the rival chiefs, Christophe and Petion, we have indeed the sorrowful evidence of division, between the blacks and the men of color or mulattoes, the seeds of which was planted in the days of slavery. Nevertheless in that mutual good understanding that existed between them by which it was agreed to unite together whenever a foreign foe invaded the island; and in the contemptuous manner that both chiefs rejected the perfidious overtures of Bonaparte, we have still the evidence of that, conservative good sense which fully exhibits the negros ability to take care of himself. In the next administration of Boyor where we find these divisions in the French part of the island happily healed; and the Spanish colony also united in one government with the French.

After Boyer's administration there were some slight manifestations of disorder, arising from the smouldering feud between the blacks and men of color that the ancient regime of slavery had created among them; the baneful influence of which the work of freedom and independence has not yet had time to entirely efface. In this disorder we find the Spanish part of the island secede and set up a separate nationality.-But we find every thing in the French part soon settling down into order again, under the vigorous sceptre of the present ruler, Faustin I.

Here we shall rest the evidence in proof of the competency of the negro race for self-government which we have drawn out to rather a protracted length for the space assigned to a single Lecture;   and turn our attention now to some of the evidences of civilized progress evinced by that people.

EVIDENCES OF CIVILIZED PROGRESS

Under the administration of Dessalines aside from the Military preparations we have noticed, he continued the Code Rural of Toussaint as the law of the land, there by demonstrating that the negro in independence could carry forward measures of industry for his own benifit as well as for the whites when he governed for and in the name of France; for such was the case during the Governor Generalship of Toussaint. He also established schools in nearly every district of his dominions.

In the constitution that he promulgated, it was declared that he who was not a good father, a good husband, and above all a good soldier, was unworthy to be called a Haytian citizen. It was not permitted fathers to disinherit their children; and every person was required by law to exercise some mechanical art or handicraft.

The overthrow of the government of Dessalincs, by the spontaneous uprising of the people in their majesty, when it had become a merciless and tyrannical despotism, may also be noted here as another evidence of progress in political freedom of thought that made the race scorn to be tyrannized over by an oppressive master, whether that master was a cruel white tyrant, or a merciless negro despot.

Passing on to the two-fold government of Prtion and Christophe, we not only discover the same military vigilance kept up by the construction of the tremendous fortification called the Citadel Henry that was erected by Christophe, under the direction of European Engineers, mounting 300 cannons; — but we also find both of these chiefs introducing teachers from Europe in their respective dominions; and establishing the Lancasterian system of schools.

We discover also during their administration, Protestant Missionaries availing themselves of the tolerant provision in regard to religious worship that had been maintained in the fundamental laws of the country since the days of Dessalines. These Missionaries commenced their work of evangelization with the approbation of the negro and mulatto chieftains; —and Christphe went so far as to import a cargo of Bibles for gratuitous distribution among his people.

Thus do we find that progress continued to make its steady steps of advancement among these people, not withstanding the political divisions that had now taken place among them.

The succeeding administration of General Jean Pierre Boyer, under whom these divisions were happily healed, was fraught with stupendous projects of advancement.

The whole of the laws of the island were codified and made simple, under six different heads, viz: The Code Rural, the Civil Code, the Commercial Code, the Criminal Code, and the Code of Civil and Criminal procedure, regulating the practice in the several courts of the island. Thus, by this codification of her laws, did Hayti execute over thirty years ago, that which the States of this Union are just arousing to the necessity of doing. Boyer also set on foot a project of emigration, for the purpose of inducing the colored people of the United States to remove to Hayti, in order to replenish and accelerate the growth of the Haytian population. This project resulted in the removal of 6000 colored people to that island from this country.

In addition to this important movement, various enterprises were undertaken by men of public spirit, during this administration, to promote industry among the people of Hayti.

A company was formed to carry on a mahogany saw mill, which expended $20,000 in the purchase of the necessary machinery from France. The mill was erected at St. Marc's. Judge Lespinasse, chief justice of the Court of Cassation, was President of the Company; and it was under the special patronage of General Boyer, the President of the Republic.

Another company was also formed, under the presidency of Senator Jorge, for tanning purposes, and expended $10,000 in preparations for carrying on the business. A saw mill was also erected at Port-au-Prince, by a private individual, at the cost of $15,000.

Thus were the most vigorous efforts of progress manifested during the administration of Boyer.

In the subsequent administration of Guerrier, Pierrot, and Riviere, which followed each other in quick and rather chaotic succession, the work of industrial progress did not abate. Two steamers were purchased by the government, a model agricultural farm was established under a scientific director from France; and English architects, carpenters, and stone masons were hired to come in the country to improve the style of building.

Finally, we also discover the same evidences of gradual progress, when we come down to the present administration of Faustin I. A navy of about twenty armed vessels have been created. Thirteen steam sugar mills have been erected. The system of education improved and extended. And a house of industry erected at Port au Prince, for the purpose of instructing boys in the mechanic arts.

And here let me add, that during the whole period of these successive administrations, that we have thus summarily passed under review, a thrifty commercial trade has been maintained between that island and the maritime nations of Europe and America, amounting in the aggregate, to several millions of dollars per annum.

Hence these evidences of educational and industrial development, expanding continually as years roll onward, we regard as the most irrefragable proof of true civilized progress on the part of the Haytian people.

STABILITY OF THE GOVERNMENT.

But in addition to these facts, we may adduce the general stability of the government they have maintained, as another evidence of civilized progress. There have been but eight rulers in Hatyi since 1804. And in the United States, since 1809, there have been ten different chief magistrates-a period of forty-eight years. Thus, this country has had two more rulers than Hayti, within a period five years less than the Haytian sovereignty.

The fact is, there is no nation in North America, but the United States, nor any in South America, except Brazil, that can pretend to compare with Hayti, in respect to general stability of government.

Some exceptions might be taken, by the over scrupulous partizan of popular institutions, at the tendency manifested to vacillate between a Republican and Monarchial form of government, that has constantly been exhibited in Hayti, since the days of Dessalines.

The desire for Republican institutions has its rise in the Cosmopolitan ideas and example of France, at the time of the Haytian Revolution. The proximate example of the United States may also influence this desire for republicanism to some extent.

On the other hand, Monarchy is an ancient traditionary predilection of the race derived from Africa, which ancient continent maintains that form of government in common with the rest of the old world. The gorgeous splendor and august prestige of aristocratic rank and title, always attendant on this form of government, hold an imperious sway over the minds of this race of men who have such a keen appreciation of the beautiful. With these monarchical instincts on the one hand, and those powerful republican influencies on the other, Hayti has continually oscillated between a republican and monarchial form of government.

Permit me, however, to urge with due deference to the republican ideas which surround me, that it matters not in the eternal principles of morality, what the form of government may be, so long as the ruling powers of a nation maintain the inviolability of personal liberty, exact justice and political quality among all of its honest citizens and subjects. If these things are not so maintained, a republic is as great, nay a greater despotism that an autocracy.

A popular despotism therefore, whose rulers are composed of political gamblers for the spoils of office and burglarious plunderers of the public treasury that tyranizes over any class of its citizens and subject, is less tolerable than a monarchical or an aristocratic despotism, even though its rulers are a hereditary class of blood-titled paupers pensioned from generation to generation, on the public bounty of the nation. Among this latter class of rulers there is not to be found such a desperate and reckless set of lawless adventurers as will be found among the former. And should such monsters present themselves, they are in a more tangible shape to be got at and disposed of in a government of the few, than in that of the many.

The Haytian people when governed by the crowned and imperial Dessalines testified their love of liberty, by destroying the tyrant when he violated the constitution and over stepped the laws of his country.

The American people under a republican form of government manifest their want of a love of true liberty, when they permit a vagabond set of politicians, whose character for rowdyism disgraces the nation, to enact such an odious law as the Fugitive Slave bill, violating the writ of Habeas Corpus, and other sacred guarantees of the Constitution; -and then tamely submit to this high handed outrage, because such unprincipled scoundrels voted in their insane revelry, that it must be the Supreme law of the land.

If there was one-half of the real love of liberty among even the people of the professedly free northern states, as there is among the negroes of Hayti, every one of their national representatives who voted for that infamous bill, or who would not vote instantaneously for its repeal, would be tried for his life, condemned and publicly executed as accessory to man stealing. Thus would a free people, determined to preserve their liberties, rid themselves of a brood of petty tyrants who seek to impose their unhallowed partizan caprices upon the country, as the supreme law of the land, over-riding even the Higher Law of God.

If such was the real love of liberty among the northern people of this vain-glorious Republic, we should soon annihilate that morally spineless class of politicians, who need decision of character, when they got to Washington, to legislate for freedom.

But such a determined spirit of liberty does not exist here, and honest men must submit therefore with lamb-like patience to this republican despotism of irresponsible political partizans who violate every just principal of law, because these unrighteous decrees are perpetrated in the name of the sovereign people.

Hence there is far more security for personal liberty and the general welfare of the governed, among the monarchical negroes of Hayti where the rulers are held individually responsible for their public acts, than exists in this bastard democracy.

The single naked despot is soon reached by the keen avenging axe of liberty, for any acts of despotism among the Haytian blacks; but here its dull and blunted edge lays useless; for it might be hurled in vain and fall powerless among a nameless crowd of millions.

CONCLUSION

But our historical investigations are at an end, and we must hasten to bring our reflections to a conclusion. I have now fulfilled my design in vindicating the capacity of the negro race for self-government and civilized progress against the unjust aspersions of our unprincipled oppressors, by boldly examining the facts of Haytian history and deducing legitimate conclusions therefrom. I have summoned the sable heroes and statemen of that independent isle of the Caribbean Sea, and tried them by the high standard of modern civilization, fearlessly comparing them with the most illustrious men of the most enlightened nations of the earth; - and in this examination and comparison the Negro race has not fell one whit behind their contemporaries. And in this investigation I have made no allowances for the negroes just emerging from a barbarous condition and out of the brutish ignorance of West Indian slavery. I have been careful not

to make such an allowance, for fear that instead of proving negro equality only, I should prove negro superiority. I shun the point of making this allowance to the negro, as it might reverse the case of the question entirely, that I have been combatting and instead of disproving his alledged inferiority only, would on the other hand, go farther, and establish his superiority. Therefore as it is my design to banish the words "superiority" and "inferiority" from the vocabulary of the world, when applied to the natural capacity of races of men, I claim no allowance for them on the score of their condition and circumstances.

Having now presented the preceding array of facts and arguments to establish, before the world, the Negro's equality with the white man carrying forward the great principles of self-government and civilized progress; I would now have these facts exert their legitimate influence over the minds of my race, in this country, in producing that most desirable object of arousing them to a full consciousness of their own inherent dignity; and thereby increasing among them that self-respect which shall urge them on to the performance; of those great deeds which the age and the race now demand at their hands.

Our brethren of Hayti, who stand in the vanguard of the race, have already made a name, and a fame for us, that is as imperishable as the world's history.

It becomes then an important question for the negro race in America to well consider the weighty responsibility that the present exigency devolves upon them, to contribute to the continued advancement of this negro nationality of the New World until its glory and renown shall overspread and cover the whole earth, and redeem and regenerate by its influence in the future, the benighted Fatherland of the race in Africa.

Here in this black nationality of the New World, erected under such glorious auspices, is the stand point that must be occupied, and the lever that must be exerted, to regenerate and disenthrall the oppression and ignorance of the race, throughout the world. We must not overlook this practical vantage ground which Providence has raised up for us out of the depths of the sea, for any man-made and utopian scheme that is prematurely forced upon us, to send us across the ocean, to rummage the graves of our ancestors, in fruitless, and ill-directed efforts at the wrong end of human progress. Civilization and Christianity is passing from the East to the West; and its pristine splendor will only be rekindled in the ancient nations of the Old World, after it has belted the globe in its westward course, and revisited the Orient again. The Serpentine trial of civilization and Christianity, like the ancient philosophic symbol of eternity, must coil backward to its fountain head. God, therefore in permitting the accursed slave traffic to transplant so many millions of the race, to the New World, and educing therefrom such a negro nationality as Hayti, indicates thereby, that we have a work now to do here in the Western World, which in his own good time shall shed its orient beams upon the Fatherland of the race. Let us see to it, that we meet the exigency now imposed upon us, as nobly on our part at this time as the Haytians met theirs at the opening of the present century. And in seeking to perform this duty, it may well be a question with us, whether it is not our duty, to go and identify our destiny with our heroic brethren in that independent isle of the Carribean Sea, carrying with us such of the arts, sciences and genius of modern civilization, as we may gain from this hardy and enterprising Anglo-American race, in order to add to Haytian advancement; rather than to indolently remain here, asking for political rights, which, if granted a social proscription stronger than conventional legislation will ever render nugatory and of no avail for the manly elevation and general well-being of the race. If one powerful and civilized negro sovereignty can be developed to the summit of national grandeur in the West Indies, where the keys to the commerce of both hemispheres can be held, this fact will solve all questions respecting the negro, whether they be those of slavery, prejudice or proscription, and wheresoever on the face of the globe such questions shall present themselves for a satisfactory solution.

A concentration and combination of the negro race, of the Western Hemisphere in Hayti, can produce just such a national development. The duty to do so, is therefore incumbent on them. And the responsibility of leading off in this gigantic enterprise. Providence seems to have made our peculiar task by the eligibility of our situation in this country, as a point for gaining an easy access to that island. Then let us boldly enlist in this high pathway of duty, while the watch-words that shall cheer and inspire us in our noble and glorious undertaking, shall be the soul-stirring anthem of GOD and HUMANITY.

ADVERTISEMENT.

AFRIC-AMERICAN PRINTING COMPANY.

This is an association formed for the purpose of publishing negro Literature. It is formed under the auspices of the National Emigration Convention, of the colored people of the United States and Canada, and under the special patronage of the Board of publication, created by that Convention, for publishing the Afric-American Repository. This company, in pursing its object, intend primarily to publish the literary productions of colored authors; and incidentally to publish the writings of any other class of authors, when the same shall be deemed serviceable to the great cause of humanity.

It is hoped that the efforts of this company will be so well sustained by the public, that its objects will continually augment, until a complete set of measures shall be introduced among the colored people of the United States and of the American Continent, and carried out in practical operation among them, until this oppressed race shall be completely redeemed from and elevated above all of their political and social disabilities.

As to what such a train of measures should be, it is not material now to speculate upon. It is sufficient to announce the programme of the practical measure already set on foot by the company; and if this is sustained, as it is hoped it will be, time will decide what may be done in the future.

Source: Rev. Jas. Theo. Holly, *A Vindication Of The Capacity Of The Negro Race For Self-Government, and Civilized Progress, As Demonstrated By Historical Events Of The Haytian Revolution; And The Subsequent Acts Of That People Since Their National Independence.* (New Haven: John P. Anthony, Agent. William H. Stanley, Printer, 1857)

24

Alexander Crummell

Alexander Crummell (1819–1898) is best known as the early voice of Pan Africanism in Liberia and America. Born and raised in New York City, he attended the African Free School, and was drawn to the Protestant Episcopal church by the influential African-American leader, the Reverend Peter Williams, Jr. Educated for a time at Oneida Institute, he was later rejected by his church's General Theological Seminary. He turned to private tutors, and was finally ordained a priest in 1844. In 1847 he traveled to England to raise money for his church and stayed to attend Cambridge University, receiving a bachelor's degree in 1853. While getting what benefit he could from white institutions, Crummell was nevertheless a firm "race man" who believed in the efficacy of separate black organizations.

Crummell had shown no interest in the American Colonization Society, and he surprised many when he moved to the African-American colony of Liberia in 1853. But for Crummell, frustrated by racism at home, Liberia was the African-American frontier, a land of opportunity where African Americans would become the vanguard of Christianity and "civilization" in West Africa. For nearly twenty years in Liberia, Crummell served as a missionary, educator, and spokesperson for Liberian settlers. He hoped the founding of a college in Liberia would promote higher education for young Liberians, and he sought to bring education and Christianity to the African natives to further integrate them into the young republic. But mostly his aims were frustrated by the poverty of the country and the rising African-American mulatto leadership that excluded the dark-skinned and native-born from Liberia's leadership ranks. Crummell returned to the United States in 1871. For the remainder of his life he lectured widely on African-American affairs and, in 1897, founded the American Negro Academy to promote higher education among African Americans by publishing scholarly black works. He may be best remembered by W. E. B. Du Bois's affecting elegy in his 1903 classic, *The Souls of Black Folks*.

Crummell's lecture brilliantly captures his view of what the American slave experience meant for the displaced descendants of Africa. In some ways Crummell's essay is an example of the "happy fall" seen in several other pamphlets, but in this case it was not religion but language that helped to compensate for the pains of slavery. For Crummell, the English language conveyed the richness of the democratic ideas that culminated in the American Revolution and articulated the fundamental concepts of liberty and human rights. Cleansed of white racism, the English language, promoted by the African-American settlers, would be the unifying force in their efforts to bring Africa into the modern world. Crummell's essay is also noteworthy for its strong endorsement of education for women.

"The English Language in Liberia"

(1861)

HARPER, CAPE PALMAS,
Aug. 18, 1860.

Rev. A. CRUMMELL,

      Dear Sir,

          Will you be kind enough to favor us with a copy of your Oration on the 26th ult. We desire to have it published, for the benefit of our fellow citizens throughout the Republie, and of our Race, generally. We hope you will let us have it as early as possible. We have the honor to be

Your humble servants,
S. B. D'LYON,
J. M. THOMPSON, } *Committee.*
J. M. WILLIAMS.

MT. VAUGHAN, CAPE PALMAS,
20th Aug. 1860.

Gentlemen,

          I have many misgivings that the Address you ask for publication, may tend more, itself to exhibit the defects it points out, than to illustrate the commanding theme I have ventured to treat of. But even in that event, it is possible that I may be able to fasten attention upon the great language we speak, and thus help to advance the cause of Intelligence and Letters in the land: and therefore 1 shall comply with your kind request, and place the manuscript at your disposal.

          I am, Gentlemen, your faithful Serv't,

ALEX. CRUMMELL.

S. B. D'LYON, M. D.
J. M. THOMPSON, Esq. } *Committee.*
J. M. WILLIAMS, Esq.

    This address was repeated by request, before a large and most respectable audience, in the Hall of Representatives, Monrovia, on the Evening of February 1861, Gen. J. N. LEWIS, Sect. of State, in the Chair: and its publication was then requested by many of the leading citizens of that town.

Language, in connection with reason, to which it gives it proper activity, use and ornament; raises man above the lower orders of animals; and in proportion as it is polished and refined, contributes greatly, with other causes, to exalt one nation above another, in the scale of civilization and intellectual dignity."

ANON.

"Our language is a part and a most important part of our country. * * * * Nobody who is aware how a nations feelings and opinions, and whatever characterizes it, are interwoven with its language by myriads of unperceptible fibres, will run the risk of severing them. Nobody who has a due reverence for * * * * his own spiritual being, which has been mainly trained and fashioned by his native language, nobody who rightly appreciates what a momentus thing it is to keep the unity of a people entire and unbroken, to preserve and foster all its national recollections, what a glorious and inestimable blessing it is to "speak the tongue that Shakspeare spake" will ever wish to trim that tongue according to any arbitrary theory-"

Rev. J. C. HARE.

"So may we hope to be ourselves guardians of its purity, and not corrupters of it; to introduce, it may be, others into an intelligent knowledge of that with which we shall have ourselves more than a merely superficial acquaintance—to bequeath it to those who come after us not worse than we received it ourselves."

DEAN TRENCH

Address.

Two years ago to-day, when we were assembled together here, as now, to celebrate our National Anniversary, I was called up, after the Orator of the day, to make a few remarks. And perhaps, some who are here, may remember that, in setting forth a few of the advantages we pilgrims to these shores possess for a noble national growth and for future superiority; I pointed out among other providential events the fact, that the exile of our fathers from their African homes to America, had given us, their children, at least this one item of compensation, namely, the possession of the Anglo Saxon tongue; that this language put us in a position which none other on the globe could give us: and that it was impossible to estimate too highly the prerogatives and the elevation the Almighty has bestowed upon us, in our having as our own, the speech of Chaucer and Shakspeare, of Milton and Wordsworth, of Bacon and Burke, of Franklin and Webster. My remarks were unpremeditated, and they passed from my thoughts as the meeting was dismissed, and we went forth to the festivities of the day. But it happened that, shortly afterwards, I had occasion to seek health by a journey up the Cavalla. There, on the banks of that noble river, fully 80 miles from the ocean, I met with hospitality from a native trader, a man who presented all the signs of civilization, and who spoke with remarkable clearness and precision, the English language. The incident struck me with surprise, and started a crowd of thoughts and suggestions concerning the future; among these came back the lost and forgotten words of our Anniversary of 1858. More than once since, in conversations, speeches and sermons, have I expressed the ripened convictions which that occurrence created in my mind; and the other day, after I received the invitation to speak before you on this occasion, I concluded to take this for the subject of remark:

"THE ENGLISH LANGUAGE IN LIBERIA"

I shall have to ask your patience this day, for, owing to that fatality of tardiness which seems to govern some of our public movements, I have had but a fortnight to prepare for this duty, and hence I cannot be as brief as is desirable. I shall have to ask your attention also, for I can promise you nothing more than a dry detail of facts.

I trust, however, that I may be able to suggest a few thoughts which may be fitted to illustrate the responsibilities of our lot in this land, and to show forth the nature and the seriousness of the duties which arise out of it.

1. Now, in considering this subject, what first arrests attention is the bare simple fact that here, on this coast, that is, between Gallinas and Cape Pedro, is an organized negro community, republican in form and name; a people possessed of Christian institutions and civilized habits, with this one marked peculiarity, that is, that in color, race and origin, they are identical with the masses of rude natives around them; and yet speak the refined and cultivated English language—a language alien alike from the speech of their sires and the soil from whence they sprung, and knowing no other. It is hardly possible for us fully to realize these facts. Familiarity with scenes, events, and even truths, tends to lessen the vividness of their impression. But without doubt no thoughtful traveller could contemplate the sight, humble as at present, it really is, without marvel and surprise. If a stranger who had never heard of this Republic, but who had sailed forth from his country to visit the homes of West African Pagans, should arrive on our coast; he could not but be struck with the Anglican aspect of our habits and manners, and the distinctness, with indeed undoubted mistakes and blunders, of our English names and utterance. There could be no

mistaking the history of this people. The earliest contact with them vouches English antecedents and associations. The harbor master who comes on board is perhaps a Watts or a Lynch; names which have neither a French, a Spanish, nor a German origin. He steps up into the town, asks the names of storekeepers, learns who are the merchants and officials, calls on the President or Superintendent or Judge; and although sable are all the faces he meets with, the *names* are the old familiar ones which he has been accustomed to in the social circles of his home, or on the signs along the streets of New York or London, viz.: the *Smiths*, (a large family in Liberia as every where else in Anglo-Saxondom,) and their broods of cousins, the Johnsons, Thompsons, Robinsons and Jacksons, then the Browns, the Greens, the [paradoxical] Whites, and the [real] Blacks; the Williams', James', Paynes, Draytons, Gibsons, Roberts', Yates,' Warners, Wilsons, Moores, and that of his Excellency President Benson.

Not only names, but titles also are equally significant, and show a like origin. The streets are Broad, and Ashmun, and as here, Griswold. The public buildings are a Church, a Seminary, a Senate House, and a Court House.

If our visitor enters the residence of a thriving, thoughtful citizen, the same peculiarity strikes him. Everything, however humble, is of the same Anglo-Saxon type and stamp. On the book-shelves or tables, are Bibles, Prayer or Hymn Books, Harvey's Meditations or Bunyan's Pilgrim's Progress, Young's Night Thoughts or Cowper's Poems, Walter Scott's Tales or Uncle Tom's Cabin. In many places he will find well-used copies of Shakspeare and Milton. Not a few have enriched themselves with the works of Spenser and Wordsworth, Coleridge and Campbell, Longfellow and Bryant, Whittier and Willis, and of that loftiest of all the bards of the day, Alfred Tennyson. Should it happen to be a mail-day, or the "Stevens" has just glided into our waters, he would find at the Post Office, papers from America and England: "The Times," "Illustrated London News," "Daily Advertiser," "The Star," "The Guardian," "The New York Tribune," and "Commercial Advertiser," the "Protestant Churchman," and the "Church Journal." In one heap, "Littell's Living Age; in another, "Chambers' Journal." Here, "Harpers Monthly;" there, "The Eclectic." Amid the mass of printed matter he would see, ever and anon, more ambitious works: Medical and Scientific Journals, Quarterly Reviews, the "Biblioth&oeca Sacra," "Blackwood's" and other Magazines.

Such facts as these, however, do not fully represent the power of the English tongue in our territory. For, while repressing all tendencies to childish vanity and idle exaggeration we are to consider other telling facts which spring from our character and influence, and which are necessary to a just estimate of the peculiar agency we are now contemplating. And here a number of facts present themselves to our notice. Within a period of thirty years, thousands of heathen children have been placed under the guardianship of our settlers. Many of these have forgotten their native tongue, and know now the English language as their language. As a consequence, there has sprung up, in one generation, within our borders, a mighty army of English speaking natives, who, as manhood approached, have settled around us in their homes from one end of the land to the other. Many of these take up the dialect of the other tribes in whose neighborhood their masters lived, but even then English is their speech. Thus it is that every where in the Republic, from Gallinas to Cape Palmas, one meets with a multitude of natives who have been servants in our Liberian families, and are daily in the utterance of English. A considerable number of these have enjoyed the opportunity of school instruction, and have carried back to the country the ability to read and to write English. In many cases, it is, in truth impossible to say whether their attainments should be suggestive of sorrow or of joy. I have had naked boys working for me on the St. Paul, who, when they wanted any thing, would write a note with as much exactness as I could. We all here know *one* native man, over the river, who is a leader in Devil-dances, and yet can read and write like a scholar. A friend of mine, traveling in the bush, nigh 200 miles from Monrovia, stopt one night, exhausted, at the hut of a native man, who brought him his own Bible to read, but alas! it was accompanied by a decanter of rum! The moral of such facts I shall not enter upon; but here is the simple fact, that by our presence, though in small numbers, we have already spread abroad, for scores of miles, the English language, written as well as spoken, among this large population of heathen.

The trading schemes of merchants and settlers is another powerful auxiliary in disseminating this language.

At every important point on the coast, Liberian, English and American merchants have, for years, established their factories between Cape Palmas and Monrovia, there cannot be less than 30 factories. In each of these depots, some three or four English-speaking persons—Liberians—are living; in a few cases families have made them their permanent abodes; and thus, what with the native servants, the natives in neighboring towns, the more remote natives who flock hitherward for trade, and the few happy cases where pious young men devote a portion of their time to teaching, there is, and has been, a powerful, a wide spread system in operation for the teaching and extension of English.

Another process has been for some time at work to spread our language. The interior natives have found out that a home in our vicinity is equivalent to an act of emancipation; and as a consequence, remnants of tribes who for centuries have been the prey of their stronger neighbors, for the slave trade; and boys and men, upwards of 100 miles inland, who have been held in slavery, crowd in upon our neighborhood for freedom. Behind our settlements, on the St. Paul, there is the most heterogeneous mixture conceivable, of divers tribes and families, who have thus sought the protection of our commonwealth. Numbers of the Bassas, Veys, Deys, Golahs, and especially the Pessas, the hereditary slaves of the interior, have thus come to our immediate neighborhoods. Although I am doubtful of the *moral* effect of this movement upon *ourselves*, yet I feel no little pride in the fact that this young nation should become, so early, a land of refuge, an asylum for the oppressed! And I regard it as a singular providence, that at the very time our government was trumpeted abroad as implicated in the slave trade, our magistrates, in the upper counties, were adjudicating cases of runaway slaves, and declaring to interior slave holders that, *on our soil*, they could not reclaim their fugitives!

Just here another important item claims attention, that is the *Missionary* agency in propogating this language. The reference here will be, chiefly, to the two uppermost counties of Liberia. Their younger sister, Sinou, I am sorry to say, has not, as yet, made any marked impression upon her surrounding heathen; more we believe through youth and weakness, and suffering, than through indifference or neglect. Missionary operations, though participated in by others, have been chiefly carried on, in Bassa, by the Baptists. The means which have been employed have been preaching and schools. On the St. John's they have had for years a Manual Labor School, instructed by white Missionaries. This school has passed into the hands of a native Teacher, educated at Sierra Leone—a man who is the son of a prominent chieftain, and who possesses unbounded influence, as far as the Bassa tongue reaches. He has, moreover, these three prominent qualities, that is, he is a well-trained English scholar, a thoroughly civilized man, and a decided and well-tried disciple of the Lord Jesus Christ. His earnestness is evidenced in the fact that his work is unaided and self-supporting, and numbers of his tribe are glad to send him their children.

Besides this means of influence, ministers have been accustomed to visit numerous towns and villages, preaching the Gospel. And thus, by preaching and schools, a multitude of the Bassas have gained the English tongue, with many of its ideas and teachings.

The same Anglicising influence has been carried on, but on a larger scale, in Montserrada County, but mainly through the Methodists; and they have spread our language widely abroad through that county, by the means of native schools, native children in their American schools, and Missionaries residing in country towns, teaching and preaching as far back as the Golah tribe, and now among the Veys: native preachers too, men converted to the faith, and moved by the Spirit to proclaim the glad tidings to their needy parents, brothers and kin. I must not fail to mention the fact, that during the last two years one of their ministers has carried the English tongue some 200 miles in the interior,* and has spread it abroad amid the homes of the mild Pessas; thus preparing the way for legitimate trade, for civilization, for the Gospel of Jesus Christ, by the means of the spoken Word and the English Bible.

Thus, fellow-citizens, by these varied means the English language has been pushing its way among the numerous tribes of our territory. And thus, in a region of not less than 50,000 square miles, there are few places but where an English-speaking traveller can find some person who can talk with him in his own language.

And now I beg you to notice one point: this English, which we are speaking, and likewise teaching the heathen to speak, is not our native tongue. This Anglo-Saxon language, which is the only language ninety-nine hundredths of us emigrants have ever known, is not the speech of our ancestors. We are here a motley group, composed, without doubt, of persons of almost every tribe in West Africa, from Goree to the Congo. Here are descendants of Jalofs, Fulahs, Mandingoes, Sussus, Timmanees, Veys, Congos, with a large intermixture every where of Anglo-Saxon Dutch, Irish, French and Spanish blood—a slight mingling of the Malayan, and a dash, every now and then, of American Indian. And perhaps I would not exaggerate much, if I ended the enumeration of our heterogeneous elements in the words of St. Luke—"Jews and Proselytes, Cretes and Arabians."

And yet they all speak in a foreign tongue, in accents alien from the utterance of their fathers. Our very speech is indicative of sorrowful history; the language we use tells of subjection and of conquest. No people lose entirely their native tongue without the bitter trial of hopeless struggles, bloody strife, heart-breaking despair, agony and death! Even so we. But this, be it remembered, is a common incident in history, pertaining to almost every nation on earth. Examine all the old histories of men—the histories of Egypt, China, Greece, Rome and England—and in every case, as in ours, their language reveals the fact of conquest and subjection. But this fact of humiliation seems to have been one of those ordinances of Providence, designed as a means for the introduction of new ideas into the language of a people; or to serve, as the transitional step from low degradation to a higher and nobler civilization.

2. And this remark suggests, in the 2d place, the query—"What is the nature, and if any, the advantage of the exchange, we have thus, in God's providence, been led to make?

The only way in which in a fit manner I can answer this question is, by inquiring into the respective values of our native and our acquired tongue. Such a contrast will set before us the problem of "Loss and Gain" which is involved therein. The worth of our fathers' language will in this way stand out in distinct comparison with the Anglo-Saxon, our acquired speech. And *first*, lest us speak of the African dialects. I refer now to that partic-

---

* The lamented Rev. George L. Seymour, Missionary and Traveler.

ular group of African aboriginies who dwell in West Africa, from the Senegal to the Niger, and who have received the distinctive title of "Negro."

Within this wide extent of territory are grouped a multitude of tribes and nations with various tongues and dialects, which doubtless had a common origin, but whose point of affiliation it would be difficult now to discover. But how great soever may be their differences, there are, nevertheless, definite marks of inferiority connected with them all, which place them at the widest distance from civilized languages. Of this whole class of languages, it may be said, in the aggregate that (a) "They are," to use the words of Dr. Leighton Wilson, "harsh abrupt, energetic, indistinct in enunciation, meagre in point of words, abound with inarticulate nasal and guttural sounds, possess but few inflections and grammatical forms, and are withal exceedingly difficult of acquisition."* This is his description of the Grebo, but it may be taken, I think, as on the whole, a correct description of the whole class of dialects which are entitled "Negro." (b) These languages, moreover, are characterised by lowness of ideas. As the speech of rude barbarians, they are marked by brutal and vindictive sentiments, and those principles which show a predominance of the animal propensities. (c) Again, they lack those ideas of virtue, of moral truth, and those distinctions of right and wrong with with which we, all our life long, have been familiar. (d) Another marked feature of these languages is the absence of clear ideas of Justice, Law, Human Rights and Govermental Order, which are so prominent and manifest in civilized countries; and (e) lastly—These supernal truths of a personal present Deity, of the moral Government* "Western Africa, &c." 457, By Rev. J. L. Wilson, D. D. of God, of man's Immortality, of the Judgment, and of Everlasting Blessedness, which regulate the lives of Christians, are either entirely absent, or else exist, and are expressed in an obscure and distorted manner.

Now, instead of a language characterized by such rude and inferior features as these, we have been brought to the heritage of the English language. Negro as we are by blood and constitution, we have been, as a people, for generations, in the habitual utterance of Anglo-Saxon speech. This fact is now historical. The space of time it covers runs over 200 years. There are emigrants in this country from the Carolinas and Georgia, who, in some cases, come closer to the Fatherland; but more than a moiety of the people of this country have come from Maryland and Virginia, and I have no doubt that there are scores, not to say hundreds of them, who are unable to trace back their sires to Africa. I know that, in my own case, my *maternal* ancestors have trod American soil, and therefore have used the English language well nigh as long as any descendants of the early settlers of the Empire State.* And, doubtless, this is true of multitudes of the sons of Africa who are settled abroad in the divers homes of the white man, on the American continent.

At the present day, be it remembered, there are 10,000,000 of the sons of Africa alien from this continent. They live on the main land, and on the islands of North and South America. Most of them are subjects of European and American Governments. One growing prominent section of them is an independent Republic.† They speak Danish, Portuguese, Spanish, French and English; the English speaking portion of them, however, is about equal to all the rest together. The sons of Africa under the Americans, added to those protected by the British Flag, number 5,000,000.

Now what is the peculiar advantage which Anglo-Africans have gained by the loss of their mother tongue? In order to answer this query, we must present those direct and collateral lingual elements in which reside the worth and value of the English language, especially in contrast with the defective elements of the African dialects.

---

* New York.   † Hayti.

I shall not, of course venture to any extent, upon the etymological peculiarities of the English language, for even if I had time, I lack the learning and ability for such disquisition. Moreover the thoughts presented on such a day as this, should have a force and significance pertaining to national growth and a people's improvement. I shall therefore point out some of those peculiarities of the English language which seem to me specially deserving notice, in this country, and which call for the peculiar attention of thoughtful patriotic minds among us.

The English language then, I apprehend, is marked by these prominent peculiarities;— (a) *It is a language of unusual force and power.* This I know is an elemental excellence which does not pertain, immediately, to this day's discussion; but I venture to present it, inasmuch, as you will see presently, it has much to do with the genius and spirit of a language. The English is composed chiefly of simple, terse and forcible, one and two-syllabled words; which make it incomparable for simplicity and intelligibleness. The bulk of these words are the rich remains of the old Saxon tongue, which is the main stream, whence has flowed over to us the affluence of the English language. It is this element which gives it force, precision, directness and boldness; making it a fit channel for the decided thoughts of men of common sense, of honest minds and downright character. Let any one take up the Bible, the Prayer-Book, a volume of Hymns of any class of Christians, the common proverbs, the popular sayings:—which strike deep into the hearts of men and flow over in their common spontaneous utterances; and he will see everywhere these features of force, perspicuity and directness. Nor is it wanting in beauty, elegance and majesty; for, to a considerable extent, this same Saxon element furnishes these qualities; but the English, being a composite language, these attractions and commanding elements are bestowed upon it, in fullness, by those other affluent streams which contribute to its wealth, and which go to make up its "well of English undefiled." (b) Again, the *English language is characteristically the language of freedom.* I know that there is a sense in which this love of liberty is inwrought in the very fibre and substance of the body and blood of all people: but the flame burns dimly in some races; it is a fitful fire in some others; and in many inferior people it is the flickering light of a dying candle. But in the English races it is an ardent, healthy, vital, irrepressible flame; and withal normal and orderly in its development. Go back to the early periods of this people's history, to the times when the whole of Europe seemed lost in the night of ignorance and dead to the faintest pulses of liberty—trace the stream of their descent from the days of Alfred to the present time, and mark how they have ever, in law, legislation and religion, in poetry and oratory, in philosophy and literature, assumed that oppression was an abnormal and a monstrous thing! How when borne down by tyranous restraint, or lawless arbitrary rule, discontent and resistance have—

"Moved in the chambers of their soul"

How when misrule became organic and seated, tyranny unreasoning and obstinate, they have demonstrated to all the world, how trifling a thing is the tenure of tyrants, how resistless and invincible is the free spirit of a nation.!

And now look at this people—scattered, in our own day, all over the globe, in the Great Republic, in numerous settlements and great colonies, themselves the germs of mighty empires; see how they have carried with them every where, on earth, the same high, masterful, majestic spirit of freedom, which gave their ancestors, for long generations, in their island home—

— "the thews of Anakim,
The pulses of a Titan's heart ;"

and which makes them giants among whatever people they settle, whether in America, India or Africa, distancing all other rivalries and competitors.

And notice here how this spirit, like the freshets of some mighty Oregon, rises above and flows over their own crude and distorted obliquities. Some of these obliquities are prominent. Of all races of men, none I ween, are so domineering, none have a stronger, more exclusive spirit of caste, none have a more contemptuous dislike of inferiority: and yet in this race, the ancient spirit of freedom, rises higher than their repugnances. It impels them to conquer even their prejudices: and hence, when chastened and subdued by christianity, it makes them philanthropic and brotherly. Thus it is that in England this national sentiment would not tolerate the existence of slavery, although it was Negro slavery. Thus in New Zealand and at the Cape of Good Hope, Statesmen, Prelates, Scholars, demand that a low and miserable aboriginal population shall be raised to their own level; and accept, without agonies and convulsions, the providence and destiny which point plainly to amalgamation.* Thus in Canada it bursts forth with zeal and energy for the preservation and enlightenment of the decaying Indian. And thus in the United States, rising above the mastery of a cherished and deep-rooted spirit of caste; outrunning the calculations of cold prudence and prospective result; repressing the unwrought personal feeling of prejudice, it starts into being a mighty religious feeling which demands the destruction of slavery and the emancipation of the Negro! (c) *Once more I remark, that the English language is the enshrinement of those great charters of liberty which are essential elements of free governments, and the main guarantees of personal liberty.* I refer now to the right of Trial by Jury, the people's right to a participation in Government, Freedom of Speech, and of the Press, the Right of Petition, Freedom of Religion. And these are special characteristics of the English language. They are rights, which in their full form and rigid features, do not exist among any other people. It is true that they have had historical development: but their seminal principles seem inherent in the constitution of this race. We see in this people, even in their rude condition, the roots from which have sprung so fair and so beautiful a tree. And these conserving elements, carefully guarded, deepened and strengthened in their foundations from age to age, as wisdom and sagacity seemed to dictate, illustrated and eulogized by the highest genius, and the most consumate legal ability; have carried these states, the old country, the Republic of America, and the constitutional colonies of Britian, through many a convulsive political crisis; the ship of state, rocked and tossed by the wild waves of passion, and the agitations of faction; but in the end leaving her to return again to the repose of calm and quiet waters!

In states thus constituted, no matter how deep may be the grievances, how severe the suffering, the obstructive element has to disappear; the disturbing force, whether man or system, must be annihilated!—for freedom is terrible as well as majestic; and the state emerges from the conflict with a fresh acquisition of strength, and with an augmented capacity for a nobler career and loftier attainments. This fact explains the progressive features of all Anglican political society. Revolution seems exoteric to it; but the tide of reform in legal constitutional channels, sweeping away obstructive hindrances, goes onward and upward in its course.

I quote here a remark of a distinguished writer, a lady:—"The original propensities of race are never eradicated, and they are no where more prominent than in the progress of the social state in France and England. The vivacity and speculative disposition of the Celt, appear in the rapid and violent changes of government and in the succession of

---

* "See Church in the Colonies, No. xxii. A Journal of the visitation of the Bishop of Capetown. Also, letters of the Bishop of New Zealand, etc. etc."

theoretical experiments in France; while in Britain the deliberate slowness, prudence and accurate perceptions of the Teuton are manifest in the gradual improvement and steadiness of their political arrangements. (Here she quotes a passage from Johnson's Physical Atlas) "The prevalent political sentiments of Great Britain is undoubtedly *conservative*, in the best sense of the word, with a powerful undercurrent of democratic tendencies which give great power and strength to the political and social body of this country, and makes revolutions by physical force almost impossible. * * * * Great Britain is the only country in Europe which has had the good fortune to have all her institutions worked out and framed by her in a strictly organic manner: that is, in accordance with organic wants which require different conditions at different and successive stages of national development—and not by theoretical experiments, as in many other countries, which are still in a state of excitements consequent upon these experiments. The social character of the people of this country, besides the features which they have in common with other nations of Teutonic origin, is, on the whole, domestic, reserved, aristocratic, exclusive."*

The spirit of the above contrast is truly and accurately reproduced in the lines of a great poet:—

> "A love of freedom rarely felt,
> Of freedom in her regal seat
> Of England; not the school-boy heat,
> The blind hysterics of the Celt."

And another of England's great poets, the calmest, quietest, the least impassioned of all her bards: moved by this theme, bursts fourth in the burning words:—

> ——"We must
> Be free or die! who speak the language
> Shakspeare spake; the faith and morals hold
> Which Milton held!"

(d) Lastly, in pointing out the main features of the English language, I must not fail to state *its peculiar identity with religion*. For centuries this language has been baptized in the spirit of the Christian faith. To this faith it owes mostof its growth, from a state of rudeness and crudity to its present vigor, fullness, and expressiveness. It is this moreover which has preserved its integrity, and kept it from degenerating into barren poverty on the one hand, or luxuriant weakness on the other. The *English Bible*, more than any other single cause has been the prime means of sustaining that purity of diction, that simplicity of expression, that clearness of thought, that earnestness of spirit, and that lóftiness of morals which seem to be distinctive peculiarities of this language. Its earliest ventures for a true life, were wrestlings with the spirit of the Word. Previously to the invention of printing, pious Kings and holy Priests made their first attempts in English in their rude essays, to write "in their own language," the words and precepts of the Gospels. Its first lispings were in scriptural translation, its earliest stammerings in fervent prayers, holy Primers, and sacred minstrelsy. Then when the Press unfolded its leaves, its first pages were vernacular readings of the word of God From thence, ever since, as from a fountainhead, has flowed a mixed stream of thought and genius and talent, in all the departments of science, of law and of learning: but the whole has been coloured and leavened. and formed by, and under the plastic influence of Christianity. The Bible and its precepts, has been the prompting spirit of its legal statutes, its constitutional compacts, its scientific ventures, its poetic

---

* "[Mrs.] Somerville's Physical Geography." Ch. 33.

flights, its moral edicts. But above and beyond all these, this language has delighted to expand and express itself in Tracts and Tales and Allegories; in Catechisms and Homilies and Sermons; in heavenly Songs, sacred Lyrics, and divine Epics: in Liturgies and Treatises, and glowing Apologies for the Faith; sweeping along in a pure and gracious flood, which in the end shall empty itself into a blessed eternity!

These then are the main peculiarities of this language, and these some of the rich gifts it bestows upon us. But while, indeed, dwelling as I do, with delight, upon the massy treasures of this English tongue, I would not have you to suppose that I forget the loss which has accompanied all this gain. Do not think, I pray you, that I am less a man. that I have less the feelings of a man; because I would fain illustrate a favouring providence,

— "And justify the ways of God to man."

No! I do not forget that to give our small fraction of the race the advantages I have alluded to, a whole continent has been brought to ruin; the ocean has been peopled with millions of victims; whole tribes of men have been destroyed; nations on the threshold of civilization reduced to barbarism; and generation upon generation of our sires brutalized! No, my remarks, at best, are discordant; and I avoid collateral themes in order to preserve as much unity as possible, while endeavouring to set forth the worth and value of the English language.

And this is our language. But notice here the marks of distinctive providence. Our sad and cruel servitude has been passed among men who speak this tongue; and so we have been permitted, as the Israelites of old, to borrow "every man of his neighbour, and every woman of her neighbour, jewels of silver and jewels of gold."* But now on the other hand, as to that portion of our race whose lot has been cast among other sections of the European family; what advantages, what compensation have they reaped which can compare with our riches and our gain? Where do we find among them a Bill of Rights, the right of trial by Jury or, an act of Habeas Corpus? Where do they know clearly and distinctly the theory of Free Speech, of a Free Press, of Constitutional Government?—where are they blessed with such a noble heritage as the English Bible, and all the vast wealth, both religious and political, of the literature of England and America? It is not in Cuba, nor in Porto Rico. Not in Gaudalope, not in Martinico. Even in Brazil these ideas are but struggling for life; and their continued existence is doubtful. Time is yet to show whether either the white or black race there, will ever rise to their full height and grandeur. With all our hopes of, and pride in Hayti, her history shows how sad a schooling she has had! In truth how could France or Spain train the Negro race to high ideas of liberty and of government, when all their modern history has been an almost hopeless effort, to learn the alphabet of freedom,—to tread the first steps of legal self-restraint.? I grant that not unfrequently they present the individual black man, refined, elegaut, accomplished and learned, far beyond any that spring up on American or English soil. But in capacity for free government, and civil order, the British West India Isles, Sierra Leone, the free coloured men of America, and our own Republic are, without doubt, far in advance of all the rest of the children of Africa, under the sun. Indeed it is only under the influence of Anglo-Saxon principles that the children of Africa, despite their wrongs and injuries, have been able to open their eyes to the full clear quiet heavens, of freedom far distant though, at times they were!

3. I venture now to call your attention to a few remarks upon the probable destiny of this English language, in this country, and throughout this continent.

---

* Exodus Ch xi, 2.

And here, as every where else on the globe, one cannot but see the most magnificent prospects for this noble language.* Its thought, its wisdom, its practicality, its enterprising spirit, its transforming power, its harmonizing influence, and its Christian leavening, have gone out every where in our territory, and are changing and fashioning, not only our small civilized communities, but also gradually lifting up and enlightening our heathen neighbors. By a singular power it is multiplying its own means and agencies for a reproduction of its own influence, and a further extension of power in wider circles. As an illustration of this, we have here present to-day, by a remarkable providence, as guests—and we are glad to see them in our midst—the Captain and this large company of officers, of the little Steamer "Sunbeam," bound for the upper waters of the Niger; there to introduce trade and civilization, to pioneer letters and culture, and to prepare the way for the ENGLISH LANGUAGE and RELIGION.†

One cannot but mark the finger of marvellous providence, in the divers ways, in which this language is getting mastery over and securing hold upon, the masses of natives through all Liberia. Look for instance at the fact, that the only people these Krumen trust and rely upon, and with whom alone they are willing to ship for sea, are men who speak the English language. And consider here the bearing of this fact upon the increase of this speech throughout the country. They come from all that section of the coast which lies between Bassa and Beribi, and inland upwards of 60 miles, and offer themselves as seamen. Indeed, the desire for this service is almost a passion among them; boys in scores, run away from their parents for sea-service; I have seen here, in Harper, fully that number together, on a Steamer day; and notwithstanding the hindrances and the monopoly of the coastwise natives, the interior people run all risks to reach the coast to go to sea. The vessels in which they ship as sailors are English-speaking vessels. And in this way a multitude of them are acquiring the habitual use of English. On the coast, between Bassa and this point, there are many large towns where, among adults, it is almost as constantly employed as in our civilized communities.††

Notice here another fact: among all the industrious pursuits of our citizens, trading absorbs as much attention as any other pursuit. Scores of our youth, soon after leaving school, start, with their cloth, guns, powder and tobacco, for the factory, whether on the coast or in the country. Added to this is the other fact, that from Sierra Leone to the Equator, the master commercial influence is English. Liverpool and Bristol, Boston, Salem and Baltimore rule this coast. The numerous factories which now exist, and those which are starting up every where along the coast and up our rivers, are English-speaking. So

---

* I quote the following from a learned English Journal:—"And as of all the works of man language is the most enduring, and partakes the most of eternity, as our own language, so far as thought can project itself in the future, seems likely to be coeval with the world, and to spread vastly beyond even its present immeasurable limits, there cannot easily be a nobler object ambition than to purify and better it." Rev. J. C. Hare, Philological Museum, Vol. I. 665.

† The Steamer "Sunbeam" came into the Roads of Harper, Wednesday, 25th of July, and the Captain, and his Officers and Company, joined in the procession on the 2?th, having fired a salute in the morning. They all participated in the festivities at a public party, in the evening, and went off to their Steamer at 11 o'clock at night, amid the loud cheers of the citizens, who accompanied them to the water's side.

††"Three-fourths of the male population of the Kru country speak imperfect, but intelligible English."—"Western Africa," &c. p. 103. By Rev. J. L. Wilson, D. D.

almost universally is this the case, that Dutch, French and Sardinian vessels find an acquaintance with English an absolute necessity, and are lost without it.

Thus, by these varied means the English language is gradually extending itself throughout this country, and rivaling the rude native tongues of an aboriginal population. Now all these divers streams of influence, operating daily and hourly all through the country, upon thousands of our native population, disclose to us a transforming agency, which is gradually subverting these native languages of our tribes. The influence is here; it is in operation; it is powerful. Every day by trading, by adventure, by the curiosity of the natives, by war at times, by the migration of tribes, by the hasty footsteps of fugitives—this English language is moving further and further interiorwards its centre, and sweeping abroad with a wider and wider circumference. Nor can it be resisted. It carries with it two mighty elements of conquest: it is attractive, and it is commanding: (1) it is *attractive*, in that it brings cloth, iron, salt, tobacco, fish and brass rods, and all the other divers articles which are wealth to the native, and excite his desires. Poor, simple, childish, greedy creature! he cannot rest satisfied with the rudeness of nature, nor with the simplicity of his sires; and therefore he will part at any moment with the crude uncouth utterances of his native tongue, for that other higher language, which brings with its utterance wealth and gratification.

It is *commanding* too as well as attractive. When used merely as the language of trade, it brings to these people the authority of skill, ingenuity, and art in tasteful fabrics, in finely-wrought domestic articles, in effective instruments of warfare. The acquisition of it is elevation. It places the native man above his ignorant fellow, and gives him some of the dignity of civilization. New ideas are caught up; new habits formed, and superior and elevating wants are daily increased. Then when the instruction in schools and service in our own families for a few years, put the native boy so far in advance of his tribe that he must either become head-man or revolutionist; and if the latter, dividing the nation and carrying his party to a higher mode of living, and to a closer connection with Liberians or foreign traders.

As to the future results of this rivalry there can be no doubt; for, first of all, it is a superior tongue; and in all the ideas it expresses it comes to the native man with command and authority; next, it appeals to him in the point of his cupidity, and his selfish nature yields to an influence which gratifies his desires and his needs. And it is thus, by the means of commerce, and missions, and government, that this language is destined to override all difficulties, and to penetrate to the most distant tribes, until it meets those other streams of English influence which flow from Sierra Leone on the north and from Abbeokuta on the east; and so at the last the English language and the English religion shall rule for Christ, from the Atlantic to Timbuctoo, and all along both the banks of the Niger!*

Powerful as are these divers agencies in working out the end suggested, they are far inferior to one other, which I must hold up to distinctive notice. Christianity is using the English language on our coast as a main and mighty lever for Anglicising our native population, as well as for their evangelization.

I have already referred, in part, to the work of Missions: but there are some peculiarities in this work which clearly show that Christ is going to put all this part of the coast in possession of the English language, English law, and the English religion, for his own

---

* There seems every probability that the whole of that part of Africa, called Nigritia, which includes what is termed the Negro race proper; is to be brought under the influence of the English language, by the agency of black men, trained under Anglo-Saxon influences, at the Pongas Mission, Sierra Leone, Mendi Mission, Liberia, English Accra, Lagos, and Abbeokuta.

glory. Hundreds of native youth have acquired a knowledge of English in Mission Schools, and then in their manhood have carried this acquisition forth, with its wealth and elevation, to numerous heathen homes. Throughout the counties, Bassa and Montserrada, the Methodists have raised up numbers, in the wilderness, whose daily utterance is English; and they are doing this more at the present time than ever before. We who are living in this county, know well what a disturbing element, Missions, here, have been, both to heathenism and to the Grebo tongue. But how great has been this Missionary transformation of the Grebo to English, very few, I judge, have stopt to calculate. For instance, the Episcopal Mission, in this neighborhood, comprises at least 12 stations; and this has been its status for, at least, 12 years. At these stations, what with day-schools and night-schools, for a dozen scholars each; and, remembering that, at Cavalla, 100 children, at least, are always under training, in Reading, Writing and Arithmetic; you can see that several thousands, of our aboriginal population, have received a common school education, in the English language. And numbers of these persons show their appreciation of their advantages by securing the same for their children, and coveting them for their kindred.

And thus, every year, wave after wave dashes upon the weak intrenchments of heathenism, and is wearing them away; and thus, also, to change a figure, we have illustrated the noble truth, that a great language, like the fruitful tree, "yields fruit after its kind; and has its seed in itself;"* by which it is not only reproduced in its own native soil, but also takes possession of distant fields, and springs up with all its native vigor and beauty, in far off lands, in remote and foreign regions!

And now, lest this subject should seem to have but slight connection with the rejoicings of the day, let me point out a few practical teachings which flow from it, and which clearly pertain to our nation's advancement, political and moral, and to its future usefulness and power.

1st. Then I would say, that inasmuch as the English language is the great lingual inheritance God has given us for the future; let us take heed to use all proper endeavors *to preserve it here in purity, simplicity and correctness.* We have peculiar need to make this effort, both on account of our circumstances and our deficiencies: for the integrity of any and all languages is assailed by the newness of scenes in which an emigrant population is thrown by the crudity of the native tongue, with which it is placed in juxtaposition; and by the absence of that corrective which is afforded, in all old countries, by the literary classes and the schools. Here, in our position, besides the above, we have the added dangers to the purity of our English, in the great defect of our own education; of a most trying isolation from the world's civilization; in the constant influx of a new population of illiterate colonists ;† and in the natural oscillation from extremely depressed circumstances to a state of political democracy, on the one hand, and an exaggeration of the "ologies," and "osophies" of school training, at the expense of plain and simple education, on the other. The correctives to these dangers are manifest. (a) *In our schools we must aim to give our children a thorough and sound training in the simple elements of common school education.* Instead of the too common effort to make philosophers out of babes, and savans out of sucklings; let us be content to give our children correctness, accuracy, and thoroughness, in spelling, reading, writing, arithmetic and geography. I cannot but regard it as a serious defect in the schools in Liberia, that so many teachers undertake to instruct their pupils in Chemistry,

---

* Gen. 1. ii.

†Since the delivery of this Address a new element has been added to our population. The American Govornment is now sending recaptured Africans to Liberia.

Botany and Natural Philosophy before they can write and spell with accuracy. It seems to me the wiser course is to ground our youth well in the elements of the simple branches, before any thing higher is undertaken. Where it is convenient and desirable, teachers may aim at something more. We are, most certainly, in need of learned men and accomplished women. The State moreover is not too young, nor our circumstances too humble for us, even now, to gather around us the fruits of the highest culture and of the profoundest attainments. But all learning in our schools should be built upon the most rigid and thorough training in those elements which enable people to spell and read correctly, and to understand and explain, such simple reading as comes before them in the Bible, the Prayer Book, devotional books, and common newspapers. (b) But besides this, COMMON SCHOOl *education must needs be made more general, superior masters secured, and the necessities of the case be put more directly within the control of the citizens, than it is at present.* Perhaps there is no defect in our political system so manifest and so hurtful, as that its arrangements allow no local interests, whether it be in the election of a Constable, or the appointment of a Schoolmaster. As a consequence, all our growth seems to be the result of national, in the place of local enterprise; a feeling of dependence upon the Capital is exhibited every where; and there exists, universally, a lack of municipal pride and energy. It would be quite beyond the limits I have set before me, to enter upon this subject, or, I should venture to point out great and growing evils which are the result of this state of things; in the points, that is, of political ambition, local improvements, Roads, and civil order. I confine myself, however to the subject of education; and I would fain call the attention of public men to the necessity of putting the power of common school education *in the hands of the people,* in townships* with whatever measure of government aid can be afforded; if, indeed they wish to see inaugurated a common school system in our country, and desire the continuance in the land of sound English speech, thought, manners and morals. (c) In addition to the above, let every responsible man in the country, and by responsible man, I mean Government Officers, Ministers, Teachers and Parents, strive to introduce among our youthful citizens a sound and elevating English Literature. In this respect we are greatly endangered. There is going on, continually, a vast importation among our young men, of the vilest trash conceivable, in the form of books. They are, moreover, as poisonous as they are trashy. As trade and commerce increase this evil will increase, and magnify itself; and it is a manliest duty to ward off and forestall this danger, as soon, and as effectually as possible. Happily the antidote to this evil is simple, and easily available. There are a few standard English books which, some for generations, some in recent times, have served the noble purpose of introducing the youthful mind to early essays to thought and reflection; to the exercise of judgment and reason; and to the use of a chaste and wholesome imagination. It is the nature and the office of books, to produce these grand results. "For books," to use the lofty periods of Milton, "are not absolutely dead things, but do contain a potency of life in them, to be as active as that soul whose progeny they are—nay, they do preserve, as in a vial, the purest efficacy and extraction of that living intellect that bred them! I know they are as lively, and as vigorously productive, as those fabulous dragons' teeth, and being sown up and down, may chance to spring up armed men."†

The particular works to which I refer, are so masterly, and have become so much the staple of the Anglo-Saxon mind, that in England, America, and the British colonies,

---

* The wide diffusion of education, which has distinguished New England from her earliest times, is owing to this arrangement. Its great, and divers advantages are pointed out by De Tocqueville. See "Democracy in America" Ch. V.

† John Milton. Oration for "Unlicensed Printing."

numerous editions of them have been stereotyped, and may be had almost as cheap as palm leaves. I do not speak of the brilliant Essayists, of the profound Historians, of the sagacious Moralists. I am refering to another class of books, not less distinguished indeed, but more level to the common taste: works which have been scattered broadcast through the whole of Anglo-Saxondom, and the possession of which is attainable by the humblest persons, by the simplest investment. Any one of these books, which I shall mention, can be bought by any one, if he will practice a simple act of self-denial, for a few hours, or put by, occasionally, a single twelve and a half cents. My catalogue would include the following works:

Locke on the Mind.	Life of Ben Franklin.
Bacon's Essays.	Life of James Watt.
Butler's Analogy.	Life of Mungo Park.
Paley's Natural Theology.	History of Rome.
Wayland's Moral Philosophy.	History of England.
Banyan's Pilgrim's Progress.	Milton's Poems.
Robinson Crusoe.	Cowper's Poems.
Alison on Taste.	Burder's Self-Discipline.
Watt's on the Mind.	Todd's Student's Manual.
Channing's Self-Culture.	

The entire list, as several of them are abridged, may be purchased for less than three dollars. But the value of such a Library to a youth, just starting into life would be incalculable. And no better service could be done the cause of pure speech, correct diction, and earnest thought, than a general effort to put a Library of this kind, within the reach of every intelligent boy in the country, of 15 years of age.*

(d) But besides the correct training of the young, I beg to insist upon the great necessity of special care being bestowed upon the culture of the female mind, in Liberia. I feel that I cannot exaggerate the importance of this duty. The mothers, sisters, and daughters of the land, are to train the whole of the rising generation, now growing up around us, down, forever through all the deep dim vistas of coming ages. The influence of woman in this great work is deeper and more powerful than that of man; and especially in those years of our life when we are most susceptible. But no one who looks carefully at the state of things in this country, can suppose, for a moment, that either justice is done to the intellect of this sex, or, that women, in this land, feel the burden of obligation which rests so heavily upon them. The latter fact, however, peculiarly affects me. I must confess myself amazed at the general frivolousness of the female mind in this country. It is one of the most astonishing problems that my mind has ever been called upon to solve, how women can live such trifling, unthinking lives as they do in this land. When I look at the severe and rugged aspects of actual existence in this young country, I find it difficult to understand how it is that Parisian millinery can maintain such a tyranous control, as it does, over the sex, from Cape Mount to Palmas.

I do not blame the women so much for this state of things; nor do I forget the somewhat pardonable fact that dress is the only Fine Art, we have in Liberia. The world has been six thousand years in existence, and it has hardly yet begun to do justice to the intel-

---

* Just here, while speaking of books, it is no more than duty to acknowledge the vast debt of obligation, Liberian citizens ow BENJAMIN COATES, Esq. of Philadelphia, U. S. A. Scores of persons in Liberia will join in this expression of gratitude. The families are not a few, who, as in my own case, beside other books, have, likewise their valuable COATES' LIBRARY.

lect of woman.* Here, on this soil, this injustice cannot be perpetuated with safety. What with the present state the census,—more than half of the population being females, and the colonization ships, from the necessities of the case, sending us every six months, two women to one man; we shall, by and bye, reach a state of moral shipwreck; and the sad examples of the heathen, will, ere long, begin to act injuriously upon our social and domestic state, if we are not careful and foresighted. This will surely be the case, especially in the humblest walks of life, if we do not strive to raise our daughters and our sisters to become the true and equal companions of men, and not their victims. He who keeps wide open, the eyes God has given him, cannot be blind to some sad tendencies which already show themselves in our social state. And reform, in this particular, cannot commence too soon. Two or three things can be done immediately. (1) Let every respectable householder make the effort to put in his wife's hand some thoughtful Literary Journal, such as "Littells Living Age," or "Chambers' Journal;" by which both taste and thought may be cultivated, and the mind be started on the track of reflection. (2) Let some influential persons attempt to gather, in clubs or a society, the aspiring matrons and young women, in our communities, for reading, composition and conversation upon improving topics. Let the scheme projected be humble and simple: let it be elementary, even in its nature; and by gradual steps, rise to something more ambitious; why indeed, may not ministers of the Gospel lead classes of their congregations in this intellectual effort? There is certainly nothing unholy in it: there is surely *much* that may lead to, and foster piety in it: much that would have the sanction of Scripture. Indeed is not the religion of Christ to be the great regenerating agent in all *mental*, as well as all spiritual things? Is not the CHURCH to take the lead in all things that are to elevate and dignify man.? In any event, and by all means, do not let us go on in the dull, unthinking way we are now treading; and leave the minds of children and youth, in our families, unblessed by that pure speech and strong Anglo-saxon thought, which come with the most impressive force, from the graceful mind, and the tender voice of cultivated womanhood.* (3) But the master need in Liberia is that of a FEMALE SEMINARY, of a high order, for the education of Girls. Already our wives and daughters are in the rear of ourselves and sons, in training and culture; humble as we all are, in this country, in acquirements, yet there is a class of men in Liberia who are fully fifty years in advance of our women, that is, intellectually. The operations of High Schools, now in existence, the High Schools for boys projected, the other educational preparations going on, for Colleges and Seminaries, the return, ever and anon, of the professional young men, Lawyers, Doctors, Ministers, who are sent to America to be educated, with the mental training afforded men in mercantile pursuits, political contests, legal affairs and

---

* "It seems needful that something should be said specially about the education of women. As regards their interests they nave been unkindly treated—too much flattered, too little respected. They are shut up in a world of conventionabilities, and naturally believe that to be the only world. The theory of their education seems to be, that they should not be made companions to men, and some would say they certainly are not." "Friends in Council" B. 1, Ch. viii. 4

* I cannot resist the temptation to add here another fine extract from the learned English Journal before quoted:—It is a most happy and beautiful provision that children should imbibe their native language primarily and mainly from their mothers, should suck it in, as were, along with their milk; this it is that it is that makes it their mother tongue. For women are much more dutious recipients of the laws of nature and society; they are much less liable to be deluded by fantastical theories: and it is an old and very true remark, that in order to feel all the beauty and purity of any language, we must hear it from the lips * * * * * of a sensible, well educated woman." [Rev.] J. C. Hare. Philological Museum, Vol. 1. 644.

Legislative duty; will place men before long, a century ahead of our women. Such mental inequality will be a dangerous state for the interests of education and for social well-being. The mental inferiority of women will retard the progress of our children and youth. The intellectual force of the country will more and more decline: Learning and Letters will be without influence; material interests will every where predominate: we shall lose the freshness and the force of all our anglo-saxon antecedents: and at length, men every where, will rise up and weigh their paltry purses in the scale, over against the strongest brains: and all manhood shall cease in the land! No better correction to this sad tendency can be found than a good, sound, moral English Education for those especially, who will be entrusted with the rearing and training of our unborn children. I beg therefore to urge upon public attention, the immediate need of raising the standard of female education in this country. I beg to insist upon the deep necessity of elevating the mind of woman in the republic, and directing it to noble and commanding themes. I beg to enforce the duty of making woman in this land as superior intellectual and dignified as we all would have her, beautiful and attractive and moral. And to this end, all heads of families should strive, at the earliest day, to fall upon some plan, to found a FEMALE SEMINARY, with an able staff of officers and teachers.*

2. The subject we have been considering, teaches the duty of National care and effort, that our heathen neighbours be trained to the spirit, moral sentiments, and practical genius of the language we are giving them.

I have already affirmed that more natives speak English in Liberia than Anglo-Africans. I wish to add to this, the almost certain fact, that by the arrival of Imigrants, by the opening of interior Stations, by Missionary Societies in America, the number of native men and women who will read and write will, ere long, overwhelmingly predominate over us; so that for one civilized Liberian, there will be ten native men who will then speak English. Already our fellow-citizens have, at times, to make strange comparisons. It was only yesterday a respectable citizen told me that his hired woman expressed unwillingness on a recent occasion, to attend prayers in his family, because his native boys could read and she could not. Her ignorance of letters shamed her, "and made her feel," to use her own wise expression, "more than ever before the importance of education." These comparisons are becoming too frequent; and by and bye they will extend to communities as well as individuals, unless we provide more fully for the improvement of our own colonists. But I only mention the above facts in order to show, how rapid is the advance of the heathen within our own knowledge and acquaintance. And now the question arises, are these people to be quickened by letters to become only intelligent heathen.? Are we, by contact with them, to give them only an intellectual paganism.? Is our influence upon them to touch only the brain, and not life, manners, the family society? or rather should we not as a Nation, take upon us the duty of so training these people, that as they receive the language, so they may likewise receive the civilization, the order, the industry, and the mild, but transforming influences of a regulated Christian state.? The Mission of Liberia,

---

* I feel sure that, for the accomplishment of this end, we can, if necessary, look to that anxious and painstaking benevolence, in America, which so very generally anticipates the Intellectual needs of Liberia. But there are men of means enough in Liberia to start such an undertaking; and there are scores who are able to pay a good sum annually, to give their daughters a substantial and at the same time, a refined education.

Since the delivery of this address, Rev. Mr. Blyden has been acting in accordance with the above suggestion, in England; and has succeeded, I learn, in raising a considerable amount of funds for a Female High School in Liberia.

in its civil aspects, is clear to my mind. This nation is to restore society all along our coast; and by restoring society to regulate social life, to quicken in its growth the "tender plant of confidence," in both a direct and indirect manner to elevate the domestic state, and to give rise to industrial activity, and to establish good neighbourhood. However humble the effort may be, still it seems to me, that we ought to have, in each county, an industrial School for native boys who are fugitives, or wanderers, or who have been convicted of crime; where they could be trained to the use of the plough and hoe, and receive a good, but simple English education. Our neighbours too, that is, those who live near our settlements should be bound by law, to make broad and substantial roads for travel, to keep the Sabbath, and to conform more to our habits of dress than they now do. Moreover we cannot be too early in giving them the benefit of the great Saxon institutions of Trial by Jury, and personal protection. Life should be made sacred among them in the neighbourhoods of our larger towns. The Sassy-wood Ordeal should be put an end to, and a due process of law guaranteed to all criminals and suspected parties among them. This I know could not be done in remote places; but in the vicinity of our towns and settlements, sanguinary retaliation, envy and revenge should not be allowed to show themselves as they now do; nor the awful scenes which take place, almost under our eyes, be suffered to barbarize our children. Indeed both for their benefit and our own, law and authority cannot be too soon established among them on a firm basis, and *with full legal forms*. It is a matter alike of policy and of duty for us to attempt, though at a humble distance, the same legal reformation among this people that the English have, with great success effected in India. There is no greater disparity *here* in our relative numbers, than *there*, between the Christian power and the heathen masses: while here we have a population at once simple and unenlightened to deal with, and the presence and protection of the three chief naval powers of the world. Moreover we have this encouragement in any such undertaking, namely, that our heathen neighbours are ambitious of improvement, and always welcome the changes and the regulations, which tend to make them "Americans."

3. Finally let us aim, by every possible means, *to make indigenous, in this infant country, the spirit and genius of the English language*, in immediate connection with its idiom.

You all doubtless remember the solemn utterance of St. James that "the body without the spirit is dead." So likewise a language without its characteristic features, stamp, and spirit, is a lifeless and unmeaning thing, and must ere long, degenerate into a crude, mongrel, discordant jargon. If the English had educated their West India blacks they would never have committed so great a blunder, as they did before emancipation, as the publication of the Bible for them, in broken English:—a miserable caricature of their noble tongue. All low, inferior, and barbarous tongues are, doubtless, but the lees and dregs of noble languages, which have gradually, as the soul of a nation has died out, sunk down to degradation and ruin. We must not suffer this decay, on these shores, in this nation. We have been made, providentially, the deposit of a noble trust; and we should be proud to show our appreciation of it. Having come to the heritage of this language we must cherish its spirit, as well as retain its letter. We must cultivate it among ourselves; we must strive to infuse its spirit among our reclaimed and aspiring natives. And what that spirit is, we have witnessed in the character of the people among whom we have lived, across the waters; in their strong institutions; in the history of their ancestors; in the distinctive features of their governmental antecedents, in their colonies; their religion, letters and commerce. The spirit of the English language is the spirit of Independence, both personal and national; the spirit of free-speech and a free press, and personal liberty;

---

*St. James, ii. 26.

the spirit of reform and development; the spirit of enterprise; the spirit of law, of moral character, and spiritual beneficence.

With these ideas we have been familiar from our youth. Wherever the English language is spoken these sentiments are the daily utterances of men. Even in those cases where there is the widest separation between theory and practice, even there the idea of freedom exacts and secures expression. The American black man, even in the States of slavery, has been in a school of freedom, from which even the Italian, the German, the Frenchman, the Russian and the Sardinian, have been separate and alien. He has had unfolded to him, in harangues, in public speeches, in grand orations, in the social talk of the table and the fire-side, in the august decisions of Courts and Legislatures; and in the solemn utterances of State papers, all the sublime abstractions of human rights and civil freedom.

You and I have been accustomed to the utterance of the noblest theories of liberty, the grandest ideas of humanity all our life time; and so were our fathers. And although we have been shorn of our manhood, and have, as yet, attained only a shriveled humanity; still there is some satisfaction in the remembrance, that ideas conserve men, and keep alive the vitality of nations. These ideas, alas! for the consistency of men! though often but abstractions there, have been made realities here. We have brought them with us to this continent; and in this young nation are striving to give them form, shape, and constant expression. With the noble tongue which Providence has given us, it will be difficult for us to be divorced from the spirit, which, for centuries, has been speaking through it. For a language acts, in divers ways, upon the spirit of a people; even as the spirit of a people acts with a creative and spiritualizing force upon a language. But difficult though it be, such a separation is a possibility. And hence arises the duty of doing all we can to keep alive these grand ideas and noble principles. May we be equal to this duty—may we strive to answer to this responsibility! Let us endeavor to live up to the sentiments breathed forth in all the legal charters, the noble literature, the religious learning of this tongue. Let us guard, even here, the right of FREE SPEECH. Let us esteem it one of the proudest boasts of this land, and to appropriate the happy language of a heathen—esteem it "the rare felicity of our times that, in this country, one can think what he pleases, and speak what he thinks."* Let us prize the principle of Personal Liberty, as one of the richest jewels of our constitutional diadem. Let us not shrink from the severest test to which a heathen and degraded population around us, may at times strain it. Let us, amid all the extravagances of their crude state, guarantee, even them, the full advantage of it. Conscious of the nobleness of this great constitutional principle, may we allow it full force and unrestricted expression. Let us rejoice that our Republic, diminutive as it is in the group of nations, is already a refuge for the fugitives; and congratulate one another on the fact that we can already apply to our state and position, the proud lines of Whittier:—

> "No slave-hunt in our borders, no pirate on the strand,
> No fetters in Liberia! no slave upon our land."

Let us endeavor, by the reading of their Journals, by close observation of that venturesome enterprize of theirs, which carries them from "beneath the Arctic circle, to the opposite region of Polar cold;"—by a careful inspection of their representations, who visit these shores, and by a judicious imitation of their daring and activity; let us strive to catch and gain to ourselves somewhat the SPIRIT OF ENTERPRIZE AND PROGRESS which characterizes them, in all their world-wide homes. Moreover, let us cultivate the principle

---

* "Rara temporum felicitate, ube sentire quse velis, et quse sentias dicere licet." Tacitus, Hist. Lib. 1 Cap. 2.

of Indefendence, both as a nation and as individuals, and in our children; as, in itself a needed element of character, as the great antidote to the deep slavishness of a three centuries' servitude, and as a correction to the inactivity, the slothfulness, and the helplessness, which are gendered by a tropical clime. I am well aware of the exaggeration to which all men are liable to carry this sentiment; but this, indeed is the case with all the other noble principles which I have alluded to. This possibility of excess is one of the conditions of freedom. You cannot leave it in, nor any of its accessories, within the line of strict propriety, to the rigid margin of cold exactitude. And the spirit of independence, the disposition to modest self-reliance, the feeling of one's being sufficient for one's own needs, and temporal requirements; is just one of those golden elements of character, which needs to be cultivated every where among our population. It is conservative, too, as well as democratic; and if it does overflow, at times, its banks; it will not be long ere it will delight to come back to, and run in, its proper channel. An antidote to its extravagancies, will, moreover, be found, in the cultivation of another prime characteristic of the English language, that is, ITS HIGH MORAL AND SPIRITUAL CHARACTER. Remembering that "righteousness exalteth a nation, but that sin is a reproach to any people;" let us aim at the cultivation among us, of all that sensitive honor, those habits of honesty, that purity of manners and morals, those domestic virtues, and that evangelical piety, which are peculiarly the attributes of Anglo-Saxon society, States and homes.

So, by God's blessing, shall we prove ourselves not undeserving of the peculiar providence God has bestowed upon us; and somewhat worthy of the inheritance of the great and ennobling ENGLISH LANGUAGE.

Source: Rev. Alexander Crummell, B.A., *The English Language in Liberia* The Annual Address Before the Citizens of Maryland County, Cape Palmas, Liberia—July 26, 1860. (New York: Bunce & Co., 1861)

25.

T. Morris Chester

Thomas Morris Chester (1834–1892) was a most restless activist. Born in 1834 in Harrisburg, Pennsylvania, to a black abolitionist family (his father sold *The Liberator*) and educated in Pennsylvania, Vermont, Liberia, and England, Chester traveled the world in search of liberty. He worked throughout the United States, lectured in England, Europe, and Russia, settled in Liberia, and then returned finally to America after the Civil War to live in New Orleans and Pennsylvania. Chester traveled far in his philosophy too: although imbued with his parents' integrationist ethos, he became frustrated with an America that would not end slavery or embrace black achievement. And so, in the 1850s, he supported black emigrationists, rejecting American shores in favor of Africa. During the Civil War, as a correspondent for a white paper, Chester returned and saw new opportunities for blacks in Lincoln's America. By the time he died in 1892, Chester was characterized as somewhat of a racial conservative. Yet, the bedrock of his thought, wonderfully captured here, was a firm belief that oppressed blacks had to learn racial pride; only this would allow them to navigate the difficulties of American racism. And this required a self-conscious teaching of black historical achievements, something Chester argued would occur only when African Americans began writing their own national histories and biographies.

"Negro Self-Respect and Pride of Race"

(1862)

"When I reflect over the uprising of an injured and oppressed people,
I can conceive of no grander spectacle of moral courage,
nor a brighter exhibition of liberty or the pride of race."

Mr. PRESIDENT AND GENTLEMEN OF THE PHILADELPHIA LIBRARY COMPANY, LADIES AND GENTLEMEN:—As you have been well entertained by the interesting introductory of the President, (Mr. D. Bowser) and the logical disquisition, not unmingled with eloquence, of my friend, (Mr. S. Morgan Smith,) and as he (Rev. Alston) that cometh after me is mightier than I, (merriment) whom you are all anxious to hear, I shall respect your patience.

I congratulate you, Mr. President and Gentlemen, on the passage of another year, which marks the twenty-ninth anniversary of your institution. Its popularity and influence are evident in the large audience here assembled to commemorate the day which gave it existence. Sir, as your polemic season opens tonight under the most favorite auspices, let me trust that its close may be made memorable by its brilliant results. I have always understood that the intelligence of this city has very generally attended your lectures and participated in your discussions; and that you are always favored by the inspiring smiles of the ladies, who present this evening a scene of clustering beauty which resembles a magnificent garden of variegated flowers. (Laughter and applause.)

While other speakers have very fully entertained you upon the troubled state of the country, and pointed out the cheering beacons which illuminate the political pathway of the Afro-American's future, I propose to make a few remarks upon SELF-RESPECT AND PRIDE OF RACE, in which I shall exhort the Library Company to contribute to the development of these virtues.

You are aware that an association of individuals to promote a worthy object will, if composed of good materials, and its aims vigorously prosecuted, eventually triumph. It matters not what may be the opposition, when fully alive to the importance of its mission, and putting into operation the appliances which it can command, it is bound to succeed. They may be organised for a good subject—but under the influence of injudicious consellors, they may prostitute their labors to unworthy purposes. Every society is responsible for the influence which it circulates. However little they may deteriorate from the grand principles which called them into existence, they must answer at the bar of public opinion for the consequences. Literary societies are essential to promote general information and give a high tone to moral sentiment.

Gentlemen, if I understand the object for which you have associated yourselves together, it is to respond to the wants of the people who are seeking literary knowledge, and to infuse a moral purity into the community's intellectual growth.—You cannot be insensible to the important relationship which you may sustain to society, nor the influences which your acts will have on future ages. Too much caution cannot be exercised in the advancement of sentiments. Far better is it for you to listen to the humblest member in your institution upon practical truths, than to hear the most profound scholar in the city upon speculative theories. An error in fundamental doctrine, germinated under your auspices, may go down to posterity with all of its blighting consequences.—You are regarded as the source of literary intelligence to whom the people look for instruction. Like the tender plants, drawing their nourishment from the earth and opening their buds under the genial warmth of the sun, the Afro-Americans receive their inspiration from such institutions, and are quickened into mature growth by the glow of an advanced civilization. Guard against every error which, when once introduced, too often pervades every phase of society. Just as weeds spring up all over a garden, impeding the growth of cultivated plants, so are false theories germinated in the most improved society, which are subversive of great truths and sublime principles. You should act as the gardener of the social circle—weed out every budding error—pluck up every growing evil, and nourish every fundamental doctrine. Then the intellectual development of man will be radiated by all the moral attributes, and the fair plants which need gentler care will be fully cultivated to a purified and refined growth. (Applause.)

It is to your intelligence and discretion that a proper public sentiment is entrusted. A deep regard for ethics should pervade your association, and the concealed facts of the past should be reproduced to vindicate our susceptibility to a high order of excellence. Schools and colleges are instituted to discipline the mind for thought—churches are to inspire a faithful observance of holy orders, and literary societies, besides being beneficiary, diffuse a fund of general knowledge which tend to the ethical development of communities.

When we consider that our fathers were dragged from their sunny homes and brutalized by an American institution, which exceeds in its unblushing outrages the combined villanies of christendom, and now look at their descendants who have advanced in intelligence and christianity, despite the malicious efforts of our unscrupulous foes, there is not a man with one drop of Negro blood in his veins but has cause to be proud of the superiority which the race has displayed under the most humiliating and disheartening circumstances. (Loud applause.) In direct opposition to the wishes and prejudices of our oppressors, to public sentiment and the laws of the land, we have come up from the house of bondage where every effort was made to brutalize and corrupt us; and as we advanced along the track of time, uncheered by the quickening beacons of good schools and churches we were nerved on by nothing else under Heaven but the transcendent superiority of our nature. (Applause.) The more they imposed heavy burdens upon us, the more we have increased and prospered. The greater the efforts to prevent the diffusion of knowledge, the more gratifying has been our intelligent growth. (Applause.) The deeper the curses for our degradation, the brighter have been the blessings for our elevation. (Applause.) The stronger the resolutions to perpetuate our servitude, the more transparent has been the power of God to break the yoke of the oppressed.—(Applause.) The stronger the resolutions to perpetuate our servitude, the more transparent has been the power of God to break the yoke of the oppressed.—(Applause.) The more extensive the villanies to crush our impulses, the higher have sprung our aspirations of manhood.—(Applause.)

There is still room for improvement, but none that will justify any reflection from our enemies. There is one virtue, however, of which as a people we are somewhat deficient in this country, owing to the industrious efforts of the advocates of slavery to produce so unfortunate a result. It cannot be denied that we need a higher cultivation of self-respect and pride of race. Public sentiment and legislation have been sufficiently ungodly to somewhat distract the councils of Afro-Americans—to suppress every manly attribute, and cast doubts upon the superiority of our people. These influences have been so unfortunate that they have prevented a thorough union of feeling and sympathy among all classes.

The instincts which Almighty God implanted in our nature to unite us by the bonds of a common cause and a common destiny, have, in some instances, only been suppressed, not eradicated. Events sometimes develop the fact that these virtues are only slumbering, and when awakened they disclose a self-respect and love of race which no people can excel. You may call public meetings, announce interesting lectures, build splendid churches and open excellent schools, and you will scarcely awaken an echo in certain misguided localities, for which the patriarchal institution is wholly responsible in blunting our sensibilities. But if you want to arouse our latent manhood, and see a grand development of moral courage in opposition to public sentiment and unjust laws—a love of race that is not surpassed by any people, and our united efforts supporting the principles of liberty,—let it be announced that a fugitive slave is arrested by the revolting vampires who exist by sucking our blood, and you will witness a magnificent gathering together of the Afro-Americans in their physical strength. (Loud applause.)

Such an event would spread with the rapidity of lightning, and from Seventh street, and St. Mary, and Lombard, and Shippen, men and women would march up grandly to the tune of John Brown, to fight, if necessary, for the god-given rights of the race. (Loud applause.) From up town and down town would come the more intelligent cohorts for mortal resistance, who recognize no law that attempts to legalize a stupendous wrong (Loud applause.) Dining rooms would be deserted and culinary apartments vacated, while their tenants went forth to rescue one of God's images from the curse of slavery (Applause.) Under such circumstances, the high and the low, the rich and the poor, the virtuous and the vicious would all rally harmoniously and enthusiastically, to attest their devotion to the principles of liberty. (Applause.) When I consider that public opinion, a vile prejudice and unchristian laws are against us—when I think of the consequences which are likely to follow– and when I reflect over the uprising of an injured and oppressed people, I can conceive of no grander spectacle of moral courage, nor a brighter exhibition of the love of liberty, or the pride of race. (Applause.) Such a union is complete, effective and sublime in the rapidity of its formation, and serves as an index to the latent feelings and impulses of our people. Every phase of social existence is always under such circumstances represented in full force; not by substitutes, but by men who are ever ready to drive from the soil of the North, the hunting blood-hounds of the South.

I refer you to these grand and spontaneous spectacles to clearly demonstrate that there are a latent self-respect and pride of race existing among all classes, which unfortunately have only been developed by extraordinary occasions:—and now, Gentlemen, I must insist that you will, through your institution, adopt such measures as will tend, in this city, to the full development, on all occasions, of those nobler virtues with which we have been endowed.

In your efforts to contribute to the literary advancement of this community, you should exert yourselves to draw out these qualities of our nature which, when earnestly and unitedly enlisted in our just cause, will culminate in the most satisfactory results. I do not counsel any violation of law, or breach of good order, but I beseech you to organize among all classes a more effective union upon every question which involves your rights, your privileges, or your happiness. I would not persuade you to like the white race less, but to love the black race more.—(Applause.) Remove as far as practicable, from all observation and association, every influence which tends to weaken your self-respect. Take down from your walls the pictures of WASHINGTON, JACKSON and MCLELLAN; and if you love to gaze upon military chieftains, let the gilded frames be graced with the immortal TOUS-SAINT, (great applause) the brave GEFFRARD, and the chivalrous BENSON, (applause) three untarnished black generals whose martial achievements are the property of history. (Applause.) Remove from the eyes of the rising generation the portraits of CLAY, WEBSTER and SEWARD, and if superior intellects present any attractions, hang in the most conspicuous place the great WARD, the unrivalled DOUGLASS and the wise ROBERTS, (loud applause) all of whom were born in the South, and under the most disadvantageous circumstances attained the highest order of statesmanship.—(Loud applause.) Tear down the large paintings in which only white faces are represented, and beautify your walls with scenes and landscapes connected with our history, which shall win our praise and inspire our admiration. (Continued applause.) If you wish bishops to adorn your parlors, there are the practical ALLEN, the pathetic PAYNE, the logical BURNS and the eloquent CLINTON—(applause) if you want priests, there are the lamented DOUGLASS (applause) the gifted GARNET (applause) and the popular SCHUREMAN. (Laughter and applause.) If your tastes are of a literary character, and you desire to frame professors, there are the classical FREEMAN, (applause) the polished REASON, (loud applause) the talented CRUMMEL (applause) and the cultivated BASSET. (Applause.) The medical faculty can be represented by the likenesses of the skilful SMITH, the active WILSON, the attentive DUNBAR and the successful ROBERTS. (Applause.) If you would gaze upon eminent members of the legal profession, there are the cunning MORRIS, the sagacious PAYNE, the able BENEDICT and the graceful ROCK.—(Applause.) The lovers of music can gem their drawing rooms with the highly applauded members of the LUCA and BOWERS family, (loud applause) and the melodious SAWAN, (applause) whose soft successions, blended with richest harmony, culminate to the summit of musical perfection. (Long continued applause.) Let your children look upon such public speakers as the brilliant DELANY, the chaste REMOND, the polemic WEIR and the rising CATTO. The wealth can be represented by the penetrating SMITH, the economical WATSON and the close-calculating WHIPPER—(applause) the martyrs by the intrepid GREEN and the undaunted COPELAND of Harper's Ferry fame, (applause) who cheerfully died for the good of the race—(long continued applause) the men of a moral and holy influence by the upright PECK, the beloved WRIGHT and the modest BISHOP—(applause) those of a high order of female excellence by the highly respected SARAH DOUGLASS, the accomplished JOANNAH HOWARD, and the sainted MRS. BENSON—(Loud applause) the artists of the stage by the famous ALDRIDGE and the beautiful Mrs. D'MORTI—the artists of the brush by the sanguine BOWSER, the gallant CHAPMAN and the distinguished R. DOUGLASS. If you would have your children gaze upon greatness and glory, hang up the portraits of ALEXANDER DUMAS, the brilliant author (applause) CRISPUS ATTUCKS, the first martyr of the American Revolution (great applause) BENJAMIN BANEKER, the mathematician (long and continued applause) NAT TURNER, the emancipationist, (great applause) JOSEPH CINQUES, the god-like hero (loud applause) ROBERT SMALL, the unrivalled strategist of the present war, (thunders of applause) and a host of others whose deeds have immortalized their names.—And especially whose place in conspicuous places the likenesses of men who without education, and in the face of a violent prejudice, by honest industry and the natural superiority which belongs to the race, raised themselves from the humblest walks of life to the highest positions among the gay circles of this fashionable city. (Applause.)

Point out the special virtues and qualities of all, and tell the rising generation that they can go and do likewise.

The great and good men and women, with beautiful associated scenes in our history, looking down from the walls, will awaken a high degree of self-respect and an exalted pride of race. The lives and usefulness of such persons would be examples for all time to come, and stimulate others to earn a place upon the scroll of fame. Impress the youths with the moral goodness and sacrificing devotion of our representatives, and you will quicken, at the intention of their honored names, the liveliest emotions of respect and veneration. (Applause.)

I am aware that your newspapers are not as interesting as the Saven's, yet every family should subscribe for one if it is only to acquire the habit of supporting one of your own enterprises (Applause.) They express your sentiments on all the great questions under discussion, and that should be enough to commend them to your support. (Applause.) In subscribing for one, you not only encourage a sentinel guarding your liberties, but you manifest a laudable desire to contribute to the success of your own literature. (Applause.) Every dollar you spend for a Saxon journal is put down to their credit, and it is now time that the thousands of dollars annually expended for the pro-slavery papers, should be cheerfully given to support a morning periodical controlled by your talent,—from which daily you could draw such manly inspiration as would effectually organise you into an unbroken union for the best interests of the race. (Applause.)

Unfortunately, the same books which are used in the white schools to impress them with the superiority of their race and, in many instances, the inferiority of ours, are introduced into our academics with about the same results. Neither the geographies nor the histories are calculated to awaken either pride of self-respect; and as they both represent us in a subordinate position, destitute of noble impulses, or lofty aspirations, their teachings have a very embarrassing effect upon the youths, which not unfrequently extend to riper years. This is a great evil, but time will remedy it. Histories and geographies, adapted to the use of your schools, written by one of you, with a view to inspire and cheer the youths in their difficult ascent up the hill of knowledge, are much needed. The man who supplies this great want, will do the race a service for which posterity will bless him. I believe that the hour can produce the man, and am confident that if this great responsibility were entrusted to my friend, MR. J.C. WHITE, Jr., (loud applause,) that he would fully satisfy public expectation. You should immediately yoke him in the harness—for I do not believe that he will kick in the traces—in justice to your children and the welfare of the race. (Applause.)

In your libraries let the most conspicuous shelf be honored with the works of black authors, or the records which point to our worth and superiority. Place into the hands of the youths only those works which transmit the lives and public services of our eminent men, their heroic daring and unbending integrity. Commit to the flames all of your books which ignore our superiority; and do not permit your children to reach the standard literature of the age, in which there are no sentiments to inspire them with pride, until they are first deeply imbued with an unwavering confidence of self-respect and an exalted pride of race with no partial writings can effect. (Applause.) The American religion, American politics and American literature have ever, to the lasting disgrace of the American people, been prostituted to ignore our virtues.—Henceforth discard such religion as illegitimate and hypocritical, such politics as corrupt and infamous, and such literature as versatile and dangerous. Follow only the christianity of the Bible which diffuses good will to man, rally only in support of that policy which recognizes God as our Father and as all mankind as brethren, and study only that literature which enriches and ennobles the mind. (Applause.)

I would not hesitate to adopt every means to bring our people up to a high standard of personal esteem and dignified deportment. I would stimulate and encourage you, that as one drop of Negro blood consigns all alike to a mortifying subordination, to organize a thorough union, with Negro blood for a basis.—(Applause.) I believe, though you may bleach us to the whiteness of snow, that if one drop of the royal blood of Africa remains, there is purity enough in that small particle to counteract any improper impulses which may be suggested by the unfortunate mixture. (Laughter and applause.) While I would not engender any hostile feelings between the African and Saxon, I would suggest by every means at your command, the inoculation of such feelings and sentiments as will cause our hearts to rejoice and radiate our countenance with you, when we hear of a worthy act performed by one of the race—whether he is one of the untarnished blacks, or his brow is bleached by the peculiarities of the climate. (Laughter and applause.) As it is a mere speculation what is the color of the inhabitants of the celestial and infernal regions, I am confident that if the developments of the two races are an index to their complexion, that God and his winged seraphs are black, while the Devil and his howling imps are white. (Merriment.) The Italians have very properly represented his satanic majesty as white. Now when you want a scene from the Bible, and this cloven-footed personage is painted black, say to the vender, that your conscientious scruples will not permit you to support so gross a misrepresentation, and when the Creator and his angels are represented as white, tell him that you would be guilty of sacrilege, in encouraging the circulation of a libel upon the legions of Heaven.

Fully believing in the complete triumph of our rights and privileges—in the inauguration of a brighter and purer era—in the practical application of religion and liberty—in the glorious epoch that will develope our latent virtues which history will perpetuate—in the good times coming when black brows will be a passport of respectability and a certificate of intelligence, and in the dawn of that promised period when we shall see Ethiopia stretch her hands unto God and princes come out of Egypt, I call on you all here assembled, in the name of the martyrs who are now looking down from the battlements of Heaven, and in the name of virtue, religion and liberty, to cultivate a high degree of self-respect and an exalted pride of race which, with the superiority of other developed qualities, will eventually radiate this continent with our moral and intellectual grandeur.—(Loud applause.)

Source: T. Morris Chester, Esq., *Negro Self-Respect and Pride of Race*, Delivered at the Twenty-Ninth Anniversary of the Philadelphia Library Company, December 9, 1862.

Index